KASTOM, PROPERTY AND IDEOLOGY

LAND TRANSFORMATIONS IN MELANESIA

.

KASTOM, PROPERTY AND IDEOLOGY

LAND TRANSFORMATIONS IN MELANESIA

EDITED BY SIOBHAN MCDONNELL,
MATTHEW G. ALLEN AND COLIN FILER

Australian
National
University

PRESS

STATE, SOCIETY AND GOVERNANCE IN MELANESIA SERIES

ANU PRESS

Published by ANU Press
The Australian National University
Acton ACT 2601, Australia
Email: anupress@anu.edu.au
This title is also available online at press.anu.edu.au

National Library of Australia Cataloguing-in-Publication entry

Title: Kastom, property and ideology : land transformations in
            Melanesia / Siobhan McDonnell (editor);
            Matthew G. Allen (editor); Colin Filer (editor).

ISBN: 9781760461058 (paperback) 9781760461065 (ebook)

Series: State, society and governance in Melanesia.

Subjects: Land use, Urban--Melanesia.
            Land tenure--Melanesia.
            Land reform--Melanesia--Political aspects.
            Religion and culture--Melanesia.
            Melanesia--Religious life and customs.
            Melanesia--Social life and customs.

Other Creators/Contributors:
            McDonnell, Siobhan, editor.
            Allen, Matthew G., editor.
            Filer, Colin, editor.

Cover design and layout by ANU Press. Cover photograph by Michelle Nayahamui Rooney.

Contents

Tables

Figures

Contributors

Matthew G. Allen is a Fellow in the State, Society and Governance in Melanesia Program at The Australian National University.

John Connell is Professor of Human Geography in the School of Geosciences at the University of Sydney.

George N. Curry is Professor of Geography in the Department of Planning and Geography at Curtin University.

Colin Filer is an Associate Professor in the Crawford School of Public Policy at The Australian National University.

Joseph D. Foukona is a Lecturer in the School of Law at the University of the South Pacific and a PhD candidate at The Australian National University.

Jennifer Gabriel is a Research Fellow in The Cairns Institute at James Cook University.

Emmanuel Germis is a socio-economic researcher at the Papua New Guinea Oil Palm Research Association in Kimbe.

Philip Hirsch is Professor of Human Geography in the School of Geosciences at the University of Sydney.

Gina Koczberski is a Senior Research Fellow in the Department of Planning and Geography at Curtin University.

Siobhan McDonnell is a Research Fellow in the National Centre for Indigenous Studies and the State Society and Governance in Melanesia Program at The Australian National University.

Sarah Mecartney was formerly the Pacific Programme Manager of the United Nations Human Settlements Programme (UN-Habitat), and is currently an independent consultant specialising in urban development, investment and policy.

Rebecca Monson is a Lecturer in the College of Law at The Australian National University.

Anna Naupa was formerly a Senior Program Manager in AusAID's Vanuatu Land Program, and is currently a policy adviser in the Pacific Islands Forum Secretariat.

Paul N. Nelson is an Associate Professor in the Centre for Tropical Environmental and Sustainability Studies at James Cook University.

John Numapo was formerly the Chief Magistrate of Papua New Guinea, and is currently the Chief Magistrate of Solomon Islands.

Georgina Numbasa is a Lecturer in the Department of Environmental Sciences and Geography at the University of Papua New Guinea.

Michelle Nayahamui Rooney is a Research Fellow in the Crawford School of Public Policy at The Australian National University.

Rachel E. Smith is a Postdoctoral Fellow in the Department of Anthropology at Stanford University.

Victoria Stead is a Postdoctoral Fellow in the Alfred Deakin Institute for Citizenship and Globalisation at Deakin University.

Michael Wood is a Senior Lecturer in the Department of Anthropology, Archaeology and Sociology at James Cook University.

Foreword

Access to land remains central to the livelihoods of Melanesians. I welcome this important volume and the contribution that it makes to the discussion of land issues in the Melanesian region.

The movement for independence in various Melanesian countries was galvanised by the demand to return alienated land to the indigenous populations. The constitutions of Vanuatu, Papua New Guinea and Solomon Islands reflect this aspiration by retaining customary control over most land. In Vanuatu, for example, the Constitution has specifically maintained the jurisdiction of customary institutions over land. Since Independence, however, customary land has again been parcelled, commodified and leased. The recent land rush in Papua New Guinea and in Vanuatu demonstrate the potential impacts of land leasing on the customary system. These land transformations are discussed at length in this publication, and as such the volume offers important insights into understanding land issues in Melanesia.

A number of chapters in this volume deal with the implications of increasing urbanisation across Melanesia. While the problems associated with urbanisation look different across the region, all countries have faced challenges in trying to provide suitable land for the expanding populations around urban centres. These are difficult issues, but Melanesian policy makers must recognise that not everyone living in urban areas has an island or village to which they can return. The state has an obligation to try and provide its population with access to urban services, and necessarily this will involve the creation of new state land through the acquisition of new areas of customary land, which often requires substantial funds.

In discussing urbanisation in the Melanesian region, I think we need to challenge the idea of 'squatter' settlements on customary land. In my experience in Vanuatu, very few people are 'squatters' on customary land;

almost everyone has an agreement that they have entered into that allows them to live on the land. When people with customary agreements are evicted, I believe there is a role for the state in trying to relocate people and find them alternative areas of land to live on.

The research in this book contributes greatly to our understanding of how people are living on land in Melanesia in urban, peri-urban and rural areas. Many of the chapters in this book describe the various forms of transactions that take place over land, from customary agreements to formal leasing.

Policy makers from the Melanesian region need to learn from applied case studies of land issues in their own countries, and more broadly from across the region. Research findings must always be condensed into a form that policy makers can read and learn from. As such, I am pleased that this is an open-access digital publication, which should make it widely available throughout Melanesia.

I am delighted to see the large number of Melanesian women represented in this volume, and of Melanesian voices more broadly. It is essential that people from the region write about land issues in their own countries. It is important to see our own academics and practitioners writing about land issues that are so central to our Melanesian identity.

I commend the essays in this volume to anyone interested in the future of people living in the Melanesian region. Access to land is central to sustainable development. Maintaining adequate land access is a major social justice issue. Land is essential to the maintenance of *kastom*, kinship structures and language. The title of this book encapsulates the way in which people across Melanesia today find themselves at a crossroads, caught between the idea of land as property and the concept of land as life, which is central to *kastom*.

Ralph Regenvanu
Minister for Lands
Republic of Vanuatu
December 2016

1

Powers of Exclusion in Melanesia

Colin Filer, Siobhan McDonnell and Matthew G. Allen

Introduction

In the recent explosion of academic literature devoted to the study
of what has been described as a new global 'land rush' or 'land grab',
reference is often made to the process that Karl Marx called 'primitive
accumulation', and especially to his observation that '[t]the expropriation
of the agricultural producer, of the peasant, from the soil is the basis of
the whole process' (Marx 1976: 876). That is because the new 'land rush'
or 'land grab' is sometimes understood as a process that has resulted from
a massive increase in the amount of transnational investment in large-scale
agricultural projects, especially in 'developing' countries where peasant
farmers constitute a large part of the rural population (Cotula et al. 2009;
Borras and Franco 2010; Deininger and Byerlee 2010; Zoomers 2010;
Alden Wily 2011; Oxfam 2011). This can be construed as the agrarian
aspect of a global process of 'accumulation by dispossession' (Harvey
2003), since it entails the foreign acquisition of land rights previously held
by local or indigenous communities. However, many scholars have argued
that the idea of a generic 'global land grab' conceals a wide variety of more
specific types of social, political and economic change in the distribution
of landed property (Peluso and Lund 2011; Borras and Franco 2013;
Hall 2013; Wolford et al. 2013). In this respect, they echo the point that
Marx himself made when he said that the process of separating peasants
from land 'assumes different aspects in different countries, and runs through

its phases in different orders of succession, and at different historical epochs' (Marx 1976: 876). But beyond this, many scholars also argue that the ideas of 'expropriation' and 'dispossession' do not suffice to describe or explain the changes that are actually taking place in the distribution of landed property in different parts of the contemporary world.

In their book, *Powers of Exclusion*, Derek Hall, Philip Hirsch and Tania Murray Li argue that the concept of 'exclusion' is rather more useful as a point of entry to understanding the variety of such transformations in the countries of Southeast Asia. They define exclusion as a generic form of social process that has the effect of transforming landed property relations at various geographical scales or levels of political organisation. However, they do not define it as the opposite of a social process of *inclusion*, but as a process that consists of a denial of *access* to previous, current or potential users of the land in question (Hall et al. 2011: 7). In this respect, they regard it as an essential condition of any form of landed property or productive land use in any part of the world at any moment in history. But while this process may take a variety of specific forms in certain places at certain times, it is always a process that is 'structured by power relations' (ibid.: 4) that are understood to be broader than property rights (ibid.: 8). Specific forms of exclusion are therefore related to different forms of power.

The aim of the present volume is to test the application of their conceptual framework, which we shall henceforth call the Exclusion Framework, to the neighbouring region of Melanesia. The countries with which we are mainly concerned in this volume are the four Melanesian Spearhead states—Papua New Guinea (PNG), Solomon Islands, Vanuatu and Fiji. Given our interest in the relationship between state formation and transformations of landed property, we have excluded consideration of New Caledonia (still a French territory), Papua and West Papua (two provinces of Indonesia) and the islands of the Torres Strait (in the Australian state of Queensland). The combined population of the four Spearhead states is less than 10 million, which is very much smaller than the total population of the Southeast Asian nations in which Hall, Hirsch and Li situate their argument. It is not clear whether this difference in scale makes any difference to the suitability of any conceptual framework for finding answers to the 'land question', but there is no doubting the political and economic significance of this question in the Melanesian regional context.

The chapters in this volume derive from a collection of papers presented at a workshop designed to consider land transformations in Melanesia in light of the Exclusion Framework. The workshop was held during the biennial conference of the Australian Association for the Advancement of Pacific Studies in April 2014. It was chaired by Vanuatu's Minister for Lands, Ralph Regenvanu, and was also addressed by PNG's High Commissioner to Australia, Charles Lepani. The workshop was attended by academics, policy makers, advocates and activists, and functioned as an engaged space for policy discussion around land issues in Melanesia. During the workshop, Minister Regenvanu and High Commissioner Lepani challenged scholars to present their research on important land issues in a way that would be accessible to policy makers in Melanesia. This volume constitutes a response to that challenge.

The authors of papers presented at the workshop were asked to deal with one or more of a range of questions derived from our reading of the Exclusion Framework:

1. Who are the actors promoting or opposing key changes in landed property relations?
2. Who wins and who loses as a result of the changes that actually take place?
3. How are specific types of change informed by particular political or historical contexts?
4. Is it possible to identify processes of inclusion, as well as exclusion, in a broader process of transformation?
5. Does the transformation of landed property look different at different levels of political or social organisation?
6. What is the role of the state in changing the relationship between people and landscapes?
7. How is the transformation of landed property related to the process of state formation?

In the remainder of this introduction, we elaborate on the ways in which such questions may be addressed in the Melanesian context. The nature of the Exclusion Framework itself entails that we divide this discussion into two main parts. The first has to do with the way in which property relations are conceived as social relations, and, therefore, the way in which the transformation of property relations is conceived as a type of social process. The second has to do with the way that power is exercised in this type of social process.

Land, Property and Society

Hall, Hirsch and Li name seven different types of exclusion by reference to the types of people involved and the types of things they do:

1. '*Licensed* exclusion' is a process by which governments award legal land titles to some people but not others (Hall et al. 2011: 27).
2. '*Ambient* exclusion' is a process by which people are denied access to land that is reserved for the 'common good' or 'public interest' (most notably in the form of protected areas) (ibid.: 60).
3. '*Self*-exclusion' is a process by which 'local communities' are persuaded to limit the use of the land that they already occupy (as in various forms of 'community-based natural resource management') (ibid.: 71).
4. '*Volatile* exclusion' is a process by which small farmers lose access to large areas of land that are converted to a single land use to meet the market demand for specific agricultural commodities (ibid.: 111).
5. '*Post-agrarian* exclusion' is a process by which small farmers lose access to agricultural land that is converted to non-agricultural use (ibid.: 118).
6. '*Intimate* exclusion' is a process by which villagers exclude relatives or neighbours from land to which they formerly had access (ibid.: 145).
7. '*Counter*-exclusion' is a process by which poor people (or indigenous people) resist their own dispossession or repossess land from which they have previously been excluded (ibid.: 172).

They do not claim that this is an exhaustive list of all the specific forms of exclusion that can be found in the countries of Southeast Asia. There seems to be a fairly obvious bias towards the forms of exclusion that can be found in rural areas. All of these processes have been documented in Melanesia, and some are documented in this volume. The question we ask is whether this sort of typology is the best way to understand the current transformation of landed property relations as a universal phenomenon. Although we pose this as a question about Melanesia, we do not assume or propose that Melanesia has some unique social or cultural characteristics that entail a special answer to this question. Whatever the relationship between land, property and society in the recent history of this particular region, some aspects of this relationship are likely to be found in other regions as well. What we aim to do here is to unpack some of the concepts conventionally applied to an understanding of this relationship and see whether the Melanesian evidence makes more sense if we add the concept of exclusion to the mix.

Property Relations

Property is conventionally understood as a bundle of rights in resources that are necessarily embedded in the social relations through which some people do or do not recognise the rights of other people (Blomley 2003; von Benda-Beckmann et al. 2006). All property relations, including landed property relations, are therefore social relations, although many social relations are not property relations. At the same time, it can be argued that the very concept of property conceals social relations (between people) by representing them as rights that people can exercise independently of each other (Rose 1994). In the four Spearhead states of Melanesia, this concealment is accomplished by the Western legal principle known as Torrens Title, whereby the act of registration creates an 'indefeasible' private property right that trumps all customary rights of access to a circumscribed area of land, and thus constitutes the legal basis for the use of state power as a power of exclusion (see Chapters 3 and 9, this volume). This is an instance of what Hall, Hirsch and Li call 'licensed exclusion'.

In his analysis of commodity fetishism, Marx elaborated on this idea of concealment by proposing that social relations between people in a market (or capitalist) economy are completely disguised as economic relations between commodities. Following this line of argument, many anthropologists would argue that there was no (abstract) concept of property in traditional Melanesian societies, even if there were all sorts of economic transactions between people, some of which (like barter) were quite impersonal, and some of which could involve the alienation of what might be described as 'land rights' (Carrier 1998).

We have no quarrel with the idea that property relations should be conceived as a set of social processes rather than a set of 'things' that are either present or absent in a certain type of economy or society. This remains the case when a traditional society is somehow combined with a capitalist economy. The question is whether the generic concept of exclusion, rather than some alternative concept like alienation, throws more light on the place of landed property relations in this combination.

Hall, Hirsch and Li try to avoid the reduction of social relations to what Marx or Weber would recognise as class relations, even though they are dealing with transformations of landed property. That is because social classes have traditionally been distinguished as the parties to an economic relationship that only has two sides to it. An example would be the distinction between landlords and tenants as two sides to the economic relationship represented by the payment of rent, or the distinction between capital and labour as two sides to the economic relationship represented by the payment of wages.

Marx defined the social relations of production as a combination of property relations and labour relations. Hall, Hirsch and Li are less concerned with the combination of these two types of social relation, and more concerned to show that the transformation of property relations may involve more than two classes of people (or social actors) in a single social process, especially when that process is analysed at more than one geographical scale or political level. They are trying to get beyond the traditional Marxist analysis of agrarian class formation or social differentiation at the level of the village, involving landlords and tenants, merchants and moneylenders, or rich and poor peasants.

Nineteenth-century social theorists were much impressed by the seeming impersonality of market forces in a capitalist economy. Marx himself distinguished between social relations—by which he meant relations between social classes—and what he called 'personal and local' relations. This was similar to the distinction that other social scientists have made between society and community, where local communities are built out of personal (or 'face-to-face') relations such as friendship, kinship or patron–client relations. While Marx might have seen the distinction between economy and society as a product of capitalist (or liberal) ideology, this second distinction has been institutionalised in the separation of economics from sociology as two distinct branches of social science. Polanyi (2001) reacted against this second distinction by insisting that all economies are 'embedded' in societies, by which he meant that economic processes are a subset of social processes, while social relations include both economic and personal relations.

If economic relations are regarded as a subset of social relations, then it is hard to maintain the argument that all social relations are also class relations. In a broader definition of social relations, it can instead be argued that social relations are the relations constructed between the different characters who participate in specific social (or economic) processes. In a Melanesian social context, the separation of social and economic relations from personal relations is nowhere near as complete as it is in the idealised model of a capitalist economy. What some scholars describe as a 'moral economy' (Gregory 1982; Ballard 1997) or a 'relational economy' (Curry and Koczberski 2009) could otherwise be described as a type of society (or community) in which economic relations are also personal relations.

Anthropologists have come to use the word 'transaction' as a broad label for traditional or pre-capitalist social relations that perform economic functions—or what Maurice Godelier (1986) would call the functions of relations of production—without having any obvious counterpart in a modern capitalist economy. The various forms of 'gift exchange' would constitute an obvious example in the Melanesian context (Strathern 1996, 1999). These could be described as economic relations if it were not for the argument that there was no separation of economy from society (or economic from social relations) in pre-capitalist societies, and it is certainly not possible to see any such separation in traditional Melanesian societies.

How then should we describe the relationship between different types of transaction in land and the different types of social process designated by words like exclusion, dispossession or expropriation? In our view, this is essentially a question of spatial and temporal scale. It may take weeks or months (or even years) for different actors to negotiate the sale or lease of a particular block of land. This is a social (and economic) process, but still one that has fairly narrow spatial and temporal limits, and therefore one that is likely to involve 'personal and local' relations. In the bigger scheme of things, it is just one instance of a social (and economic) relation that may be more or less common across a wider region or a longer period. For example, when we write about the 'transition from feudalism to capitalism', we refer to a process that may last for decades or centuries, in which a society (and economy) based on the relationship between landlords and tenants is replaced by one based on the relationship between capital and labour. The problem then is to determine the spatial and temporal scale at which it makes sense to make general statements about a general process called 'exclusion' or a number of more specific forms of this same process.

Land-Based Livelihoods

The majority of the people or households in each of our four Melanesian countries are smallholders united by their dependence on what we shall here call 'land-based livelihoods'. There has been much debate about the best way to designate this social class. The word 'smallholder' is far from perfect, but it is preferable to the word 'peasant', which is hardly ever used in Melanesian political discourse, and even preferable to words like 'villager' or 'farmer' (MacWilliam 1988). The critical feature of a land-based livelihood is that the land on which it is based is not just the space occupied by a house or a workshop or a trade store, but an area, however small, from which natural resources are extracted. These resources include the nutrients in the soil cultivated by a farmer or gardener, but they also include the timber harvested from a native forest, or the metal derived from an underground ore body.

Smallholders do not necessarily derive their livelihoods from the land through the application of their own labour. They might also make a living from the collection of compensation or royalty payments from a mining company or a logging company that operates on their land. To obtain this sort of income, they must normally be able to assert their status as 'customary landowners' (Filer 1997; Holzknecht 1999).[1] The owners of customary land, or holders of customary land rights, may also rent land to an agribusiness company, or more frequently to other smallholders who cultivate it for a living (Ward 1981; Curry and Koczberski 2009). Although many smallholders aspire to be petty landlords, the number of households that actually collect some sort of resource rent is relatively small. For most of these households, a resource rent is only one component of their land-based livelihood, and in some cases—as with logging royalties—it may not last too long.

---

1   'Customary landowners' may be thought of as customary groups, or as groups holding customary rights, or as individuals holding customary claims to membership of such groups. The ambiguities of this phrase are an inherent property of what Filer (2006) calls the 'ideology of landownership'. In Vanuatu, such people are generally called 'custom landowners'—a phrase that connotes an additional element of reification.

Although these petty landlords constitute a minority within the larger class of smallholders, their number could be comparable to the number of people who are formally and directly employed by mining companies, logging companies, or other companies that extract natural resources from the land. These wage-earners also have land-based livelihoods, but they do not count as smallholders. When the companies involved in this type of business are extracting resources from customary land, they occasionally try to employ the customary owners of that land to do this kind of work, but they are not always successful because the customary owners may regard such work as an affront to their own status as petty landlords.

There is another subclass of smallholders who do not count as 'villagers' because their labour is applied to land-based livelihoods in urban or peri-urban areas. Most of them are engaged in the production of food crops for sale in urban markets or cash crops for export to overseas markets. Furthermore, most of them do not have customary rights to the land from which their livelihoods are derived. This group includes the so-called block-holders who cultivate oil palm on allotments of state land in state-sponsored resettlement schemes in PNG and sell their crops to the operators of a nearby nucleus estate, but it also includes migrants who have made arrangements with customary landowners to access some of their land for the same purpose (Ploeg 1999; Koczberski et al. 2009).

There are numerous instances of this kind of informal tenancy arrangement between petty landlords and migrants or 'settlers' who have been separated from their own customary land for periods of time that may be long enough to entail a complete loss of customary land rights in their places of origin (see Chapter 5, this volume). Whether or not the tenants have land-based livelihoods, their numbers have almost certainly grown in step with the growth of the urban and peri-urban population as a whole, but it is hard to determine the prevalence of such arrangements from official census and survey data because information on household economic activities is not normally accompanied by information on land rights. Nevertheless, the number of households involved in this type of arrangement seems to be larger than the number involved in the type of informal labour contract by which customary landowners employ other people to work their land. This second type of arrangement is generally confined to areas in which customary landowners can obtain a reasonable cash income from other sources while still living on their own land.

As a general rule, the dependence of smallholders on the value of resources extracted from their own customary land can be expected to increase with the distance of their normal place of residence from an urban centre or a decent road that leads to one. The more remote a rural settlement, the larger the proportion of households with land-based livelihoods, the more likely that these will depend entirely on the exercise of customary rights, and the smaller the opportunity for landowners to supplement their subsistence by selling some of the fruits of their labour (Hanson et al. 2001; Gibson et al. 2005; Bourke and Harwood 2009). At the other end of the spectrum, in urban and peri-urban areas, households with land-based livelihoods may only account for a minority of the total population, and some of them are likely to contain members who derive a livelihood from something other than the use of land—as wage-earners, shopkeepers, artisans, criminals, and so forth. The transformation of landed property relations should therefore take different forms at different points along a line of accessibility that leads from the most remote rural villages to the biggest urban centres. The exchange value or 'price' of a given quantity of land should vary along the same continuum, but so should the capacity to realise that value in some sort of monetary transaction such as rent collection. Exceptions to this rule normally arise with the discovery of a natural resource in a 'remote' area which has a higher market value than the land with which it is associated—oil, gold, timber, and so forth—which makes for the creation of a new resource frontier (Tsing 2005; Li 2014).

Hall, Hirsch and Li clearly think that people who qualify as smallholders are the principal victims of different forms of exclusion, even if they can also be perpetrators in the process of 'intimate' exclusion. They do not try to calculate the number of households or people whose land-based livelihoods are disrupted or destroyed by different forms of exclusion, and that is not surprising, given the size of the national populations in Southeast Asia and the uninformative nature of national census data. The statistical issue is no less problematic in Melanesia, but the populations are much smaller, so anecdotal evidence or subnational survey data can tell us more about the rate of absolute or relative decline in the size of the smallholding population and the different reasons for this type of social change.

The Urban Question

Hall, Hirsch and Li have little to say about the transformation of landed property relations in urban areas, mainly because their central concern is with various types of 'agrarian transition'. In the Melanesian political context, it is not possible to separate the land question from the problem of urbanisation, because struggles over access to land are generally more intense in urban and peri-urban areas than they are in rural areas. This is not simply a function of population growth or population density, but is also due to the fact that some of the land in urban areas is still customary land or is subject to customary claims. As a result, urban spaces are rather like patchwork quilts, with some parts covered by formal land titles, some parts occupied by their customary owners, and some parts whose legal status is quite uncertain. From this point of view, urban spaces are condensed versions of the rural spaces in which the patches tend to be much larger, with much lower population densities.

It is difficult to measure the rate of urbanisation, or the growth of the urban population relative to the rural population, mainly because census data continue to divide the two populations on the basis of town boundaries established during the colonial period. Some of the areas now defined as 'peri-urban' areas result from the expansion of a single urban space beyond the limits of these boundaries (Storey 2003), but these new urban areas are still officially designated as parts of a surrounding rural area. This does not mean that urban or peri-urban areas can be defined in material terms by the exclusion of land-based livelihoods. As we have seen, there is a class of smallholders in these areas who make some sort of a living out of the practice commonly known as 'urban gardening' (Thaman 1977, 1995), even if they form a small minority of the total urban population.

It is currently estimated that the urban and peri-urban population of PNG accounts for roughly 20 per cent of the total national population. The proportion is more than 25 per cent in Solomon Islands and Vanuatu, and as much as 50 per cent in Fiji (see Chapter 2, this volume). Between 30 and 50 per cent of the people who live in such areas are housed in so-called squatter settlements (Connell 2011), and so 'squatters' are represented in the national political discourse as a distinctive (and problematic) social class.

One of the main reasons for the growth of informal settlements in urban areas has been the inability of national or local governments to acquire, secure, subdivide and service additional land for residential development. This has entailed an increase in the cost of accommodation in the private housing market, well beyond the general rate of inflation reflected in the consumer price index, and a corresponding decline in the proportion of the urban population who can afford to pay rent to a private landlord or pay off a mortgage obtained from a bank. While some employers (including government agencies) subsidise the housing costs of their employees, a growing number of full-time wage-earners in the formal economy have joined the population of the settlements. It is not the source of people's livelihoods that distinguishes the settlements from other residential areas, or distinguishes one settlement from another. Instead, the residents of each settlement are more likely to share common origins in a particular province or district or 'tribal group' (Oram 1976; Jackson 1977; Foukona 2015; Moore 2015; also Chapter 4, this volume).

In theory, a general distinction can be drawn between settlements located on government land that has been alienated from its customary owners, but not yet leased out to other users, and those located on customary land, where the settlers have entered into an informal purchase or tenancy arrangement with the customary owners (Numbasa and Koczberski 2012). In practice, the distinction is blurred by legal uncertainties surrounding the original process of alienation, or by the resurrection of customary claims over land left 'waste and vacant' by the state. In both cases, settlers have good reason to escape their identity as 'squatters' by constructing personal and local relations with the customary owners or their descendants (Chand and Yala 2008). Alternatively, those in occupation of vacant public land may seek to establish a quasi-customary right of adverse possession to protect themselves against the threat of eviction (Chapter 3, this volume), or even claim an entirely new kind of right on the basis of their economic contribution to national development (Chapter 2, this volume).

Despite these efforts, the threat of eviction is a very real one, and the practice has grown more common with the rise in the real market value of urban land and the intensity of competition for new leasehold titles (Koczberski et al. 2001; Connell 2003). In some cases, evictions have only been temporary demonstrations of state power, and settlers have been allowed to reoccupy the land from which they have been removed (Goddard 2001). In other cases, they have been 'compensated' with an allocation of land, and even the promise of formal land titles, in another part of the same town. But because of the way that settlements have been socially constructed, the process of eviction can easily take on the character of an 'ethnic cleansing' exercise, in which squatters are demonised as alien intruders who should be forced to return to the province or district from which they originated (Allen 2012). In this version of 'intimate exclusion', the 'customary owners' of an urban or peri-urban space may well repudiate their social connections with settlers from other parts of the country or reprimand each other for selling or renting the land on which the outsiders have settled (Monson 2015).

Dispossession and Expropriation

One of the main reasons that Hall, Hirsch and Li have opted to portray the transformation of landed property in Southeast Asia as a mixture of different forms of exclusion is their desire to question the idea that there is just one form of dispossession or expropriation that is a necessary condition of capitalist development. They recognise that the process known as enclosure in British and European history is indeed a specific form of dispossession or expropriation, and one that may well have supported the accumulation of agricultural and industrial capital, but this does not entail that dispossession or expropriation is invariably part of a process of (primitive) capital accumulation, nor does it necessarily involve the privatisation of communally owned land (Hall et al. 2011: 13–14).

When people say that 'possession is nine-tenths of the law', they imply a contrast between possession (in practice) and ownership (in law). The same contrast appears in the distinction often made between land use and land tenure. The contrast sometimes disappears when people talk or write about dispossession and expropriation, as if these were just two different words for the same sort of social process, but the distinction is significant. When 'squatters' have been evicted from an informal settlement, they have been dispossessed. They might also believe that they have been expropriated, if they think that their occupation and improvement of the land has created a legal entitlement to it. But the people who evict them will commonly justify the act of dispossession by saying that they had no such entitlement, and so they have not been expropriated. Dispossession is a physical process whose occurrence can be observed 'on the ground'. Expropriation is a change in the distribution of property rights that can be, and often is, contested in law. In some circumstances, a process of expropriation may constitute the legal basis for a subsequent process of dispossession that often involves the application of physical force. However, dispossession can occur without a prior process of expropriation, and expropriation does not necessarily lead to a process of dispossession (Borras and Franco 2013). Numerous examples exist in Melanesia of land titles being created without any subsequent material possession of the land.

A distinction between the possession and appropriation of land, and hence between the dispossession and expropriation of people, does not make much sense in a stateless society. In the pre-colonial societies of Melanesia, the possession or appropriation of land was intimately linked to the practice of shifting cultivation (Rimoldi 1966; Lea 1969; Panoff 1970; Brown and Podolefsky 1976; Mitchell 1976; Healey 1985). The members of a single 'tribe' or political community had various ways of deciding which households would clear which plots of (normally forested) land to make new gardens in any particular year. The act of cultivation was generally an act of exclusive possession during the brief period in which most of the crops were harvested and planted, but in the longer term, it did not enable the household to appropriate the land itself. Personal property rights were normally confined to the products of people's own labour. This explains why the ownership of planted trees was typically vested in the individuals who planted them, while the ownership of the land on which they grew was vested in a larger social group. In this property regime, acts of dispossession within a political community were a threat to its existence as a community, and when they did occur, they were often acts of expulsion. The dispossession of people in other communities was commonplace, but 'tribal warfare' did not necessarily entail a change in the territorial boundaries of these communities (Reay 1967); it could just involve the appropriation of other people's heads or bodies.

It is a moot point whether (and where) the 'alienation' of customary land during the colonial period counted as an act of dispossession or expropriation. Each of the four colonial regimes in our region—British, French, German and Australian—had its own way of recognising or not recognising 'native land rights' (Mair 1948; Rowley 1958; Brookfield 1972; Crocombe 1972; Firth 1983; Bennett 1987; Van Trease 1987; Ward and Kingdon 1995). There were also considerable differences in the way that British colonial authorities dealt with this issue in their four Melanesian possessions in the late nineteenth century. In the early years of colonial rule, when land was supposedly 'purchased' from its native owners with the proverbial beads and trinkets, it barely makes sense to ask whether the 'sellers' knew what they were doing, or whether they had a customary 'right' to engage in such transactions. On the other hand, the idea of a 'colonial land grab' obscures the fact that colonial annexation of these territories was partly justified by the need to regulate the appropriation of native land by European planters, miners and missionaries (Harris 1981; Quinn 1981). The colonial authorities constructed a legal concept of native land rights through the very same process by which they constructed the capacity of individual native leaders (often designated as 'chiefs') to act as group representatives in the alienation of native land. This process was accomplished far more rapidly in Fiji than it was in the other colonial territories (France 1969), but in all cases it led to the creation of specific institutions, policies and procedures for the investigation of native land rights as a precondition for the purchase of native land (Holmes 1953; McGrath 1964). White anthropologists were more or less active participants in this legal and political process (Mair 1948; Bell 1953; Rimoldi 1966; Lawrence and Hogbin 1967; Panoff 1970).

This process was markedly different from what happened in the white settlement of Australia, where the legal doctrine of Terra Nullius deprived the Aboriginal population of any form of landed property rights. In Melanesia, the colonial authorities generally accepted the evidence of shifting cultivation as evidence of appropriation, as well as possession, although it took them some time to appreciate the extent to which the landscape had been modified by this practice, and even longer to appreciate that it was not wasteful and destructive (Allen and Filer 2015). The recognition of native land rights did not prevent the colonial authorities from appropriating large areas of land that were declared to be 'waste and vacant', and some of these areas may well have qualified as a sort of 'no man's land' for one reason or another. However, these declarations were generally invalidated at the end of the colonial period, as the political leaders of the newly independent states insisted that any land that had not been purchased from its customary owners must still belong to the realm of customary tenure (Sack 1974).[2] In Vanuatu, they went even further, by insisting that all alienated land must still be customary land in some sense, because the very nature of customary tenure did not allow for the permanent alienation of communal ownership, only for the temporary

---

2   This complete rejection of the principle of Terra Nullius had obvious links to the simultaneous demands being made for the recognition of native title in Australia.

grant of use rights (Larmour 1984). This idea has since gained ground in all four Spearhead states, creating a version of Polanyi's 'double movement' in which the principle of Torrens Title is continually challenged by the reassertion of customary rights (Filer 2014; also Chapter 12, this volume). This has come to resemble the process that Hall, Hirsch and Li call 'counter-exclusion' when the descendants of customary landowners whose land was alienated during the colonial period actually repossess the land from which their ancestors were excluded (Filer and Lowe 2011).

This does not mean that the rate of expropriation has diminished, or that it has not taken a variety of new forms. In urban areas, 'land grabbing' may involve the expropriation of persons holding leasehold titles over public (state) land through the fraudulent grant of new leasehold titles over the same land—an activity that often leads to lengthy legal battles. In cases where the fraudulent grant of titles does not affect the rights of an existing title holder, it may still be deemed an act of expropriation, rather than misappropriation, if people with customary claims over the land are able to maintain that they were not consulted about the transaction, or if the new title holders proceed to evict the current occupants of the land, whether or not they have customary claims over it. These types of 'licensed exclusion' have flourished with the 'corruption' of government agencies responsible for land administration in response to the boom in urban land values (see Chapter 9, this volume).

The same types of fraudulent activity have also been recorded in rural areas, especially in places where the economic value of the land has suddenly risen with the prospect of some form of large-scale 'resource development', but in rural areas, they are more likely to involve the expropriation of customary landowners, and less likely to lead to the dispossession of the current occupants. A notable example is the abuse of the so-called lease-leaseback scheme in PNG, whereby huge areas of customary land have ended up in the hands of foreign 'developers' operating in partnership with landowner company directors (Filer 2011a, 2011b, 2012; also Chapter 7, this volume). In this case, all customary rights to the land in question have been legally abrogated for the period of the lease, which is normally 99 years, without the knowledge of the customary landowners who have supposedly consented to the transaction (see Chapter 6, this volume). This would count as an example of what Hall, Hirsch and Li call 'volatile exclusion' if the customary owners were to be dispossessed, as well as expropriated, since most of the leases have been granted for agricultural purposes, even if many of the leaseholders are more interested in harvesting logs than in planting cash crops. A similar form of expropriation has flourished in some rural areas of Vanuatu, albeit with a different collection of investors and local collaborators, and with a much greater risk of dispossession for the customary owners (Van Trease 1987; Scott et al. 2012; McDonnell 2013). This would count as an example of what Hall, Hirsch and Li call 'post-agrarian exclusion', since most of the leases have been granted for the construction of tourist resorts or residential property.

There are other forms of expropriation and dispossession that take place in rural areas, even when customary land is not legally alienated through the creation of new leasehold titles. That is because customary landowners or their representatives can alienate specific types of use right, such as timber harvesting rights, or can consent to the grant of mining rights by governments that claim ownership of subsurface mineral resources. The four Spearhead states have different policy regimes in place to regulate different types of extractive industry, and these contain different provisions for the establishment of what is nowadays called 'free, prior and informed consent'. But even when serious efforts are made to establish the consent of customary landowners to the logging or mining of their land, they can still be expropriated through the misappropriation of the compensation and rental payments to which they are entitled by the development agreements signed on their behalf (Zimmer-Tamakoshi 1997; Koyama 2005; Golub 2007; Lattas 2011; Hviding 2015).[3] Large-scale mining operations are liable to involve a distinctive form of dispossession, when the customary owners and occupants of land covered by mining leases are subjected to the process of 'involuntary resettlement', but the compensation they receive for their loss is not so easily stolen from them.

Alienation and Incorporation

Hall, Hirsch and Li make hardly any use of the word 'alienation', either because they think that their concept of exclusion is a better way to think about the transformation of landed property relations, or because the concept of alienation is open to many different definitions and interpretations. The distinction commonly made between alienated and customary land rests on a narrow legal definition by which the owners

---

3   Hviding describes this as an instance of 'accumulation by dispossession', but he recognises that the misappropriation of logging royalties in Solomon Islands does not involve what we would call the dispossession of customary landowners.

of land rights can either choose to alienate them to other people by various means, or else these rights can be alienated by other people without the knowledge or consent of their rightful owners, in which case the owners are expropriated. However, there is a much broader philosophical or sociological interpretation of the concept that is concerned with the way that ideas about the relationship between people and property have developed in different types of society.

The vernacular languages of Melanesia rarely contain a word that is used in the same way as the word 'land' is used in English, let alone a phrase equivalent to 'land rights'. This does not exactly mean that they had no such ideas; it just means that the arrangements by which people gained access to specific places or resources could not be spoken of in isolation from a larger bundle of local and personal relations that were represented, or embedded, in the biophysical landscape (Weiner 1991; Leach 2003). In recent decades, the advocates of indigenous land rights in all corners of the world have come to encapsulate this form of attachment in a variety of slogans with the common theme that 'land is life'.[4] The construction of land as an alienable form of property is thus conceived as a universal social process that destroys the special attachment of indigenous people to something that is much more than this. From this point of view, the alienation of land from people is not a process of expropriation but a process of reification. Land is separated from human labour, local livelihoods and personal relationships, and made into a substance that can be mapped and surveyed, quantified and measured, divided and subdivided, without any necessary reference to its cultural and natural attributes (see Chapter 12, this volume). As we have seen, the process by which land was turned into a new kind of legal object was the same as the process by which the 'native' was turned into a new kind of legal subject—the 'customary landowner' whose rights could be recorded and, perhaps, eventually registered. However, the fixed idea that native land rights must, by definition, be collective or communal land rights meant that the subdivision of native territory had to be matched by a parallel subdivision of native society. This was a regional variant of the process that some scholars call territorialisation (Vandergeest and Peluso 1995).

---

4   The original version of the slogan was probably coined in the Philippines around 1970. It made its first known appearance in PNG in a book published in 1974 (Dove et al. 1974: 182). The preferred version of this mantra in contemporary Vanuatu is 'my land, my life'.

The suppression of tribal warfare often entailed the demarcation of territorial boundaries between neighbouring tribes, especially in areas of high population density (Brookfield and Brown 1963; Allen and Giddings 1982; Gordon 1985; Curry 1997). Once this task had been accomplished, the colonial authorities could envisage the subdivision of each tribal territory between the constituent elements of each territorial community. In doing so, they were inclined to regard each tribe as a combination of 'clans', and each clan as a combination of smaller social units, such as 'lineages'. Each of the entities in this social and spatial hierarchy was conceived as a group of people with exclusive rights to its own territorial domain, and each group would ideally be represented by a greater or lesser 'chief' whose status allowed him (or very occasionally her) to deal in the rights of the whole group (see Chapter 11, this volume). Most of the vernacular languages of the region contained a set of proper nouns that could be read as the names of such groups,[5] and many contained words that could be read as the titles of their leaders. The key point about such acts of translation is that they took away the significance of proper nouns that were not the names of groups that could dispose of land, but were the names of the roles played by different groups in some other kind of social activity, like the practice of marriage or the conduct of mortuary ceremonies. At the same time, they took away the significance of words that referred to positions of leadership in any kind of social activity that could not be construed as an allocation of rights to the use of land. It is in this sense that the process of territorialisation was also a process of alienation, even when customary land was not legally alienated from its customary owners.

As we have seen, the process of territorialisation was a form of uneven development. In Fiji, tribal territories were subdivided into the properties of clans and lineages in the 1880s, and a corresponding hierarchy of chiefly titles was established at the same time (France 1969). In PNG, the colonial authorities made no serious attempt to demarcate the boundaries of 'landowning groups' until the 1960s, and even then they failed to get the job done (Hide 1973). Nevertheless, the idea that clans and lineages are corporate groups of landowners, in which the rules of membership are also the rules that govern access to customary land, was firmly entrenched

---

5   In some areas, the names were derived from words that represented different species of animals or plants, and were thus part of a system of totemic classification. In other areas, the names were derived from the names of founding ancestors, or the names of places where those people once lived, and therefore sounded more like the names of descent groups.

in the colonial legacies of all four Spearhead states. As a result, post-colonial laws and policies that have aimed to protect or enhance the powers and rights of customary landowners have generally made these corporate groups take on more and more of the characteristics of a private company. By this means, the 'chief' of such a group is liable to be recast as the chairman or managing director of a board whose other directors have a lesser claim to chiefly status.[6]

The incorporation of customary groups and the formalisation of their customary rights count as separate moments in the alienation of land from people because most of the people who notionally belong to such groups or hold such rights progressively lose control over the pieces of paper that represent their membership or ownership. Certificates of incorporation are not used to accomplish anything like a traditional economic transaction; they are more like a form of paper currency that can be used as evidence of the right of an individual office-holder—say a chairman or secretary—to act on behalf of a group that may only exist on paper. When survey plans and title deeds are added to this currency, the process of alienation is taken to another stage, as individuals are then able to accomplish the transfer of legally recognised 'customary rights' to third parties that bear no resemblance to any sort of customary group, and in so doing, strip away their customary quality (Cooter 1989, 1991; also Chapter 6, this volume). In this respect, the formalisation of customary land rights is not just a process of 'licensed exclusion' in which governments award legal titles to some people in preference to other people. It can also be a process of 'intimate exclusion' in which the possession of titles and offices is used by powerful men to exclude other members of the customary group from decisions about the use of customary land (see Chapters 10, 11 and 13, this volume). This is one of the main reasons why the advocates of indigenous land rights in Melanesia have been opposed to the registration of customary land titles, even under laws that prohibit the outright sale of customary land.

Even when customary land rights have somehow been converted into this peculiar form of 'private collective property', their privacy is no guarantee that the owner is internally coherent or clearly distinguished from others

---

6 This process of incorporation has been taken much further in PNG than it has in Solomon Islands or Vanuatu. In Solomon Islands, the corporate group is legally conceived as a collection of trustees and beneficiaries, rather than a collection of directors and shareholders. In Vanuatu, the creation of land trusts after Independence resulted in legal conflict that led to most of the trusts being disbanded.

of its kind, whether they be households or clans, incorporated land groups or private companies. People who argue that this type of property is an obstacle to economic development are not making a point about the privacy of the property right, but about the governance of the corporate body that owns it (Gosarevski et al. 2004; Hughes 2004; Lea and Curtin 2011). By representing the transformation of landed property as a set of gains and losses made by the parties to an unequal or asymmetrical relation of alienation or exclusion, we may be led to overlook the multiple forms of agency that exist on both sides of the fence. If the fence is construed as a denial of access, the social process by which it is built does not have to be construed as one that only contains two types of actor, the winners and the losers. Just as people now disown the right of some distant ancestor to sell customary land to white settlers or government officers, so they can contest the right of today's title holders and office holders to dispose of customary land in an un-customary manner. In this sense, a process of counter-exclusion is built into the process of incorporation that alienates some customary landowners from their customary rights, since the alienation is always incomplete.

The Gender of Tenure

It is easy enough to argue that land cannot be completely alienated from people or by people so long as the people in question are unable or unwilling to exclude themselves from customary social institutions. However, this does not entail that all such institutions are equally capable of sticking to the land that now constitutes the basis for land-based livelihoods or has acquired some kind of exchange value in a market economy. If we take the view that land *as such* had no market value in the pre-colonial economy, or that there was no pre-colonial 'economy' distinct from pre-colonial society, it is not even clear how any customary social institutions could retain their influence over economic transactions in land without being changed beyond recognition.

When transactions in land are embedded in the local and personal relations of kinship and marriage, the transformation of landed property relations becomes a transformation of gender relations and intergenerational relations. The social reconstruction of clans and lineages as corporate groups of customary landowners was often accompanied by an expectation (on the part of colonial authorities) that these should be what anthropologists call unilineal descent groups. In 'patrilineal societies', people inherit membership of such groups from their fathers; in 'matrilineal societies', from their mothers. While the process of territorialisation was accompanied by a distinction between areas occupied by patrilineal and matrilineal 'tribes', and this distinction has since become part of the common sense of public discourse in the Spearhead states, the contrast between these two types of society makes more sense under Western laws of inheritance than it does in customary social practice (Goddard 2011).

To be sure, it was commonly the case that most people inherited membership of named social groups or categories from either their fathers or their mothers. Even in these cases, it was common practice for people to be adopted or incorporated into groups to which they had no 'right of membership' by birth. But there were many other cases in which the transmission of membership between generations did not follow such simple rules, or in which there were no such rules at all because 'descent groups' had no social or economic function (Ogan 1971; Wagner 1974; Guddemi 1997; Jorgensen 1997; Ernst 1999; Filer and Lowe 2011). And even where they did have a social or economic function, there is no reason to assume that this function was primarily defined by their collective ownership of exclusive property rights, rather than by the substance of the transactions that took place between the members of these groups. In all Melanesian societies, this was a thoroughly gendered substance, in the sense that all the people and things involved in such transactions had masculine or feminine properties (Strathern 1988).

If seen through the lens of 'property rights', this means that men and women had different types of rights in land and other types of property. But it does not necessarily mean that women in matrilineal societies had *more* rights in land than women in any other type of society. From a gender perspective, the difference between one society and another lay primarily in the means by which male and female rights and powers, like other male and female things, were transacted between people. And that included the means by which they were transmitted from one generation to the next. In the majority of communities where descent groups did perform some social or economic function, marriage was the customary social institution through which the groups 'leased' male or female bodies to each other for reproductive purposes. At the end of the day, when the bodies were no longer living, they were normally buried in the ground of their own group. On the other hand, insofar as these groups were the collective owners of both male and female land rights, funeral or mortuary ceremonies were the primary social institution through which such rights could be transferred from one group to another (Rodman 1987; Damon and Wagner 1989; Foster 1995). No sense can be made of customary rules of descent and inheritance in abstraction from the transactions in reproductive capacities—the social relations of reproduction—that take shape through the human life cycle (Strathern 1972, 1988; Leach 2003; Hirsch and Strathern 2004).

These considerations help to explain why two things that used to puzzle anthropologists no longer seem to be so puzzling. The first is the puzzle posed by the construction of women in matrilineal societies as the 'landowners' who could not convert their property rights into political power (Maetala 2008; Naupa and Simo 2008). The second is the puzzle posed by the failure of men to dispense with the custom of matrilineal inheritance in a legal and economic system suffused with the values of possessive individualism (Nash 1974, 1987; Lomas 1979; Sykes 2007; Bainton 2008; Eves 2011; Martin 2013). When there is a contest between the property rights of individuals and those of customary groups, there is no reason to suppose that a difference in the rules that govern membership of the customary groups—matrilineal, patrilineal, or otherwise—should make a difference to the outcome of the contest. On the other hand, the difference between the collective property rights exercised in 'matrilineal' and 'patrilineal' societies, if they are now to be conceived as 'rights' in the modern legal sense, cannot simply be taken to reflect the customary balance of power between women and men.

Regardless of the rules that determine membership of customary social groups, the incorporation of such groups as the legally recognised owners of customary land does seem to be a process in which the balance of rights and powers has been tipped in favour of the male members—or at least some of them. Melanesia seems to be fertile ground for the sort of triangular process in which male leaders seek to demonstrate their own personal authority over other group members by alienating collective land rights to outsiders (see Chapter 13, this volume). This propensity may well have been encouraged by the patriarchal bias of European outsiders who sought to acquire such rights during the colonial era, but it has not disappeared when other aspects of the colonial legacy have been rejected. If anything, it is more likely to be represented as a continuation of pre-colonial customary practice, even when the transactions in question have no traditional counterpart.

The right of male leaders to engage in this particular form of 'intimate exclusion' is commonly conflated with their right to make public speeches on those traditional social occasions, such as mortuary ceremonies, when people or things are transferred from one group to another (see Chapter 11, this volume). And yet there is a world of difference between the social process that encompasses this type of event and the one that is involved in a decision to dispose of rights to the use of customary land in return for some form of 'development'. Women are routinely excluded from this type of decision-making process, even in those matrilineal societies where they are acknowledged as the 'true landowners', because they are not allowed to speak for the land (Naupa and Simo 2008; also Chapter 10, this volume). And what often follows is their further exclusion from the process in which the benefits of 'development'—in the form of compensation, rental or royalty payments—are distributed by the decision makers (McDonnell 2013). Given that this is not a customary social process, governments can only use the power of the law to create a right for women to participate.

Power, Politics and Ideology

Hall, Hirsch and Li suggest that there are four 'powers of exclusion', which they call *regulation, force, the market* and *legitimation* (Hall et al. 2011: 4). They say that the separation of these four powers is an analytical device, but in practice they tend to be combined in one way or another in a range of more specific social processes (ibid.: 197). Their seven different *types* of exclusion may therefore be distinguished from each other, not only by reference to the types of people involved and the types of things they do, but also by reference to the types of power that are exercised in each case. What is not entirely clear is whether each of the four powers that they identify is understood to be a power that some people exercise over other people, or something more abstract and impersonal.

When someone is forcibly dispossessed or evicted from a piece of land, it is normally possible to identify someone else who is responsible for this use of force. It might be a landlord who has hired a group of thugs to evict a tenant whose rental payments have fallen in arrears, or it might be a judge who has ruled that the current occupant of the land has no right to be there and should therefore be removed by the police. In the first case, the power of the market may also be at work, since the tenant's inability to pay the rent could result from his or her loss of income from the sale of some commodity. In the second case, the power of regulation would seem to be at work, since there will normally be some law that justifies the ruling made by the judge. But the landlord does not exactly *use* the power of the market to evict the tenant, unless we say that his capacity to pay the thugs is itself a manifestation of this power, or unless it turns out that he was responsible for cutting off the tenant's income in the first place. In the same way, the judge does not exactly *use* the power of regulation to dispossess the illegal occupant, unless perhaps we assume that he or his associates have some personal interest in the achievement of this outcome. But if we say that the power of the market or the power of the law is something more abstract and impersonal, does it make sense to say that the 'power of force' is something of the same sort?

Consider this question from the point of view of a (male) person who wishes to exclude someone else from a piece of land. If he uses force, and is successful, then he will have exercised the sort of interpersonal power that political philosophers recognise when they say that person A has exercised power over person B if and when A has got B to do what A wants B to do (Lukes 2005). It is not force that has the power; it is the person who has used it. There may be several ways in which force can be applied in the exercise of power. In the present case, person A could hire a bunch of thugs to do the job, or he could take person B to court in the hope of securing a judgement that would lead the police to exercise force on his behalf. Or he could pay the police to be his bunch of thugs, or bribe the judge to make a ruling in his favour. But force might not need to be used at all. If a court instructs person B to vacate the property, the order itself may have the desired result. Or the money that person A might otherwise use to pay the police or bribe the judge could just as well be offered to person B as the price of compliance.

These might seem like fairly trivial examples in the wider scheme of things, but regardless of scale, any social process that involves the transformation of landed property relations is likely to be a political and legal process as well as an economic process. Interpersonal power is not only exercised in the context of local and personal relations; it is also exercised on a broader social stage, where groups or classes of people exhibit their power by making laws or policies or rules that serve to advance their own interests at the expense of other members of society. Hall, Hirsch and Li attribute a specific power of regulation to the set of (formal and informal) rules that govern access to land or exclusion from land, and thus create different forms of landed property or types of land use (Hall et al. 2011: 15).

They connect the power of regulation to the 'power of force' by pointing out that regulations generally entail sanctions, one of which may be the use (or threat) of force, usually state force (ibid.: 16).

They recognise that force is not always used in the service of regulation, and might even be used to oppose it, but it is also important to recognise that regulations are not always enforced, even by the people who are responsible for their production. If regulation is conceived as a process comparable to the one that Peluso and Lund (2011) call 'legalisation' or 'institutionalisation', then it is easier to see that the power to make laws or policies or rules that relate to the ownership and use of land may be matched or countered by the power to ignore such things and find another way to deny access. In very simple terms, the power to *break* the rules may be no less important than the power to make them. Indeed, the powers to make, enforce, bend, break or contest a body of rules may all be applied quite differently, either in the process of excluding people from land or in the alternative process that Hall, Hirsch and Li call 'counter-exclusion'. The exercise of such powers may or may not involve the use of force, and it is hard to see why they should be represented as examples of one type of political and legal process that deserves the name of 'regulation'.

So what about the power of the market? When Hall, Hirsch and Li describe the market as a 'power of exclusion', they are not only talking about the market in land or land rights, but also the market in other things like agricultural outputs or inputs. The operation of these markets can easily lead to the loss of land rights on the part of smallholders who can no longer afford to keep hold of them, while the accumulation of capital in the form of landed property can proceed on the basis of multiple forms of unequal exchange. However, land markets do not emerge spontaneously in societies where other things already have an exchange value; they must first be established and maintained through the application of state power. That is why Marx (1976: 871) described the 'so-called primitive accumulation' as a myth. Marx developed a complex theory of 'ground rent' in what proved to be an unsuccessful attempt to show that his labour theory of value could be applied to the price of commodities like land and other natural resources that are not the products of human labour. Polanyi (2001) called such things 'fictitious commodities' because they are not produced for the purpose of exchange, and argued that the markets in such things are more unstable than normal commodity markets, even when they are central to the operation of a capitalist economy. From his point of view, land markets are not simply created by acts of 'so-called primitive accumulation', but remain the sites of an enduring contest between people who use the power of the state to keep them in operation and other people who use the same power to limit the negative effect of their operation on social relations and the natural environment (Kelly and Peluso 2015: 474). The commodification of land or land rights is therefore subject to what Polanyi called a 'double movement', in which different actors are continually attempting to remove or reassert political limits on market transactions (Cotula 2013).

This type of contest is all the more likely to take place in states where the majority of people have what we call land-based livelihoods, and have not yet been subject to a process of accumulation by dispossession. In these circumstances, other kinds of power get applied to the operation of a land market, and if one of these is to be defined as the power of 'market forces', it is best understood as the use of money or other commodities (aside from land) to secure some change in the distribution of landed property. Rather than talk about the 'power of the market' as an abstract and impersonal force, we might instead consider the ways in which some political actors use their existing wealth to secure the transformation of landed property relations, whether or not they use it in combination with the use of force.

And where does this leave our fourth and final 'power of exclusion'? Hall, Hirsch and Li define the power of legitimation as the power of arguments about what is right or wrong (or fair or reasonable) in the distribution (or denial) of access to land. Legitimation can also be understood as the social or political process through which the transformation of landed property relations is justified. But if it is conceived as an instrument in the exercise of interpersonal power, comparable to the use of force or money, then words like 'authority' or 'persuasion' could be adopted to describe it. And if it is conceived as the articulation of ideas that confuse the current state of affairs with moral judgements about the way that land or land rights ought to be transacted or distributed, then we could equate it with the power of ideology. Hall, Hirsch and Li do not have a great deal to say about ideology. Their book is notable for the absence of terms like nationalism, populism, socialism, or other 'isms' that are the conventional labels for such things. However, they do make several references to neoliberalism, which they clearly regard as the dominant ideology in the countries of Southeast Asia. Maybe six of their seven specific forms of exclusion are justified by reference to neoliberal principles, but the process of 'counter-exclusion' must surely be justified in some other way.

In his account of the transition from feudalism to capitalism, Polanyi recognised that the landed aristocracy had sometimes used its political power to defend the interests of the emergent working class against the capitalists who exploited them. This observation formed the basis of his argument that markets in 'fictitious commodities', including the land market and the labour market, are subject to an ongoing political and ideological contest between free market principles and what he called the principle of 'social protection' in all capitalist economies and societies. Liberal and neoliberal ideologies have largely retained the argument of classical political economy that landowners are little more than parasites if their incomes are largely derived from the rental value of a natural resource, whether it be undeveloped land or native forests or subsurface mineral resources. The removal of political constraints on the market in such things is therefore justified by the profits and wages that can be earned when 'developers' are free to invest capital and labour in the transformation of natural spaces or resources into genuine commodities, and in so doing, reduce the economic significance of 'unearned' rental incomes and the political influence of the rent collectors, whether they be private landlords or government agencies.

Nowadays, the defence of such political constraints is justified in two different ways. First, there is the long-standing argument against the alienation of land from people, or labour from land, that now tends to be framed by the discourse of human rights. Second, there is a more recent argument against the logic of 'resource development' that relies on environmental values, like the protection of biological diversity or the sustainability of ecosystem services. To update Polanyi's terminology, we could therefore say that the other side of the double movement is represented by a combination of social *and environmental* protectionism. The relative importance of these two aspects of the counter-movement is then likely to depend on the relative significance of land-based livelihoods in each national economy. As the alienation of land from people proceeds apace, the alienation of land from nature, or natural resources from the natural environment, becomes a bigger political issue.

Let us now consider how these reflections on the relationship between power, politics and ideology apply to current arguments about land rights in Melanesia.

The Dominant Ideology Thesis

The world of Melanesian politics is sometimes described as a world without ideology because it is hard to distinguish between the policies and programs of different political parties (Rich et al. 2006). This could be taken to mean that all elected politicians subscribe to a single (dominant) ideology, or that ideologies are not distinguished from each other in a way that makes it possible for politicians in parliament to align themselves with one side or the other, or that assemblies of elected politicians do not constitute the sort of space where major political choices are made. We can certainly allow for the existence of multiple ideologies in one political space without having to treat each of them as the exclusive property of one political party or one social class. Indeed, we might even allow that different ideologies can be espoused by one individual in different political contexts.

There is a neoliberal argument which states that economic growth in Melanesia has been obstructed by the prevalence of customary land rights (Gosarevski et al. 2004; Hughes 2004; Curtin and Lea 2006; Lea and Curtin 2011). Elements of neoliberalism can also be detected in the policy prescriptions of international financial institutions and bilateral aid agencies, but their interest in the privatisation of state-owned enterprises has not been matched by a comparable level of interest in the privatisation of landed property. That is partly because the aid industry has a parallel interest in the protection of human rights and the natural environment, and partly because neoliberal economic policies are not popular with regional politicians or members of the general public (Kavanamur 1998; Fingleton 2005).

What seems rather more popular is an 'ideology of development' that supposedly takes inspiration from the experience of the Asian 'tiger' economies, since it is partly concerned to favour the interests of a national business elite in their dealings with foreign investors, and partly concerned to protect small business owners from foreign competition. While foreign investors dominate some sectors of each national economy, they do not share a common interest in the privatisation of landed property. Property developers may seek to secure the permanent expropriation and dispossession of customary landowners in order to turn a profit, but mining and logging companies only need to gain specific use rights for the time it takes to conduct the business of resource extraction.

Different groups of foreign investors also have quite different levels of public commitment to the principles of social and environmental justice, or what some companies now describe as their 'social licence to operate'.

Many national politicians might seem to have a common interest in the 'mobilisation' of customary land for so-called 'impact projects' in rural areas (see Chapter 8, this volume), but most of the people who vote them into (and out of) office have land-based livelihoods that depend on the maintenance of customary rights. If these people also subscribe to an 'ideology of development', it is not because they favour the accumulation of capital at their own expense, but because they believe (rightly or wrongly) that 'developers' will provide them with rental incomes, business opportunities, or even some of the public goods and services, from roads to scholarships, that cannot be obtained from their governments (see Chapter 7, this volume). Their aspirations should not be confused with those of the smaller class of people with wage-based livelihoods, mostly living in urban and peri-urban areas, who want the price of land to be reduced to the point at which they can afford to buy their own homes. When regional politicians talk about 'land reform', it is this second constituency to which they often seem to be appealing.

Hall, Hirsch and Li use the phrase 'land reform' to describe a social and political process in which land is taken away from its current legal owners and granted to people who previously owned little or no land. The redistribution of land rights through such a process is virtually unknown in Melanesia. Instead, the phrase is generally used to refer to a policy process that is either concerned with the formalisation or registration of customary land rights, or else with the adoption of legal measures to prevent the misappropriation of customary land or public land, or to restore such land to its rightful owners.[7] Both of these activities can be represented as forms of counter-exclusion that are meant to challenge the abuse of political or bureaucratic power to bend or break the formal or informal rules that already apply to the allocation of landed property. Both can therefore be justified by reference to the principles of human rights and good governance, and both are therefore likely to win support from the donor community and some of the more enlightened members of the business community. However, both need broad public support in

---

7   It is the second of these aims that has dominated the recent land reform agenda in Vanuatu, where it has been pursued by the Graon mo Jastis (Land and Justice) party led by Ralph Regenvanu.

order to overcome the symbiotic relationships formed between politicians and less scrupulous investors with an interest in land speculation or other forms of resource extraction (see Chapter 9, this volume).

If neoliberalism does not exactly count as the dominant ideology in this region, it might still be counted as one of the several variants of a capitalist or 'pro-business' ideology that dominates the land policy domain. Other variants include the economic nationalism or economic populism that both seek to exclude foreigners from the ownership of some types of property or the conduct of certain types of business. They also include the sort of possessive individualism that is espoused by wage-earners or small business owners who wish to secure their own possession of the small areas of land on which they live or work. There are even forms of social and environmental protectionism that operate in partnership with the 'right' sort of business against the 'wrong' sort of business. However, those forms of social and environmental protectionism that are actively supported by the donor community and some members of the business community do not constitute the strongest form of opposition to the neoliberal agenda. That honour could be reserved for Christianity, which has a pervasive influence on all aspects of social life in Melanesia, but few of its many denominations have a distinctive outlook on the land question. The strongest form of counter-movement is a form of cultural conservatism that defends all customary institutions, including customary land rights, as components of what we propose to call a 'neo-traditional social order' that is partly accommodated by the institutions of the nation-state but partly opposed to them.

The Neo-Traditional Social Order

There has been a long debate about the extent to which Melanesian 'custom' or 'tradition' has been modified by the introduction of new concepts, institutions and practices by the colonial authorities and the agents of post-colonial 'development' (Keesing and Tonkinson 1982; Keesing 1989; Jolly 1992; Otto and Pedersen 2005; Filer 2006). Much of this debate fails to take account of the full range of meanings ascribed to 'custom' (*kastom* or *kastam*) or the variety of institutions or practices that are said to be 'customary'. These things are defined in various ways in the national legislation of different Melanesian countries, but legal definitions of 'custom' do not exhaust the range of meanings found in public debate. We do not propose that there is a single 'ideology of custom' at work in

Melanesia, nor do we propose that every form of cultural conservatism has been exclusively concerned with the promotion or defence of customary land rights, even if that is our main concern in the current context. Some links might be drawn between the growing prominence of this issue in Melanesian politics and the growth of international concern with the rights of indigenous peoples, but these links still seem quite tenuous in regional political debates because of a widespread perception that 'customary landowners' have a higher social status and greater political power than people who are merely 'indigenous'.[8]

In our view, the neo-traditional social order is a set of social institutions whose justification lies in the combination of the twin ideologies of *landownership* and *chieftainship*. These are not exactly two sides of the same coin, since their mutual relationship varies between Spearhead states in ways that reflect the distinctive features of their economic and political trajectories. But both have their roots in a segmentary mental model of traditional social organisation derived from the process of territorialisation we have already described. The veracity of this model is not the point at issue here. What matters is the process by which these twin ideologies have been legalised or institutionalised as part of the process of state formation, and the manner in which they have been applied to the transformation of landed property relations.

The fundamental tenet of the ideology of landownership is that every automatic (or indigenous) citizen counts as a 'customary landowner' by virtue of his or her membership in one of the multitude of customary social groups (tribes or clans or lineages) that supposedly have exclusive customary rights over land. Even land that was alienated during the colonial period can still be represented as the subject of these customary claims, and no land anywhere is wholly free of them (Filer 2014). In this conception of the world, it is these customary groups that constitute the 'real' units of social and political organisation within the nation-state, and not those 'modern' groups whose members have the right to vote for individuals to represent them in a national parliament, provincial assembly, local council, or civil association (Anderson and Lee 2010).

---

8   In New Caledonia, Kanak political parties have been wary of the idea that Kanaks belong to separate 'indigenous communities' in case this weakens the political case for independence from France.

The fundamental tenet of the ideology of chieftainship is that 'politics' (or political conflict) reflects the corruption by alien values and institutions of a traditional social system in which the authority of chiefs is the only legitimate form of personal power. In the post-colonial era, the institution of chieftainship has been granted various forms of legal recognition, but this has necessarily created some tension in the distribution of power between elected politicians and unelected chiefs (White 1992; White and Lindstrom 1997). This tension cannot be resolved unless these two classes of people can somehow be merged into one, which has not been the case in any part of Melanesia, even if some individuals have managed to perform both roles at once. If chiefs are understood to be the representatives of groups of customary landowners, and hence to have a specific form of traditional authority over the allocation of customary land rights, it is then a moot point whether bodies of elected politicians can interfere with this allocation without recognising that authority.

Both ideologies may be understood as forms of nationalism insofar as they construct the idea of 'the nation' in specific ways (as a nation of customary landowners or a nation represented by traditional chiefs), but they do not resemble the nationalisms of European history because they do not treat state institutions (including modern legal codes) as legitimate expressions of this cultural identity. Both can be used to legitimate or justify the exclusion of outsiders at any level of political organisation—not just at the level of the nation-state but at various levels below it—and can therefore be expressed in forms which some observers have described as 'micro-nationalism' (May 1982). Both can therefore be mobilised to make what Hall, Hirsch and Li call 'ethno-territorial claims' within the boundaries of any jurisdiction, and hence to justify the exclusion of outsiders, including other indigenous citizens, from specific areas of customary land.

The neo-traditional social order was an integral component of British colonial rule in Fiji (Macnaught 1982). However, the government of Frank Bainimarama has distinguished itself from all previous regimes by dismantling these customary institutions on the grounds that they are obstacles to national unity and economic development (Lawson 2012). Bainimarama's version of economic nationalism is shared by some of the political leaders in other Spearhead states, but there is less enthusiasm for his attack on the ideologies of landownership and chieftainship since these have not been so deeply entrenched in their political systems for such a long period of time, nor have they been used to counter the economic interests of such a large population of citizens as the Fijian population of Indian descent.

In Vanuatu, the ideology of chieftainship has acquired a problematic relationship with the ideology of landownership. This is partly because of the extent to which the native population was both decimated and dispossessed during the colonial era, and partly because of the way that some 'chiefs', acting as if they were individual 'landowners', have more recently been involved in acts of 'intimate exclusion' that have alienated the land of the customary social groups they are supposed to represent. McDonnell (2013) calls these men 'masters of modernity', rather than 'masters of tradition' (Rodman 1987), because of the way that they have used the power of the state, as well as their claims to customary authority, to authorise their own dealings with foreign or non-indigenous real estate developers. Claims to chiefly status have thus defied the ideology of landownership and the 'power of custom' because they have been used to justify the alienation of customary land. However, these activities have given rise to a form of 'counter-exclusion', and a process of land reform, in which the ideology of landownership and some of the institutions of the neo-traditional social order, including the National Council of Chiefs, have been mobilised against this process of alienation.

In PNG and Solomon Islands, by contrast, the ideologies of landownership and chieftainship have both acquired most of their contemporary force from the extent of foreign investment in the extraction of natural resources from customary land. In PNG, the legal incorporation of more than 13,000 'landowning clans' over the past 25 years has clearly been tied to specific legal and political processes through which customary land rights have been partially alienated to the government in return for the prospect of some kind of 'resource development' (Filer 2007). In those parts of the countryside where the social relations of 'resource compensation' have come to the fore, either in reality or in local people's expectations, land group chairmen, landowner company directors and political office holders have struggled to establish themselves as 'chiefs' who can claim some traditional right to control the distribution (or misappropriation) of 'landowner benefits' (May 1997). This is even true of areas where anthropologists could only identify 'big men' or 'great men', not 'chiefs', as traditional figures of political authority (Keesing 1968; Golub 2007; Martin 2013).

Landed Property and State Formation

The ideological forces that have already been discussed may be sufficient to account for the specific nature of the legal and political processes involved in the transformation of landed property relations in the four Spearhead states. Yet we still need to consider the extent to which the 'power of the state' is (or is not) applied to these processes, or the extent to which the exercise of interpersonal power by 'state actors' *and other actors* in the transformation of landed property relations *is also* part of the broader process of state formation. That broader process appears to be constrained by the existence of a neo-traditional social order whose inhabitants regard the state as a large but illegitimate tenant from which everyone is entitled to extract as much rent as they can, by whatever means are available to them. Indeed, the wealth owned by the state is the magnetic force that impels so many citizens to compete for election to public offices from which they can dispose of it. Those who succeed can make the institutions of the state look weak when they either break existing rules or make up new ones that enable them to consolidate their own personal power through the allocation of public wealth, including public land. But the state looks even weaker when their interpersonal rivalries prevent them from consolidating their collective power as a political class from which new members are excluded. And in countries where the institutions of the modern democratic state can still be cast as foreign impositions, this form of exclusion is not easily achieved.

In some respects, the Melanesian countries are comparable to the Asian 'frontier regions' that Hall, Hirsch and Li characterise as areas of traditionally low population density, occupied by ethnic minority or indigenous groups of shifting cultivators (or even hunter-gatherers), which have been subject to colonisation by migrants from densely settled areas of permanent rice cultivation over the course of the last 60 years (Hall et al. 2011: 28–9). The whole of West Papua (or what the Indonesian government now calls the provinces of Papua and West Papua) would count as a frontier in this sense. The Spearhead states have not been subject to colonisation by migrants from densely settled areas of permanent rice cultivation, but their largely uncharted rural areas are still occupied by indigenous groups of shifting cultivators with population densities that are still low by Asian standards. And even if the ideology of landownership resists the very idea that anyone has a right to colonise anyone else's customary land, it is still the case that foreign investors have obtained the right to exploit much of this land in one way or another. In these circumstances, we should not be surprised if the application of state power to the business of rural or resource development has distinctive limitations.

Three of the four Spearhead states possess a severely truncated form of territoriality in which the distribution of customary land rights between customary social groups was only partially documented by the colonial authorities and remains a bone of deep contention whenever anyone proposes to formalise or legalise such rights for the purpose of public or private investment. As we have seen, the colonial authorities made some efforts to demarcate the physical boundaries between tribal territories in order to limit the incidence of territorial disputes, but the delineation of land boundaries by means of cadastral surveys was mostly confined to those areas of land that were alienated from customary tenure. What the colonial authorities bequeathed to their successors was a set of procedures to be followed by government officers in the acquisition of rights to customary land that had not already been alienated. These typically involved the physical inspection of land boundaries in the company of leading men from neighbouring customary groups and the negotiation of a price or compensation package that would persuade the owners to part with their rights. This aspect of the colonial legacy was transformed in somewhat different ways in each of the newly independent states of the region. However, the institution of legal procedures for the alienation of customary land rights has generally not been matched by any effective capacity to regulate the subsequent distribution of 'landowner benefits' between the people who purport to represent the original owners.

The truncated form of territoriality in these three countries could either be taken as evidence of popular resistance to the exercise of state power or as evidence of a fundamental lack of capacity on the part of relevant government agencies. On one hand, the 'illegibility' of national and subnational landscapes has created more opportunities for people to engage in illegal or fraudulent land transactions and protracted legal disputes. On the other hand, it has motivated foreign aid agencies to try and fill the capacity gap by funding the production of new policies and laws that aim to limit such opportunities. The efforts of the World Bank and other aid agencies to strengthen the administration of the forestry, mining and petroleum sectors in PNG would be a case in point. Yet these efforts to enhance the 'power of regulation' commonly fail because they are based on an assumption of 'national ownership' that proves to be false. That is one reason why the architects of the recent land reform process in PNG, which resulted in the legislation that now allows incorporated land groups to register titles to their own land, insisted on keeping foreign aid agencies and consultants at arm's length (see Chapter 6, this volume). What is not so clear is whether such assertions of national sovereignty can serve to prevent the sort of irregular behaviour that has come to be associated with the alienation of customary land rights in all three countries.

In these three countries, the 'rule of law' seems to be seriously compromised because of widespread ignorance of what the law says, wilful misinterpretation of the law by politicians and public servants engaged in a 'culture of complicity' (see Chapter 9, this volume), and a basic lack of enforcement capacity on the part of the courts and the police. When big companies end up behaving like proxy states in their dealings with representatives of the neo-traditional social order, this is not because of any great desire to assume such responsibilities, nor because governments have been persuaded to adopt a neoliberal policy agenda, but rather because politicians themselves have a habit of turning into 'chiefs' or 'landowners' when making their own demands on these companies, while public servants sit in their offices, read the newspapers, and possibly dream of their own election. In these circumstances, the 'power of regulation' will always be problematic. When the production of new laws seems almost like a way of compensating for the inability to make them work in practice, there is no reason to suppose that a change in the rules will effect a change in the balance of power between different groups of political actors. But if legal reform can only be one part of the solution to a political problem, there may be no solution without it. Whatever the means by which actors evade or subvert the rules at different levels of political organisation, a change in their legal identities can still effect some change in the ways that land is transacted.

Two Points about Scale

If Weber's ideal type of bureaucratic authority makes little sense in these circumstances, we need to ask what other qualities—apart from the occupation of neo-traditional leadership roles or the possession of personal charisma—enable individual actors or characters to exercise authority in land matters. Rebecca Monson (Chapter 13, this volume) echoes Sikor and Lund (2009) in arguing that (landed) property and (political) authority are 'mutually constitutive', by which she means that people who can demonstrate a capacity to transform landed property relations, often to their own personal advantage, acquire additional authority by doing so. On the other hand, Michelle Rooney (Chapter 4, this volume) suggests that 'big people' (men or women) may gain additional authority over land matters because of their level of education or the nature of their employment in the formal economy, and may use this authority to resist the expropriation or dispossession of other, 'smaller' people. But all the stories told by the contributors to this volume should serve as a reminder that any analysis of the exercise of authority over the distribution of land rights is liable to vary with the geographical and political scale at which the analysis is undertaken, regardless of differences in the laws and policies that belong to specific jurisdictions. One of our reasons to question what is meant by the 'powers of exclusion' in a Melanesian context is that Melanesian jurisdictions are so small by comparison to those of Southeast Asia, however large they might appear in a Pacific Island context. The smaller the jurisdiction, the harder it is to distinguish social and economic relations from interpersonal relations, and the greater the scope for individual actors to exercise or modify the 'powers of regulation'. This may be one reason why the Lands Minister in Vanuatu seems to have more political power and personal authority than his counterpart in PNG (see Chapter 9, this volume).

Hall, Hirsch and Li allow that individuals or organisations or even 'social movements' may be actors in the transformation of landed property relations, depending on the scale at which the process is analysed. Since they are mainly concerned with large groups or classes of social actors, they do not make the conventional distinction between actors and the roles they perform or the characters they play in a social process. Yet this distinction can be helpful in the analysis of social processes in which actors are able to represent themselves in different ways. Thus, for example, a (male) public servant involved in approving some process of exclusion or expropriation may subsequently get elected to parliament and then use his position as a politician to try and reverse the process that he formerly endorsed. To say that he is simply continuing to operate as a 'state actor' does not encapsulate such a change of character. In Melanesian countries, it is also quite common for actors to swap roles or characters without the need for any change in their material circumstances, as when politicians (or public servants) represent themselves as customary landowners (or landowner representatives) even while they act in the interests of foreign investors who are seeking to exclude customary landowners from their land. That is why people sometimes say that 'conflict of interest' is a concept unknown in Melanesian politics. But perhaps it also counts as evidence that the political process in Melanesia has elements of flexibility or instability that are less prominent in other countries.

While Hall, Hirsch and Li are clearly aware of the possibility that different 'powers of exclusion' can be exercised in different ways at different geographical scales or levels of political organisation, they do not seem to entertain the alternative understanding of scale as a social and political construct in its own right (Leitner et al. 2008). The emergence of the 'landowning group' as the fundamental unit of social and political organisation within the nation-state, and the changing balance of power between 'customary landowners' and government bodies in the negotiation of benefit-sharing agreements, are examples of the scale-making powers of extractive industry projects in resource frontiers or resource-dependent economies (Tsing 2005). While the flow of revenues from such projects has not induced the same degree of political fragmentation in PNG and Solomon Islands as has been documented in Nigeria (Watts 2004), it has still induced an escalation of ethno-territorial claims by representatives of the neo-traditional social order (Allen 2013).

The instances of violent conflict that erupted on the island of Bougainville in 1988, and on the island of Guadalcanal 10 years later, both serve to illustrate the way in which struggles over the distribution of the benefits and costs of large-scale resource development become struggles over the scale at which ethno-territorial claims should be made, customary property rights should be recognised, and new political settlements should be forged. From these examples, it would seem to be the scale of customary land rights that is most productive of violent conflict in Melanesia, and hence responsible for the realignment or 're-scaling' of political boundaries, as the ideology of landownership insinuates itself into the national imagination as a shifting bundle of claims to exclude other citizens from the benefits of large-scale resource development. The question we can then pose, but not so readily answer, is whether the relationship between this type of scale-making activity and the process of state formation (or deformation) varies between the four Spearhead states as a function of their relative dependency on large-scale resource development, or as a function of some other factor, like the relative size of their national populations.

Exclusion Reviewed

The concept of exclusion, as expounded by Hall, Hirsch and Li, is undoubtedly a useful addition to the vocabulary that is required for an understanding of all the social processes entailed in the transformation of landed property relations, and this is just as true of Melanesia as it is of Southeast Asia. That is mainly because the loss or denial of access to land is not invariably coupled with a process of dispossession or expropriation, but has sometimes been accomplished by means of another kind of social process, like the process of territorialisation in which Melanesian 'clans' have been reconstituted as the collective and exclusive owners of customary land rights. Yet this example suggests that we should not simply abandon the idea that a process of exclusion may be countered by a process of *in*clusion, rather than the process that Hall, Hirsch and Li call 'counter-exclusion', since clans are still capable of including or incorporating people who do not have an automatic right of membership by virtue of descent from some founding ancestor.

We do not believe that the concept of exclusion is sufficiently powerful or comprehensive to displace the concepts of dispossession and expropriation from the vocabulary that is needed. Indeed, we find that the concept of exclusion tends to elide the distinction between the physical and legal forms of social process that is entailed in the distinction we have drawn between acts of possession, dispossession and repossession on the one hand, and acts of appropriation, expropriation and reappropriation on the other. Furthermore, the opposition of a generic process of 'counter-exclusion' to several specific types of exclusion does not appear to us to encompass the full range of possibilities encompassed in Polanyi's concept of a 'double movement', once this is conceived as an oscillation or alternation in both physical and legal transformations of landed property relations, and not just as a contest between opposing ideologies. We would certainly argue that the reassertion of customary land rights has been a more powerful and diverse social (and political) process in Melanesia than it has been in Southeast Asia. On the other hand, there are some aspects of the long-term, large-scale process of alienation and territorialisation that do not seem to be reversible, but constitute aspects of a process of state formation and capital accumulation that constitutes the stage on which different actors perform their double movements.

When we come to consider the six different types of exclusion (excluding counter-exclusion) that Hall, Hirsch and Li have chosen to highlight in their own discussion of the agrarian transition, we find that such highlights are liable to vary from one region to another, as they themselves concede. For example, this volume contains no discussion of the process they call 'self-exclusion', and very little discussion of the process they call 'ambient exclusion', because these forms of exclusion are relatively insignificant in Melanesia. Although there have been a number of donor-funded nature conservation projects whose proponents have tried to change customary land use practices, they have not had much success because the creation of new protected areas has not been taken as a valid pretext for the alienation of customary land rights (Filer 2012). National governments have sometimes used their legal powers to alienate customary land for the construction of public infrastructure, but have rarely been able to do so without protracted arguments about the identity of the customary owners and the contents of their compensation package (Manning and Hughes 2008). On the other hand, the chapters in this volume illustrate a variety of different forms of 'intimate exclusion' on the part of men posing as the representatives of customary land groups, and it is not clear that their actions are coherent enough to warrant the adoption of a single label for what they do.

Finally, we find that the four 'powers' distinguished by Hall, Hirsch and Li are not really things of the same general type, and this becomes apparent when we ask how individual actors exercise power in settings where it is not only the actions of ordinary people that can be subject to detailed scrutiny at a purely local scale, but also the actions of foreign investors, government ministers, public servants, and so forth. In the Melanesian context, we find that the distinction that Hall, Hirsch and Li make between the powers of 'regulation' and 'legitimation' fails to take account of the importance of the sort of ideological contest that Polanyi highlighted in his own version of the double movement. In this context, we do not find it helpful to assume that 'neoliberalism' is the dominant ideology, or the dominant form of political economy, but find it more helpful to think of power through the lens of legal pluralism (Merry 1988). Instead of opposing the power of 'the market' to that of 'the state', we find that it makes more sense to see how the power of 'custom' has entered into a complex and dynamic relationship with the power of 'the law' in the regulation of a variety of economic transactions in this fictitious commodity.

References

Alden Wily, L., 2011. *The Tragedy of Public Lands: The Fate of the Commons under Global Commercial Pressure.* Rome: International Land Coalition.

Allen, B.J. and C. Filer, 2015. 'Is the "Bogeyman" Real? Shifting Cultivation and the Forests, Papua New Guinea.' In M.F. Cairns (ed.), *Shifting Cultivation and Environmental Change: Indigenous People, Agriculture and Forest Conservation.* London: Routledge.

Allen, B.J. and R. Giddings, 1982. 'Land Disputes and Violence in Enga: the "Komanda" Case.' In B. Carrad, D.A.M. Lea and K.K. Talyaga (eds), *Enga: Foundations for Development.* Armidale (NSW): University of New England.

Allen, M.G., 2012. 'Land, Migration and Conflict on Guadalcanal, Solomon Islands.' *Australian Geographer* 43: 163–180. doi.org/10.108 0/00049182.2012.682294.

———, 2013. 'Melanesia's Violent Environments: Towards a Political Ecology of Conflict in the Western Pacific.' *Geoforum* 44: 152–161. doi.org/10.1016/j.geoforum.2012.09.015.

Anderson, T. and G. Lee (eds), 2010. *In Defence of Melanesian Customary Land.* Sydney: Aid/Watch.

Bainton, N.A., 2008. 'Men of Kastom and the Customs of Men: Status, Legitimacy and Persistent Values in Lihir.' *Australian Journal of Anthropology* 19: 194–212. doi.org/10.1111/j.1835-9310.2008. tb00122.x.

Ballard, C., 1997. 'It's the Land Stupid! The Moral Economy of Resource Ownership in Papua New Guinea.' In P. Larmour (ed.), *The Governance of Common Property in the Pacific Region.* Canberra: The Australian National University, National Centre for Development Studies and Resource Management in Asia-Pacific Program.

Bell, F.L.S., 1953. 'Land Tenure in Tanga.' *Oceania* 24: 28–57. doi. org/10.1002/j.1834-4461.1953.tb00588.x.

Bennett, J.A., 1987. *Wealth of the Solomons: A History of a Pacific Archipelago 1800–1978.* Honolulu: University of Hawaii Press (Pacific Islands Monograph 3).

Blomley, N., 2003. 'Law, Property, and the Geography of Violence: The Frontier, the Survey, and the Grid.' *Annals of the Association of American Geographers* 93: 121–141. doi.org/10.1111/1467-8306.93109.

Borras, S.M. Jr and J.C. Franco, 2010. 'Towards a Broader View of the Politics of Global Land Grab: Rethinking Land Issues, Reframing Resistance.' Rotterdam: Erasmus University, Initiatives in Critical Agrarian Studies (Working Paper 1).

——, 2013. 'Global Land Grabbing and Political Reactions "From Below".' *Third World Quarterly* 34: 1723–1747. doi.org/10.1080/01 436597.2013.843845.

Bourke, R.M. and T. Harwood (eds), 2009. *Food and Agriculture in Papua New Guinea.* Canberra: ANU E Press.

Brookfield, H.C., 1972. *Colonialism, Development and Independence: The Case of the Melanesian Islands in the South Pacific.* Cambridge: Cambridge University Press.

Brookfield, H.C. and P. Brown, 1963. *Struggle for Land: Agriculture and Group Territories among the Chimbu of the New Guinea Highlands.* Melbourne: Oxford University Press.

Brown, P. and A. Podolefsky, 1976. 'Population Density, Agricultural Intensity, Land Tenure, and Group Size in the New Guinea Highlands.' *Ethnology* 15: 211–238. doi.org/10.2307/3773132.

Carrier, J.G., 1998. 'Property and Social Relations in Melanesian Anthropology.' In C.M. Hann (ed.), *Property Relations: Renewing the Anthropological Tradition.* Cambridge: Cambridge University Press.

Chand, S. and C. Yala, 2008. 'Informal Land Systems within Urban Settlements in Honiara and Port Moresby.' In AusAID (Australian Agency for International Development) (ed.), *Making Land Work—Volume Two: Case Studies on Customary Land and Development in the Pacific.* Canberra: AusAID.

Connell, J., 2003. 'Regulation of Space in the Contemporary Postcolonial Pacific City: Port Moresby and Suva.' *Asia Pacific Viewpoint* 44: 243–257. doi.org/10.1111/j.1467-8373.2003.00213.x.

——, 2011. 'Elephants in the Pacific? Pacific Urbanisation and Its Discontents.' *Asia Pacific Viewpoint* 52: 121–135. doi.org/10.1111/j.1467-8373.2011.01445.x.

Cooter, R., 1989. 'Issues in Customary Land Law.' Port Moresby: Institute of National Affairs (Discussion Paper 39).

——, 1991. 'Kin Groups and the Common Law Process.' In P. Larmour (ed.), *Customary Land Tenure: Registration and Decentralisation in Papua New Guinea*. Port Moresby: National Research Institute (Monograph 29).

Cotula, L., 2013. 'The New Enclosures? Polanyi, International Investment Law and the Global Land Rush.' *Third World Quarterly* 34: 1605–1629. doi.org/10.1080/01436597.2013.843847.

Cotula, L., S. Vermeulen, R. Leonard and J. Keeley, 2009. *Land Grab or Development Opportunity? Agricultural Investment and International Land Deals in Africa*. London: International Institute for Environment and Development.

Crocombe, R., 1972. 'Land Tenure in the South Pacific.' In R.G. Ward (ed.), *Man in the Pacific Islands*. Oxford: Clarendon Press.

Curry, G.N., 1997. 'Warfare, Social Organisation and Resource Access amongst the Wosera Abelam of Papua New Guinea.' *Oceania* 67: 194–217. doi.org/10.1002/j.1834-4461.1997.tb02604.x.

Curry, G.N. and G. Koczberski, 2009. 'Finding Common Ground: Relational Concepts of Land Tenure and Economy in the Oil Palm Frontier of Papua New Guinea.' *Geographical Journal* 175: 98–111. doi.org/10.1111/j.1475-4959.2008.00319.x.

Curtin, T. and D. Lea, 2006. 'Land Titling and Socioeconomic Development in the South Pacific.' *Pacific Economic Bulletin* 21(1): 153–180.

Damon, F.H. and R. Wagner (eds), 1989. *Death Rituals and Life in the Societies of the Kula Ring*. DeKalb (IL): Northern Illinois University Press.

Deininger, K. and D. Byerlee, 2010. *Rising Global Interest in Farmland: Can It Yield Sustainable and Equitable Benefits?* Washington (DC): World Bank.

Dove, J., T. Miriung and M. Togolo, 1974. 'Mining Bitterness.' In P.G. Sack (ed.), *Problem of Choice: Land in Papua New Guinea's Future.* Canberra: Australian National University Press.

Ernst, T., 1999. 'Land, Stories, and Resources: Discourse and Entification in Onabasulu Modernity.' *American Anthropologist* 101: 88–97. doi. org/10.1525/aa.1999.101.1.88.

Eves, R., 2011. 'Puzzling over Matrilineal Land Tenure and Development in New Ireland, Papua New Guinea.' *Pacific Studies* 34: 350–373.

Filer, C., 1997. 'Compensation, Rent and Power in Papua New Guinea.' In S. Toft (ed.), *Compensation for Resource Development in Papua New Guinea.* Port Moresby: Law Reform Commission (Monograph 6).

——, 2006. 'Custom, Law and Ideology in Papua New Guinea.' *Asia Pacific Journal of Anthropology* 7: 65–84. doi. org/10.1080/14442210600554499.

——, 2007. 'Local Custom and the Art of Land Group Boundary Maintenance in Papua New Guinea.' In J.F. Weiner and K. Glaskin (eds), *Customary Land Tenure and Registration in Australia and Papua New Guinea: Anthropological Perspectives.* Canberra: ANU E Press (Asia-Pacific Environment Monograph 3).

——, 2011a. 'New Land Grab in Papua New Guinea.' *Pacific Studies* 34: 269–294.

——, 2011b. 'The New Land Grab in Papua New Guinea: Case Study from New Ireland Province.' Canberra: The Australian National University, State Society and Governance in Melanesia Program (Discussion Paper 2011/2).

——, 2012. 'Why Green Grabs Don't Work in Papua New Guinea.' *Journal of Peasant Studies* 39: 599–617. doi.org/10.1080/03066150. 2012.665891.

——, 2014. 'The Double Movement of Immovable Property Rights in Papua New Guinea.' *Journal of Pacific History* 49: 76–94. doi.org/1 0.1080/00223344.2013.876158.

Filer, C. and M. Lowe, 2011. 'One Hundred Years of Land Reform on the Gazelle Peninsula: A Baining Point of View.' In V. Strang and M. Busse (eds), *Ownership and Appropriation*. Oxford and New York: Berg (ASA Monograph 47).

Fingleton, J. (ed.), 2005. *Privatising Land in the Pacific: A Defence of Customary Tenures*. Canberra: Australia Institute (Discussion Paper 80).

Firth, S., 1983. *New Guinea under the Germans*. Melbourne: Melbourne University Press.

Foster, R., 1995. *History and Social Reproduction in Melanesia: Mortuary Ritual, Gift Exchange, and Custom in the Tanga Islands*. Cambridge: Cambridge University Press.

Foukona, J., 2015. 'Urban Land in Honiara: Strategies and Rights to the City.' *Journal of Pacific History* 50: 504–518. doi.org/10.1080/00223 344.2015.1110328.

France, P., 1969. *The Charter of the Land: Custom and Colonization in Fiji*. Melbourne: Oxford University Press.

Gibson, J., G. Datt, B. Allen, V. Hwang, R.M. Bourke and D. Parajuli, 2005. 'Mapping Poverty in Rural Papua New Guinea.' *Pacific Economic Bulletin* 20(1): 27–43.

Goddard, M., 2001. 'From Rolling Thunder to Reggae: Imagining Squatter Settlements in Papua New Guinea.' *Contemporary Pacific* 13: 1–32. doi.org/10.1353/cp.2001.0007.

——, 2011. 'Bramell's Rules: Custom and Law in Contemporary Land Disputes among the Motu-Koita of Papua New Guinea.' *Pacific Studies* 34: 323–349.

Godelier, M., 1986. *The Mental and the Material: Thought, Economy and Society* (transl. M. Thom). London: Verso.

Golub, A., 2007. 'From Agency to Agents: Forging Landowner Identities in Porgera.' In J.F. Weiner and K. Glaskin (eds), *Customary Land Tenure and Registration in Australia and Papua New Guinea: Anthropological Perspectives*. Canberra: ANU E Press (Asia-Pacific Environment Monograph 3).

Gordon, R.J., 1985. *Law and Order in the New Guinea Highlands.* Hanover (MA): University Press of New England.

Gosarevski, S., H. Hughes and S. Windybank, 2004. 'Is Papua New Guinea Viable with Customary Land Ownership?' *Pacific Economic Bulletin* 19(3): 133–136.

Gregory, C.A., 1982. *Gifts and Commodities.* London: Academic Press.

Guddemi, P., 1997. 'Continuities, Contexts, Complexities, and Transformations: Local Land Concepts of a Sepik People Affected by Mining Exploration.' *Anthropological Forum* 7: 629–648. doi.org/1 0.1080/00664677.1997.9967477.

Hall, D., 2013. 'Primitive Accumulation, Accumulation by Dispossession and the Global Land Grab.' *Third World Quarterly* 34: 1582–1604. doi.org/10.1080/01436597.2013.843854.

Hall, D., P. Hirsch and T.M. Li, 2011. *Powers of Exclusion: Land Dilemmas in Southeast Asia.* Singapore: NUS Press.

Hanson, L.W., B.J. Allen, R.M. Bourke and T.J. McCarthy, 2001. *Papua New Guinea Rural Development Handbook.* Canberra: The Australian National University, Research School of Pacific and Asian Studies, Department of Human Geography.

Harris, G.T., 1981. 'Papuan Village Agriculture 1884–1960.' In D. Denoon and C. Snowden (eds), *A Time to Plant and a Time to Uproot: A History of Agriculture in Papua New Guinea.* Port Moresby: Institute of Papua New Guinea Studies.

Harvey, D., 2003. *The New Imperialism.* Oxford: Oxford University Press.

Healey, C.J., 1985. *Pioneers of the Mountain Forest: Settlement and Land Redistribution among the Kundagai Maring of the Papua New Guinea Highlands.* Sydney: University of Sydney (Oceania Monograph 29).

Hide, R.L., 1973. *The Land Titles Commission in Chimbu: An Analysis of Colonial Land Law and Practice, 1933–68.* Port Moresby and Canberra: The Australian National University, Research School of Pacific Studies, New Guinea Research Unit (Bulletin 50).

Hirsch, E. and M. Strathern (eds), 2004. *Transactions and Creations: Property Debates and the Stimulus of Melanesia.* New York: Berghahn Books.

Holmes, I.A., 1953. 'The Legal Recognition of Native Land Rights.' *South Pacific* 7: 666–675.

Holzknecht, H., 1999. 'Customary Property Rights and Economic Development in Papua New Guinea.' In T. van Meijl and F. von Benda-Beckmann (eds), *Property Rights and Economic Development: Land and Natural Resources in Southeast Asia and Oceania.* London: Kegan Paul International.

Hughes, H., 2004. 'Can Papua New Guinea Come Back from the Brink?' Sydney: Centre for Independent Studies (Issue Analysis 49).

Hviding, E., 2015. 'Big Money in the Rural: Wealth and Dispossession in Western Solomons Political Economy.' *Journal of Pacific History* 50: 473–485. doi.org/10.1080/00223344.2015.1101818.

Jackson, R.T., 1977. 'The Growth, Nature and Future Prospects of Informal Settlements in Papua New Guinea.' *Pacific Viewpoint* 18: 22–42.

Jolly, M., 1992. 'Spectres of Inauthenticity.' *Contemporary Pacific* 4: 49–72.

Jorgensen, D., 1997. 'Who and What Is a Landowner? Mythology and Marking the Ground in a Papua New Guinea Mining Project.' *Anthropological Forum* 7: 599–628. doi.org/10.1080/00664677.1997.9967476.

Kavanamur, D., 1998. 'The Politics of Structural Adjustment in Papua New Guinea.' In P. Larmour (ed.), *Governance and Reform in the South Pacific.* Canberra: The Australian National University, National Centre for Development Studies (Pacific Policy Paper 23).

Keesing, R.M., 1968. 'Chiefs in a Chiefless Society: The Ideology of Modern Kwaio Politics.' *Oceania* 38: 276–280. doi.org/10.1002/j.1834-4461.1968.tb00973.x.

——, 1989. 'Creating the Past: Custom and Identity in the Contemporary Pacific.' *Contemporary Pacific* 1: 19–42.

Keesing, R.M. and R. Tonkinson (eds), 1982. *Reinventing Traditional Culture: The Politics of Kastom in Island Melanesia.* Special issue 13(3) of *Mankind.*

Kelly, A.B. and N.L. Peluso, 2015. 'Frontiers of Commodification: State Lands and Their Formalization.' *Society and Natural Resources* 28: 473–495. doi.org/10.1080/08941920.2015.1014602.

Koczberski, G., G.N. Curry and J. Connell, 2001. 'Full Circle or Spiralling out of Control? State Violence and the Control of Urbanisation in Papua New Guinea.' *Urban Studies* 38: 2017–2036. doi.org/10.1080/00420980120080916.

Koczberski, G., G.N. Curry and B. Imbun, 2009. 'Property Rights for Social Inclusion: Migrant Strategies for Securing Land and Livelihoods in Papua New Guinea.' *Asia Pacific Viewpoint* 50: 29–42. doi.org/10.1111/j.1467-8373.2009.01379.x.

Koyama, S.K., 2005. '"Black Gold or Excrement of the Devil"? The Externalities of Oil Production in Papua New Guinea.' *Pacific Economic Bulletin* 20(1): 14–26.

Larmour, P., 1984. 'Alienated Land and Independence in Melanesia.' *Pacific Studies* 8(1): 1–47.

Lattas, A., 2011. 'Logging, Violence and Pleasure: Neoliberalism, Civil Society and Corporate Governance in West New Britain.' *Oceania* 81: 88–107. doi.org/10.1002/j.1834-4461.2011.tb00095.x.

Lawrence, P. and I. Hogbin, 1967. *Studies in New Guinea Land Tenure.* Sydney: Sydney University Press.

Lawson, S., 2012. 'Indigenous Nationalism, "Ethnic Democracy" and the Prospects for a Liberal Constitutional Order in Fiji.' *Nationalism and Ethnic Politics* 18: 293–315. doi.org/10.1080/13537113.2012.707495.

Lea, D.A.M., 1969. 'Access to Land among Swidden Cultivators: An Example from New Guinea.' *Australian Geographical Studies* 7: 137–152. doi.org/10.1111/j.1467-8470.1969.tb00206.x.

Lea, D. and T. Curtin, 2011. *Land Law and Economic Development in Papua New Guinea.* Newcastle-upon-Tyne: Cambridge Scholars Publishing.

Leach, J., 2003. *Creative Land: Place and Procreation on the Rai Coast of Papua New Guinea.* New York: Berghahn Books.

Leitner, H., E. Sheppard and K.M. Sziarto, 2008. 'The Spatialities of Contentious Politics.' *Transactions of the Institute of British Geographers* 33: 157–172. doi.org/10.1111/j.1475-5661.2008.00293.x.

Li, T.M., 2014. 'What Is Land? Assembling a Resource for Global Investment.' *Transactions of the Institute of British Geographers* 39: 589–602. doi.org/10.1111/tran.12065.

Lomas, P.W., 1979. 'Malanggans and Manipulators: Land and Politics in Northern New Ireland.' *Oceania* 50: 53–66. doi. org/10.1002/j.1834-4461.1979.tb01931.x.

Lukes, S., 2005. *Power: A Radical View.* Basingstoke: Palgrave Macmillan (2nd edition). doi.org/10.1007/978-0-230-80257-5.

Macnaught, T.J., 1982. *The Fijian Colonial Experience: A Study of the Neo-Traditional Order under British Colonial Rule Prior to World War Two.* Canberra: Australian National University Press.

MacWilliam, S., 1988. 'Smallholdings, Land Law and the Politics of Land Tenure in Papua New Guinea.' *Journal of Peasant Studies* 16: 77–109. doi.org/10.1080/03066158808438383.

Maetala, R., 2008. 'Matrilineal Land Tenure Systems in the Solomon Islands: The Cases of Guadalcanal, Makira and Isabel Provinces.' In E. Huffer (ed.), *Land and Women: The Matrilineal Factor.* Suva: Pacific Islands Forum Secretariat.

Mair, L.P., 1948. *Australia in New Guinea* (intro. Lord Hailey). London: Christophers.

Manning, M. and P. Hughes, 2008. 'Acquiring Land for Public Purposes in Papua New Guinea and Vanuatu.' In AusAID (Australian Agency for International Development) (ed.), *Making Land Work—Volume Two: Case Studies on Customary Land and Development in the Pacific.* Canberra: AusAID.

Martin, K., 2013. *The Death of the Big Men and the Rise of the Big Shots: Custom and Conflict in East New Britain.* New York: Berghahn Books.

Marx, K., 1976 [1867]. *Capital: A Critique of Political Economy—Volume One* (transl. B. Fowkes). Harmondsworth: Penguin Books.

May, R.J. (ed.), 1982. *Micronationalist Movements in Papua New Guinea*. Canberra: Australian National University, Research School of Pacific Studies, Department of Political and Social Change (Monograph 1).

May, R.J., 1997. '(Re?)Discovering Chiefs: Traditional Authority and the Restructuring of Local-Level Government in Papua New Guinea.' Canberra: The Australian National University, Research School of Pacific and Asian Studies, Department of Political and Social Change (Regime Change and Regime Maintenance in Asia and the Pacific, Discussion Paper 18).

McDonnell, S., 2013. 'Exploring the Cultural Power of Land Law in Vanuatu: Law as a Performance That Creates Meaning and Identities.' *Intersections* 33.

McGrath, W.A., 1964. 'Notes for the Guidance of Administration Officers Engaged in the Investigation of Rights to Native Land and Purchase of Native Land.' Port Moresby: Department of Lands, Surveys and Mines.

Merry, S.E., 1988. 'Legal Pluralism.' *Law and Society Review* 22: 869–896. doi.org/10.2307/3053638.

Mitchell, D.D., 1976. *Land and Agriculture in Nagovisi, Papua New Guinea*. Port Moresby: Institute of Applied Social and Economic Research (Monograph 3).

Monson, R., 2015. 'From *Taovia* to Trustee: Urbanisation, Land Disputes and Social Differentiation in Kakabona.' *Journal of Pacific History* 50: 437–449. doi.org/10.1080/00223344.2015.1106642.

Moore, C., 2015. 'Honiara: Arrival City and Pacific Hybrid Living Space.' *Journal of Pacific History* 50: 419–436. doi.org/10.1080/00223344.2015.1110869.

Nash, J., 1974. *Matriliny and Modernisation: The Nagovisi of South Bougainville*. Port Moresby and Canberra: The Australian National University, Research School of Pacific Studies, New Guinea Research Unit (Bulletin 55).

———, 1987. 'Gender Attributes and Equality: Men's Strength and Women's Talk among the Nagovisi.' In M. Strathern (ed.), *Dealing with Inequality: Analysing Gender Relations in Melanesia and Beyond.* Cambridge: Cambridge University Press.

Naupa, A. and J. Simo, 2008. 'Matrilineal Land Tenure in Vanuatu— *"Hu i Kaekae long Basket?"*: Case studies of Raga and Mele.' In E. Huffer (ed.), *Land and Women: The Matrilineal Factor.* Suva: Pacific Islands Forum Secretariat.

Numbasa, G. and G. Koczberski, 2012. 'Migration, Informal Urban Settlements and Non-Market Land Transaction: A Case Study of Wewak, East Sepik Province, Papua New Guinea.' *Australian Geographer* 43: 143–161. doi.org/10.1080/00049182.2012.682293.

Ogan, E., 1971. 'Nasioi Land Tenure: An Extended Case Study.' *Oceania* 42: 81–93. doi.org/10.1002/j.1834-4461.1971.tb00306.x.

Oram, N.D., 1976. *Colonial Town to Melanesian City: Port Moresby 1884–1974.* Canberra: Australian National University Press.

Otto, T. and P. Pedersen, 2005. 'Disentangling Traditions: Culture, Agency and Power.' In T. Otto and P. Pedersen (eds), *Tradition and Agency: Tracing Cultural Continuity and Invention.* Aarhus: Aarhus University Press.

Oxfam, 2011. 'Land and Power: The Growing Scandal Surrounding the New Wave of Investments in Land.' Oxford: Oxfam GB for Oxfam International.

Panoff, M., 1970. 'Land Tenure among the Maenge of New Britain.' *Oceania* 40: 177–194. doi.org/10.1002/j.1834-4461.1970.tb01089.x.

Peluso, N.L. and C. Lund, 2011. 'New Frontiers of Land Control: Introduction.' *Journal of Peasant Studies* 38: 667–681. doi.org/10.108 0/03066150.2011.607692.

Ploeg, A., 1999. 'Land Tenure and the Commercialisation of Agriculture in Papua New Guinea.' In T. van Meijl and F. von Benda-Beckmann (eds), *Property Rights and Economic Development: Land and Natural Resources in Southeast Asia and Oceania.* London: Kegan Paul International.

Polanyi, K., 2001 [1944]. *The Great Transformation: The Political and Economic Origins of Our Time*. Boston (MA): Beacon Press.

Quinn, P.T., 1981. 'Agriculture, Land Tenure and Land Law to 1971.' In D. Denoon and C. Snowden (eds), *A Time to Plant and a Time to Uproot: A History of Agriculture in Papua New Guinea*. Port Moresby: Institute of Papua New Guinea Studies.

Reay, M., 1967. 'Structural Co-Variants of Land Shortage among Patrilineal Peoples.' *Anthropological Forum* 2: 4–19. doi.org/10.1080/00664677.1967.9967214.

Rich, R., L. Hambly and M. Morgan (eds), 2006. *Political Parties in the Pacific Islands*. Canberra: Pandanus Books.

Rimoldi, M., 1966. *Land Tenure and Land Use among the Mount Lamington Orokaiva*. Port Moresby and Canberra: The Australian National University, Research School of Pacific Studies, New Guinea Research Unit (Bulletin 11).

Rodman, M., 1987. *Masters of Tradition: Consequences of Customary Land Tenure in Longana, Vanuatu*. Vancouver: University of British Columbia Press.

Rose, C.M., 1994. *Property and Persuasion: Essays on the History, Theory, and Rhetoric of Ownership*. Boulder (CO): Westview Press.

Rowley, C.D., 1958. *The Australians in German New Guinea 1914–1921*. Melbourne: Melbourne University Press.

Sack, P.G. (ed.), 1974. *Problem of Choice: Land in Papua New Guinea's Future*. Canberra: Australian National University Press.

Scott, S., M. Stefanova, A. Naupa and K. Vurobaravu, 2012. 'Vanuatu National Leasing Profile: A Preliminary Analysis.' Washington (DC): World Bank, Justice for the Poor Program (Briefing Note 7.1).

Sikor, T. and C. Lund (eds), 2009. *The Politics of Possession: Property, Authority, and Access to Natural Resources*. Chichester: Wiley-Blackwell.

Storey, D., 2003. 'The Peri-Urban Pacific: From Exclusive to Inclusive Cities.' *Asia Pacific Viewpoint* 44: 259–279. doi.org/10.1111/j.1467-8373.2003.00214.x.

Strathern, M., 1972. *Women in Between: Female Roles in a Male World (Mount Hagen, New Guinea)*. London: Seminar Press.

——, 1988. *The Gender of the Gift: Problems with Women and Problems with Society in Melanesia*. Berkeley: University of California Press.

——, 1996. 'Cutting the Network.' *Journal of the Royal Anthropological Institute* (NS) 2: 517–535. doi.org/10.2307/3034901.

——, 1999. *Property, Substance and Effect: Anthropological Essays on Persons and Things*. London: Athlone Press.

Sykes, K., 2007. 'The Moral Grounds of Critique: Between Possessive Individuals, Entrepreneurs and Big Men in New Ireland.' *Anthropological Forum* 17: 255–268. doi.org/10.1080/00664670701637727.

Thaman, R.R., 1977. 'Urban Gardening in Papua New Guinea and Fiji.' In J.H. Winslow (ed.), *The Melanesian Environment*. Canberra: Australian National University Press.

——, 1995. 'Urban Food Gardening in the Pacific Islands: A Basis for Food Security in Rapidly Urbanising Small-Island States.' *Habitat International* 19: 209–224. doi.org/10.1016/0197-3975(94)00067-C.

Tsing, A.L., 2005. *Friction: An Ethnography of Global Connection*. Princeton (NJ): Princeton University Press.

Vandergeest, P. and N.L. Peluso, 1995. 'Territorialization and State Power in Thailand.' *Theory and Society* 24: 385–426. doi.org/10.1007/BF00993352.

Van Trease, H., 1987. *The Politics of Land in Vanuatu: From Colony to Independence*. Suva: University of the South Pacific.

von Benda-Beckmann, F., K. von Benda-Beckmann and M. Wiber, 2006. *Changing Properties of Property*. New York: Berghahn Books.

Wagner, R., 1974. 'Are There Social Groups in the New Guinea Highlands?' In M.J. Leaf (ed.), *Frontiers of Anthropology*. New York: Van Nostrand.

Ward, A., 1981. 'Customary Land, Land Registration and Social Equality.' In D. Denoon and C. Snowden (eds), *A Time to Plant and a Time to Uproot: A History of Agriculture in Papua New Guinea*. Port Moresby: Institute of Papua New Guinea Studies.

Ward, R.G. and E. Kingdon (eds), 1995. *Land, Custom and Practice in the South Pacific*. Cambridge: Cambridge University Press.

Watts, M., 2004. 'Resource Curse? Governmentality, Oil and Power in the Niger Delta, Nigeria.' *Geopolitics* 9: 50–80. doi.org/10.1080/1 4650040412331307832.

Weiner, J.F., 1991. *The Empty Place: Poetry, Space and Being among the Foi of Papua New Guinea*. Bloomington: Indiana University Press.

White, G.M., 1992. 'The Discourse of Chiefs: Notes on a Melanesian Society.' *Contemporary Pacific* 3: 73–108.

White, G.M. and L. Lindstrom (eds), 1997. *Chiefs Today: Traditional Pacific Leadership and the Postcolonial State*. Stanford (CA): Stanford University Press.

Wolford, W., S.M. Borras Jr, R. Hall, I. Scoones and B. White, 2013. 'Governing Global Land Deals: The Role of the State in the Rush for Land.' *Development and Change* 44: 189–210. doi.org/10.1111/ dech.12017.

Zimmer-Tamakoshi, L., 1997. 'When Land Has a Price: Ancestral Gerrymandering and the Resolution of Land Conflicts at Kurumbukare.' *Anthropological Forum* 7: 649–666. doi.org/10.1080 /00664677.1997.9967478.

Zoomers, A., 2010. 'Globalisation and the Foreignisation of Space: Seven Processes Driving the Current Global Land Grab.' *Journal of Peasant Studies* 37: 429–447. doi.org/10.1080/03066151003595325.

2

Urban Melanesia: The Challenges of Managing Land, Modernity and Tradition

Sarah Mecartney and John Connell

Introduction

All Melanesian countries exhibit rapid urbanisation, and yet, in development, policy, and academic discussions, they are often regarded as simply rural, since a large proportion of the population lives in rural areas and there is a strong cultural affiliation to the land. However, half of the Fijian population, more than a quarter of that in Solomon Islands and Vanuatu, and substantial numbers of Papua New Guineans are urban residents. Growing numbers, often now extending beyond formal urban boundaries, emphasise the need to recognise urbanisation and urbanism, and its permanency, and understand these new urban contexts, the processes utilised by different communities to access land and services, and how this influences and requires urban development and management.

Modernisation and globalisation have brought fundamental changes to Pacific societies, affecting values, goals and social norms. In 2008, the Pacific Islands Forum Secretariat, through its Land Management and Conflict Minimisation Project, recognised:

a shift taking place from communal lifestyles, to lifestyles where there is a greater emphasis on individual economic wealth accumulation, leading to increasing pressures to derive economic benefits from customary land. Basic human follies of greed and personal power influence people who are in positions of power, so that their decisions are at times being made for their own personal gains, and not in the interest of the landowning group as a whole (PIFS 2008: 19).

It did not, however, address the question of how non-customary owners and nationals access land, the varying notions of property rights in urban environments and their hinterlands, and how and why urban land issues have otherwise rarely been at the forefront of development planning. Although Melanesian towns and cities house increasingly larger proportions of national populations, they have become 'the elephants in the room—ignored in policy and practice, perhaps an aberration, a circumstance in transit—hopefully not really there and surely not the "real Pacific"' (Connell 2011: 121; see also Wittersheim and Dussy 2013). Policy, practice and perception largely ignore urban growth, despite its obvious centrality and underwhelming visibility.

It is scarcely surprising that policy makers have struggled with urban land. Land issues have made urban development particularly difficult, notably where land is mainly owned by local indigenous groups, as it is throughout Melanesia. Like other states, the current Solomon Islands government maintains land acquisition as a priority area for the broader development of the country and seeks 'to continue to pursue customary land mobilization and reform by looking at ways to bring customary land into productive usage as land remains fundamental in the country' (GoSI 2014: 6). That is a major challenge since access to land is zealously guarded as a critical, unique and enduring source of wealth, especially in towns and near urban boundaries where it seems most under threat, and problems have confronted external efforts to encourage land registration and privatisation, and thus an 'orderly, regulated and planned' urban development. Consequently, a distinctive form of urbanisation has developed, associated with the rights, or lack of rights, of residents to land in urban areas. Urban centres are increasingly characterised by a core 'modern city' and rapidly growing uncontrolled fringes of peri-urban customary land, settlements on marginal lands, and pockets of traditional villages swallowed up in the expanding modern town. This chapter examines these issues and the questions they raise about how rapidly changing cities can be managed, how they can contribute to national development, who have 'rights to the city', and what public policies might most effectively enable a more managed urban growth that can create space for the inclusion of multiple, diverse urban communities.

Urbanisation in Melanesia

Melanesia is rapidly urbanising at a pace that has increased significantly in this century, with accelerating social, economic and environmental changes placing pressure on access to urban land. Part of this urbanisation consists of suburbs and tower blocks (increasingly in gated communities) with formal tenure, that would not be out of place anywhere in the world; part consists of settlements largely constructed by the residents with diverse forms of formal and informal tenure; and part is composed of 'urban villages', where established villages—famously at Hanuabada in Port Moresby—have become surrounded and engulfed by expanding cities. The three parts symbolise the juxtaposition of modern and traditional, formal and informal, homogeneous and heterogeneous, whether of culture, housing or employment (Jones 2011a). Each part is composed of people and communities with social networks, governance structures, and various ways of life. Urban residents, short-term and long-term, are born there or come from all islands and provinces; they include professionals, unskilled people, migrants, customary landowners and squatters, all with different formal and informal tenure arrangements, on state-owned or custom-owned land, and with different reasons for being in the city.

All Melanesian towns and cities have informal and squatter settlements, with each of the four independent Melanesian states having 30–50 per cent of their urban populations living in these communities in 2010 (Connell 2011). Informal settlements are growing particularly quickly as the supply of land and formal housing is inadequate to meet needs. Informality occurs where incomes are low and irregular, public housing policies fail to meet demand for low-cost housing, and urban planning and management are weak. It is unsurprising that settlements are thus widely perceived as social, economic and environmental problems, and that there is opposition to rural–urban migration. Vanuatu and Solomon Islands have the highest current rates of urban growth in the Pacific at 2.8 per cent and 3.7 per cent per annum respectively. Such growth rates mean a doubling of population size in less than

20 years. In Honiara, this means about 1,500 additional residents looking for housing and land every year. In Port Vila, the minimum official area of residential plots is 600 square metres, and an additional 10,000 residential plots will be required in the next 16 years. Pressures on land are already obvious, in terms of demands on government authorities, extension of housing into more distant areas, inadequate infrastructure and service delivery, pollution and problematic environmental management. The geographical spread and spatial pattern to the distribution of changes in land use highlight a rapid rate of lease 'sales' in and around towns and cities, which is matched by increased struggles over land and growing political opposition to land sales. Pressure on land for commercial, agricultural and residential purposes produces a highly competitive environment, accompanied by increasing inequality, rising informality and, in some communities, a lower quality of life, especially where informal settlements are built on marginal, hazard-prone land, as land shortages necessitate, so contributing to a 'coastal squeeze' and intense pressures on land and housing in such areas (Jones 2011b; Connell 2013; Bryant-Tokalau 2014).

Over time, urbanisation has become more permanent, especially where urban residents or their ancestors have come from small and remote islands (Connell 2011). It is a tired romanticism that everyone has land to 'go back to' or, indeed, wishes to return to traditional villages. Many urban households have effectively severed connections with rural areas (or their distant rural kin have severed connections with them), have come from places where little land is available (even were they to seek to 'return'), or have children who have grown up without the language, aptitude and social connections for rural life, and who have relatively permanent urban employment. Urban residents may contemplate return but remain in town for their children's sake (Mecartney 2001). In some places an urban middle class has emerged with only tenuous connections to rural areas (Gewertz and Errington 1999). The importance of towns and cities for the future of Pacific Island states is inescapable, whether as drivers of economic growth, centres of social conflict, or simply centres of modernity. Yet national political leadership and urban bureaucracies are often still unwilling to accept the reality that urban populations will not only stay, but will continue to increase. Without that acceptance and more effective management, conflict may become more evident than economic growth. Resolving underlying land issues is thus crucial.

Contemporary Customary Complexities and the Right to the City

Within most Melanesian towns and cities, and especially the largest ones, multiple forms of land tenure exist, accompanied by even more ways of thinking about and owning urban and peri-urban land. Claims to land may come from colonial or post-colonial law, possession, purchase, customary ownership, or recognition by customary owners. That diversity, and the entanglements of ideologies, raise basic and severe challenges for governments for effective planning and controlling urban development and management. Government ownership is common in urban areas, dating from colonial era acquisition, with smaller but significant areas under customary tenure or individual freehold. On the fringes of towns, where expansion has become significant, customary tenure is much more important, and poses problems for the conversion of rural land to urban uses. A general problem exists in 'adapting tenures which derive from combined customary and colonial precedents, to serve the needs of non-customary, post-colonial societies' whilst 'traditional precedents are not relevant to modern urban living' (Crocombe 1987: 386, 390). The unresolved task of bringing customary land into a modern realm has resulted in substantial areas of capital cities especially being quarantined from urban development, whether for housing, garbage dumps, or other modern uses.

Melanesian countries place great store on the continuing role of customary land in support of national values. After Independence, Vanuatu went further than any other country in abolishing all freehold land tenure and returning land to traditional owners; in urban areas land titles were converted to automatic leases on the assumption that land rents would pass to customary owners (Rodman 1995). Customary landowners fear the loss of ownership of their land, and seek to protect it from alienation, yet feel they have little control over urban migrants who have settled on their land, even though, in most cases, permissions and some form of agreement have been made. Simultaneously, many feel threatened by overcrowding, lack of employment, and the rise of facets of contemporary life that are seen as problematic, such as excessive drinking, drugs, new diseases and brash youth, that challenge perceptions of tradition and the good life. Some traditional owners, such as the Motu-Koitabu in Port Moresby, have thus fought strenuously to prevent further settlement and gain more adequate compensation for land alienation (Connell and

Lea 2002: 131–2). However, over time, migrant groups have grown in number, size and authority, by dint of their growing power and status in urban society. Conversely, despite the growing semblance of permanency attached to the gradual acquisition of services and improvement to housing, settlers often have no security of tenure. Acquisition of secure land title is the most basic and greatest single need for most residents (Kiddle 2010), in itself also an indication of the extent of intended urban permanency. Uncertainty has resulted in their unwillingness to invest in housing and infrastructure, and so improve their quality of life.

Land issues are further complicated both by uncertainties about the nature of group ownership of particular tracts of land, and by indecision, uncertainty and division between landowners concerning the future of the land. In urban areas, local 'communities' are increasingly dispersed, leadership is fragmented, putative 'real owners' multiply and, via marriage and migration, once unknown 'others' may claim some form of ownership. The fact that there are multiple classes of claimants to a particular parcel of land, no strong tradition of delegated authority, and no statute of limitations with regard to customary claims, means that it is extremely difficult to come up with schemes by which landowners can pool resources to convert customary land into modern, alienable property (Fukuyama 2008: 21).

Such complexities can seem insuperable and have posed severe problems for urban development. At Blacksands settlement (Port Vila), some landowners lived in the settlement while others were quite distant; more distant landowners wished to legally subdivide the land to lease to possible investors, others sought to increase the number of settlers paying rent, some preferred the removal of settlers, and still others had no desire for any change (Mecartney 2001). Some customary landowners acknowledge the mutual benefits of opening up land for development on one side of the scale (for example, the Ifira Land Trust in Vanuatu), while others aggressively curtail any consideration of urban expansion or use of custom land for residential purposes. All were conscious that their need for land was likely to grow in the future, but there was no organisation, formal or informal, for them to articulate sentiments, fears and plans. Insecurity of tenure poses problems for landowners, settlers and urban managers.

That is further complicated where footholds in the city are tenuous, for example, where landowners who have negotiated leases with urban settlers die and new arrangements are negotiated. This has sometimes resulted in landowners attaching more stringent regulations on land, for example, banning some economic strategies such as fishing, using mangrove swamps for collecting crabs, shells and wood, and restricting gardening, numbers of houses (and ethnic groups), and the establishment of trade stores (Numbasa and Koczberski 2012). Such changing practices attest to increased competition for land (for housing and agriculture), marine access, and other urban resources. Many urban residents survive rather than prosper in the city, sometimes by holding several jobs, a situation of 'occupational multiplicity', or holding none at all, and merely 'killing time' (Mitchell 2013). Claims on the city vary substantially, urban dreams can remain elusive, and the city can seem a threatening place of strangers.

Since land is much more than an economic asset, were that not enough, and society is 'written on the ground', landownership is complex, embedded in cultural and personal relations, and not easily amenable to translation into Western codes and conventions. Even claiming exclusive rights to land for oneself or one's group can negate long-standing elements of reciprocity. Clarification of land tenure, however necessary for the working of a capitalist economy, can threaten the tenuous achievement of community and unity where land tenure remains cloudy and thus flexible, and even subject to competing claims, rather than be finalised and fossilised and a source of overt contention (McDougall 2005). That is, however, incompatible with most forms and processes of urban development.

Much attention on land in Melanesia is focused on the protection and benefits of land dealings for *in situ* landowners, and ignores how this may impact on national citizens who live and work on land with which they are not culturally associated. Customary landowners (and their relatives), governments (with access to public land) and smaller numbers of people who have been able to purchase land usually have superior urban status in terms of permanence and stability. By contrast, those who are relatively recent migrants, with temporary tenure (either negotiated or claimed by squatting), and who are usually relatively poor and without good access to employment, have weaker prospects for stability or access to services. That is accentuated where they are of different ethnicity, or with distinctive cultural characteristics, from the dominant urban population group. One consequence has been opposition to urban newcomers.

KASTOM, PROPERTY AND IDEOLOGY

In many of the larger Melanesian cities especially, deliberate efforts have been made by established urban residents, and urban and national governments, to exclude more recent migrants from urban permanency or simply refuse to grant access to such services as electricity and water supplies. In some sense this is a legacy of colonial 'apartheid' policies that sought to exclude 'inappropriate' natives from urban residence, and that were not overturned until the eve of Independence. The rise of urban populations, poverty and the informal sector (sometimes perceived as the 'infernal sector'), has been marked by new repressions of the poor and marginalised in anti-urban policies, where residents are forced out of urban areas, most dramatically by evictions and the bulldozing of settlements, and by attempts to devolve responsibilities from the state, for example to churches, rather than efforts to devise welfare and employment policies to reduce urban problems (Koczberski et al. 2001; Connell 2003, 2011; Russell 2009; Mitchell 2011). Even urban markets (especially for betel nuts) and market vendors have been opposed by urban and national governments, despite their ability to provide food and substantial employment, and thus livelihoods, albeit insecure, for youths and women. For two decades, Port Moresby food vendors have been harassed rather than provision made for them (Connell and Lea 2002). In Honiara, governments were bulldozing markets at the same time as formal reports were recognising them as invaluable for employment generation (Maebuta and Maebuta 2009; Russell 2009). Such opposition has occurred even while urban residents experienced reduced access to garden land and coastal fishing (Wittersheim 2011). Anti-urbanism is not, however, matched by pro-ruralism.

In a form of wishful thinking, residents of informal settlements are often perceived as temporary and/or not really belonging to the city, and thus unworthy of rights and services. Beyond this conceptualisation, quintessentially in Port Moresby, settlers are seen by the wider public, and by such agencies as the police, as 'violent and volatile' people, responsible for most urban crime, and a security threat who should therefore be repatriated to their rural villages (Mawuli and Guy 2007: 109–11). Ideally, they should be out of sight and out of mind—rather than becoming beneficiaries of positive policy formation. Such a pervasive and long-standing moral panic has taken various forms in the past. In some cases, this sense of 'not truly belonging' has resulted in conflict and forced removal of urban communities. As early as 1977, opposition to settlers in Bougainville resulted in several groups of squatters being repatriated to the New Guinea mainland (Connell and Lea 2002: 64–5). Attitudes have not fundamentally changed since then. Migrants in Port Vila, whether from Ambrym, Tanna or smaller islands, are seen as problematic and disruptive (Widmer 2013). In Honiara, violence erupted partly because of competition between different ethnic groups for scarce urban land (and equally scarce livelihoods) (Allen 2012). A correlation between urban crime levels and migration has been frequently voiced but lacks any demonstrable proof, whereas it is not implausible that social disorganisation and crime are a function of substantial inequalities in access to land, housing and other services. Practices opposing settlers have remained in the guise of achieving order and cleanliness, reducing crime and unemployment, freeing land for business development, and demonstrating that the state was not weak. No practices have contributed to developing a more inclusive city, or recognising the contribution of these residents through the provision of informal goods and services.

Opposition to settlers, and the lack of rights for customary owners, emphasise that cities are places of both inclusion and exclusion. The gradual emergence of post-colonial Melanesian 'revanchist cities' (Smith 1996) is characterised by discourses and actions directed at minorities, squatters, informal workers and recent migrants, creating an exclusionary version of civil society, nominally directed towards control and safety but designed to remove symptoms of poverty and difference from sight. In so doing, revanchist urban practices have displaced already marginalised people into more difficult circumstances, evaded the possibility of creating a more inclusive urbanism, and effectively denied the right to the city to a substantial proportion of the urban population. In other parallel contexts, this has resulted in calls for more substantive forms of participation and urban citizenship (Holston 2009; Stead 2015). Certain present and potential residents, and national citizens, have thus been more or less excluded from the city and its services and from the potential benefits of urban life, emphasising issues of contention, conflict and uneven power relations (Hall et al. 2011). Moreover, intensified competition over land and shifts in governance affect land use in ways that introduce new injustices (Sikor et al. 2013), while the sensitivity of land issues is a powerful political and economic tool—maximising the paradox of cultural protection and integrity against responsibility for fair land dealings for all. Modernisation has introduced new concepts and new dimensions to the use and management of customary land and the distribution of benefits derived from it. For example, resource extraction and infrastructure investment projects, such as those in Papua New Guinea (PNG) and Solomon Islands, offer compensation payments for alienated land that have often given rise to community conflict over compensation and a recent escalation in demands, even where that land has been used for the benefit of the local community (Banks 1998). The combination of disputes over landownership, increased claims for compensation by those who often perceive this to be their most valuable asset, the individualisation of property rights previously held in common (Gilberthorpe 2007) and mismanagement have all slowed the process of urban development.

Intensified competition and struggles over land 'coupled with shifts towards flow-centred governance has generated land uses involving new forms of social exclusion, inequity and ecological simplification' (Sikor et al. 2013: 522). Increased demands for land that surrounds towns have created a parallel increase in land 'ownership' claimants (just as around mine sites). Such land has high value due to demand, and is also the site of blurred civic responsibilities. Little clarity on the roles and rights of involved actors exists in the absence of clear national or cultural guidance in this growth space, so that, as in Southeast Asia, 'claims to land on the basis of indigenous or ethno-territorial basis in which one group asserts precedence and the right to exclude on the grounds of historical and affective claims to place, raise especially troubling dilemmas' (Hall et al. 2011: 11). The resultant urban fracture zones are evident, as in Vanuatu, with the creation of the Vete Indigenous Land Association, a 'registered' group of individual and group claimants primarily from the island of Tongoa and the Shepherd Islands, who state that they have been excluded from land decision processes on Efate, which they assert is their traditional land (Wilson 2011). Once again an increased number of claimants, using different strategies for claiming landownership, in urban sites where land is obviously becoming more valuable and in demand, does nothing to ease the task of urban management and development.

The Trouble with Land

Balancing the rights and needs of customary owners and migrant citizens represents a critical challenge for urban management, and, other than in Fiji, there has been a marked reluctance of government to intervene in customary land matters. Politicians deliver promises rather than plans.

Urban land has, to date, been conscientiously placed in the 'too hard basket' due to a lack of recognition of its contribution to development finance, and because cultural politics threaten future plans and vested interests oppose change. Nonetheless, throughout Melanesia, land mobilisation strategies have been pursued that would secure land for urban development, and in PNG finance has been secured for land development through the state becoming the lessee of customary land enabling lease-leaseback schemes for customary land mobilisation, bringing land into use without it becoming alienated (see Chapter 6, this volume). However, if land policies are piecemeal, exclude the role of the resource 'owner' and 'user', and fail to deal with the underlying systems for land rights allocation, land use planning and the land market, inefficiency and discontent may prevail.

Larger cities, greater urban permanency and environmental concerns raise new challenges, but especially the need for appropriate and accessible land for residential purposes and the management of growth (planning, infrastructure investment). There is a widespread and growing perception that institutions—whether state, customary or hybrid—are ineffective in managing land issues, and fail to deliver equitable or durable outcomes, hence their legitimacy is increasingly questioned. This imposes multiple stresses and costs on three critical fronts:

- restricted business development, whether small or large, local or foreign, through inadequate guarantees of security, making this less profitable, less durable and more uncertain;
- inefficient delivery of public assets—roads, schools, clinics, water and electricity—where disputes over rights, compensation and lease payments result in higher costs and delays; and
- decreased social cohesion, with intra-community and intergenerational tensions as a consequence of unresolved contests over benefit-sharing arrangements.

Thomas Sikor and colleagues (2013) note a discernible trend in land governance away from the classic territorial forms that had become dominant with the rise of the modern nation state, such as land use regulations made by central governments, land use planning conducted by local governments, and land management undertaken by local communities to guide access to and development of land. In Melanesian towns and cities, communities do not have a strong role in land management, nor is there clear action or an articulated role for customary landowners in contributing substantially to land management or use in peri-urban environments, the contemporary zones of crisis (Storey 2003).

Many urban land managers—land use and physical planners, housing and environmental officers—in Melanesia are confronted with multiple land challenges when seeking to address sustainable urban development issues. Land issues offer problems of:

- ambiguous and inadequately defined rights;
- frequent and unrecorded land use changes;
- land conflicts;
- land grabbing by powerful elites (access to urban land being a prime area of corruption);
- a lack of information (sometimes none at all or simply not in digital form);
- ambiguous and/or outdated, and poorly monitored and implemented land use plans;
- outdated legislation;
- over-regulation (with rules that are unknown and unenforceable with current staff capacity or without the technical ability to assess non-compliance);
- a lack of effective development control;
- fraudulent valuations; and
- a weak private land sector and market.

Whereas urban land management needs to be systemic to produce sustainable development, urban land managers are constantly forced to make instant, non-sustainable decisions about fundamental issues such as environmental concerns, climate change, and the occupation of vulnerable and disaster-prone locations. Beyond such problems there are few enough land managers or supportive institutions.

Tim Anderson (2011) and others downplay the need for land reform, promoting the productivity of customary land, its social value and the livelihood opportunities it supports. While this remains crucial in rural areas—especially in the face of land grabs (Filer 2011)—it is less valid in densely populated, fast growing, heterogeneous urban communities. Virtues exist in recognising flexibility, but what works in rural areas among largely homogeneous cultural groups is impossible to implement in cities. Here 'fuzzy boundaries have the virtue of enabling flexible accommodations', yet lack of clarity enables officials at various levels to 'act as tyrants, using the power invested in them erratically to evict, intimidate [and] make a grab for resources' (Hall et al. 2011: 12). Such 'regulatory fuzziness' poses greater problems at the peri-urban interface. Regulating access to land and exclusion from it are carried out by both state actors and customary groups, involving at least four areas of regulation that determine boundaries between pieces of land, prescribe the types of land use that are acceptable, determine the kinds of ownership and usufruct claims made with respect to different areas of land, and make claims about which groups have rule-based claims to any particular piece of land. Unsurprisingly, in such circumstances, regulation is not always effective, as reflected in the lack of compliance with land use plans, zoning strategies and local planning schemes that exists in both Port Vila and Honiara. Typically, therefore, in Honiara, although the Town and Country Planning Act allowed for stakeholders to take part in the development of a local planning scheme, the city council planners were not effectively implementing this provision (Hou and Kudu 2012: 25).

The two key actors promoting (and also opposing) changes in land relations are currently limited to national governments and customary landowners—the latter being dominated by male representatives (both individuals and as collective groups). The blurred administrative lines and boundaries of urban centres and their peripheries result in fuzzy responsibilities that allow state actors and customary owners to exclude urban settlements and their communities from access to services and fair land dealings. There is a need to address current urban boundaries and how any potential redefinition impacts on the rural edge, with its stronger traditional governance structures and norms, like the large settlement of Blacksands near Port Vila, which is largely ignored by all levels of government in Vanuatu. In recent years, there has been investment in institutional strengthening of state and subnational agencies to improve delivery for development planning, but customary landowners have not benefited from this, despite their relevant knowledge, being excluded from the more intimate but formal interactions of urban contexts. However, at a rather different scale from capital cities, a unique arrangement has been gazetted for the small urban centre of Lenakel (Tanna, Vanuatu), where the town's administrative area has been declared a 'physical planning area', and thus subject to national planning and zoning regulations, whilst the ownership of the land remains with the 12 customary land claimants. The management of the town is overseen by 13 councillors comprising representatives of the landowners, youth, women, churches and business houses. Its success remains to be seen, and what is possible in a town of no more than 4,000 people may not be easy to transfer elsewhere.

Remarkably, neither urban nor state land has expanded spatially since independence was gained, but few significant changes followed, beyond exceptional cases such as the gazetting of Nasinu as a new township in Fiji (within the Suva-Nausori corridor), and also Rakiraki. With rapid growth, there have been increasing calls to expand city and municipal boundaries (as in the case of Port Vila). The Solomon Islands government has listed, among its top 10 priorities, a desire 'to see the Honiara Boundary issue resolved so that sensible discussions can begin to occur about developments outside the original Honiara Boundary' (GoSI 2014: 6). This has been identified as a priority in recognition of the need for urban equity, social stability and economic growth, but will not be easy to implement in a contested area. Generally, there have been reactions rather than positive responses to expansion statements (emanating largely from government and private sector sources that seek economies of scale and social protection views). Local communities have demonstrated concern over land use, access and affordability, whilst landowners fear a minimisation of their roles as resource custodians, and a perceived loss of both cultural identity and a source of revenue. However, dialogue has often been maintained 'offline', outside formal meetings and often on an individual basis, and while many officials agree on the nature of the problems associated with land use, needs and management, few evince any real confidence that they can be overcome. A lack of enterprise, initiative and domestic leadership is difficult to ignore, and bodes ill for improving urban land governance and for development in a broader sense.

Towards Strategic and Inclusive Urban Planning

In Melanesia, public policy has largely been formally directed at rural development, transport and service provision. Policy or action for urban spaces is often absent, and the social ramifications of this are not well understood by national decision makers or citizens. Attempts at urban planning are scarcely new, and even flourished on the eve of decolonisation, and yet, half a century later, in rapidly changing cities with no tradition of planning and management, there are no demonstrable Melanesian success stories.

Urban planning—even land use planning—is rare in Melanesia, and unregulated urban expansion has increased the costs of urbanisation, especially for infrastructure provision. Public space and recreational space are scarce. Many settlements are entirely unregulated, and governments simply cannot keep pace with service provision, producing anarchic, dysfunctional and partial housing and land markets. Policies that once had some ephemeral success have been overwhelmed by rapid changes, especially urban population increases, bureaucratic inefficiency and, again, land shortages (Jones and Lea 2007). Management has worsened rather than improved. Few effective housing policies exist, and state housing is undeveloped and beyond the reach of the poor, so that people have had little option but to provide for themselves. Even 'site and service' schemes have become rare. In PNG, the National Capital District Commission's *Settlements Strategic Plan, 2007–2011* focused on upgrading settlement areas and developing site-specific plans related to distinctive land tenure situations, but it made little progress (Jones 2012). Basic infrastructure is rarely the result of public initiatives. Governments have demolished as much as constructed, so that many people are in effect urbanising the towns themselves, in the face of formal intransigence and neglect. Even then, urban communities find it increasingly difficult to access land for housing and other individual purposes. Five key challenges are the lack of access to land, acute competition for land, variable knowledge of land tenure, affordability, and the availability of adequate housing. These are most prevalent in the peri-urban interface where land markets are subject to competitive pressure as urban centres expand and speculation is frequent. Fiji's National Housing Policy (GoF 2011) therefore adopted a fundamental shift in the role of government, from provider to enabler of both affordable housing and improved access to land through innovative partnerships.

Recognition of the considerable challenges and the disappointments of urban planning and management brought belated external intervention to coordinate and exchange ideas, strategies and plans for urban development that culminated in the Pacific Urban Agenda (PUA). The PUA was developed in 2003, endorsed by the Pacific Islands Forum Leaders in 2005, and further accepted by the Pacific Urban Forum in 2007 (and again in 2011), as an effective mechanism for raising awareness and improving understanding of urban matters at country and regional levels, and one that could be used as a basis for the inclusion of urban issues in national development plans. The PUA was never formalised as a document, but was buried within the Pacific Islands Forum Secretariat's *Pacific Plan* (PIFS 2007), and without any regional agency tasked with putting it into place. Nonetheless, the PUA provided moral and practical support for effective urban policies and enshrined a set of themes and guidelines for establishing institutional frameworks, building technical capacity, and raising political awareness. In a region devoid of institutional support for urban management, it was a necessary development.

A set of interventions centred on four thematic areas:

- institutional framework: strengthening capacities (particularly local government);

- urban environment: integrating environmental and disaster management issues into urban development decision making;

- access to serviced shelter: strengthening provision of serviced land for urban development; and

- urban quality of life: recognising community and traditional decision-making structures where appropriate; engaging with vulnerable groups; addressing livelihood and employment; community-based safety nets.

The PUA did not directly advocate improved access to land for all, instead taking a less confrontational approach within the goal of improving institutional structures for better management of urban growth and the provision of infrastructure for basic services for urban communities. Land and housing were identified as priority areas in the PUA and reinforced at various meetings, such as a national urban forum in Vanuatu (2010), national housing policy consultations in Fiji (2011), the Papua New Guinea National Urban Forum (2012), the Pacific Housing Workshop (2012), and the Rights to Housing in Melanesia Workshop (2013). However, conspicuous in their absence at such meetings, or with limited representation, have been traditional landowners and leaders, the private sector and the community (in numerous possible versions of civil society)—three critical groups of actors who have significant influence in shaping their space and managing its use, and with their own rights to the city, but who have not always been organised or recognised. A key challenge within the PUA has been that of government agencies not proactively seeking dialogue with the identified customary landowners and the local community. Dual challenges of workload and regulatory responsibilities, along with uncertainty over how to actually engage with landowners and community alike, have frequently resulted in a lack of action or dialogue. Different ministerial portfolios do not support effective urban management or forward planning, such as city development strategies, and fragmentation of responsibilities is not conducive to effective and cohesive responses, especially where managerial expertise is scarce. Urban management requires a multisectoral coordination with governance, land, planning, investment, environment and community components, which allows interactions with people and politics.

Despite obvious constraints, the PUA has enjoyed some success as an advocacy platform, but its implementation at the regional level has suffered from limited technical and human capacity, a lack of (multipartner) commitment, and inadequate resources to implement priorities such as access to land and housing in the wider Pacific Plan. The difficulty of mobilising land for urban development deterred widespread embrace of the PUA, and enabled only limited efforts at participatory governance and the application of innovative skills and approaches required for unlocking customary land for urban growth. This reflected caution by both governments and politicians in evaluating the social, economic, environmental and political implications of urban change, rather than a conscious decision not to address urban issues. The weighing up of the implications of urban change (including evaluating financial costs), assessing the ramifications of urban improvements versus deferred expenditure in rural areas, the costs of the conditions and caveats attached to development loans and grants (more difficult to access for those not in the finance sector) and their impacts on local landowners, were all paramount considerations. Urban development was constantly deferred.

Some selected lessons learned through the application of the PUA are that Pacific Island countries require committed and active leadership (and champions), along with well-articulated, resourced and integrated plans for (urban) development. Such plans and strategies need to be developed through effective community consultations and then strong partnerships between national and local governments, public corporations (service providers), traditional leaders and landowners, community-based organisations, the private sector and development partners. These partnerships are critically important in addressing potential threats that undermine living standards, sustainability and economic growth, and in creating healthy and safe living environments across urban and peri-urban areas. That is no small challenge.

Management, Public Policy and Dialogue

The limited impact of the PUA has emphasised how urban plans and policies have been piecemeal and largely ineffective in managing rapid expansion at the urban fringe. Throughout Melanesia, national frameworks to guide urban growth and promote a more equitable share of the benefits of development are required. Partial land use and urban policies have been formulated in Vanuatu, Fiji and PNG, but with varying degrees of participation and sectoral integration affecting their impact. PNG has recently endorsed an Urbanisation Policy (GoPNG 2010), which clearly sets out the benefits and advantages of planned and managed urbanisation, but may be destined to become another moral statement rather than an effective practical plan. Nonetheless, settlement assessment and upgrading is being undertaken, and is supported by political leaders, while communities are organising themselves into collective associations to dialogue with state actors and better understand what their rights are within regulated and political urban environments.

Since 2007, several Pacific Island countries have commenced actions to manage urban growth. These have included the establishment of Planning and Urban Management Agencies (in Samoa, Tonga and Kiribati) with integrated work plans with land agencies, several policy dialogues, and policy formulation in consultation with other national government agencies, but these initiatives are yet to be effectively extended to the larger Melanesian states. Solomon Islands has continued to regularise temporary occupation licences in Honiara, thus giving settlers more security of tenure. Many such efforts have been conducted with little support from other sectors, thus highlighting the critical need to extend participation, since a key lesson is that exclusion of interest groups results in slow progress and a lack of a holistic ownership for improved urban management.

Fiji, by contrast, has a more active program (in partnership with land trusts, local governments, non-governmental organisations and communities) aimed towards eradicating poverty by the provision of housing and land opportunities for all. Fiji has recently clarified the role and responsibilities of the state in urban environments, settlements and accessing iTaukei (customary) land in a manner that strives for equitable benefits. However, the cost of management is high, both financially and politically, for the state, and the implementation of actions for improved access to land for all has commenced cautiously on a small scale, primarily directed at vulnerable communities in the Greater Suva Area. In 2014, the Ministry of Local Government, Urban Development, Housing and the Environment launched its Town-Wide Settlement Upgrading Programme, which targets settlements on iTaukei land within urban areas. The implementation strategy has been established by:

- facilitating the provision of basic infrastructure services and affordable and decent housing opportunities;
- providing some form of security of tenure (communal leases and regulated subdivisions as two options); and
- improving compliance with the Urban Policy Action Plan (2004), Urban Growth Management Plan (2006), and National Housing Policy (2011).

As this clearly demonstrates, numerous agencies and institutions must work together in urban areas.

The role of urban and peri-urban formal and informal settlements in policy dialogue has been marginalised, affecting well-intentioned but ill-formed policy goals and implementation. For 'fuzzy governance' at the peri-urban interface, hybrid systems—legal or perceived—are likely to be required, like those set up in the small town of Lenakel. Some states are moving in this direction. Thus the Constitution of Vanuatu (1980) recognises custom, and a range of statutory and regulatory instruments prescribe governance roles for several organisations rooted in custom, such as the National Council of Chiefs (Malvatumauri), the Vanuatu Cultural Centre, and Customary Land Tribunals. These arrangements have so far enabled Ni-Vanuatu to reaffirm local identity and *kastom* while pursuing economic and political liberalisation in ways that have eluded other Melanesian nations. Necessarily, though, this hybridity is incomplete, leaving gaps, overlaps and inconsistencies in the framework as the rapid pace of transformation from pre-market customary institutions to global institutions throws up unresolved policy contests, and also challenges the capability of existing institutions to effectively regulate and mediate transactions and ensure the affordability of both land and housing. Continuing globalisation of the economy, and the expected acceleration of investment and development affecting customary land, will pose additional challenges. The institutions responsible for managing these stresses—governmental, commercial and traditional—are coming under increased pressure (see Chapter 6, this volume).

Little can be achieved without advocacy and champions, and the involvement of landowners and settlers in more robust processes. Advocacy, public policy and dialogue are all being used to varying degrees to address improved access to land, property and services, and to resolve land conflicts. The experience of attempts at Pacific urban management over the last decade clearly indicates that there is a need to develop pragmatic and culturally acceptable solutions to packaging native and customary land for urban development, as little formal land supply has been provided. The task of developing relevant and robust planning responses to these challenges rests not with urban experts, but with the ability of central, provincial and local government to work *with* rather than *for* landowners and urban communities and respond to their needs rather than define their needs on their behalf. Recognising local community needs on the one hand, whilst integrating regional and international concerns on the other, calls for good communicators. Public policy can provide guidance when well formulated and inclusive dialogue contributes to developing practical goals and the sustainability of policy actions. However, such effective integrated activity is rare in any country, let alone in Melanesia.

Political urban champions are emerging but require more technical and financial support to implement the socially inclusive development they advocate. Without collective action to elevate urban and land challenges on development agendas, resource commitment will remain low. The additional challenges posed by natural disasters, and the adverse impacts of climate change that affect settlements and residential patterns, also demand the recognition of a continuum of land rights and action. For example, following the 2007 tsunami in Gizo, Solomon Islands, many did not want to return to their previous places of residence due to the perceived risks they would face if there were repeated natural disasters. However, due to land disputes and lack of clarity over land tenure, permanent places for resettlement were not identified. The government appeared unable or unwilling to take an active role in settling the disputes, and three years later security of tenure remained an issue, since the land disputes had not been formally settled and many of the affected population had rebuilt on Crown land with no legal permission. Such problems of resettlement are familiar throughout Melanesia and the wider Pacific (Connell 2012) and, yet again, indicate the land constraints to modern development.

Capacity constraints within both national and municipal governments affect the ability to get policy 'right', and its implementation remains a significant challenge. Despite genuine and considerable efforts in Melanesia, no single entity exists that can deliver on targeted and effective urban policy on its own. Greater integration and coordination need to be recognised across government agencies alongside genuine engagement with non-government actors, supported by greater political commitment and stronger administration, since these cannot be sustained by external partner support or on the moral basis of the PUA. More home-grown options must examine the role of the private sector and how it engages with the city and customary landowners. The voices of many people— notably the youth, women and urban residents (including non-customary landowners)—are muted in public consultation, where that exists. Community participation in urban discourse has been piecemeal and limited. While some urban communities are not as socially cohesive as rural and outer island communities, though these too lack cohesion, greater efforts need to be made in engaging affected urban communities in the planning, design and development of their locales.

The invisibility of communities is most marked in fringe squatter communities, such as Burns Creek on the edge of Honiara, where thousands are without the most simple access to water and sanitation facilities, living in conditions of poverty but not demanding improved access and opportunities either from the state (national and subnational) or from landowners for fear of violence or eviction. On the other hand, recent (February 2014) land reforms in Vanuatu insist on the inclusion of women and youth in decision dialogue with an Ombudsman for Land as a mediator should the case arise. A hybrid system, where modernity meets *kastom*, offers promising ways forward, but this too requires courageous champions and leaders. Customary landowners and indigenous structures will have a greater means of influence than they have exercised in the past and over a larger area. This requires governments to be sensitive to this scenario and less reliant on their own prerogatives. The cost of avoiding 'sensitive' land issues is too high a price to pay.

In this century, land summits and similar meetings have tended to focus on customary landowners, providing little space for the local population residing on or wishing to access non-state lands for residential/family purposes. Indeed, urban residents are caught between a place-of-living versus a place of traditional identity, in many ways disempowering their contribution to decision making. They may elect local councillors and national members of parliament, yet their engagement as 'non-customary' landowners in policy and other decision-making processes is currently limited. Greater efforts are needed to nurture the inclusion of urban residents in national land dialogues if a more equitable and people-centred development is to be achieved. Provision for dialogue has not been adequately provided in urban settings that at best operate symbolically, with chiefly representatives to mediate social situations that do not include access to 'foreign' land. People in the Pacific, regardless of where they live, have cultural knowledge of successful ways of resolving land-related conflict. This knowledge needs to be recognised, respected, supported and extended. Extra care needs to be taken to protect the interests of local people and to establish open dialogue and capacity building so that all involved parties understand the full consequences of development and investment and can make informed decisions.

Future Challenges

Land is a ubiquitous and problematic feature of development throughout the Pacific, and land management is unusually challenging in Melanesia, yet it is at the core of sustainable urban and increasingly national development. Limited understanding exists of the roles that towns and cities play in national development, and whether there is sufficient engagement of landowners, the private sector and the community in the management of this growth. Immediate urban problems may stem from land issues, absent policies and management limitations, but underpinning these are circumstances of limited economic growth, political instability and diverse development priorities. Customary land has tended to be a nation divider rather than a foundation for state building—ironic given that land tenure was a unifier in paths to independence in Melanesian countries. In PNG, where urbanisation was relatively late, towns were anticipated, on the eve of Independence, to become centres of national social, economic and political development—nothing less than 'crucibles of nationhood' (Ward 1970, cited in Connell 2011: 121). That optimistic era has long gone. Identity remains inseparable from land and, in revanchist cities, crucibles boil over. Over time, attitudes to urbanisation have hardened, through prejudice against squatter settlements rather than any idealist vision of rural development policy. There is no going back to *taem bifo*. People have moved and will continue to move, and genuine efforts between customary landowners, the state and community must recognise changed ways of living, and broader rights to the city.

The Pacific future is decidedly urban. Recognising this reality will help focus the efforts of governments and traditional leaders, and ordinary citizens, on practical measures to manage this growth, as well as address the critical discussions and decisions in relation to land. Yet for several decades, antipathy to migrants and settlers has been pervasive, emphasising how:

> The identity of the modern city is created by what it keeps out … In order to determine itself as the place of order, reason, propriety, cleanliness, civilisation and power, it must represent outside itself what is irrational, disordered, dirty, libidinous, barbarian and cowed (Mitchell 1988: 165).

Melanesians are rarely easily cowed, but such pervasive representations emphasise exclusion and denial of agency and minimise the possibility of comprehensive and strategic urban planning and management. There is an urgent need for practical discourse on the mutual benefits of accessing and developing customary land whilst respecting customary tenure systems. Just as urbanisation evolves and changes over time, so does custom, requiring modalities that recognise cultural protection and the need to provide basic services for all citizens while also taking into account equitable access to land. Critically, Pacific cities and their management demonstrate and require elements of hybridity that offer solutions in other realms of development and change (Connell 2013). The modern city must be built, grounded and inspired by traditional foundations. This is particularly significant where the physical boundaries of urban areas do not coincide with their administrative boundaries, and peri-urban areas play an important role in the provision of food, water resources and land. This peri-urban interface is also where processes of urbanisation are most intense, and where some of the most obvious social and environmental impacts are located. If well managed, the interactions between town and village provide the basis for a balanced regional and sustainable development. Yet, despite a greater engagement with the broader community for management approaches that are grounded in the principles of equity, justice and human rights, and the right to the city, inevitable problems exist in seeking to embrace competing philosophies of land tenure, under pressure and in contexts of rapid change and mobility, respecting different groups with varied interests, knowledge, wisdom and objectives, but among whom consultation and collaboration are required.

Committed political and traditional leadership is needed to accept the reality that urban populations will continue to increase and urbanisation will intensify. Urban solutions depend on economic growth, slower population growth, more effective service provision and management, and innovative approaches to land provision. The level of protection and respect of human rights will be tested as countries continue to urbanise. Advocacy for the recognition of increasing urban permanency, public policy for managing urban growth, and creating space for the inclusion of urban communities in land discussions are crucial. Champions, plans, and skilled, competent and neutral managers, and considerable general goodwill and political will, are all required. Actions must work for both short and long-term periods. There needs to be genuine collaboration across multiple stakeholder groups for meaningful actions in managing urban growth whilst ensuring fair land dealings for all and not just for a selected few. That is no gentle challenge or easy agenda where economic prospects are constantly changing. But the consequences of continued inaction and an imbalanced discourse may result in conflict and increased poverty in both urban and rural environments.

References

Allen, M., 2012. 'Land, Identity and Conflict on Guadalcanal, Solomon Islands.' *Australian Geographer* 43: 163–180. doi.org/10.1080/00049 182.2012.682294.

Anderson, T., 2011. 'Melanesian Land: The Impact of Markets and Modernisation.' *Journal of Australian Political Economy* 68: 86–107.

Banks, G., 1998. 'Compensation for Communities Affected by Mining and Oil Developments in Melanesia.' *Malaysian Journal of Tropical Geography* 29: 53–67.

Bryant-Tokalau, J., 2014. 'Urban Squatters and the Poor in Fiji: Issues of Land and Investment in Coastal Areas.' *Asia Pacific Viewpoint* 55: 54–66. doi.org/10.1111/apv.12043.

Connell, J., 2003. 'Regulation of Space in the Contemporary Postcolonial Pacific City: Port Moresby and Suva.' *Asia Pacific Viewpoint* 44: 243–258. doi.org/10.1111/j.1467-8373.2003.00213.x.

——, 2011. 'Elephants in the Pacific? Pacific Urbanisation and Its Discontents.' *Asia Pacific Viewpoint* 52: 121–135. doi.org/10.1111/j.1467-8373.2011.01445.x.

——, 2012. 'Population Resettlement in the Pacific: Lessons from a Hazardous History.' *Australian Geographer* 43: 115–126.

——, 2013. *Islands at Risk: Environments, Economies and Contemporary Change.* Cheltenham: Edward Elgar.

Connell, J. and J. Lea, 2002. *Urbanisation in the Island Pacific: Towards Sustainable Development.* London: Routledge. doi.org/10.4324/9780203453070.

Crocombe, R., 1987. *Land Tenure in the Pacific.* Suva: Institute of Pacific Studies (3rd edition).

Filer, C., 2011. 'New Land Grab in Papua New Guinea.' *Pacific Studies* 34: 269–294.

Fukuyama, F., 2008. 'State Building in Solomon Islands.' *Pacific Economic Bulletin* 23(3): 18–34.

Gewertz, D. and F. Errington, 1999. *Emerging Class in Papua New Guinea The Telling of Difference.* Cambridge: Cambridge University Press. doi.org/10.1017/CBO9780511606120.

Gilberthorpe, E., 2007. 'Fasu Solidarity: A Case Study of Kin Networks, Land Tenure and Oil Extraction in Kutubu, Papua New Guinea.' *American Anthropologist* 109: 101–112. doi.org/10.1525/aa.2007.109.1.101.

GoF (Government of Fiji), 2011. *The National Housing Policy.* Suva: Ministry of Local Government, Urban Development, Housing and Environment.

GoPNG (Government of Papua New Guinea), 2010. *National Urbanisation Policy for Papua New Guinea, 2010–2030.* Port Moresby: Office of Urbanisation.

GoSI (Government of Solomon Islands), 2014. Statement by the Prime Minister, the Honourable Gordon Darcy Lilo. Honiara, 21 January.

Hall, D., P. Hirsch and T.M. Li, 2011. *Powers of Exclusion: Land Dilemmas in Southeast Asia*. Singapore: NUS Press.

Holston, J., 2009. 'Insurgent Citizenship in an Era of Global Urban Peripheries.' *City and Society* 21: 245–267. doi.org/10.1111/j.1548-744X.2009.01024.x.

Hou, T. and D. Kudu, 2012. 'Solomon Islands: Honiara Urban Profile.' Nairobi: United Nations Human Settlements Programme (UN-Habitat).

Jones, P., 2011a. 'Urbanisation in the Pacific Islands Context.' *Development Bulletin* 74: 93–97.

———, 2011b. 'Urban Poverty in Pacific Towns and Cities and the Impact from the Global Financial Crisis: Insights from Port Moresby, Papua New Guinea.' *Australian Planner* 48(3): 32–45.

———, 2012. 'Pacific Urbanisation and the Rise of Informal Settlements: Trends and Implications from Port Moresby.' *Urban Policy and Research* 30: 145–160. doi.org/10.1080/08111146.2012.664930.

Jones, P. and J. Lea, 2007. 'What Has Happened to Urban Reform in the Island Pacific? Some Lessons from Kiribati and Samoa.' *Pacific Affairs* 80: 473–491. doi.org/10.5509/2007803473.

Kiddle, G.L., 2010. 'Perceived Security of Tenure and Housing Consolidation in Informal Settlements: Case Studies from Urban Fiji.' *Pacific Economic Bulletin* 25(3): 193–213.

Koczberski, G., G. Curry and J. Connell, 2001. 'Full Circle or Spiralling out of Control? State Violence and the Control of Urbanisation in Papua New Guinea.' *Urban Studies* 38: 2017–2036. doi.org/10.1080/00420980120080916.

Maebuta, H. and J. Maebuta, 2009. 'Generating Livelihoods: A Study of Urban Squatter Settlements in Solomon Islands.' *Pacific Economic Bulletin* 24(3): 118–131.

Mawuli, A. and R. Guy (eds), 2007. *Informal Social Safety Nets: Support Systems of Social and Economic Hardships in Papua New Guinea*. Port Moresby: National Research Institute (Special Publication 46).

McDougall, D., 2005. 'The Unintended Consequences of Clarification: Development, Disputing, and the Dynamics of Community in Ranongga, Solomon Islands.' *Ethnohistory* 52: 81–109. doi.org/10.1215/00141801-52-1-81.

Mecartney, S., 2001. Blacksands Settlement: Towards Urban Permanence in Vanuatu. Sydney: University of Sydney (MA thesis).

Mitchell, J., 2011. '"Operation Restore Public Hope": Youth and the Magic of Modernity in Vanuatu.' *Oceania* 81: 36–50. doi.org/10.1002/j.1834-4461.2011.tb00092.x.

——, 2013. 'Tuer le Temps dans une Ville Postcoloniale: Les Jeunes et les Quartiers à Port-Vila, Vanuatu.' In D. Dussy and E. Wittersheim (eds), *Villes Invisibles: Anthropologie Urbaine du Pacifique.* Paris: L'Harmattan.

Mitchell, T., 1988. *Colonising Egypt.* Berkeley: University of California Press.

Numbasa, G. and G. Koczberski, 2012. 'Migration, Informal Urban Settlements and Non-Market Land Transactions: A Case Study of Wewak, East Sepik Province, Papua New Guinea.' *Australian Geographer* 43: 143–161. doi.org/10.1080/00049182.2012.682293.

PIFS (Pacific Islands Forum Secretariat), 2007. *The Pacific Plan for Strengthening Regional Cooperation and Integration.* Suva: PIFS.

——, 2008. *Improving Access to Customary Land and Maintaining Social Harmony in the Pacific.* Suva: PIFS.

Rodman, M., 1995. 'Breathing Spaces: Customary Land Tenure in Vanuatu.' In R.G. Ward and E. Kingdon (eds), *Land, Custom and Practice in the South Pacific.* Cambridge: Cambridge University Press. doi.org/10.1017/CBO9780511597176.004.

Russell, L., 2009. 'Stayin' Alive: A Report on Urban Livelihoods in Honiara, Solomon Islands.' Sydney: APHEDA.

Sikor, T., G. Auld, A.J. Bebbington, T.A. Benjaminsen, B.S. Gentry, C. Hunsberger, A.M. Izac, M.E. Margulis, T. Plieninger, H. Schroeder and C. Upton, 2013. 'Global Land Governance: From Territory to Flow?' *Current Opinion in Environmental Sustainability* 5: 522–527. doi.org/10.1016/j.cosust.2013.06.006.

Smith, N., 1996. *The New Urban Frontier: Gentrification and the Revanchist City*. New York: Routledge.

Stead, V., 2015. 'Homeland, Territory, Property: Contesting Land, State, and Nation in Urban Timor-Leste.' *Political Geography* 45: 79–89. doi.org/10.1016/j.polgeo.2014.05.002.

Storey, D., 2003. 'The Peri-Urban Pacific: From Exclusive to Inclusive Cities.' *Asia Pacific Viewpoint* 44: 259–279. doi.org/10.1111/j.1467-8373.2003.00214.x.

Widmer, A., 2013. 'Diversity as Valued and Troubled: Social Identities and Demographic Categories in Understandings of Rapid Urban Growth in Vanuatu.' *Anthropology and Medicine* 20: 142–159. doi.org/10.1080/13648470.2013.805299.

Wilson, D., 2011. *Vete*: The Emerging Movement on Efate, Vanuatu Politics and Indigenous Alternatives. Honolulu: University of Hawaii (PhD thesis).

Wittersheim, É., 2011. 'Paradise for Sale: The Sweet Illusions of Economic Growth in Vanuatu.' *Journal de la Société des Océanistes* 133: 323–332. doi.org/10.4000/jso.6515.

Wittersheim, É. and D. Dussy, 2013. 'La Question Urbaine en Océanie.' In D. Dussy and É. Wittersheim (eds), *Villes Invisibles: Anthropologie Urbaine du Pacifique*. Paris: L'Harmattan.

3

Urban Land in Solomon Islands: Powers of Exclusion and Counter-Exclusion

Joseph D. Foukona and Matthew G. Allen

Introduction

Donovan Storey has observed that urban growth in Melanesia 'has created an unabated demand on services, shelter, infrastructure and land—all of which are in limited supply' (Storey 2003: 259). There can be no doubt that the supply of, and demand for, land as a commodity is a salient driver of exclusion from land in urban Honiara, the capital of Solomon Islands. In keeping with this volume's mandate to engage with the *Powers of Exclusion* framework developed by Derek Hall, Philip Hirsch and Tania Murray Li (2011), we apply it, first, to an analysis of the processes by which people—both settlers and those 'indigenous' to the island of Guadalcanal, which hosts Honiara—are being prevented from accessing urban land; and second, to an analysis of the strategies that the subjects of this exclusion are employing to claim, or claim back, access to land within the city boundaries. In other words, we are interested in examining powers of both exclusion and counter-exclusion as they apply to contemporary Honiara. In doing so, we suggest that the powers of exclusion and counter-exclusion at play in Honiara can only be fully understood against the backdrop of an encompassing political economy characterised by patronage networks and personalised forms of political and administrative governance; and with reference to the particular histories and social relations of Solomon Islands.

That said, we find much of heuristic value in Hall, Hirsch and Li's framework. Of the four powers of exclusion they identify—regulation, force, the market and legitimation—regulation and the market (and, to a much lesser extent, force) provide useful lenses on the processes of exclusion that are playing out in Honiara. In the case of powers of counter-exclusion (Hall et al. 2011: 170–91), we find that legitimation plays a central role, as evidenced by collective mobilisations around discourses such as indigeneity, customary landownership, nation-building and citizenship. While force has not, to date, emerged as a salient power of counter-exclusion in urban Honiara, contemporary urban land struggles are set against the backdrop of the so-called 'Ethnic Tension' of 1998–2003, which saw the violent eviction of settlers from rural and peri-urban areas immediately adjacent to Honiara at the hands of Guadalcanal militants whose agenda could be broadly characterised as 'ethno-territorial' (Hall et al. 2011: 175–80). In the contemporary post-conflict setting, lingering tensions and grievances, including in relation to the original alienation of the land that now hosts Honiara, cast a spectre of violence over the city. Moreover, the increasingly violent character of Honiara's settlements, most of which are organised along ethnic lines, and previous incidents involving the mobilisation of settlement youth in overt acts of collective political violence, raise the possibility that force could yet become more salient as a power of counter-exclusion in urban Honiara.

In applying the *Powers of Exclusion* framework to our examination of processes of exclusion in urban Honiara, and in particular to the interaction between regulation and the market, we arrive at a broadly similar set of conclusions to those reached by Hall, Hirsch and Li, namely that the formal rules often bear little resemblance to on-the-ground realities (Hall et al. 2011: 16), that public officials frequently 'act as tyrants' in the administration of land (ibid.: 14), and that the market for land is not a product of 'some abstract space of supply and demand' (ibid.: 18). We demonstrate how the abuse of discretionary powers vested in the Commissioner of Lands has seen property rights in urban land allocated in ways that distort the market and abrogate formal legal procedures. Once such allocations have been made, the courts have tended to rule in favour of registered titleholders, and, on occasion, these rulings have been enforced by the state's security apparatus. It is within this realm—the 'fuzzy zone of compromise, accommodation and bribery' (ibid.: 16)—that Solomon Islands' distinctive political economy, characterised by patronage networks and highly personalised forms of political and administrative governance, becomes paramount in understanding how exclusion plays out in urban Honiara.

Moreover, this political economy is also evident in some of the powers of counter-exclusion. We shall elucidate cases in which settlers have been able to successfully mobilise political and patronage networks in order to secure their access to urban land. Counter-exclusion has also seen the deployment of discursive strategies that are familiar from Southeast Asia, for example in competing narratives of settlers as citizens and nation-builders, on the one hand, and the rights of indigenous people on the other (Allen 2012). But again, these discourses are inflected by the particular histories and social relations of Solomon Islands. For example, the discourse of customary landownership (Filer 1997), which we conceptualise as sitting at a scale below indigeneity (which, in the case of Solomon Islands, is often nested at the scale of the island or province), has become a powerful ideology of both exclusion and counter-exclusion; while settler narratives, especially those of the nation's largest group of migrant-settlers—Malaitans—are firmly rooted in histories of labour migration and workers' struggle. We also demonstrate how settler narratives of counter-exclusion have recently begun to invoke the colonial construct of 'waste lands', with its obvious connections to the overarching discursive themes of citizenship and nation-building.

We begin by discussing the historical context of Honiara, and the rapid expansion of the city and its settlements that has occurred over the past several decades. We then examine the processes by which people have been excluded from accessing land in urban Honiara, focusing on the role of the Commissioner of Lands in both abrogating legal processes and distorting the urban land market. We then move to an analysis of the ways in which groups and individuals, including both settlers and indigenous landowners, have sought to counter their exclusion from the urban space. We conclude by reflecting upon the utility of the *Powers of Exclusion* framework in the case of urban Honiara and by discussing a recent change to the law designed to curb the discretionary powers of the Commissioner of Lands.

Historical Context of Honiara

The Honiara landscape once upon time was under customary land tenure. The tenure arrangements were in accordance with the rules of custom. The rights to customary land were exercised by individuals, a family or group who belong to a clan or tribe (Allan 1957). How a person accessed customary land was through membership of a line, tribe or clan. Access and use of customary land could also be allowed based on special arrangements such as compensation, marriage, warfare or gifts (Zoleveke 1979). However, in the case of Honiara, the customary landscape changed over time into an urban space as a consequence of land alienation prior to and during the colonial period.

The site of the present city of Honiara was 'partly occupied by the village of Mataniko which consisted of a group of leaf houses' (BSIP 1968: 5). The alienation of this core landscape originates from three land transactions negotiated between traders and people categorised as landowners prior to the establishment of Solomon Islands as a British Protectorate in 1893 (Moore 2013). The core area from Lunga to Point Cruz, referred to as Mataniko, was alienated through sale by Woothia (or Uvothea), Chief of Lunga, Allea, Chief of Nanago, and the latter's son, Manungo, to Thomas Gervin Kelly, John Williams and Thomas Woodhouse (who were trading partners) for £60 of trade goods in November 1886 (Moore 2013; WPHC n.d.). The other area to the west, bordering on Point Cruz, referred to as Ta-wtu (or Mamara plantation), was alienated to Karl Oscar Svensen and his partner Rabuth. The third land transaction was the alienation of the 'area to the east, named "Tenavatu"' to William Dumply, an employee of Svensen (Moore 2013).

These land areas were further alienated by the traders to other commercial actors, such the Levers plantation company, following the introduction of a leasing system by the colonial government soon after 1893. This process of alienation resulted in the exclusion of the original landowners from their land because of the new owners asserting their property rights. These land alienation processes have been sources of contestation since the 1920s, which resonates with Colin Filer's concept of a 'double movement' of property rights in the context of Papua New Guinea. He argues that 'steps taken towards the partial or complete alienation of customary rights are continually compensated or counter-balanced by steps taken in the opposite direction, towards the reassertion of such rights' (Filer 2014: 78). The double movement provides a useful framing for the ongoing assertion and reassertion of claims to land in and around Honiara.

The Kukum or Mataniko land, the core land area where Honiara is situated, was contested by landowners as an unfair purchase, and this was investigated by Gilchrist Gibbs Alexander, who was appointed in 1919 as Lands Commissioner to investigate previous land alienations in the Protectorate.[1] The Lands Commission recommended that the land claim be settled as follows:

> (a) A survey should be made at the expense of Levers Pacific Plantation Ltd of all land to the east of the Matanikau River, all such land to be included in the title of the company, the Matanikau river to be the western boundary and the line run south west from Ilu to the back boundary of the Matanikau river; (b) the land to the west of the Matanikau River including all coconut trees planted by Levers Pacific Plantation Ltd to revert to native custom owners and to be excluded from the title of the [company]; (c) the natives to move the village of Matanikau to the west of the Matanikau river but to have the produce of the native gardens on the east side of the river so long as the present crops are bearing; (d) Levers to pay 50 pounds to the natives; (e) on completion of the survey a validating Regulation should be passed confirming the freehold title of Levers in the land shown on the survey plans as finally approved by the Resident Commissioner (WPHC 1922).

The Secretary of State confirmed this recommendation by publishing it in the *Pacific High Commission Gazette* in 1924, which gave it a force of law. This state-sanctioned process legitimated the property rights of Levers Pacific Plantation Ltd. It also authorised the return of land to the west of the Mataniko River to landowners.

Honiara did not exist prior to 1942. The decision by the colonial administration to relocate the capital from Tulagi to Honiara appeared to be influenced by a number of factors. One was the existence of critical infrastructure left behind by the departing United States forces in 1945, such as the airfield at Henderson. Another was the 'anticipated agriculture potential of the Guadalcanal Plains and the dry healthy nature of the climate' (Bellam 1970: 70). During this period, Honiara was an

---

1   Alexander resigned towards the end of 1920 after investigating 29 out of 55 land claims. He was replaced by Frederick Beaumont Philips to complete the work of the Land Commission, which then came to be known as the Philips Commission.

'underpopulated and largely alienated hinterland' (ibid.). The land area on the east side of the Mataniko River, which was alienated by Levers Pacific Plantation Ltd and held as a freehold estate title known as Kukum, was acquired by the colonial administration in 1947 through a land acquisition process prescribed by law. The colonial administration acquired the land to the west of the Mataniko River through a process of negotiation with landowners who occupied it. Consequently, the landowners relocated to the fringes of the Honiara town boundary and the state assumed a 'monopoly of ownership of land in Honiara. On this clean new tenurial slate the capital was built' (ibid.: 70).

However, in 1964, Baranamba Hoai of Mataniko village disputed the state's title to land comprising the Honiara town. He made a claim on behalf of himself and the Kakau and Hebata lines of Mataniko village, reasserting ownership rights over a part of the Honiara town land. Hoai and four others gave evidence to substantiate their land claim. But the Registrar of Titles rejected the claims on the basis of a lack of *prima facie* evidence and forwarded the case for decision by the Western Pacific High Court. In his ruling, Chief Justice G.G. Briggs also rejected Hoai's claim due to lack of reliable evidence. The High Court further held that Hoai's claim was the same claim that was settled in 1924, and remained binding on the parties concerned (Anon. 1964; Moore 2013). To this day, this remains the key court decision that legitimises the state's property rights to land in Honiara.

Post-War Migration and the Growth of Honiara's Settlements

Due to Honiara's status as a city situated on alienated land over which the state has proprietary rights, it has attracted migrants from other islands to be part of this state landscape. The pattern of internal migration was influenced by the uneven distribution of 'development' and social and economic opportunities. The concentration of education, medical and employment opportunities in Honiara and the surrounding areas of north Guadalcanal was a major factor in attracting people to the island of Guadalcanal.

Although people from various islands have migrated and settled in Honiara, the largest number have come from Malaita (Gagahe 2000: 53, 63–5). This is because it was Malaitan labour that was exploited in the development projects that took place on Guadalcanal, in the Western Solomons, and in other parts of the country. Part of the reason was that Malaita had a bigger population that could supply labour to the colonial plantations, and, later, to the industries in Honiara. John Connell, in a study commissioned by the former South Pacific Commission (now the Secretariat of the Pacific Community), pointed out that migration to Guadalcanal and the Western Solomons was high in the period from 1978 to 1981 because of the employment opportunities available in these two provinces (Connell 1983). Nicholas Gagahe also noted that, according to the 1970, 1976 and 1986 national censuses, Malaita had a large number of out-migrants to Honiara, Guadalcanal, Western and Central Provinces (Gagahe 2000: 53, 63–5).

This has resulted in an increasing number of informal Malaitan settlements located in every corner of Honiara. Most of these settlements evolved from the temporary housing schemes that were introduced in the 1960s, and their names reflect their ethnic composition based on either dialect or regions of Malaita. For instance, settlements in Honiara having Malaita dialect names are Ada'liua, Aekafo, Fera'ladoa, Matariu, Koa Hill, Lau Valley, Kwaio Valley, Fulisango and Tolo. Other settlements that comprise a mixture of people from various regions of Malaita include Burns Creek, Sun Valley, Borderline, New Mala, Kobito (1, 2 and 3), Green Valley, Gilbert Camp, Kaibia and Mamulele. While these settlements lack a guarantee of tenure security, with their residents therefore susceptible to processes of exclusion, some residents have built permanent houses and have subsequently successfully applied to the Commissioner of Lands to transfer the fixed-term estate title to them. We discuss this further in a later section of the chapter.

In 1960, the state introduced 'temporary housing area' (THA) schemes on public or state land within the Honiara town boundary to cater for the influx of people to the town and to address the emergence of squatter settlements (Storey 2003). People were allowed to settle on public land and build temporary housing for a nominal fee of SB$5 or SB$10 per annum for a 'temporary occupation licence' (TOL) (Tozaka and Nage 1981: 115–8; Storey 2003). The system was intended to provide people some form of legal security in relation to urban land use while simultaneously discouraging 'large scale illegal settlement on other urban lands' (Storey 2003: 269).

By the mid-1980s, 'THAs accommodated 23 per cent of Honiara's population ... those THAs outside the town's boundaries numbered around 15, with an estimated population of 1,308 persons' (Storey 2003: 269). Over the years, however, the THA system has broken down, due in part to the significant increase in rural–urban migration. Other factors that have contributed to its decline include inadequate town planning, unaffordable housing and the maladministration of urban land. A household survey in 2006, funded by AusAID through the Solomon Islands Institutional Strengthening Lands and Administration Project, reported that only 10 of the 3,000 households surveyed had a valid TOL.

During the Ethnic Tension, which was mainly restricted to the island of Guadalcanal, some 30,000 settlers, most of whom were of Malaitan origin, were violently evicted from their places of residence in the rural and peri-urban areas west and especially east of Honiara. These displaced people either returned to Malaita or sought refuge in Honiara, where the city boundaries were secured by police and Malaitan militias. In the wake of the Ethnic Tension, Malaitan settlers have been unwilling to return to their former homes in rural and peri-urban Guadalcanal, even in the case of those who had obtained legal titles to land (Allen 2012). Honiara, on the other hand, continues to be seen as a safe and legitimate space to take up residence—a factor that has contributed to the rapid growth of both the city and its settlements since the restoration of peace and law and order in mid-2003.

Occupying an area of only 22.73 square kilometres, Honiara is easily the largest urban centre in Solomon Islands, accounting for around 78 per cent of the total urban population. The 2009 census recorded the city's population as 64,606, which increases to around 80,000 when its peri-urban fringes are included (Allen and Dinnen 2015: 391). Honiara's population has increased fivefold since Independence in 1978 (Moore 2015), and there are now around 30 informal settlements within the town boundary, six of which have encroached on customary land (Hou and Kudu 2012). Most of the residents in these settlements are considered as 'squatters' in the eyes of the state and city authorities because they 'lack legal title to the city land they occupy' (Englund 2002: 141).

Powers of Exclusion in Contemporary Honiara

Drawing upon the *Powers of Exclusion* framework, we see regulation, the market and, to a lesser extent, force as the key drivers of exclusion in contemporary Honiara. However, as we shall demonstrate below, the two main powers of exclusion considered here—regulation and the market—can only be understood with reference to a political economy characterised by patronage relations and the personalised nature of political and administrative practices. Exclusion from land in Honiara is produced through a dynamic interaction between regulation, the market and social and power relations that resonates strongly with the observation that the formal rules governing land and property rights often bear little resemblance to on-the-ground realities (Hall et al. 2011). We now consider each of the powers of exclusion in turn, but within a cross-cutting context of political economy.

Regulation

Title to Honiara city land is vested in the state as perpetual estate regulated by the Land and Titles Act. Following the definition of regulation in the *Powers of Exclusion* framework, this legislation governs which 'individuals, groups or state agencies have rule-backed claims to any particular piece of land' (Hall et al. 2011: 16). Under this legislation, the state has exclusive property right claims to Honiara city land by vesting perpetual estate titles in the Commissioner of Lands, who holds them in trust for the state.

This means that the Commissioner of Lands, as an agent of the state, has exclusive legal right to determine Honiara city land use, to benefit from the services of this land, and to transfer portions of the property rights at mutually agreeable terms. He has the legal right to dispossess people, or turn individual claimants without legal titles into squatters.

> Private property in land, other than customary land, is created by the Commissioner making a grant out of a perpetual estate over public land ... [and the] derivate interests, technically terms of years, are called Fixed Term Estates. The Commissioner of Lands is also responsible for approving all transfers of Fixed Term Estates and for approving long subleases (Williams 2011: 2).

This process of allocating private property rights depends entirely on the Commissioner of Lands' discretionary powers. These discretionary powers have been interpreted as giving him the authority to transfer or allocate plots of Honiara city land to private individuals, politicians or investors, regardless of the merits of such allocations. There have been numerous instances of the Commissioner of Lands exercising his discretionary powers in ways that appear to be beyond the textual legal meaning of how such powers should be exercised as prescribed by the Land and Titles Act. For example, the Honiara City Mayor, Andrew Mua, was reported on 7 June 2013 as complaining that the Commissioner of Lands had sold plots of land that were part of the Honiara dumpsite to Asian investors and other individuals (Namosuaia 2013).

The print media also reported that a small park in the centre of Point Cruz was allocated for transfer to a businessman. The Solo Environment Beautification Group claimed that they had started making a garden in the park after receiving assurance from the Permanent Secretary of the Ministry of Lands, Housing and Survey that the land would not be sold because drainage and sewerage lines lay under the area (Namosuaia 2013). Officers from the ministry, however, advised the group to stop any gardening work because the land had been sold for a commercial purpose. In August 2013, the media reported that a plot of land next to the Mataniko bridge, which had been set aside for possible future expansion of this urban transport infrastructure, was transferred by the Commissioner of Lands to an Asian businessman (Dawea 2013).

These examples show how the Commissioner of Lands' exercise of discretion, as provided by law, can easily be manipulated by 'uncodified and informal socio-political forces' (Pelto 2013). While the exercise of discretion by the Commissioner of Lands over urban land is often alleged to be an abuse of discretionary powers, there have been few court challenges or prosecutions. What is certain, however, is that the abuse of these discretionary powers has meant that a majority of Solomon Islanders find it challenging to acquire property rights in Honiara. This has seen the emergence over time of a range of strategies to acquire property rights in Honiara, which we discuss in the second part of this chapter as an instance of the powers of 'counter-exclusion'.

The continual media reports and public complaints to the effect that the Commissioner of Lands has repeatedly abused his discretionary powers by leasing Honiara city land to politicians and investors for his own benefit has resulted in a recent amendment of the Land and Titles Act as part of the government's land reform program. This legislative amendment abolished the discretionary powers of the Commissioner of Lands and provides the Land Board with the 'powers and functions relating to the allocation of interest in land, the development of land and to ensure the administration of land is carried out in a fair, transparent and equitable manner'.[2] We return to this recent development in the conclusion.

The Market

The market as a process of exclusion establishes land as a commodity that can be bought and sold. The market depends on regulation to define the process of ownership and legal title to the city land that residents occupy. The land in Honiara has been accessed, controlled and leased for government and commercial offices, private homes, stores, hotels and small-scale business. With the rapid increase in rural–urban migration and population growth, land supply as a marketable commodity in Honiara has become a limited resource. As a result, within and around Honiara, people coming from other parts of the country continue to struggle to acquire private property.

One reason is that the government insiders, or those associated with the Ministry of Lands, Housing and Survey, have secured patches of land within the Honiara town boundary, and are transferring their property rights to these lands at very high market values that are only affordable to the highest income earners and investors. There have been constant allegations from the public that numerous officers in the Ministry of Lands, including the office cleaner, have more than one fixed-term estate title to land in Honiara. This suggests that these lands officers know the system well and are heavily involved in land deals by inflating land market prices. The consequence of this is the exclusion of many low or middle-class Solomon Islanders—who make up the majority of the Honiara population—from acquiring property rights because they cannot afford the increasing price of urban land.

Individual market transactions in land are occurring in Honiara at price levels that many Solomon Islanders cannot afford. For example, in 2010, the Premier of Guadalcanal, when commenting on the sale of

---

2   Section 8A, *Land and Titles (Amendment) Act 2014*.

plots of land in the Lunga area, stated: 'We learn that there are parcels of land sub-divided and registered and are ready for sale [that] are very expensive for potential individuals and business investors' (Palmer 2010). He recommended that Levers Solomon Limited, which holds the fixed-term estate title to the land in the Lunga area, 'reduce the current value of land sales at reasonable and affordable prices for individuals and businesses who would want to invest in Guadalcanal Province' (Palmer 2013). These land transactions are unregulated, so individuals or groups could easily be excluded by those with fixed-term estate titles due to unregulated market competition.

Force

Force, as a process of exclusion, concerns acts or threats of violence such as forceful eviction (Hall et al. 2011: 4–5; see also McDonnell 2013). The Commissioner of Lands, as an agent of the state, and the Honiara Town Planning Board are the main actors who play an important role in determining people's access to, and development of, Honiara city land, including when to decide on the application of force as a process of exclusion.

Section 5 of the Town and Country Planning Act provides that there 'shall be a Town and County Planning Board in each Province and in Honiara'. The Honiara Board has jurisdiction to establish a planning scheme and to regulate any development within the Honiara town boundary, including any material change of use of any building or land. The legislation prescribes that the Board must consider the planning scheme apart from any other material consideration when considering applications for building permits or any development within the Honiara town boundary (Foukona and Paterson 2013). However, 'the enforcement of planning requirements is, in practice, not very strong' (ibid.: 75). This has given many people the impression that, as citizens, it is legitimate to first construct buildings on any vacant plot of land or any Honiara city land they have acquired, and later apply for building permits if they are required by the Board to do so.

Due to the increase in informal settlements and the construction of houses without proper building permits, the Honiara City Council has recently started issuing notices to demolish such buildings as a measure to enforce its regulations (Namosuaia 2014). For example, an Asian businessman continued to build on a patch of land on the western side of the Mataniko bridge, despite the Honiara Board turning down his proposed development application (Piringi 2013a). However, a Honiara city councillor challenged the decision of the Board, claiming that it was legitimate for the Asian businessman to develop the site because it was 'given by the Minister of Lands, Housing and Survey, Joseph Onika, who was one of the joint owners of that fixed term estate' (Piringi 2013b). The strategy used by the private businessman was to use the Honiara city councillor to challenge the decision of the Board, and to highlight that the Minister of Lands, Housing and Survey was involved by leasing this land to the businessman, and thus it was legitimate. However, the Board stood its ground, and issued an order for the private business investor to demolish his building.

The decision of the Board concerned the demolition of the private business investor's building rather than the title to the land. Once the Commissioner of Lands exercises his power in leasing urban land and a registered title is created, the property rights of the owner of registered title are indefeasible,[3] or 'not liable to be defeated except as provided by the Land and Titles Act' (*Levers Solomon Ltd v Attorney General* 2013).[4] As highlighted by the Solomon Islands High Court:[5]

> once a person becomes registered owner of an interest under the Act, he has absolute liberty to deal with that interest according to the title which attaches to it under the Act. An innocent party … is not bound to look beyond the register.

Although the discretionary power of the Commissioner of Lands to create property rights has been questionable, and in some instances aggrieved settlers have challenged it, in most instances the courts in Solomon Islands have upheld the proprietary rights of the registered owner of land within the Honiara town boundary.

One example is the case of *Kee v Matefaka*,[6] in which the defendants in this case were five families who had occupied and built semi-permanent houses on land the Commissioner of Lands had allocated to two Asian investors, Sia Kee Ching and Lau Khing Hung (Theonomi 2014).

---

3   The principle of indefeasibility and the conclusiveness of the Register are covered under Parts VIII and IX of the Land and Titles Act.
4   *Lever Solomon Ltd v Attorney General* [2013] SBCA 11. Note that all court judgements cited in this volume are available from www.paclii.org.
5   *Maneporaʼa v Aonima* [2011] SBHC 79.
6   *Kee v Matefaka* [2014] SBHC 112.

These two investors applied to the Solomon Islands High Court in order to evict the defendants from the land. The High Court upheld their application and a notice was issued to the families to voluntarily vacate the land, but they failed to do so. An enforcement order was subsequently issued, which the Sheriff of the High Court, with the assistance of the police, acted on to demolish the houses of the defendants and order them to vacate the land.

The defendants applied to the High Court seeking a stay of the enforcement orders due to 'maladministration by the Commissioner of Lands, no payment of stamp duty, and the issue of right of occupation'. The defendants claimed that they 'were not given sufficient time to prepare before vacation, and the manner in which the eviction orders were carried out was contrary to their rights and freedom from forced eviction' (*Kee v Matefaka* 2014). Edward Matefaka, a spokesperson for the families, claimed that they had 'submitted applications to the Commissioner of Lands' but while their 'applications are still pending before the Commissioner of Lands … two foreigners' have come in and 'out rightly acquired the land' (Theonomi 2014). Matefaka questioned 'whether Solomon Islanders are entitled to apply for state land and why the two foreigners—is it because of money?' The actions of the agents of the state can easily translate into a conflict between the settlers and the state, particularly when the police are involved and perceived to be protecting the property interests of foreigners.

Despite the circumstances surrounding the way in which the land was acquired, the implicit force sanctioned by the court, as a process of exclusion, which was used by the agents of the state to evict the settlers, indicate that the Commissioner of Lands' land dealings are legal unless challenged otherwise on the basis of fraud or mistake.[7] The High Court upheld the property rights of the two investors, since they were the titleholders of the registered interest in the land, and ordered the eviction of the settlers.

Administration and management of Crown land is a function vested in the Commissioner of Lands and the Registrar of Titles. That function includes the allocation and grant of titles, and can only be questioned through the Court challenging the validity of a title. Whoever is occupying Crown land without going through the formal processes, and without

---

7   See Section 229, Land and Titles Act.

the consent and approval of the Commissioner of Lands, occupies that land illegally, and can be forced to vacate it in the event of resistance or unwillingness to do so.

Powers of Counter-Exclusion in Contemporary Honiara

Legitimation

Hall, Hirsch and Li describe legitimation as 'establishing the moral basis for exclusive claims' (Hall et al. 2011: 5). They see legitimation playing a central role in counter-exclusions, which they define as 'collective mobilisation by groups of people seeking to counter their exclusion from land as territory or productive resource, and to assert their own powers to exclude' (ibid.: 170). Attempts to counter the powers of exclusion that we have already elucidated, including the historical alienation of the land on which Honiara now sits, have seen the deployment of two overarching—and competing—discursive narratives, each of which seeks to establish a morally legitimate claim to property rights in Honiara. On one hand, Malaitan settlers cast themselves as 'workers and builders of the nation, thereby linking themselves to the legitimacy of the state and its broader modernising project' (Allen 2012: 172), while on the other, 'a Guale "landowner" narrative invokes indigeneity as the paramount fount of legitimacy in the spheres of land and resource development' (ibid.: 164). While Allen describes these competing discourses of legitimation in the context of the Ethnic Tension, with a particular focus on rural areas east and west of Honiara, we suggest that they are also discernible in the context of Honiara itself. Moreover, the strategies that are being deployed to counteract urban exclusion are inflected by Solomon Islands' political economy, as well as by local histories and social relations.

We have already seen that historical patterns of rural–urban migration explain why a significant proportion of settlers who have occupied land in Honiara are from Malaita. Allen (2012, 2013) describes how Malaitan identity narratives are embedded in the history of labour relations. Due to historical patterns of uneven development, and the lack of economic opportunities on Malaita, Malaitans have a long history of labour migration that stretches back to the international labour trade of the nineteenth and early twentieth centuries. It is with some legitimacy, then, that Malaitans portray themselves as the workers and builders of Solomon Islands. In the wake of the Ethnic Tension, Malaitans have been reluctant to return to rural Guadalcanal. However, as Allen argues, their identity narrative nevertheless remains tied to the legitimacy of the state: 'The state underpins the rights of Malaitans to live within the Honiara town boundary—where they continue to comprise a significant proportion both of the urbanised elite and the town's overall population' (Allen 2012: 175).

A recent development that fits neatly into this nation-building and modernising narrative is the appeal by settlers in Honiara to the colonial concept of 'waste land'. This concept was introduced as part of the early colonial government's land policy, both to regulate land speculation and to make land available to investors. Section 10 of the Solomons (Land) Regulation No. 4 of 1896 defined waste land as 'land being vacant by reason of the extinction of the original native owners and their descendants'. Following the enactment of the Waste Land Regulation of 1900, as amended by Queen's Regulation No. 1 of 1901, repealed and consolidated by Queen's Regulation No. 2 of 1904, the definition of waste land was amended to mean land that was not owned, cultivated or occupied by any native (see Bennett 1987: 131; see also Foukona 2007). The legal implication of this was that more land in the Protectorate became available for acquisition and alienation. This process contributed to the transformation of customary land into state land in Honiara.

Today the term 'waste land' is no longer recognised in law, but some settlers, mainly from Malaita, are still using the concept to assert their claim to vacant spaces in Honiara.[8] To some of these settlers, 'waste land' is perceived as land that is not needed by Guadalcanal landowners or land in and around Honiara that is underdeveloped. In other words, some settlers justify their claims by asserting that, since the land is 'waste land', it is all right to occupy and build on it because it is not useful for any other development purpose. The fact that people continue to consider areas such as swampy places, valleys, river banks or steep gullies as waste land to legitimise their land claims is a basis for future land exclusion and contestation (Chand and Yala 2008).

---

8   This view is often expressed by settlers from Malaita who have recently built informal houses on undeveloped urban land situated in valleys and swampy areas, such as behind the King George and Panatina Ridge east of Honiara.

In many instances, the Commissioner of Lands has knowledge of these occupiers, who are usually defined in law as squatters, but the fact that they have remained on the land for a long period could constitute a possessory title.[9] Some of these occupiers have applied to the Commissioner of Lands for a grant of fixed-term estate title to the land. Others believe that, if they are ordered to vacate the land they have occupied for a long period of time, the Commissioner of Lands, as an agent of the state, and the Honiara Town Council would come up with a scheme to relocate them.[10]

In the post-conflict context, some settlers are also attempting to justify their claims to urban land over which they do not hold registered titles on the basis of being displaced by the Ethnic Tension: to evict them, they claim, would cause another displacement.[11] Such a strategy is reinforced by the fact that most informal settlements in Honiara are based on provincial or island affiliations, which creates a strong sense of group identity, security and protection.[12] Therefore, anyone who holds a legal title to a plot of land in Honiara that is occupied by settlers may find it difficult to assert their claim, either through legal means or by extra-judicial force. While going through the courts to obtain an eviction order is possible, as we have already seen, enforcing such an order in practice, and getting people to recognise it, is a difficult process that can create additional tensions.

The proposal by the Solomon Islands National Sports Council (NSC) to build a national sports stadium in the Burns Creek area is a case in point. The NSC acquired the perpetual estate title to land in this area that was occupied by settlers three years ago. The *Solomon Star* newspaper reported that in 2012 the settlers were 'given some time to leave their homes since the NSC took title over the proposed land but have not done so since then' (Anon. 2012). The settlers continued to reside on the land, and recently, with the financial help of their member of parliament (MP), they built a clinic right in the middle of the land that the NSC had earmarked for a playing field. This seemingly reinforced the settlers' perception that, if an MP can fund the building of a clinic on the land, then it is legitimate for them to continue occupying it. The NSC criticised the MP for failing to consult the Honiara City Council to ascertain the legal status of the land before funding the construction of the clinic building

---

9   Section 225 of the Land and Titles Act deals with the principles of adverse possession.

10   See, for example, *Onika v Sevesi* [2007] SBHC 57.

11   This was the view by some settlers who moved from the Guadalcanal Plains to Malaita during the Ethnic Tension and then relocated to the Burns Creek area, east of Honiara.

12   Connell and Curtain (1982: 119–36, 127) made similar observations in Port Moresby and Lae.

(Aruwafu 2012). In October 2013, the NSC revealed that the sport stadium's 'actual ground work could not eventuate as proposed, due to settlers refusing to leave the land earmarked for the stadium despite the call to relocate' (Anon. 2013).

Another example of an MP assisting settlers to assert their property rights concerned a block of public land opposite the White River betel nut market in 2013. Reef islanders from Temotu Province have occupied the land in question for the past 20 years and have named it Karaina settlement (Palmer 2013). The settlers were aware that they did not have tenure security and could be excluded from the land by any private person or company who acquires the legal title to it. The MP claimed that the settlers had asked him to register the land during his campaign in 2010, and he promised them that he would attempt to do so if he became an MP. The Commissioner of Lands made a grant out of a perpetual estate over the land by vesting a fixed-term estate title held in trust by three prominent members of the Karaina settlement: the ward councillor, the Honiara City Mayor and the West Honiara MP (Palmer 2013). This land transaction was fast-tracked and enabled by the fact that an MP was engaged in the process, which suggests that the behaviour of the Commissioner of Lands is influenced by patronage politics.

Those people who do not have the requisite patronage networks to secure access to urban land have also adopted the strategy of building as fast as they can on any vacant plot of land that they identify in Honiara, even in the absence of any building permit approval from the Town and Country Planning Board (Diisango 2016). These vacant plots of land are public or alienated land for which the Commissioner of Lands holds perpetual estate titles from which fixed-term estates can be created.[13] Not many people who have built on these vacant plots of land have been able to acquire fixed-term estates due to a highly bureaucratic land transfer process and high land lease prices (see Keen and Kiddle 2016). Some settlers who can afford such high costs have paid brokers or middlemen, often referred to as 'land consultants', who are familiar with the system of transferring land or have connections with officers in the Ministry of Lands, Housing and Survey to fast-track the process of land transfer.

13　The Commissioner's power to deal with estates has now been transferred to a Land Board under the *Land and Titles (Amendment) Act 2014*.

Turning now to the strategies of counter-exclusion employed by indigenous people on Guadalcanal in relation to the land that hosts Honiara, we have already seen that the colonial-era land alienations that ultimately enabled the establishment of the city have been contested since the 1920s. In the post-colonial period, the return of, or compensation or rent for the use of, these lands—especially the area from Lunga to Tenaru—have featured prominently in a succession of formal demands that have been put to the national government by the Guadalcanal Provincial Government, most recently in the form of the 'demands by the bona fide and indigenous people of Guadalcanal' that were issued in January 1999 (see Fraenkel 2004: 197–203; also Sasako 2003). These demands, and the discourses of indigeneity that have framed them, operate at the scale of the island of Guadalcanal. They can be interpreted as part of a broader ethno-territorial agenda that seeks to exclude the rights of outsiders, including the state, in matters of resource access and control on Guadalcanal (Allen 2012). This agenda was one of the key underlying causes of the violent land evictions that occurred during the Ethnic Tension.

However, this island-scale ethno-territorial project is deeply problematised by territorial ambitions and agendas that operate at lower scales of socio-political organisation, specifically at the scale of customary landownership. Originally postulated by Filer (1997), the 'ideology of customary landownership' has become an increasingly pervasive and powerful strategy of territorialisation and exclusion throughout post-colonial Melanesia. In the case of Honiara, there have been claims and counter-claims among Guadalcanal landowners, and there have also been tensions between the Guadalcanal Provincial Government and individual landowner claimants.

For example, a chief called Andrew Kuvu, representing Guadalcanal indigenous tribal groups, asserted their ownership of land from Lunga to Tenaru (Anon. 2011), but another local man, Andrew Orea, alleged that Kuvu was illegally harvesting cocoa and coconut from this land, and that another landowner, Jemuel Guwas, was selling plots of land from within this contested area (Orea 2009). Another landowner, George Vari, who was chairman of the Lunga-Tenaru Trust Board, challenged the claim by Guadalcanal provincial leaders that Lunga land belongs to the province and its people, and asserted that it belongs to the Malango people (Vari 2012). These claims and counter-claims demonstrate that Guadalcanal people, despite drawing on the 'ideology of customary landownership', are not one entity, and in any case, their ownership claims are without any legal basis. The property rights to the Lunga-Tenaru land, which is part of the Tenavatu estate, is vested in Levers Solomon Limited. With the consent of the state, Levers can sell the rights to this fixed-term estate to any private individual or investor, which entails the exclusion of Guadalcanal landowners.

Force

As previously discussed, there exist, both historically and in the contemporary context, multi-scalar ethno-territorialising agendas in relation to Honiara. While there is no immediate evidence that these agendas will be pursued through some form of collective violence, the grievances that underscore them continue to be voiced by the Guadalcanal Provincial Government, by prominent Guadalcanal landowners, and by a wider network of leaders throughout the province (see Babasia 2014; Leni 2014). Given the persistence of these grievances, and in the wake of the violent evictions that occurred on north Guadalcanal during the Ethnic Tension, a spectre of ethno-territorial violence hangs over all of Honiara. However unlikely a return to widespread violence may be, the possibility that these long-standing agendas may lead to collective violence aimed at reclaiming Honiara cannot be entirely discounted (Anon. 2014a, 2014b).

Moreover, within Honiara itself, settlements are widely perceived as violent spaces in which alcohol and drug abuse are widespread and acts of interpersonal and group violence are commonplace.[14] As mentioned previously, the threat of force is ever-present and may act as a deterrent to those seeking to enforce property rights in settlement areas, including the state's security apparatus. In this sense, settlers' claims to rights of occupation or possession are backed by a spectre of violence. This threat of force is given greater weight, as well as an explicitly political dimension, by a number of well-documented cases of settlement youth being mobilised in overt acts of collective violence on the streets of Honiara. During the riots of April 2006, this collective violence effectively brought down the government of the day (see Dinnen 2007; Moore 2007). In this sense, Honiara's settlements are politically powerful spaces, at least for those political elites who are able to harness the energy and frustration of their younger residents.

---

14   One example would be the conflict between two ethnic groups in the Karaina settlement, situated in the White River area in western Honiara (Inifiri 2014).

Conclusion

In this chapter we have applied the *Powers of Exclusion* framework to an analysis of the processes by which both settlers and those 'indigenous' to the island of Guadalcanal have been prevented from accessing urban land, and to the strategies that the subjects of this exclusion have been employing to claim, or claim back, access to land within the city boundaries. We have found that the framework is broadly useful in explaining these dual processes, and we arrive at a broadly similar set of conclusions as Hall, Hirsch and Li. With regard to the powers of exclusion: the formal rules have tended to bear little resemblance to on-the-ground realities; public officials have frequently acted as 'tyrants' in the administration of land; and the market for land is not a product of some abstract space of supply and demand. In regard to the powers of counter-exclusion, legitimation has played a central role, as evidenced by collective mobilisations around discourses such as indigeneity, customary landownership, nation-building and citizenship. We have also argued, against the backdrop of the Ethnic Tension and the increasingly violent character of Honiara's settlements, that force, in the form of collective violence or the threat thereof, may yet become more salient as a power of counter-exclusion in this urban space.

However, just as the *Powers of Exclusion* framework is tailored to the particular political economy and social contexts of Southeast Asia, diverse as they are, so too, we have suggested, the powers of exclusion and counter-exclusion at play in contemporary Honiara can only be fully understood in the context of an encompassing political economy characterised by patronage networks and personalised forms of political and administrative governance, and with reference to the particular histories and social relations of Solomon Islands. Perhaps the most salient example of this political economy has been the abuse of discretionary powers vested in the Commissioner of Lands, which has seen property rights in urban land allocated in ways that distort the market and abrogate formal legal procedures. In many instances, the abuse of these powers has seen urban property rights granted to individuals on the basis of political patronage or to foreign investors for personal economic gain.

The circumstances surrounding the way that these land transactions are made are often perceived as dubious by members of the public and contrary to the expectations of occupiers. With the recent (2014) amendment to the Land and Titles Act, which abolishes the Commissioner's powers and establishes a Land Board to administer and lease land, it is anticipated that a more transparent leasing process will be introduced. It is hoped that questionable land dealings will be minimised since the discretionary power to create property rights vests in a board rather an individual who can easily be manipulated or bribed. The Board came into operation in December 2014, and produced an annual report for 2015 that was tabled in parliament in May 2016 and has recently been made accessible to the public. The report provides a list of land allocations and the names of successful applicants (GoSI 2016). This demonstrates a degree of transparency in the Board's deliberations. However, there are no records of minutes concerning how the Board has dealt with the applications, including in relation to the criteria used to assess them. Furthermore, the issue of the high cost of land transactions has remained, which means that in most cases only those with money can afford to successfully apply for urban land in Honiara. Some of the applicants to whom the Board has allocated land, as shown in the annual report, have revealed that they have not been able access the land. This is because boundary markers have been moved, the land is already occupied by someone else, or officers in the Ministry of Lands have been unhelpful in showing where the land is located and facilitating its transfer.

References

Allan, C.H., 1957. *Customary Land Tenure in the British Solomon Islands Protectorate: Report of the Special Lands Commission.* Honiara: Western Pacific High Commission.

Allen, M.G., 2012. 'Land, Identity and Conflict on Guadalcanal.' *Australian Geographer* 43: 163–180. doi.org/10.1080/00049182.201 2.682294.

——, 2013. *Greed and Grievance: Ex-Militants' Perspectives on the Conflict in Solomon Islands, 1998–2003.* Honolulu: University of Hawaii Press (Topics in the Contemporary Pacific 2).

Allen, M.G. and S. Dinnen, 2015. 'Solomon Islands in Transition?' *Journal of Pacific History* 50: 381–397. doi.org/10.1080/00223344. 2015.1101194.

Anon., 1964. 'Native Claim to Honiara Land Rejected.' *Pacific Island Monthly*, April.

——, 2011. 'Landowners Caution.' *Solomon Star* (editorial), 4 July.

——, 2012. 'NSC to Put in Work Plan.' *Solomon Star* (editorial), 27 June.

——, 2013. 'NSC Powerless.' *Solomon Star* (editorial), 30 October.

——, 2014a. 'Gov't Urged to Fix Boundary Issue.' *Solomon Star*, 23 August.

——, 2014b. 'Tandai Landowners Slash Demarcation Proposal.' *Solomon Star*, 17 September.

Aruwafu, C., 2012. 'NSC: Ete's Excuse Lame.' *Solomon Star*, 24 October.

Babasia, E., 2014. 'Lunga Land.' *Solomon Star*, 25 June.

Bellam, M.E.P., 1970. 'The Colonial City: Honiara, a Pacific Islands' Case Study.' *Pacific Viewpoint* 11(1): 66–96.

Bennett, J.A., 1987. *Wealth of the Solomons: A History of a Pacific Archipelago 1800–1978*. Honolulu: University of Hawaii Press (Pacific Islands Monograph 3).

BSIP (British Solomon Islands Protectorate), 1968. *BSIP News Sheet*, 1–14 February.

Chand, S. and C. Yala, 2008. 'Informal Land Systems within Urban Settlements in Honiara and Port Moresby.' In AusAID (Australian Agency for International Development) (ed.), *Making Land Work— Volume Two: Case Studies on Customary Land and Development in the Pacific*. Canberra: AusAID.

Connell, J., 1983. *Migration, Employment and Development in the South Pacific—Country Report 16: Solomon Islands*. Noumea: South Pacific Commission.

Connell, J. and R. Curtain, 1982. 'The Political Economy of Urbanization in Melanesia.' *Singapore Journal of Tropical Geography* 3: 119–136. doi.org/10.1111/j.1467-9493.1982.tb00235.x.

Dawea, E., 2013. 'Councillor Wants Development Stopped.' *Solomon Star*, 2 August.

Diisango, S., 2016. 'Concern over Illegal Settlements.' *Solomon Star*, 28 September.

Dinnen, S., 2007. 'A Comment on State-Building in Solomon Islands.' *Journal of Pacific History* 42: 255–263. doi.org/10.1080/00223340701461700.

Englund, H., 2002. 'The Village in the City, the City in the Village: Migrants in Lilongwe.' *Journal of Southern African Studies* 28: 137–154. doi.org/10.1080/03057070120117015.

Filer, C., 1997. 'Compensation, Rent and Power in Papua New Guinea.' In S. Toft (ed.), *Compensation for Resource Development in Papua New Guinea*. Port Moresby: Law Reform Commission (Monograph 6).

——, 2014. 'The Double Movement of Immovable Property Rights in Papua New Guinea.' *Journal of Pacific History* 49: 76–94. doi.org/10.1080/00223344.2013.876158.

Foukona, J., 2007. 'Legal aspects of customary land administration in Solomon Islands.' *Journal of South Pacific Law* 11(1): 64–72.

Foukona, J. and D. Paterson, 2013. 'Solomon Islands'. In D. Paterson and S. Farran (eds), *South Pacific Land Systems*. Suva: University of the South Pacific Press.

Fraenkel, J., 2004. *The Manipulation of Custom: From Uprising to Intervention in the Solomon Islands*. Canberra: Pandanus Books.

Gagahe, N.K., 2000. 'The Process of Internal Movement in Solomon Islands: The Case of Malaita.' *Asia-Pacific Population Journal* 15(2): 53–75.

GoSI (Government of Solomon Islands), 2016. 'Land Board Annual Report 2015.' Honiara: Ministry of Lands, Housing and Survey.

Hall, D., P. Hirsch and T. Li, 2011. *Powers of Exclusion: Land Dilemmas in Southeast Asia*. Singapore: NUS Press.

Hou, T. and D. Kudu, 2012. 'Solomon Islands: Honiara Urban Profile.' Nairobi: United Nations Human Settlements Programme (UN-Habitat).

Inifiri, J., 2014. 'Police Investigation in Karaina Row Start.' *Solomon Star*, 27 August.

Keen, M. and L. Kiddle, 2016. 'Priced Out of the Market: Informal Settlements in Honiara, Solomon Islands.' Canberra: The Australian National University, State Society and Governance in Melanesia Program (In Brief 2016/28).

Leni, N., 2014. 'Extension of City Boundary.' *Solomon Star*, 22 September.

McDonnell, S., 2013. 'Exploring the Cultural Power of Land Law in Vanuatu: Law as a Performance That Creates Meaning and Identities.' *Intersections* 33.

Moore, C., 2007. 'Helpem Fren: The Solomon Islands, 2003–2007.' *Journal of Pacific History* 42: 141–164. doi. org/10.1080/00223340701461601.

——, 2013. 'Honiara.' In C. Moore (ed.), *Solomon Islands Historical Encyclopaedia 1893–1978*. St Lucia: University of Queensland. Viewed 13 April 2014 at: www.solomonencyclopaedia.net/biogs/ E000133b.htm.

——, 2015. 'Honiara: Arrival City and Pacific Hybrid Living Space.' *Journal of Pacific History* 50: 419–436. doi.org/10.1080/00223344. 2015.1110869.

Namosuaia, D., 2013. 'Land Risk.' *Solomon Star*, 7 June.

——, 2014. 'Mass City Clean-Up—Council Sets to Demolish Illegal Buildings.' *Solomon Star*, 31 January.

Orea, A.S., 2009. 'Who is Kuvu?' *Solomon Star*, 15 December.

Palmer, E., 2010. 'Land Row … Guadalcanal Wants to Be Part of Lungga Land Sale. *Solomon Star*, 31 March.

——, 2013. 'Tran Acquire Title for Karaina Settlement.' *Solomon Star*, 17 October.

Pelto, M., 2013. 'High Value Urban Land in Honiara For Sale—Deep, Deep Discounts Available to the Right Buyer.' Devpolicy blogpost, 16 December. Viewed 12 December 2016 at: devpolicy.org/high-value-urban-land-in-honiara-for-sale-deep-deep-discounts-available-to-the-right-buyer-20131214/.

Piringi, C., 2013a. 'Defying Orders.' *Solomon Star*, 10 October.

———, 2013b. 'Maeli Hits Back.' *Solomon Star*, 14 October.

Sasako, A., 2003. 'The Day and Forces that Changed Solomon Islands.' *Fiji Islands Business*, July.

Storey, D., 2003. 'The Peri-Urban Pacific: From Exclusive to Inclusive Cities.' *Asia Pacific Viewpoint* 44: 259–279. doi.org/10.1111/j.1467-8373.2003.00214.x.

Theonomi, B., 2014. 'More Houses Demolished: Families Left Homeless as Police Tear Down Homes.' *Solomon Star*, 18 June.

Tozaka, M. and J. Nage, 1981. 'Administering Squatter Settlements in Honiara.' In P. Larmour, R.G. Crocombe and A. Taungenga (eds), *Land, People and Government: Public Lands Policy in the South Pacific*. Suva: University of the South Pacific, Institute of Pacific Studies, in association with Lincoln Institute of Land Policy.

Vari, G., 2012. 'Lunga Land Ownership.' *Solomon Star*, 16 May.

Williams, S., 2011. 'Public Land Governance in Solomon Islands.' Washington (DC): World Bank, Justice for the Poor Program (Briefing Note 6:1).

WPHC (Western Pacific High Commission), 1922. British Solomon Islands Commission Claim No. 17—Matanikau, Kookom. Auckland: University of Auckland (Special Collection WPHC 4/IV, MP 450/1922).

———, n.d. Land Claims, Register B. Auckland: University of Auckland (Special Collection WPHC MP 18/1/2).

Zoleveke, G., 1979. 'Traditional Ownership and Land Policy.' In P. Larmour (ed.), *Land in Solomon Islands*. Suva: University of the South Pacific, Institute of Pacific Studies.

4

'There's Nothing Better than Land': A Migrant Group's Strategies for Accessing Informal Settlement Land in Port Moresby

Michelle Nayahamui Rooney

The land belongs to the customary landowners before the colonial time in Papua New Guinea. But since the colonial time the land was given to the state. The land has portion numbers. We are applying for the portions. We have the documents and we've written a letter to the lands department and the former governor of NCD. We expected something from the government but nothing has been done. It is for the improvement of this community that we secure land to settle (resident of ATS settlement, January 2013).[1]

In the year 2000, the United Nations General Assembly with all the world governments' representatives agreed that by the year 2015 poverty levels must be decreased to the lowest levels. How do you achieve that with people who cannot afford to make their own living? To equip them to achieve this goal, there is nothing better than land itself. Once you get land and the title, they can mortgage it to get loans from the bank and do something to start building their level up (resident of ATS settlement, January 2013).

---

1 In order to assist with the clarity of the argument of this chapter, I have edited, summarised and translated interview transcripts while maintaining the meaning of the interviews and context. Where a particular word or phrase is important for the argument, I have kept these in their original form.

Introduction

These statements were made by two leaders of local institutions in the Air Transport Squadron (ATS) settlement in Port Moresby, the capital of Papua New Guinea (PNG) (see Figure 4.1).[2] They reflect the myriad actors, value systems and processes that migrant settlers residing in 'informal' or 'illegal' settlements in Port Moresby must engage with to secure and legitimise their 'informal' occupancy over land. They also reflect the intersections between customary and neoliberal state ideologies of land and property. Many residents of the ATS settlement moved there after being excluded from the expensive housing and property market in Port Moresby. Many cannot afford to return home or prefer to remain in the city closer to services. This chapter examines their collective strategies to secure land as actors who occupy a place at the centre of the political economy of land in the city. As the 'illegal' or 'informal' occupants of land, their tenure is challenged by customary landowners, the state and private holders of state leases.

The chapter aims to contribute to an understanding of two growing areas of concern for Melanesia, namely (1) the urbanisation process, and (2) emerging land dynamics arising from increasing internal migration and population mobility. It will contribute to an emerging body of literature that explores urban land dynamics arising from internal migration by examining the ways in which residents of urban settlements collectively act in relation to both customary landowners and the state in an urban Melanesian context.

Urbanisation in the Pacific is a challenge for development in the region. It is estimated that around 26 per cent of the region's population live in urban areas (Numbasa and Koczberski 2012; see also Chapter 2, this volume). PNG's urban population is around 13 per cent of its total population (GoPNG 2010; Jones 2011). It is estimated that up to 50 per cent of PNG's urban population lives in informal settlements (Connell 2011; Jones 2011; Numbasa and Koczberski 2012). Central to challenges of urbanisation in Melanesia is the shortage of available land for development and housing (Kidu 2002; Connell 2011; Chand and Yala 2012; Numbasa and Koczberski 2012). Housing problems faced by city

---

2   The Air Transport Squadron compound of the PNG Defence Force is adjacent to the settlement. The settlement is referred to interchangeably as the 'Oro ATS', 'ATS', 'Oro', or 'Popondetta' (the urban centre of Oro Province) settlement.

dwellers are often the result of a prohibitive combination of inadequate supply of formal housing, financial incapacity, and difficult legal and regulatory processes, leading many to take up residence in settlements. Pre-existing claims on settlement land mean that the threat of eviction is a major risk to settlers' livelihoods and well-being.

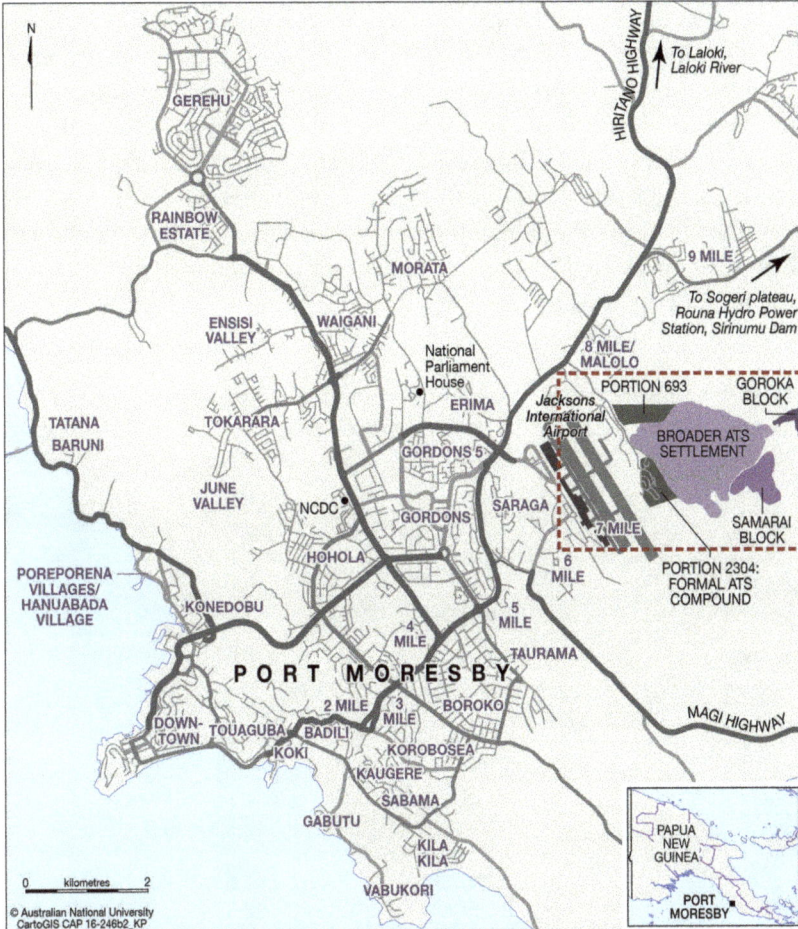

Figure 4.1 Map of Port Moresby, 2013, showing location of ATS settlement.

Source: CartoGIS, The Australian National University.

Historical factors that shaped Port Moresby's contemporary housing problems involved the spatial stratification of houses and residential areas around expatriate administrators, their national employees, low-cost housing, self-help housing for national workers, and settlement schemes for incoming migrants. In this context, housing was usually provided by employers at a highly subsidised rate. The market price of existing formal residential housing was most often beyond the financial capacity of migrants (Langmore and Oram 1970; Oram 1976; Stretton 1979; Goddard 2005: 21–32; Numbasa and Koczberski 2012; Webster et al. 2016). Between 1985 and 2010, the increasing commercial value of land has meant that formal housing allocation has evolved into a high-priced market stimulated by broader economic activity in the extractive industry sector (Tables 4.1 and 4.2). Private companies and higher-level government positions continue to offer housing as an incentive to attract the most skilled Papua New Guineans, but for most Port Moresby residents, this situation means that housing is unaffordable. Moreover, the increased land value and high property prices have also attracted property developers interested in investing capital in the city, and this is seen in the increase in investment-style properties being advertised in the city (Rooney 2015) (Table 4.3).

Table 4.1 Weekly rental costs for two- and three-bedroom houses in different suburbs of Port Moresby (in PNG kina, at constant 2010 prices), 1985–2010.

	1985	1990	1995	2000	2005	2010
Boroko, Korobosea, Gordons, Gordons 5						
Maximum	3,346	2,796	2,603	1,785	950	4,000
Minimum	797	1,048	651	470	380	650
Average	1,779	1,934	1,281	906	691	2,297
Hohola, Gerehu, Waigani, Tokarara, June Valley, Ensisi, Morata, Rainbow Estate						
Maximum	1,977	1,747	2,765	2,442	506	1,200
Minimum	608	517	325	282	380	550
Average	1,151	1,011	857	677	443	802
Downtown Port Moresby						
Maximum	n.a.	4,310	4,554	2,630	2,532	7,500
Minimum	n.a.	643	813	650	570	1,500
Average	n.a.	2,224	1,914	1,634	1,354	3,579

Source: Rooney 2015, based on *Post-Courier* newspaper advertisements published in June each year.

Table 4.2 Sale prices for two- and three-bedroom houses in different suburbs of Port Moresby (in PNG kina, at constant 2010 prices), 1985–2010.

	1985	1990	1995	2000	2005	2010
Boroko, Korobosea, Gordons, Gordons 5						
Maximum	760,393	671,023	487,976	657,511	443,166	2,500,000
Minimum	425,820	326,192	146,393	65,751	341,871	380,000
Average	554,001	450,501	366,999	358,479	389,353	1,147,692
Hohola, Gerehu, Waigani, Tokarara, June Valley, Ensisi, Morata, Rainbow Estate						
Maximum	547,483	121,157	211,456	356,934	443,166	750,000
Minimum	91,247	116,497	32,532	56,358	291,223	175,000
Average	268,875	118,827	94,003	138,051	367,194	424,654
Downtown Port Moresby						
Maximum	669,146	1,048,473	1,138,612	1,221,092	1,202,879	4,000,000
Minimum	669,146	838,778	422,913	469,651	1,076,260	2,800,000
Average	669,146	996,049	817,941	653,989	1,139,569	3,100,000

Source: Rooney 2015, based on *Post-Courier* newspaper advertisements published in June each year.
Note: 2005 figures for Downtown Port Moresby derived from advertisements published in August 2005.

Table 4.3 Sale prices of investment-style properties (in PNG kina, at constant 2010 prices), 1985–2010.

	1985	1990	1995	2000	2005	2010
Maximum	1,520,786	2,562,933	341,583	4,320,786	1,899,282	7,500,000
Minimum	316,324	279,593	123,621	216,039	215,252	230,000
Average	809,927	1,149,437	214,710	1,129,823	700,360	1,825,654

Source: Rooney 2015, based on *Post-Courier* newspaper advertisements published in June each year.
Note: 2005 figures are derived from advertisements published in August 2005.

By opting to reside in informal and low-cost land tenure and housing arrangements, evoking their shared history and engaging with their intimate network of kinship relations, residents of informal settlements are able to reposition themselves from a point of being excluded from the prohibitively expensive land and housing market into one of inclusion—albeit contested—in a settlement context. This contested inclusion provides an illustration of Hall, Hirsch and Li's (2011) framing of exclusion that focuses on access—rather than inclusion—as the opposite of exclusion. They argue that the exclusionary powers of force, regulation, legitimation and markets work to exclude some while enabling others to have access to land. Thus, exclusion from expensive formal housing leads to people seeking inclusion in informal settlements, but this inclusion also comes at the expense of excluding others. In the face of threats by prior claimants to dispossess them of the land they currently possess, migrants residing in Port Moresby's informal settlements need to legitimate their occupancy of the land or counter these threats by excluding others' claims on, and access to, the same land. The collective strategies of residents of Port Moresby's settlements demonstrate an inherent capacity to negotiate and create systems of land tenure and access that meet their needs (Hall et al. 2011: 8).

This contested inclusion also provides new insights into the discourse on urban land in Melanesia, which tends to focus on juxtaposing customary landowners with an array of 'other' actors whose counter-claims are the result of pre-colonial and colonial history, urbanisation, population growth and commercial interests. These actors include customary landowners, the state, property developers and migrants. A key challenge for policy makers, then, is negotiating with customary landowners to allow more of their land to be made available for urban development, while ensuring that their traditional rights are protected and that they benefit equitably from the use of their land (Barter 2002; Kidu 2002; Koczberski 2002; Nolan and Abani 2002; Pai and Sinne 2002; Chand and Yala 2008, 2012; GoPNG 2010; Jones 2011: 94; Numbasa and Koczberski 2012).

There is a growing body of Pacific literature that examines how migrant settlers engage with customary landowners in relation to accessing and maintaining tenure. In the context of Port Moresby, Chand and Yala (2008, 2012) have undertaken a study looking at informal arrangements for land access in settlements. Others have examined this issue in the oil palm growing regions of PNG and Solomon Islands, looking at the ways in which migrant settlers and customary landowners use adaptive strategies to create avenues for mutually beneficial land transactions (Koczberski and Curry 2004, 2005, 2009; Koczberski et al. 2009, 2012; Allen 2012; see also Chapter 5, this volume). Koczberski and Numbasa (2012) have looked at migrant access and maintenance of tenure in the urban setting of Wewak (PNG) (see also Chapter 5, this volume). Martin (2013) describes the shifting ways in which people in East New Britain (PNG) apply, in varying degrees, both custom and Western notions of exchange and reciprocity to land transactions. Thornton and colleagues

(2013) examine social change and increasing urban landlessness in Samoa. Much of this literature focuses on relationships between migrant settlers and customary landowners, with less attention being paid to the ways in which migrant settlers engage with *both* customary landowners and state and legal processes. Through a gendered lens, and in the context of Solomon Islands, Monson (2010, 2012) explores the role of customary normative processes and legal and state systems of negotiating land and property in delimiting the 'voices' of important stakeholders, such as women, in land discourses relating to disputes between customary landowners and migrant settlers (see also Chapter 13, this volume).

In the introduction to this volume, the authors adopt a broader definition of alienation that situates customary landowners in both the Melanesian ideology of landownership as well as in formal legal contexts. This definition provides a frame for this chapter to discuss how migrants residing in Port Moresby's informal settlements engage with both customary landowners and the state in Melanesian relational terms and formal legalised ways.

After describing the fieldwork and data, the chapter presents the nature of the contestation over the land that the ATS settlement. It then briefly maps the historical geography of the land area in this settlement to illustrate the multiple claims on it. It then examines various strategies that residents of this settlement deploy to secure their collective access to land. The conclusion discusses the key findings and policy implications.

Fieldwork and Data

The fieldwork for this research was conducted in the ATS settlement over the period from December 2012 to June 2013. The settlement is primarily made up of people who come from PNG's Oro Province. During the fieldwork, over 50 formal interviews were conducted with members of the ATS community, key informants and representatives of local institutions. Interviews were also conducted with representatives of other institutions in Port Moresby such as international agencies, non-governmental organisations, the Governor of the National Capital District (NCD), and other residents of Port Moresby. Further data was obtained from the Department of Lands, the National Mapping Bureau, and media reports. A household socio-economic and demographic survey was conducted with 32 households from one particular ethnic group.

The interviewees were members of the household who knew detailed information about the household. The interviews were loosely structured and conducted as conversations lasting anywhere from 45 minutes to two hours. They focused on six themes: (1) household demographic data; (2) household characteristics; (3) incomes, employment and livelihoods; (4) accessing land in the settlement; (5) main risks or threats to livelihoods affecting the community; and (6) social relations within the settlement, in Port Moresby, in people's village of origin and beyond. Apart from the formal interviews, I interacted socially and often, both with people I interviewed and with others, over the fieldwork period. I also draw on my experiences and observations as a long-term resident of Port Moresby to inform my insights and analysis.

Contested Urban Land

In January 2015, more than 18 months since I had completed my fieldwork in the settlement, the land there had escalated to become the subject of a national parliamentary debate. While this issue has attracted media attention for many years, recent developments in Port Moresby have intensified land debates. Developments include a rapidly increasing population, soaring property prices, increased traffic, and a multimillion dollar schedule of road and building construction to host the 2015 South Pacific Games and the 2018 Asia-Pacific Economic Cooperation meeting. In 2014, NCD Governor Powes Parkop announced in the media that the evictions of settlers would increase to make way for new roads (Martin 2014). In this context, in October 2014, and in response to questions about the status of land in the ATS area, the Minster for Lands is reported to have made the following statement on the floor of Parliament:

> 'Let me give the status of land at ATS … The portions … 693 up to 698, all of them have titles to them. Leases have been given from 1964 up to 2008,' Mr Allan said.

> 'And our people out there are illegally living on these portions however, looking at time and some of these titles. Some title holders have taken time to develop and we will look at the issuance of these titles.' (Anon. 2014a)

In November 2014, a Member of the Opposition, Sam Basil, posted a message to his Facebook page to say that he had presented a petition on the floor of Parliament on behalf of the residents of the ATS settlement. The petition asked the government to reconsider granting titles over the land portions in the area to a private company, and instead to consider granting the land to the residents for legal settlement (Basil 2014).

Around this time, customary landowners, who had long been raising the matter in the media, also challenged the residents of the ATS settlement:

> not to mislead the State on the initial arrangement for their permanent settlement.
>
> Clan chairman and spokesman William Tokana said the State, especially Lands and Physical Planning Minister Benny Allan and Moresby Northeast MP Labi Amaiu should be properly briefed on the history of ATS and land portion 698.
>
> He said this portion was handed over by the customary landowners to Oro settlers as a goodwill gesture through intervention by then prime minister Bill Skate and then NCD governor Philip Taku (Anon. 2014b).

In this statement, the clan spokesman clarified that the original arrangement by which land was allocated to Oro settlers involved only Portion 698. However, over time the settlement has extended well beyond the boundary of Portion 698 (see Figure 4.2), and the recent land contestation involves other parcels of land as well.

It is evident that the residents of the ATS settlement are situated at the frontier of Port Moresby's expanding sprawl. Given their physical possession of the land, they are also at the centre of the contestation between the state, private leaseholders, and customary landowners. The escalation of the matter to the level of a parliamentary petition and debate, and the associated public discussion through the media, illustrates the highly contested commercial and moral values at stake. The rest of this chapter examines the multiple ways that residents of the settlement have gone about securing their tenure over the land.

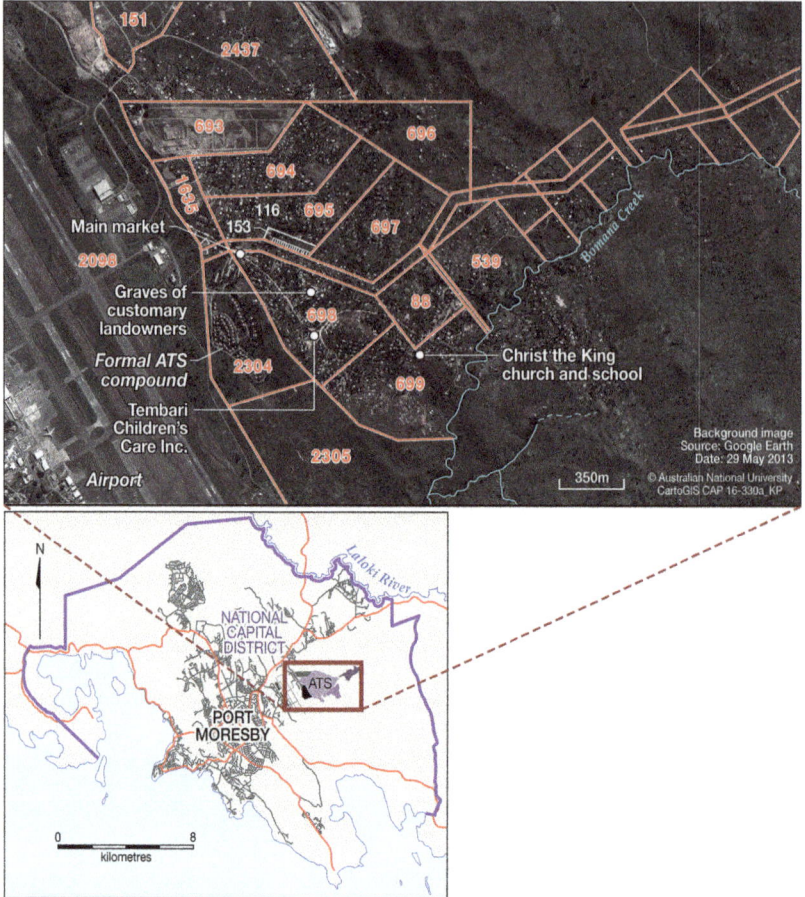

Figure 4.2 Google Earth image of ATS settlement, 2013, with cadastral overlay.

Source: CartoGIS, The Australian National University, based on Google Earth imagery and survey data from the PNG Department of Lands and Physical Planning.

History of Port Moresby Land

Customary Landowners

When I asked research participants the question, 'Who are the customary landowners of this area?', the general response was, 'the Dubara clan (of Hanuabada)'. Understanding the contemporary issues that residents of the ATS settlement face thus requires situating them in the historical context of land in Port Moresby. When the area was first visited by Europeans in 1873, the largest indigenous settlement was called Hanuabada (literally 'Big Village'), which was actually made up of five villages and two distinct ethnic groups—the Motu and the Koita (or Koitapu [sic]) people (Belshaw 1957: 11–12; Oram 1976: 11; Groves 2011: 3–9). The villages were Hohodae (Koita), Poreporena (Motu), Tanobada (Motu), Guriu (Koita) and Elevala (Motu) (Belshaw 1957; Gregory 1980, 1982). While there are variations in the history of these two groups of people, there is general consensus that the Motuans were the original coastal people, while the Koita came from the hills inland, but they have live together along the coastline of what is now Port Moresby for generations. Reflecting this long and shared history, the Motu and Koita people together are now known as the Motu Koitabu people and live within and beyond the boundary of the city as it is known today.

Though culturally distinct, the two groups have similar forms of social organisation (Belshaw 1957: 12; Oram 1976: 4). Each of the villages was divided into named *iduhu*, which were the basic residential and social units based on common descent. Each *iduhu* had several lines of houses built over the sea. Houses on the left (or eastern) side were called *laurina* and houses on the right (or western) side were called *idibana* (Belshaw 1957: 13). In Hohodae village, the main *iduhu* were known as Taurama, Geakone and Dubara (ibid.: 13). The 'Dubara clan' that the ATS settlers refer to consists of the descendants of the Dubara *iduhu* of Hohodae village. Of importance for understanding the contemporary dynamics of land in Port Moresby is the fact that *iduhu* may split for a number of reasons, such as conflict or marriage, and an affected person or group may move and reside elsewhere (Belshaw 1957: 13; Bramell 1960; Groves 2011: 24–5). This means that 'clans' may have several branches residing in different areas, but with land claims similar to those held by their Hanuabada-based kin (Belshaw 1957; Oram 1976; Goddard 2005; Groves 2011). Furthermore, although the inheritance of land in Motu Koitabu tradition is theoretically patrilineal, land may be transferred to or through women in certain circumstances and within local customs and practices (Belshaw 1957: 27–30; Bramell 1960).

Commoditisation of Land

Europeans started buying land from indigenous people in 1884, when the southern part of the island of New Guinea was declared a Protectorate of the British government (Oram 1976: 22). The Administration began buying land for Crown purposes, and by 1889, as part of planning the town of Port Moresby, land was being bought, surveyed and divided into quarter-acre blocks, then subdivided into sections and allotments (ibid.: 1976: 25–6). Over the period from 1883 to 1974, increasing tracts of Motu and Koita land were bought. The legal framework evolved to accommodate the Administration's increasing need for land. The initial policy was that Europeans were only allowed to buy 'waste and vacant' land, provided this did not impede the access rights of the indigenous population (ibid.: 24). By 1906, the Land Ordinance was enacted, giving the Administration powers to compulsorily buy land for public purposes (ibid.: 25). In 1956, a proposal that all Port Moresby land should be purchased did not succeed, although the Administration insisted that indigenous landholders had a 'moral obligation to make their land available for development' (ibid.: 175). By 1974, only one fifth of the land within the Port Moresby town boundaries remained under customary tenure.

Indigenous landowners increasingly showed signs of resentment and reluctance to sell their land, and by the 1960s, land shortage was evident. The threat to their subsistence livelihoods as a result of loss of land remains a key issue for indigenous people. As time progressed, there was increasing awareness of the long-term value of land as a means of earning cash returns (Oram 1976: 177). However, by the 1960s, the area where the ATS settlement is located was all Crown land (ibid.: 178), and by the 1980s, all the land portions in the area had been purchased by private leaseholders (see Figure 4.2).

Land Groups Incorporation Act

While this history shows that land in Port Moresby has been gradually subsumed into a commoditised market and transacted under conveyancing laws for over 100 years, increasingly marginalised customary landowners continue to assert their claims through legal instruments such as the Land Groups Incorporation Act (LGIA). The LGIA was enacted at the time of Independence in order to legalise notions of indigenous land management (Filer 2007). However, despite the noble intention to incorporate customary groups into formal land tenure regimes in order for them to realise the economic benefits of their land, the LGIA has been problematic in its application (Filer 1997, 2006, 2007; Jorgensen 2007). Such attempts to use formal legal frameworks to integrate customary land into modern economic and legal systems are discussed by McDonnell (2013), in the broader Pacific context, as instances of the 'cultural power of law' in redefining cultural and customary identities. In 2009, the LGIA was amended to enable more stringent requirements to be imposed on group membership, land boundaries, areas of dispute, management committees, annual general meetings (with 60 per cent quorums), bank accounts, registers of members and codes of conduct (Tararia and Ogle 2010: 22–3).

In the next sections, I explore how this historical and legal context, in which the ATS settlement was established in the mid-1990s, continues to have a bearing on the way that the resident navigate the land challenges that confront them.

Collective Strategies for Securing Urban Land

Engaging with Customary Landowners

Many urban settlements are formed around ethnic, provincial or regional groups (Gewertz and Errington 1999; Koczberski and Curry 2004; see also Chapters 2 and 3, this volume), involving people who have a shared history that acts as a glue for identifying criteria for inclusion in the settlement (Langmore and Oram 1970; Gewertz and Errington 1999; Barber 2003, 2010; Goddard 2005; Chand and Yala 2008; Numbasa and Koczberski 2012; Sharp et al. 2015). Similarly, the narratives of residents of the ATS settlement whom I interviewed indicate a collective effort to secure land, by people who originated from Oro Province, with both customary landowners and the state. In the mid-1990s, leaders of the Oro Province community living in Port Moresby started to look for land to form a settlement. As discussed by Koczberski and Curry (2004) and Bashkow (2006), the Oro Province 'identity' has been in the making for some time, and this would have helped to enable collective action (Rooney forthcoming).

It is not only the dichotomy between customary and state claims on the land that settlers face; they must also navigate the dynamics of customary landowners who are increasingly demanding their share of the developments on their land. Given the current contestation over the land, the prior claims of customary landowners, and the fact that, during my research, it was very difficult to obtain any written documents pertaining to the original agreement reached to establish the settlement, it is hard to reconstruct some parts of its history. This section of the chapter relies on data from interviews, incorporated land group (ILG) records, other Lands Department records, media reports, court documents and consultations with a number of key informants. The main purpose here is to demonstrate the deployment of an Oro Province identity as a collective strategy to secure urban land, and how this strategy has changed over time from an emphasis on provincial identity towards positioning themselves as citizens.

Prominent in people's recollections of how the settlement land was accessed was the story of friendships between several Oro men living in the city and members of the Dubara clan. In 1995, negotiations between these men and the Dubara clan members culminated in an agreement for Oro people to settle on Portion 698 (Figures 4.1 and 4.2). Oro leaders also liaised with the then NCD Governor, Bill Skate, and Member for Moresby North-East, Philip Taku, to allow them to settle on this same land.[3] In order to facilitate this process and to manage the movement of Oro people into the new settlement, the Oro leaders formed the Oro Community Development Association (OCDA). Its inaugural executive members included Jerry Asina and Joel Sanata, who still feature prominently in people's recollections of the early days of the settlement and in media reports.

A key figure in this history is the late Maso Henao, who was a prominent female member of the Dubara clan and the mother of William Tokana, the current clan chairman and spokesman who features in most of the recent media reports. Many people I spoke with recounted that it was Maso Henao who granted the Oro leaders permission to settle on Portion 698. However, in the land group records for the Dubara clan

---

3   Given the focus of this chapter on the importance of social relationships in the strategies of settlers, I have decided to use the real names of the key actors involved in the history of the ATS settlement, as they are already used in the public domain due to media coverage of issues in the settlement for a number of years.

of Hohodae, Hanuabada, members of the clan question Maso Henao's role in decisions over land. This is despite the same records also indicating that she had been granted customary rights over the land at the ATS settlement because of her commitment to pursuing the rights of landowners. This occurred even though the land had been state land for many years. To underscore customary landowners' connection with the land in question, Portion 698 contains the burial site of a number of the members of the Dubara clan (see Figure 4.3). Indeed, many residents of the settlement recall Henao in their stories of the history of the settlement, and several recalled attending her funeral in the settlement at Portion 698. People also recollected engaging with customary landowners by contributing funds towards, and participating in, customary events in practices similar to those described by a number of other authors (Koczberski and Curry 2004, 2005, 2009; Chand and Yala 2008, 2012, Koczberski et al. 2009, 2012; Monson 2010; Allen 2012; Numbasa and Koczberski 2012).

Figure 4.3 Cemetery of customary landowners on Portion 698, with Maso Henao's grave in the centre of the picture.
Source: Photograph by author.

On the other hand, reflecting the complexity of customary landowner identification in PNG, a few people I interviewed expressed uncertainty on this score. For example, when I asked another person if he was still in touch with the Dubara clan, he responded that the customary landowners used to:

> come up here and pick up some collection [for customary events]. But not these days. We knew that they were illegally collecting fees for their problems (Luke, ATS settlement, April 2013).

The statement that customary landowners were 'illegally collecting fees' suggests uncertainty about their claims to the land. As the history of land in Port Moresby illustrates, fissions in the customary landowning clan over the years, as well as gradual appropriation of land by colonial administrators, have contributed to this uncertainty about who are the rightful owners of the land.

This is also evident in the ILG records for Port Moresby. A search of the ILG register in the Lands Department showed that the 'Dubara clan' had two registered ILGs. The land mediation records in the files indicate that there was a split in the Dubara *iduhu* that resulted in one group relocating from Hanuabada village to Kirakira village. The latter group is registered as 'Dubara of Kirakira', while the former is registered as 'Dubara of Hohodae, Hanuabada'. This situation explains some of the uncertainty among residents of the settlement. For example, in a 2005 meeting, the chairman of the Dubara of Kirakira ILG noted that:

> [W]ith regard to the land issue with the settlers of ATS settlement. He informed the members [of the ILG] that the settlers have raised a total of (K25,000.00) Twenty-Five Thousand Kina as requested ... As the settlers are unsure as to who is the real owner of the land on which the settlement is located, they have withheld the money and have contacted [representatives of the ILG] to discuss the landownership matter with the Dubara Idibana Clan of Kira Kira.

The ILG records reveal that there was a long-standing dispute between these two groups over land around the ATS area, and land mediation was ongoing. In addition, there is a long-standing and public attempt by both groups to reclaim land or claim compensation from the state for the use of their land. The land area at the centre of this dispute includes Jacksons International Airport, which is located near the ATS settlement (see Figures 4.1 and 4.2). More recently, the media reported that another clan—the Iarogaha clan of Korobosea—was claiming ownership of the airport land (Anon. 2015), but it is not clear from the report if this clan was also claiming land in the ATS settlement area.

This historical narrative has been complicated by demographic changes, population growth and the increased land value around the settlement. Over the years, the population of the ATS settlement has grown substantially. In 2013 it was estimated that there were between 7,000 and 10,000 people now living in this area (Rooney forthcoming). The settlement is still known as ATS but now extends well beyond Portion 698 (Figure 4.2).

Patrilineal Ideologies and Inclusion

While the ATS settlement has a strong Oro Province identity and history, things are far more complicated. The social relationships that underpin the settlement's Oro identity draw on the common provincial background of its residents, and include shared histories of education, church, kinship and employment networks. As many of the settlement's residents moved there from formal zones, and still have close kin living in other areas of Port Moresby, this shared Oro Province identity predates the establishment of the settlement, and is mutually constituted by those living outside and inside the settlement.

Within the settlement, it is very clear that the population is mixed in both ethnic and socio-economic terms. Interspersed throughout the settlement, and intermarrying with people from Oro Province, are people from all over the country. There are large subsets of the population who could easily be regarded as having their own distinct settlements. For example, there is a large 'Samarai' (Milne Bay Province) block and a 'Goroka' (Eastern Highlands Province) block.

Those who primarily identified with the OCDA explained the principles by which land is allocated as being based on an Oro identity. As a general rule, originally, newcomers to the settlement arrived under the rubric of the OCDA. The OCDA charged an application fee and annual membership fee. In theory, the application fee was stratified, with men from Oro Province paying the lowest fee regardless of where their spouse came from. Higher fees were charged to non-Oro Province people, or outsiders, including Oro Province women married to outsider men. Upon establishing residency in the settlement, an annual membership fee of K30 was charged. This 'theoretical' emphasis on patrilineal principles of allocating land resonates with the 'patrilineal ideology' of different ethnic groups in the province, such as the Orokaiva (Schwimmer 1973: 95–110, 193–7) and the Korafe (Gnecchi-Ruscone 1991).

In practice, however, accessing land in the settlement diverges from this patrilineal narrative, and people who have a long association and social standing in the settlement were also evidently accepted as part of the community. Thus the moral and political basis for inclusion in the settlement is the need for accommodation and identification as a member of a patrilineal group, as well as ongoing participation in the social, economic and political sphere of the settlement. This divergence between a patrilineal ideology of land access and actual social practices, in which inclusion is based on shared lives and contiguous relationships, also resonates with traditional practices in Oro Province and other parts of PNG (Crocombe 1971: 301; Schwimmer 1973; Gnecchi-Ruscone 1991: 26; Bashkow 2006: 41).

In the actual practices of accessing land, people generally described a process whereby a relative would facilitate communication between themselves and the OCDA or other leaders in the settlement. By facilitating this process, and sometimes allowing newcomers to build a temporary shelter on their land, an existing resident implicitly vetted the arrival of a new applicant. Many people admitted that, once they had accessed land in the settlement and paid an 'application fee', they did not usually pay the annual fees. Reasons for non-payment included citing misuse of money by previous executives or, for many people, not being able to afford the K30 per annum. Another challenge for the OCDA was the influx of new settlers, including 'outsiders' who entered the settlement directly through friends without joining the association. One such category of newcomers are those referred to as 'big people', who offered amounts far in excess of the established fees, which has led to many settlers taking it upon themselves to facilitate land access in order to make money.

The term 'big people' variously refers to people in a network of kin, *wantoks*, friends, or colleagues, who live and work in formal areas of Port Moresby, and who settlers view as wealthy, educated and elite professionals with powerful networks of their own. It reflects the ways in which settlers position themselves in relation to 'others' who live and work in the formal areas of Port Moresby. 'Big people' may form a network of resources on which to draw, or potential powerful actors who can use their own networks to gain from their relationships with settlers. As far as possible, residents of the settlement try to engage with 'big people' in mutually beneficial ways, as we shall see later in this chapter.

Engaging as Citizens

Like others residents of Port Moresby, residents of the ATS settlement talked about being citizens. They are voters, clients of politicians, taxpayers, part of the labour force, beneficiaries of projects, and important development partners in the international development arena of poverty reduction. They know that, as citizens, they must be accorded equal status as their compatriots who live in formal areas of the city. This narrative of citizenship speaks to the narrative of the land being legally owned by the state. As citizens, residents of settlements throughout Port Moresby are increasingly becoming a major political interest group, and many of them maintain and nurture social and political relationships in all spheres of life. People would often tell me about how candidates made promises of services and utilities, such as water, during election periods, but did not follow through.

Reflecting the double narrative of the customary and legal status of the land, there appears to have been a shift in settlers' understanding of the status of the land they occupy. As this informant explains:

> We were told that it was customary land so we all went in blind thinking it's a customary land. Eventually I did my own investigation and I started seeing cement markers. It was telling me that this cannot be a customary land. These cement markers mean something else—that the land has been surveyed. So I started going around investigating and I discovered that all this was state land (resident, ATS settlement, January 2013).

Given the general lack of access to formal land records, it is understandable that settlers would not have known the actual legal status of the land at the time when the settlement was established. This change in knowledge, and the difficulties of dealing with fragmented landowners, as apparent in the ILG records, shape the ways that residents of the settlement legitimate their occupancy in relation to the state. It also places more emphasis on commoditised land tenure systems in which land is surveyed and parcelled into blocks. This was also evident during fieldwork, as people talked about surveyors surveying the land so that blocks of land could be allocated, bought and sold. A common sentiment was that, without land titles (collective or individual), they cannot make claims on the state for public services.

These intersecting narratives, between customary land tenure arrangements based on social relations on the one hand, and commoditised land tenure systems based on citizenship on the other hand, are woven with the narrative of collective Oro Province and ethnic identity on the one hand and citizenship on the other. With respect to securing land based on the notion of citizenship, people tended to foreground issues such as the need to 'secure the title' as a way of securing 'loans from the bank' and 'city services', such as water, instead of being treated 'as just a squatter'. Herein we see settlers nestled between, and negotiating with, two land tenure ideologies (relating to customary and commoditised land), and two social and political value systems (relating to provincial cultural identity and national state citizenship).

The emphasis on the rights of citizens to land has gained more prominence in recent years, as more evictions are taking place at the hands of property developers attracted to the increasing value of land in the city. For example, in response to a major eviction exercise in 2013, the NCD Governor Powes Parkop noted that 'it was not acceptable for a corporate company to evict PNG citizens' (Anon. 2013a). He went on to explain that, under such circumstances, city residents living in informal settlements who had been evicted or threatened with eviction tended to approach the NCD Commission, and himself as Governor, for assistance. The assistance in the particular instance involved supporting people with the costs of transporting their personal belongings to other areas, providing new tarpaulins for shelter as well 'considering assisting the people with their legal fees to take out a court injunction against the developers' (Anon. 2013a).

Threats of Eviction: Portion 695

Within the ATS settlement, residents also draw on their status as citizens in order to address challenges to their land tenure. Reflecting this nestling between two land tenure ideologies and social and political value systems is the case of Portion 695 (see Figure 4.2). Another reason for collective mobilisation is the common goal of residents who are directly affected by a threat of eviction, as in this case. This case also highlights the point that, even within the relatively small geographical spaces of settlements, risks to land tenure may be localised, and the nature of risk is related to the history and geography of the area. In this case, the cadastral boundaries creating Portion 695 rendered the settlers residing within it the subjects of an eviction notice. This case was in the courts, and is one in which I was able to directly observe and, to a limited extent, participate during my fieldwork.[4]

I was in the settlement one morning, approaching the home of a prominent settlement leader living on Portion 695, when my research assistant and I noticed a police vehicle parked beside his home. We soon found out that the police were issuing a notice of an eviction to be applied to people living on this portion. The atmosphere at the small betel nut stand where we usually congregated was sombre, as we contemplated that, just the previous day, one of the daily newspapers had reported that another Port Moresby settlement located near the Moresby Arts Theatre had been demolished by bulldozers (Sayama and Wapar 2013).

Soon after the eviction notice was issued at the ATS settlement, a number of reports appeared in the local media. One newspaper reported that:

> The policemen turned up with an eviction order from Dunlavin Limited, a Chinese company, ordering the settlers to vacate portion 1695 at 8-Mile.[5] The settlers were never informed of what was happening. The community leaders were now taking the matter to court. According to sources at the Department of Lands, the land title was given to Dunlavin Limited under suspicious circumstances in 2008. Settlers moved into this location in 1994 under a pilot resettlement project carried out by then Moresby East MP Philip Taku and the late Sir William Skate who was then the NCD Governor. The resettlement of the people was a political decision and the leaders of the settlement have documents to prove this claim (Ovasuru 2013).

---

4   I was rather taken aback at witnessing this interaction with the police first-hand, and so made contact with a local newspaper to alert them of another potential settlement demolition. As I had recently interviewed the NCD Governor, I had his contact details, so I also let him know what was happening. I also contacted the editor of one of the national newspapers to alert him of the same in the hope that journalists would cover the matter. The incident prompted me to write a blog article (Rooney 2013).

5   The reference to Portion 1695 in the newspaper is presumably a typographical error, as the cadastral maps show it as Portion 695.

Another newspaper article reported that customary landowners were

> demanding K20 million from the national government before any new
> development starts. The landowners were noted to state that the national
> government did not properly acquire parts of our customary land where
> we have ultimate customary rights over them including portions of
> land around the airport areas which extends from the ATS settlement
> towards the public cemetery land at 9-Mile. It is also very disheartening
> to see foreign companies, multi-national corporations, politicians and
> big businesses engage in land-grab using their financial powers while we,
> the customary landowners, have simply been ignored by state agents.
> The Dubara clan rejected that the Oro settlement at ATS was given as
> a pilot project by former NCD politicians Philip Taku and Sir William
> Skate. They said it was traditional owners Ova Boge, Ruma Varona and
> Maso Henao who signed the initial agreement and gave their consent
> to the late Jerry Asina in 1995 to use the land. According to the clan
> members, the settlers had not complied with the conditions of the
> agreement and after 16 years they wanted their land back (Anon. 2013b).

To underscore their claims as the original claimants of ATS land customary
landowners also assert that their:

> evidence that [they] are the true traditional landowners of the land at ATS
> area is the fact that [their] parents Maso Henao and Ova Boge lie in their
> graves with other family members buried at Portion 698 (Anon. 2013c).

The references to the breach of the arrangement between customary
landowners and Oro Province settlers is confirmed in statements from
some settlers who told me that the original arrangement was for them to
settle on Portion 698.

Although the issue of the eviction relates to the specific location of Portion
695, its coverage in the media enabled both customary landowners and
settlers to reassert their claims to the land in a public domain. They both
note the 'dubious' and 'suspicious' nature of the transfer of the title of
Portion 695. Both groups of claimants situate themselves within the
broader contemporary discourse on land grabs (see Filer 2011), and turn
the public gaze, and questions regarding 'legality', back onto the state and
the Department of Lands, which is renowned for corrupt land deals (see
Chapter 8, this volume).

The immediate problem of a 'threat of eviction' is placed in the legal
framework as a dispute between settlers and the private leaseholder.
In the Latin American context, van Gelder (2013) describes interactions

between settlers' 'illegality' and the legal domain in which settlers use the formal court processes to delay or prevent eviction. The legal framework of universal human rights, where natural laws take precedence over other forms of law, such as civil or commercial law, is often the strength of arguments against eviction. In the case of Portion 695, the legal process has so far delayed the eviction. However, the same cannot be said of other eviction exercises. For example, in 2012 a significant section of the Paga Hill settlement was demolished while settlers were in the process of seeking legal recourse to stay the eviction orders (Lasslett 2012; Wilson 2012).

The threat of eviction from Portion 695 has had the effect of uniting people of different backgrounds and ethnicity. Thus Oro Province collective identity is backgrounded in order to pragmatically address the immediate issue of eviction. Residents of Portion 695 have a common purpose of fighting a counter-claimant or face losing their homes. While their Oro identity matters for harnessing important social and political influence in their court battle, they know that the outcome in the courts will depend on legal technicalities related to their claims as citizens. Out of the households that I interviewed, 13 lived in Portion 695. One of my interviewees, Lance, who lives in a cluster of households including those of his brothers and nephew, told me that one of his brothers lives several metres from him but is located inside the Portion 695 boundary, while he lives in the adjacent Portion 697 (see Figure 4.2). Lance's brother is therefore impacted by the eviction notice, while Lance and his family are safe from eviction for the time being. The case of Portion 695 and Lance's story show that, while settlement household patterns are usually described in terms of clusters of kin living together (see Chand and Yala 2012), the risk to tenure can be highly localised in ways that render these kinship clusters temporarily irrelevant, while foregrounding relationships between those living on the same legal portions of land. In this example, Lance's brother is requested, and is obliged, to make a contribution towards the legal fees to pay for the court case to save Portion 695. Lance sympathised with his brother but, as he was unemployed, he was unable to assist.

Legal Fees to Fight Eviction from Portion 695

The leaders of the residents of Portion 695 have managed the eviction process by taking the matter to court. This has a direct impact on livelihoods, as one resident pointed out when I asked about what big issues affected the community:

Another thing with this land is that we don't have the title and sometimes they tell us we have to move from this block. This affects our well-being. The leaders call for meetings and ask the community to contribute money to address land issues in order to pay lawyers to take the case to court. Only last week we met here and each household was told to contribute K100 to meeting legal fees. This is for everyone who is affected by this eviction notice (Mick, resident of ATS settlement, 2013).

Considering the relatively low incomes and their unequal distribution, this financial contribution to secure land is a significant financial burden for most families.[6] Given the long-term process and immediate impact on housing and livelihoods, the contributions are most likely an ongoing, albeit variable, cost faced by households.

Throughout my fieldwork, the residents of Portion 695 also raised funds through barbecues and dances. Through this common goal, the eviction notice has forged a shared interest for the residents of Portion 695 whose lives are now dependent on their joint efforts. Given their low incomes, however, settlers will have to look for other means to secure legal and financial support, including their social and political networks. The long-term nature of legal battles, their impact on settlers' meagre resources, and the need to tap into social and political networks, is also noted by Lasslett (2012) in the Paga Hill settlement case. The residents of ATS settlement also told me that the Governor had agreed to assist them with their legal fees.

'Big People' as Stakeholders in Land

In asserting their rights as citizens, settlers also position themselves as equal to other PNG citizens and 'big people'. From their own life experiences as former residents of formal housing, and as former or current employees, they know that the social gap between them and other citizens living in formal areas is nominal, negotiable and subject to change. Land in Port Moresby is scarce, and already others, including elites and professionals, in the city are seeking land as their own tenure of employment comes to an end, or as they seek to broaden their livelihood and housing options. As one resident noted:

---

6   Of the 32 households I interviewed, 13 of whom lived on Portion 695, 65 per cent reported household incomes of less than K100 per person per fortnight, so a K100 contribution per household towards legal fees is a very large amount and often an ongoing cost to families.

Out there in the city there's no land. You go and apply [but] you won't get it because all the land is taken up. For this reason many 'big people' are now seeing that they will one day walk out of their jobs, so they come and help the settlement associations because in this way they may one day access land in ATS and will eventually end up owning something for ourselves (resident, ATS Settlement, 2013).

That 'big people' such as lawyers, engineers, public servants and wealthier kin and friends, who 'will one day walk out of their jobs', are interested in the settlement is also an opportunity for residents of the settlement. These relationships give settlers access to otherwise inaccessible institutions and people. 'Big people' provide legal services, surveying skills, computing support for document preparation, printing, political influence or other services to gain entry into the settlement. At the same time, the relationships are not one-way relationships, and by virtue of their 'settlement' identity, settlers know that they are in a position to reciprocate by offering support, such as introducing people to influence decision makers inside the settlement, or people who can provide housing when needed. In many ways, I myself could be considered to belong to the category of 'big people'. My research was welcomed, and people explicitly asked me to convey their stories so that others would know about life in settlements. In addition to helping raise awareness on the Portion 695 eviction, I would occasionally be asked to pass a message back to someone or other. On the other hand, I may have been viewed as an intermediary by other outsiders like myself. For example, when I mentioned that I was conducting fieldwork in the ATS settlement to an acquaintance who is a public servant, he responded that he had heard of land being sold there, and that he might accompany me during one of my visits to ascertain his own prospects of buying land. Among elites and professionals, the topic of buying land is commonly discussed.

Another settler expressed puzzlement at a professional who had approached her for land in the settlement.

They are big people. They get land but they don't come again for ten years. Why would they want land if they don't want to settle? (Summarised from interview notes, 2014)

I have met professionals in the city who mention that they have a block in the settlement and visit it periodically. Two of the participants I interviewed, who now live in the settlement, previously held senior positions in the public service while their brothers held land in the settlement. When they stopped working they relocated to the settlement.

Conclusion

In this chapter, I have sought to illustrate the multiple claims on land in Port Moresby, and the complex ways that these claims are entangled with each other. I have examined these issues from the perspective of migrants residing in a Port Moresby settlement. Much of the discourse on urban land in Melanesia juxtaposes customary landowners with an array of 'other' actors who include other customary landowners, the state, property developers and migrants.

The historical and legal framework presented in this chapter shows the multiple and competing claims on urban land and the overlapping forms of property rights. Within this context the present-day reality is that the settlers occupy the land. Efforts to assert counter-claims to the land or alter the status quo, including any policy-induced changes, will either involve an eviction process or a revision of the ways that settlers' claims, obligations and responsibilities are defined and exercised. As this will have a direct bearing on their livelihoods, settlers will also be at the forefront of dialogue, mediation and negotiations, and therefore their responses are important for understanding urban land discourse.

Residents of informal settlements legitimise their claims to land by invoking both traditional notions of access to land for subsistence and the formal international human rights framework that includes notions of citizenship and the right to shelter. Both customary and modern forms of access and maintenance of tenure through exchange and reciprocity are utilised and adapted to allow settlers to negotiate with different actors at different times. By mapping the historical processes that shape contemporary claims on land, and by a grounded examination of the ways in which settlers collectively mobilise and adapt to respond to counter-claims on land, this chapter draws out several important considerations for urban land discourse in Melanesia. Claimants to urban land—the customary landowners, the settlers, the state or the private leaseholders—are dynamic and fragmented groups. Within them disputes occur, new factions emerge and new institutions are created. This means that distinctions between them often disguise complexities that are important in shaping the challenges that settlers face—and also their responses. Another category of actors emerging in these dynamics are the 'big people' whose money and status in the city create opportunities for the residents of settlements, as well as opportunities for themselves to buy land from existing residents.

The pressure from customary landowners for fees to be paid for the use of the land led ATS residents to raise substantial fees through financial contributions. However, these were withheld when settlers realised that there was a dispute among customary landowners, and requested clarity about which customary landowning group the fees should be paid to. The realisation that the land was alienated created an opening to assert an alternative claim as citizens. The common threat of eviction created a sense of unity among residents of Portion 695 regardless of their ethnicity.

Migrants living in informal urban settlements will continue to negotiate in ways that harness the best of a myriad of strategies involving different actors, values and systems. Urban land policy needs to be cognisant that any change in the status quo, no matter how well intended, will exclude some people, and this will lead to 'counter-exclusive' responses (Hall et al. 2011). At the very least, policies or proposed developments must include provisions to identify those who will be affected and options for their resettlement. Residents of the ATS settlement evoked their shared history and identity to collectively secure land, but in the face of threats by other claimants to dispossess them of the land they occupy, their strategies to legitimate their occupancy of the land involved, by necessity, excluding other claims on, and access to, the same land.

None of this relieves the hardship that settlers face, and the ongoing difficulties and challenges of maintaining tenure, but the fact that settlers will remain a prominent part of the urban social, political, physical and economic landscape, and have sustained their efforts for so long, show that they have developed ways to do so that can inform urban land policy processes. This paper offers some partial but important insights into how settlers respond collectively to land tenure challenges.

References

Allen, M.G, 2012. 'Informal Formalisation in a Hybrid Property Space: The Case of Smallholder Oil Palm Production in Solomon Islands.' *Asia Pacific Viewpoint* 53: 300–313. doi.org/10.1111/j.1467-8373.2012.01489.x.

Anon., 2013a. 'Settlers Eviction Unacceptable.' *City Sivarai,* 23 April.

——, 2013b. 'Hanuabada ILG Claims K20mil.' *The National,* 26 April.

——, 2013c. 'NCD Landowners Want Compo.' *Post-Courier,* 26 April.

——, 2014a. 'Minister Clarifies Land Queries.' *Post-Courier,* 28 October.

——, 2014b. 'Clan Tells Squatters Not to Mislead State.' *Post-Courier,* 3 November.

——, 2015. 'Land Group Refutes NAC Claims.' *Post-Courier,* 11 May.

Barber, K., 2003. 'The Bugiau Community at Eight Mile: An Urban Settlement in Port Moresby, Papua New Guinea.' *Oceania* 73: 287–297. doi.org/10.1002/j.1834-4461.2003.tb02825.x.

——, 2010. 'Urban Households, Means of Livelihoods, and Village Identity in Moresby.' In M. Goddard (ed.), *Villagers and the City: Melanesian Experiences of Port Moresby, Papua New Guinea.* Wantage: Sean Kingston Publishing.

Barter, P., 2002. 'Land Mobilisation in Papua New Guinea.' In N. Sullivan (ed.), *Culture and Progress: The Melanesian Philosophy of Land and Development in Papua New Guinea.* Madang: Divine Word University Press.

Bashkow, I., 2006. *The Meaning of Whitemen: Race and Modernity in the Orokaiva Cultural World.* Chicago: University of Chicago Press.

Basil, S.H., 2014. 'ATS Oro Settlement Petition to Parliament.' Post to personal Facebook page, 24 November. Viewed 8 January 2015 at: www.facebook.com/#!/photo.php?fbid=10152960110846614&set=a.10152960108096614&type=1&theater.

Belshaw, C.S., 1957. *The Great Village: The Economic and Social Welfare of Hanuabada, an Urban Community of Papua*. London: Routledge and Kegan Paul.

Bramell, J.B.C., 1960. 'Notes on Native Land Custom: Port Moresby Region.' Port Moresby: Native Lands Commission.

Chand, S. and C. Yala, 2008. 'Informal Land Systems within Urban Settlements in Honiara and Port Moresby.' In AusAID (Australian Agency for International Development) (ed.), *Making Land Work — Volume Two: Case Studies on Customary Land and Development in the Pacific*. Canberra: AusAID.

———, 2012. 'Institutions for Improving Access to Land for Settler-Housing: Evidence from Papua New Guinea.' *Land Use Policy* 29: 143–153. doi.org/10.1016/j.landusepol.2011.05.013.

Connell, J., 2011. 'Elephants in the Pacific? Pacific Urbanisation and Its Discontents.' *Asia Pacific Viewpoint* 52: 121–135. doi.org/10.1111/j.1467-8373.2011.01445.x.

Crocombe, R., 1971. *Land Tenure in the Pacific*. Melbourne: Oxford University Press.

Filer, C., 1997. 'Compensation, Rent and Power in Papua New Guinea.' In S. Toft (ed.), *Compensation for Resource Development in Papua New Guinea*. Port Moresby: Law Reform Commission (Monograph 6).

———, 2006. 'Custom, Law and Ideology in Papua New Guinea.' *Asia Pacific Journal of Anthropology* 7: 65–84. doi.org/10.1080/14442210600554499.

———, 2007. 'Local Custom and the Art of Land Group Boundary Maintenance in Papua New Guinea.' In J.F. Weiner and K. Glaskin (eds), *Customary Land Tenure and Registration in Australia and Papua New Guinea: Anthropological Perspectives*. Canberra: ANU E Press (Asia-Pacific Environment Monograph 3).

———, 2011. 'The Political Construction of a Land Grab in Papua New Guinea.' Canberra: The Australian National University, Crawford School of Economics and Government (READ Pacific Discussion Paper 1).

Gewertz, D. and F. Errington, 1999. *Emerging Class in Papua New Guinea The Telling of Difference*. Cambridge: Cambridge University Press. doi. org/10.1017/CBO9780511606120.

Gnecchi-Ruscone, E., 1991. Power or Paradise? Korafe Christianity and Korafe Magic. Canberra: The Australian National University (PhD thesis).

Goddard, M., 2005. *The Unseen City: Anthropological Perspectives on Port Moresby, Papua New Guinea*. Canberra: Pandanus Books.

GoPNG (Government of Papua New Guinea), 2010. *National Urbanisation Policy for Papua New Guinea, 2010–2030*. Port Moresby: Office of Urbanisation.

Gregory, C.A., 1980. 'Gifts to Men and Gifts to God: Gift Exchange and Capital Accumulation in Contemporary Papua.' *Journal of the Royal Anthropological Institute* 15: 626–652. doi.org/10.2307/2801537.

———, 1982. *Gifts and Commodities*. London: Academic Press.

Groves, M., 2011. *The Motu of Papua: Tradition in a Time of Change*. Vancouver: Webzines.

Hall, D., P. Hirsch and T.M. Li, 2011. *Powers of Exclusion: Land Dilemmas in Southeast Asia*. Singapore: NUS Press.

Jones, P., 2011. 'Urbanisation in the Pacific Islands Context.' *Development Bulletin* 74: 93–97.

Jorgensen, D., 2007. 'Clan-Finding, Clan-Making and the Politics of Identity in a Papua New Guinea Mining Project.' In J.F. Weiner and K. Glaskin (eds), *Customary Land Tenure and Registration in Australia and Papua New Guinea: Anthropological Perspectives*. Canberra: ANU E Press (Asia-Pacific Environment Monograph 3).

Kidu, C., 2002. 'A Comment on the Work of the Special Parliamentary Committee on Urbanisation and Social Development.' In N. Sullivan (ed.), *Culture and Progress: The Melanesian Philosophy of Land and Social Development in Papua New Guinea*. Madang: Divine Word University Press.

Koczberski, G., 2002. 'Pots, Plates and Tinpis: New Income Flows and the Strengthening Women's Gendered Identities in Papua New Guinea.' *Development* 45: 88–92. doi.org/10.1057/palgrave. development.1110324.

Koczberski, G. and G.N. Curry, 2004. 'Divided Communities and Contested Landscapes: Mobility, Development and Shifting Identities in Migrant Destination Sites in Papua New Guinea.' *Asia Pacific Viewpoint* 45: 357–371. doi.org/10.1111/j.1467-8373.2004.00252.x.

——, 2005. 'Making a Living: Land Pressures and Changing Livelihood Strategies among Oil Palm Settlers in Papua New Guinea.' *Agricultural Systems* 85: 324–339. doi.org/10.1016/j.agsy.2005.06.014.

——, 2009. 'Finding Common Ground: Relational Concepts of Land Tenure and Economy in the Oil Palm Frontier of Papua New Guinea.' *Geographical Journal* 175: 98–111. doi.org/10.1111/j.1475-4959.2008.00319.x.

Koczberski, G., G.N. Curry, and J. Anjen, 2012. 'Changing Land Tenure and Informal Land Markets in the Oil Palm Frontier Regions of Papua New Guinea: The Challenge for Land Reform.' *Australian Geographer* 43: 181–196. doi.org/10.1080/00049182.2012.682295.

Koczberski, G., G.N. Curry and B. Imbun, 2009. 'Property Rights for Social Inclusion: Migrant Strategies for Securing Land and Livelihoods in Papua New Guinea.' *Asia Pacific Viewpoint* 50: 29–42. doi.org/10.1111/j.1467-8373.2009.01379.x.

Langmore, J.V, and N.D. Oram, 1970. *Port Moresby Urban Development.* Port Moresby and Canberra: The Australian National University, Research School of Pacific Studies, New Guinea Research Unit (Bulletin 37).

Lasslett, K., 2012. 'The Demolition of Paga Hill.' Undated post to the website of the International State Crime Initiative. Viewed 19 December 2016 at: www.statecrime.org/testimonyproject/pagahill.

Martin, K., 2013. *The Death of the Big Men and the Rise of the Big Shots: Custom and Conflict in East New Britain.* New York: Berghahn Books.

Martin, M., 2014. 'Parkop: More Evictions on Way.' *Post-Courier,* 5 August.

McDonnell, S., 2013. 'Exploring the Cultural Power of Land Law in Vanuatu: Law as a Performance That Creates Meaning and Identities.' *Intersections* 33.

Monson, R., 2010. 'Women, State Law and Land in Peri-Urban Settlements on Guadalcanal, Solomon Islands'. Washington (DC): World Bank, Justice for the Poor Program (Briefing Note 4.3).

———, 2012. *Hu Nao Save Tok?* Women, Men and Land: Negotiating Property and Authority in Solomon Islands. Canberra: The Australian National University (PhD thesis).

Nolan, L. and J. Abani, 2002. 'Accommodating Urban Growth in Alotau.' In N. Sullivan (ed.), *Culture and Progress: The Melanesian Philosophy of Land and Development in Papua New Guinea*. Madang: Divine Word University Press.

Numbasa, G. and G. Koczberski, 2012. 'Migration, Informal Urban Settlements and Non-Market Land Transaction: A Case Study of Wewak, East Sepik Province, Papua New Guinea.' *Australian Geographer* 43: 143–161. doi.org/10.1080/00049182.2012.682293.

Oram, N.D., 1976. *Colonial Town to Melanesian City: Port Moresby 1884–1974*. Canberra: Australian National University Press.

Ovasuru, P., 2013. 'Police Eviction Effort Shocks Oro Settlers.' *Post-Courier*, 19 April.

Pai, A. and J. Sinne, 2002. 'A Framework for Management of Customary Land for Development and Investment in Urban Centres of Papua New Guinea.' In N. Sullivan (ed.), *Culture and Progress: The Melanesian Philosophy of Land and Development in Papua New Guinea*. Madang: Divine Word University Press.

Rooney, M.N., 2013. 'Another Port Moresby Community Bulldozed.' Devpolicy blogpost, 5 April. Viewed 18 December 2016 at: devpolicy.org/another-port-moresby-community-bulldozed-2013040/.

———, 2015. 'Money and Value in Urban Settlement Households in Port Moresby—Part 2: Understanding Spatial and Income Inequality through Housing Choices.' Canberra: The Australian National University, State, Society and Governance in Melanesia Program (In Brief).

——, forthcoming. Nogat Mani: Social Safety Nets for Tufi Migrants of ATS Settlement, Port Moresby, Papua New Guinea. Canberra: The Australian National University (PhD thesis).

Sayama, A. and D. Wapar, 2013. 'NCD Settlement Bulldozed.' *The National*, 12 March.

Schwimmer, E., 1973. *Exchange in the Social Structure of the Orokaiva: Traditional and Emergent Ideologies in the Northern District of Papua.* Sydney: Angus and Robertson.

Sharp, T., J. Cox, C. Spark, S. Lusby and M.N. Rooney, 2015. 'The Formal, the Informal, and the Precarious: Making a Living in Urban Papua New Guinea.' Canberra: The Australian National University, State Society and Governance in Melanesia Program (Discussion Paper 2015/5).

Stretton, A., 1979. *Urban Housing Policy in Papua New Guinea.* Port Moresby: Institute of Applied Social and Economic Research (Monograph 8).

Tararia, A. and L. Ogle, 2010. 'Incorporated Land Groups and the Registration of Customary Land: Recent Developments in PNG.' In T. Anderson and G. Lee (eds), *In Defence of Melanesian Customary Land.* Sydney: Aid/Watch.

Thornton, A., T. Binns and M.T. Kerslake, 2013. 'Hard Times in Apia? Urban Landlessness and the Church in Samoa.' *Singapore Journal of Tropical Geography* 34: 357–372. doi.org/10.1111/sjtg.12040.

van Gelder, J.-L., 2013. 'Paradoxes of Urban Housing Informality in the Developing World.' *Law and Society Review* 47: 493–522. doi. org/10.1111/lasr.12030.

Webster, T., S. Chand and L. Kutan, 2016. 'Property and Housing Policy Development.' Port Moresby: National Research Institute (Discussion Paper 140).

Wilson, C., 2012. 'Urban Settlers Battle Eviction.' Inter Press Service News Agency, 4 June. Viewed 19 December 2016 at: www.ipsnews. net/2012/06/urban-settlers-battle-evictions/.

5

Informal Land Markets in Papua New Guinea

Gina Koczberski, Georgina Numbasa,
Emmanuel Germis and George N. Curry

Introduction

Customary land in Papua New Guinea (PNG) remains a critical livelihood asset. With less than 5 per cent of the land under freehold title or state leases, the management of present and future demands for customary land for housing, services and livelihoods in the rapidly expanding urban and rural growth centres is a critical development challenge. As elsewhere in the Pacific, Papua New Guineans are leading more mobile lives as they seek new livelihood opportunities and improved access to services in urban and select rural locations. All Pacific Island states are rapidly urbanising, with urban growth outstripping national growth rates in some Pacific nations (see Chapter 2, this volume). A large proportion of migrants, especially from remote parts of PNG, are also moving to rural agricultural and resource frontier zones to access employment, education and health services. The high rate of migration to urban and select rural locations in PNG is placing great pressure on customary land as migrants seek access to land for housing and to develop livelihoods, including subsistence food and cash crop production. The demand and willingness of migrants to pay cash for short- and long-term access to land is fuelling a dynamic land market comprising 'informal' land transactions and rental arrangements.

This chapter examines informal transactions of customary land between customary landowners (hereafter referred to as landowners) and outsiders without birthrights to the land. It identifies key principles underpinning a range of informal land transactions that could be used to inform policies of land reform. We argue that landowners are not seeking a transformation of customary tenure principles to enable them to capitalise on the rising demand for land by migrants; rather, they are seeking to retain 'ownership' and control of their land within a framework that stresses the relational dimensions of their transactions with 'outsiders'. By examining the adaptations and modifications of customary tenure that are taking place on customary land outside government structures, new approaches to land reform can be found that meet the changing demands on customary land and that move away from previous failed land reform attempts based on the notion that secure individual property rights through titling of land are a prerequisite to building a modern economy.

Background

Most people in PNG, as in other parts of the Pacific, hold an intense attachment to land. Land is at the heart of economic life, cultural and spiritual beliefs, and an individual and group's sense of social identity and belonging (Sillitoe 1999). This link to social and cultural identity underpins the common view among landowners that land is inalienable. Even customary land that has been acquired by the state or converted to freehold title is rarely seen as being alienated permanently from customary ownership (Chand and Yala 2006; Filer and Lowe 2011; Curry et al. 2012).

Customary land tenure arrangements vary across the country, but generally, under customary tenure, rights to land are based on a mixture of descent, residence and participation in communal activities (Cooter 1991; Larmour 1991; Curry 1997; Koczberski et al. 2009). Exclusive individual landownership and inheritance was limited because, in the largely horticultural societies of PNG, an individual's rights to land for the cultivation of food crops waned as the garden reverted to fallow. As the fallow period lengthened there was a gradual return of rights back to the group (Ward and Kingdon 1995; Curry et al. 2012). This system of land tenure prevented individuals from acquiring exclusive control over large tracts of land.

Another characteristic of customary land tenure was its flexibility, which permitted land rights to be modified to accommodate changing socio-political, demographic and environmental situations. The pragmatic nature of customary land tenure meant that the relative importance in land rights of descent, residency and participation in social and political activities varied, so that no single criterion, such as descent, was sufficient in itself to provide unconditional rights to land (Crocombe 1971). This flexible system ensured that most villagers had sufficient land to meet their daily livelihood requirements, and allowed temporary land rights to be transferred to individuals and lineages without birthrights to the land (Crocombe and Hide 1971; Mandeville 1979; Curry 1997; Ward 1997). Thus, members of a clan short of land were often given access rights to gardening land that belonged to another clan in the village.

Although traditional principles of land tenure are still followed throughout the country, the way in which customary land is governed by landowning groups is being modified in response to new demands and pressures related to rapid demographic and socio-economic changes. In contemporary PNG the key drivers of these changes include:

- Large-scale resource development, such as mining and plantations (Lea 1997; Gilberthorpe 2007; Weiner 2007; Banks 2008; Bainton 2010; Imbun 2013).

- Smallholder production of cash crops, particularly perennial crops like coffee and cocoa, and large-scale food production for urban markets. There is a trend in areas where perennial cash crops have been incorporated into village farming systems for customary tenure to gradually become more individualised and for land to be 'sold' to other clan members (Epstein 1969; Standish 1984; Foster 1995; MacWilliam 1988; Curry et al. 2007; Martin 2007; Koczberski et al. 2009).

- Population and land pressures. Mounting demand for land in villages and the increasing need for cash are leading to many internal adjustments to land tenure arrangements. In some cases such pressures are eroding the flexibility of customary land tenure practices, resulting in a tightening up of access rights and increasing individual/family control over land (Carrier and Carrier 1989; Zimmer-Tamakoshi 1997; Martin 2013).

- Internal migration. In PNG large numbers of people, usually from remote and poorly serviced areas of the country, are migrating to urban areas and rural resource frontier regions. These migrants are entering into informal agreements with landowners to gain access to customary land for housing and to generate livelihoods.

- Rapid urbanisation and the growth of informal settlements. Most of the recent residential growth occurring on customary land in peri-urban areas is due largely to the limited supply of state and freehold land. The demand for land by migrants is sustaining an active land market in informal land 'sales' and rental arrangements (Goddard 2005; Chand and Yala 2012; Numbasa and Koczberski 2012).

- Growing notions of individualism and changing aspirations. As PNG undergoes social and economic change, people's attitudes to land are also changing. In some parts of the country, especially where engagement with the market economy is strong and growing, social relations and values are becoming more market-orientated, with a corresponding trend towards possessive individualism (Martin 2013). This is leading some clan members to view land as a commodity that can be 'sold' to people outside the landholding group.

The adaptations and modifications to customary land tenure by landowners in response to these key drivers offer lessons to inform land reform policies. Whilst customary land tenure is recognised in PNG's Constitution, it has largely been considered problematic in discussions of land reform. Land reform in PNG and elsewhere in the Pacific has been dominated by the assertion that customary tenure is incapable of providing secure property rights necessary for facilitating investment and the commercial use of land (Lea 2002; Gosarevski et al. 2004). With communal ownership and no formal title to land, customary tenure is viewed as a major obstacle to economic development. Thus, attempts at land reform in PNG have been based on the notion that secure individual property rights through land titling and tenure conversion are a prerequisite for building a favourable investment climate and fostering economic development. This private property approach to land emerged in Africa in the 1970s when the World Bank launched its policy on land reform for developing countries, and it has since dominated land reform programs in PNG and elsewhere in the Pacific (Peters 2007; Fingleton 2008).

However, land reform is 'easier said than done' (GoPNG 2007), and the three major land reform programs that have been attempted in PNG since the 1960s have failed (Larmour 1991; Fingleton 2004; Yala and Lyons 2012). One reason for their failure was their incompatibility with people's concepts of the moral basis of land rights and the strongly held view that customary land is inalienable. The failure of past land reform programs, and the growing interest by some landowning groups to mobilise their land for development, have influenced the most recent land reform discussions that started in 2005 and have since continued under the National Land Development Program (see Chapter 6, this volume). There is now greater acknowledgment that landowners must feel a sense of ownership of the land reform agenda (GoPNG 2007; Fingleton 2008). This has led to nationwide consultations with landowning groups to obtain their views and support for proposed policies. The central goal of the reforms is to identify ways to facilitate access to customary land for economic development while providing tenure security for investors and ensuring land remains under customary ownership (individual user rights but ownership at the group level). This represents a significant shift from earlier land reform programs that sought to replace customary tenure.

A significant challenge for policy makers in PNG will be how to deal with the proliferation of informal (and sometimes illegal) land transfers taking place, as landowners develop their own arrangements for land mobilisation outside government structures, and as they seek to capitalise on the demand for urban and rural land by land-poor migrants. How policy makers can develop an effective reform program and land administration system to accommodate the range of informal and semi-formal arrangements already well established will be one of the principal challenges for land reform in PNG.

In the remaining part of this chapter, two case studies are presented to illustrate how customary land tenure has been modified to accommodate 'outsiders' without birthrights to the land. The first case study is from Wewak, the provincial capital of East Sepik Province, and focuses on migrant settlers living in informal settlements. The second is in the oil palm-growing areas around Hoskins in West New Britain Province, where migrants from other provinces are acquiring land for oil palm production (Figure 5.1). Each case study examines the informal land transactions between landowners and land-poor migrants, and in particular how settlers first obtained and continue to maintain access to the customary land of others. The key principles underpinning successful land transactions in both case studies are discussed, together with the factors contributing to disputes between migrants and their landowner hosts. Whilst anthropologists as early as the 1950s reported on individuals and lineages without birthrights being given access rights to land (Meggitt 1965, 1971; Reay 1971; Forge 1972; Mandeville 1979), few recent studies have examined how migrants into urban centres and rural and resource frontier zones maintain long-term access rights to customary land to establish new livelihoods in their adopted homes.

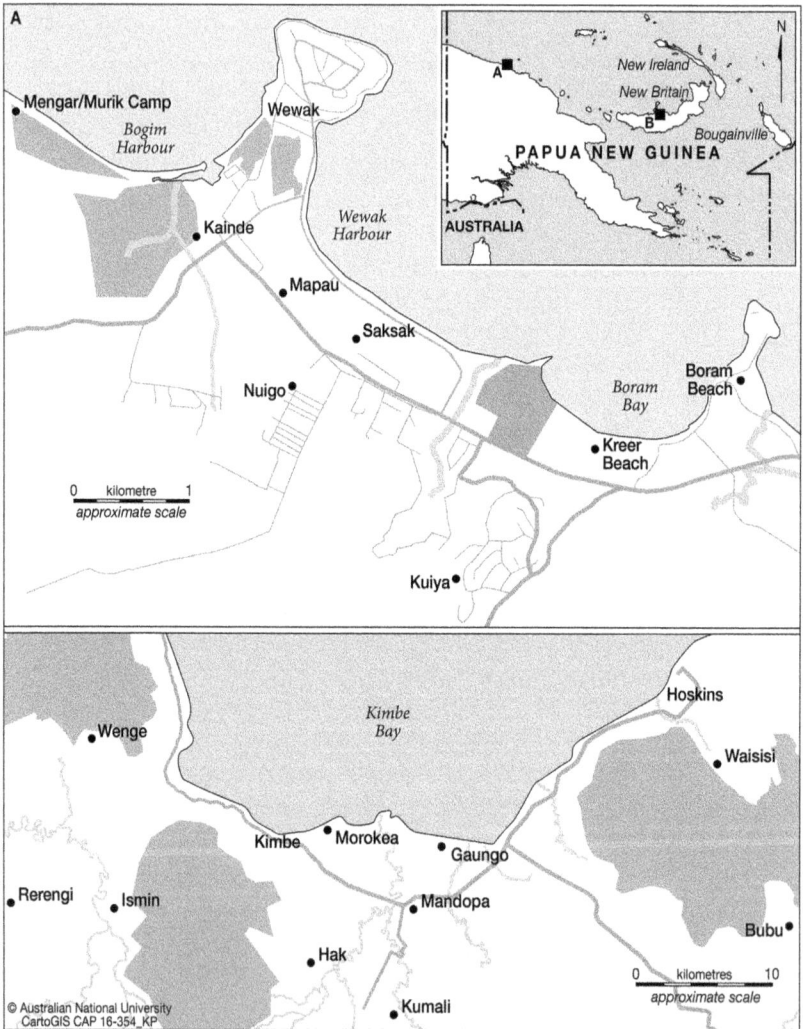

Figure 5.1 Location of study sites.

Source: CartoGIS, The Australian National University, based on PNG national census data.

Home Making in Wewak's Informal Settlements

Wewak has a population of almost 25,000, and is made up of state, freehold (largely owned by the Catholic Church) and customary land. Most of Wewak, including peri-urban areas, is on customary land. Wewak grew considerably after the Second World War through to the 1980s, as it became the administrative and commercial centre for the province. In the 1950s, several informal settlements began appearing on customary land as people from other parts of the province came to Wewak seeking employment and access to government and church services (Numbasa and Koczberski 2012). By the mid-1970s almost half of urban housing in Wewak was in informal settlements (Jackson 1977). These informal settlements on customary land have continued to expand, so that Wewak, like other towns and cities in PNG, has become a town of migrants, with over 55 per cent of the population born elsewhere (GoPNG 2001).

To examine how migrants accessed land for housing, interviews and household surveys were conducted with residents at seven informal settlements that were founded between 1950 and 1970 (Figure 5.1). Levels of services in the settlements were poor, and most do not have electricity, reticulated water or garbage collection. Each settlement was dominated by one or two cultural or ethnic groups, and while some residents were in paid employment, most made a livelihood in the informal sector selling store goods, cooked food, fish, handicrafts and wood carvings at local markets.

Table 5.1 lists the key characteristics of each settlement, including the dominant source area of migrants, the average residency period of household heads in the settlement, the type of land tenure, how settlers initially accessed the land, how they have maintained access rights to the land through time, and the range of restrictions imposed on settlers by the landowners. All the settlements are located on customary land, although some were formerly established on what was then Catholic mission-owned land. Many landowning groups who supported the establishment of the Catholic Church in Wewak donated land to the church, and some of this land was used by the church to house their workers. Over time these compounds have grown as village relatives joined family members residing in Wewak. The mission land has since been returned to the landowners, which has involved settlers entering new informal agreements and relationships with their new 'landlords'.

Table 5.1 Wewak settlement characteristics.

Name of settlement	Dominant source area of migrants	Average no. of years living in settlement	Type of land tenure	Initial arrangement to access land	Informal arrangement with landowners to maintain access rights to land	Restrictions on residents by landowners
Boram Beach Front	Schouten Islands, Murik Lakes	25.0	Customary	Traditional trading partners with landowners.	Contribute in cash & kind to customary exchange demands.	No fishing or hunting in mangroves or removal of material for house building or other purposes. Housing restrictions & control of settlement population.
Kaindi Ward 5	Yangoru, coast west of Wewak	34.8	Customary (disputed)	Customary exchange.	Contribute in cash & kind to customary exchange demands.	Restrictions on fishing or hunting in mangroves and the removal of materials for housing. Housing restrictions & control of settlement population.
Koil Island Camp	Schouten Islands	14.8	Customary	Traditional trading partners with landowners.	Informal rents/contribute in cash & kind to customary exchange demands.	No small-scale business enterprises. Housing restrictions & control of settlement population.
Kuiya Settlement	Turubu, Wosera, Dreikikir, West Sepik	23.3	Customary/ some formerly mission land	Customary exchange/mission land, compound for employees.	Contribute in cash & kind to customary exchange demands.	No large-scale business enterprises, no gardening, planting of cash crops or collecting firewood in adjoining land. Housing restrictions and control of settlement population.
Nuigo Settlement	Middle Sepik River villages	24.4	State (formerly mission land)	Mission land, compound for employees.	Formal rentals to national housing commission.	No restrictions, although warned by neighbouring landowners not to take resources on their land.
Saksak Compound	Sepik River villages	27.6	Customary (formerly mission land)	Mission land, compound for employees.	Contribute in cash & kind to customary exchange demands.	No restrictions.
Mapau Settlement	Angoram	24.3	Customary	Mission land, compound for employees.	Contribute in cash & kind to customary exchange demands.	Informal tax paid on small businesses. Housing restrictions and control of settlement population.

Source: Numbasa and Koczberski 2012.

Most settlements on customary land, such as Boram Beach, Koil Island Camp and Kaindi Ward 5 Settlement, were established initially by a person or a group of people who had some marital, friendship or long-standing traditional trading relationships with the landowning group. For example, in the 1950s, people from Wewak's offshore islands and distant coastal villages began visiting Wewak more regularly for business, to see their relatives, and to seek medical and education services (which were very limited outside the provincial capital). With the consent of landowners, the migrants established small camps on the beach, such as Boram Beach Front and Koil Island Camp at Kreer Beach. Originally, the camps were used by the visitors as places to secure their canoes during trading expeditions or when visiting the mainland to access the new services that were becoming available in the towns. Whilst the initial negotiations were between elders from the migrant source villages and members of the landowning group, later agreements tended to be between individual migrants and landowners. Over time, as residency became more long-term, the camps evolved into established permanent settlements. The traditional trading relationships that facilitated the initial residential arrangements were important for assisting later migrants to access land for more permanent settlement in Wewak, as were the initial settlers who provided a base and personal contacts within the host communities.

Since the settlements were established over four decades ago, migrants have continued to maintain their tenure rights largely through personal exchange relationships with their landowning hosts and increasingly through intermarriage (Table 5.1). Migrants maintain their access rights to the land through regular contributions in cash, food or labour to landowners' customary activities and expenses, especially funerals and brideprice payments. Three quarters of respondents reported making regular in-kind or cash contributions to landowners' customary expenses. These contributions to customary exchange are central to building and strengthening settlers' relationships with landowners, as is settlers' attendance at marriage ceremonies, funerals and other customary events in the landowning village. Socially and politically, these acts are public demonstrations by settlers of their close relationship ties with their hosts and their ongoing respect for landowners and their customs. It is through meeting their ongoing customary obligations to the landowners and maintaining good relationships with them that access rights are upheld.

In addition to maintaining ongoing customary relationships with the landowners, settlers must observe landowner-imposed land use restrictions to maintain ongoing access to land and housing (Table 5.1). Landowner regulations governing land use varied among settlements. Often restrictions included defining the types of livelihood activities migrants could and could not pursue, prohibiting the utilisation of mangrove or forest resources adjacent to settlements, and controlling house building and the numbers and demographic composition of the settler population. The most common type of landowner-imposed restriction on settlements was on who could reside in the settlement. Potential new residents had to gain approval from the landowners prior to moving into the settlement and, generally, only those closely related to existing residents were granted permission. When settlers neglected to observe these restrictions, conflicts with landowners could emerge leading to the eviction of settlers.

By engaging in exchange relationships with their landowner hosts and observing the restrictions placed on their activities, settlers were more likely to sustain stable tenure rights. Landowners engaged in a regular process of evaluating and assessing the status of their relationships with settlers, and in so doing, made judgements of the moral basis of migrants' occupancy rights. Thus, how settlers managed their relationships with landowners was critical to determining tenure status.

However, despite the relatively stable relationships between landowners and settlers, the tenure security of migrants in some settlements was being undermined. This situation was arising largely because of the changing social relationships between younger members of the landowning group and the children born in the settlement. In certain settlements, some second- and third-generation settlers resented complying with the endless requests to contribute cash and food to the customary exchanges of their landowner hosts, especially given their own household cash needs and their continuing customary obligations to relatives in their 'home' villages. Similarly, some younger members of the landowner community were reluctant to recognise the informal agreements or long-established relationship ties made by their elders with the settlers' fathers and grandfathers. From their perspective, the informal agreements established with the migrants were of the past and belonged to an older generation for whom customary obligations and practices were more strongly valued (Numbasa and Koczberski 2012). Moreover, some younger landowners viewed the new generation of settlers as the source of law and order problems, and their continued residence in the settlement was seen as an obstacle to formally leasing the land to developers. At the time of fieldwork, at least three landowning groups were holding discussions with developers about leasing their land (Numbasa and Koczberski 2012). The lure of higher returns by leasing their land to developers was stronger when the quality of the relationship between landowners and migrants was perceived to be poor. Thus the tenure security of second-generation migrants was changing as their social and exchange relationships with their landowner hosts were also undergoing reassessment.

Oil Palm and the Desire for Land

The oil palm belt along the coastal plain of Kimbe Bay in West New Britain has one of the fastest population growth rates in the country. Much of this population growth is attributable to high immigration to the province from mainland PNG. Approximately 38 per cent of the residents were born in other provinces (GoPNG 2001), many of them being concentrated around the Hoskins and Bialla oil palm land settlement schemes and plantation estates, and in the urban centres of Kimbe and Bialla.

For the past 25 years, and especially over the last decade, land-poor settlers living in the oil palm belt have been seeking customary land on which to plant oil palm. Whilst there has been a history of landowners gifting land to village non-clan members to plant oil palm, the informal 'sale' or 'renting' of land to migrants from other provinces is more recent. The 'sale' of land to settlers first emerged in the 1980s at Hoskins and in the early 1990s at Bialla. Most of those buying customary land are the children or relatives of settlers who acquired state agricultural leases on the government oil palm land settlement schemes at Hoskins and Bialla, or have been in long-term employment in the province where they also raised their children. Figure 5.1 shows the major locations where customary land is being 'sold' to outsiders. The initial land transactions between migrants and clan leaders in the Hoskins area were typically based on friendship or a marital link, similar to the close relationships associated with the early land transactions with 'outsiders' in Wewak. Also, as in Wewak, access rights were maintained through contributing to customary exchange and participating in village activities.

More recently, as the demand for customary land has grown, land dealings have increasingly been with settlers where there has been no pre-existing relationship with the landowners. Virtually all land transactions with 'outsiders' now involve payments for the land. Although there is great variation in the types of informal land sale agreements, which is partly explained by the different relationships between landowners and outsiders, typically an initial cash deposit is paid to the landowner(s), with the outstanding balance paid in cash instalments over several years after the palms come into production.

In most cases, land sales tend to be informal verbal agreements between the transacting parties, with an individual's access and use rights to the land loosely defined. Seldom are there written records of the agreed 'purchase' price and the amount and timing of payment instalments; nor are the specific rights and obligations of the migrant or landowner documented. Rarely is the size and boundary of the 'purchased' land surveyed. Members of the broader landowner group are sometimes not aware that land has been 'sold' to an 'outsider', and this can become a major source of discontent within the landowner group.

Disputes over 'purchased' customary land (and even over land initially gifted to migrants) have been increasing over the past 10 years. These disputes arise not so much because migrants and landowners have different understandings of land use rights—the right to plant oil palm—but rather because they have different concepts of land 'ownership', which means that their respective interpretations of the obligations and expectations associated with land transactions can be very different.

There are three major points of contention in migrants' and landowners' interpretations of land transactions. First, some migrants believe that the cash payments made to landowners confer on them outright ownership of the land, not unlike freehold title. These migrants therefore argue that their children should be able to inherit the land and they should have the unencumbered right to sell the land to a third party without consulting the landowners (Koczberski et al. 2009). This is rarely the view of the landowners, and nor is it the case in law as the land remains customary land with the potential to be reclaimed by the landowners on the death of the 'purchaser'. Second, those migrants who discursively construct the land transaction as a commodity transaction are of the view that, in addition to cultivating oil palm, they can establish small businesses or other income-generating activities on the land. Landowners contest this right and remind migrants that they have purchased only the use rights for oil palm cultivation, not other livelihood activities. If other income-generating activities were to be established on the land, landowners often insist on some additional payments; after all, the migrants are earning this additional income on the land of the landowners, and this wealth should be shared. Third, while many settlers do contribute cash to the customary exchange activities of the landowners, some settlers resist or reject these demands as they believe there should not be an obligation on them to maintain a social relationship with their 'hosts' through gifts of labour and wealth. These settlers strive to limit their relationships with landowners, but in doing so they undermine their moral claim to the land in the eyes of landowners.

From the landowners' perspective, land transactions must accord with customary principles concerning the inalienability of land. From this point of view, exclusive and permanent property rights are not guaranteed by full payment of the agreed 'purchase' price. Rather, migrants' land rights are less exclusive and are conditional on settlers' fulfilment of specific obligations and maintenance of good social relationships with their landowner hosts. For example, there is an expectation among landowners that they should share in the wealth generated on their land by 'outsiders', even though no landowner labour contributed to that wealth. This is most strikingly observed when oil palm prices rise and landowners expect they should also share some of income accruing from the higher prices. Thus, migrants are expected to act like clan members, share the wealth from the land, and contribute to village brideprice and mortuary payments, other forms of customary exchange, and village fundraising activities.

These demands on 'purchasers' accord more with the widespread view of landownership in PNG being grounded in relational identities. Robert Cooter's (1991) conceptual framework is relevant to an understanding of the differing interpretations of land transactions by migrants and landowners (see Table 5.2). Cooter described freehold transactions as those that occur between strangers whose only relationship with each other is commercial, where the obligations and commitments between the parties are minimal. While buyers and sellers have some obligations to each other, the transaction choices they make are not constrained by mutual social obligations. Both buyers and sellers can act to their own best advantage, and the relationship between them is short-term and concludes with completion of the sale (Koczberski et al. 2009). Cooter (1991: 41) described freehold tenure as 'property law for stranger relations'.

In contrast, land transactions occurring under customary land tenure regimes are between relatives and are based on long-term relationships of reciprocal obligations, cooperation and commitment to the kinship group. Such reciprocal obligations determine customary rights to land and constrain people's freedom to act to their own best advantage in land transactions. Under customary land tenure regimes, relational concepts of land tenure are therefore dominant. Customary land laws are thus described by Cooter (1991: 41) as 'property law for kin relations'. Migrants who construct the land transactions as being in the realm of commodity transactions, and therefore anchored in the principles of freehold title (stranger relations), are likely to see their access rights challenged as they allow their relationship with landowners to wane. Settlers accepting land access rights as being grounded in social relationships, and dependent on meeting certain exchange obligations, are better able to integrate themselves into their host communities and develop long-term stable relationships with them, with ongoing access to land.

Table 5.2 Cooter's concept of property law in PNG.

Freehold Principles (property law for stranger relations)	Customary Principles (property law for kin relations)
Relationships between people are commercial: obligations and commitments are thin	Relationships between relatives: kin networks bind people together in a web of mutual obligations and commitments
Short-term relationships between people	Long-term relationships between relatives
Concept of absolute unitary ownership	Concept of relational property and land as an inalienable resource

Source: Cooter 1991: 41.

Discussion

Informal land markets provide an important function in contemporary PNG. As highlighted above, there is a large demand for customary land by migrants desiring to secure a future in urban and rural areas of PNG where livelihood opportunities and access to services are relatively good. While there has been a long history of landowners gifting land to non-clan members, informal land agreements and the 'renting' or 'sale' of land to land-poor migrants from other provinces or districts is more recent, and presently undergoing reassessment as relationships between landowners and migrants change. The new and rapidly changing rules of access for 'outsiders' illustrate both an expanding and evolving informal land market in PNG and the profound shifts in value systems as the country becomes increasingly tied into the global economy.

A common feature across both case studies was the broad range of land transactions enabling migrants to gain access to land. Monetary land sales, rentals and 'gifted' access rights were common, with most transactions being informal verbal agreements, grounded in local forms of sociability, while some were more formal, with written documentation. In many situations there was a level of ambiguity regarding migrants' long-term tenure security, although land use rights were clearly defined and tightly circumscribed, with very specific use rights and restrictions on who can reside in the community. For example, migrants may have residence rights, but not the right to establish small businesses or harvest forest or marine products belonging to their hosts. Typically, these rights were negotiated separately from the land transaction, and sometimes incurred additional payments if they were permitted at all.

In both case studies, despite the inclusion of cash to facilitate access rights to land, ongoing tenure security was largely dependent on the creation and maintenance of social relationships. Indeed, initial settlement rights were typically granted to settlers with whom the landowners had a pre-existing relationship. In the Wewak case, this was sometimes built on long-standing trading relationships in which the leaders of the host and migrant communities arranged settlement. In West New Britain, friendships forged between migrants and landowners, sometimes while working together on plantations or in town or as neighbours, were the basis of their relationship and subsequent land transactions. More recently, as demand for land has increased, access rights to customary land have been granted to settlers with no pre-existing relationship with the landowners. This represents a deepening degree of commodification of land transactions with migrants.

However, despite the absence of pre-existing relationships with landowners, and the appearance of there being market transactions in land, recent settlers are still expected to develop relational identities with their hosts to validate access rights. These relationships are initiated and then fostered through indigenous exchange transactions in which migrants make cash, food and labour contributions to the customary and community activities of their hosts. There is also an expectation that landowners will share in the wealth generated by migrants, especially those earning regular incomes from oil palm or from full-time employment. This sharing of wealth is often portrayed as a form of indigenous exchange rather than market transactions devoid of social meaning. Being cast in the realm of indigenous exchange means that the relationship with landowners has social value and implies respect for the host group—respect for their authority as landowners, respect for their culture, and respect for their behavioural mores. Such relational conditions underpinning migrants' access rights also extend to them supporting electoral candidates from the landowner group and supporting the landowners in disputes with neighbouring groups.

This practice of landowners striving to socially embed land transactions with migrants can be considered as a form of enacting personalised 'property rights for social inclusion' or, to use Ribot and Peluso's term, as 'mechanisms of access' that allow certain actors to gain, control and maintain access to resources (Ribot and Peluso 2003: 160). These 'socially inclusive' access mechanisms create opportunities for settlers to become incorporated into networks of obligations and exchange and become a subgroup of the landowning group, which partially erases their identity as 'outsiders' and confers on them certain rights and privileges, including ongoing access to land. Similar processes of 'social inclusion' that enable migrants to validate access rights to customary land have also been reported from other urban and rural areas of PNG (Levine and Levine 1979; Goddard 2005; Martin 2013; also Chapter 4, this volume).

Whilst such access mechanisms enable migrants to move from being 'outsiders' to being 'insiders', their status is not permanent, as social relationships with members of the landowning group must be nurtured continually. Most migrants readily accept that secure and long-lasting access rights are subject to meeting certain relational conditions, and they regularly engage, sometimes begrudgingly, in the maintenance of exchange relationships with the landowning group. Others, who have 'purchased' land or pay regular rental fees, attempt to discursively construct their dealings with landowners as market transactions and resist investing in regular exchange relationships with their hosts. These migrants are most at risk of harassment and eviction.

When landowners believe that migrants are not sustaining adequate levels of investment in social relationships with their hosts, they often interpret this as a downgrading of the migrants' tenure rights with a corresponding strengthening of their own rights in the land. In oil palm, this reassessment of relationships is likely to occur on the death of either the clan leader or the migrant involved in the initial land transaction, or at the end of an oil palm planting cycle (Curry and Koczberski 2009). At these points the land rights of 'outsiders' may be renegotiated or terminated. However, as demand for land increases, and the local economic context offers more lucrative opportunities, with investors or potential new migrants willing to invest more in these relationships, migrants who have neglected their relationships with their hosts may find their tenure security weakened as they negotiate with a new generation of younger landowners eager to extract more wealth from their land. Like their Wewak counterparts keen to capitalise on new opportunities presented by developers, younger landowners' commitment to existing settlers may not be as strong as that of their parents' generation.

The potential for dispute and exclusion is greater among second and subsequent generations of landowners and migrants as social distance increases. Also, as illustrated in the case studies, conflicts are increasingly likely as population and land pressures rise, as landowners see their development options constrained by the presence of large numbers of settlers, and as long-term, intergenerational migrants develop a sense of a birthright to the land where they reside (see Chapter 12, this volume). Thus, what worked well in the past, when most settlers had a direct personal relationship with landowners, and when there were fewer land pressures and competing land uses, is coming under increasing pressure and reassessment in the increasingly market-orientated contemporary economy of PNG.

Policy Implications

What general principles and lessons do the case studies provide to inform land reform discussions? In analysing the diverse range of land transactions in place, it was clear that, whilst landowners wished to capitalise on the new economic opportunities of their land, they were not after wholesale change with a transformation of customary tenure. They wish to preserve the key aspects of customary tenure. Most contemporary land use agreements between landowners and outsiders in West New Britain and Wewak are compatible with long-existing mechanisms of transferring land rights to individuals and lineages without birthrights to the land, which have been reported by researchers from many other parts of the country. Thus, although the 'sale' of land to migrants for the cultivation of introduced cash crops such as oil palm, and the informal 'renting' of land for urban settlements, involve new types of land tenure arrangements, they are symbolically and materially modelled on old practices and customs that historically were widespread in PNG.

Further evidence that landowners do not want to see a radical change to customary tenure, despite a clear trend towards the commodification of land, is that relational identities remain central to the basis of land rights. Often the 'sale' and 'renting' of land in West New Britain, and the emergence of urban settlements in PNG, are interpreted by observers as a process of commodification of land and land rights. However, such land transactions remain, at least from the perspective of landowners, anchored in principles of customary land tenure and in long-standing concepts of clan identity, social inclusion and entitlements. It is these place-based frameworks of land tenure embedded in social relationships and non-market values that continue to play a critical role in gaining and maintaining access rights for land by 'outsiders', even if at times relationships are manipulated by landowners.

Given the enduring significance and widespread recognition of relational identities in access rights to land, new land policies should seek to align with these principles wherever possible. With the failure of previous land reform programs, there is now growing recognition among policy makers in PNG, and in other Pacific Island nations, that land reform should aim to support and build on existing customary tenure rather than replace it. As Jim Fingleton noted in a paper on land reform in the Pacific:

> there is now a general acceptance that adaptation, not replacement, of customary tenures is the way forward. The Food and Agriculture Organization (FAO) of the United Nations endorses the adaptation approach to land tenure reform. Even the World Bank, for long a critic of customary tenures, has given ground, now recognising customary tenures as a viable basis for growth and development (Fingleton 2008: 10–11).

The adaptation approach to land reform is more likely to be acceptable to landowners, and, as the case studies have shown, landowners are already one step ahead of government policy and are adapting their customary land tenure systems by entering into informal agreements with 'outsiders'. Proponents of land reform often portray customary land tenure as archaic, inflexible and inappropriate for the modern market context. They often claim that land registration and titling are necessary for raising agricultural productivity. Where there is pressure for land reform, the adaptability and flexibility of customary land tenure is often downplayed or ignored. Yet the case studies show that, in the absence of an effective land administration system and suitable state-led land reform, landowners seeking to capitalise on the demand for land are developing their own informal arrangements for land mobilisation and modifying customary land practices, in most cases successfully. Indeed, as shown in several parts of Africa, where land remains under customary tenure and demand for land by 'outsiders' is great, government efforts in land reform often lag well behind what is happening on the ground as landowners develop their own informal land arrangements (Chimhowu and Woodhouse 2006; Peters 2007; Becker 2013).

Where tenure practices are evolving rapidly, as in PNG, it is necessary, before embarking on land reform policies, that detailed empirical analysis be undertaken on how customary land tenure regimes are changing, the extent to which land is being excluded from customary ownership, and the basis and outcomes of land conflicts and dispossessions. For example, with the emergence of tensions among younger, second-generation migrants and landowners, and new forms of exclusion, both groups are seeking more formal arrangements. Landowners are seeking ways to ensure that their long-term customary tenure rights are not eroded, while some migrants are seeking to have formal recognition of their use rights to the land and more long-term security of tenure for housing and to pursue livelihoods. How will more formal or legal procedures be managed or regulated by the state, migrants, and landowner groups to provide some level of tenure security for migrants acquiring land, while recognising and preserving the underlying rights of landowners on the ground?

More challenging will be how policy makers can develop an effective reform program and land administration system to accommodate the range of informal and semi-formal arrangements already well established, and gain the cooperation and trust of landowners in the land reform agenda. Any new government system seeking to mobilise customary land for housing and livelihoods for 'outsiders' will find it difficult to compete with existing informal systems already widespread and operating for several decades in many parts of PNG. The policy aim should be to find a way to complement and build on existing informal institutions and land transaction agreements that recognise underlying customary ownership. To achieve this means developing procedures and practices, in consultation with landowning groups, local government and migrants, which ideally build on indigenous notions of land tenure to provide tenure security to both groups.

References

Bainton, N.A., 2010. *The Lihir Destiny: Cultural Responses to Mining in Melanesia*. Canberra: ANU E Press (Asia Pacific Environment Monograph 5).

Banks, G., 2008. 'Understanding "Resource" Conflicts in Papua New Guinea.' *Asia Pacific Viewpoint* 49: 23–34. doi.org/10.1111/j.1467-8373.2008.00358.x.

Becker, L.C., 2013. 'Land Sales and the Transformation of Social Relations and Landscape in Peri-Urban Mali.' *Geoforum* 46: 113–123. doi.org/10.1016/j.geoforum.2012.12.017.

Carrier, J.G. and A.H. Carrier, 1989. *Wage, Trade, and Exchange in Melanesia: A Manus Society in the Modern State*. Berkeley: University of California Press.

Chand, S. and C. Yala, 2006. 'Improving Access to Land within the Settlements of Port Moresby.' Canberra: The Australian National University, Crawford School of Economics and Government (IDEC Working Paper 07/04).

———, 2012. 'Institutions for Improving Access to Land for Settler-Housing: Evidence from Papua New Guinea.' *Land Use Policy* 29: 143–153. doi.org/10.1016/j.landusepol.2011.05.013.

Chimhowu, A. and P. Woodhouse, 2006. 'Customary vs Private Property Rights? Dynamics and Trajectories of Vernacular Land Markets in Sub-Saharan Africa.' *Journal of Agrarian Change* 6: 346–371. doi.org/10.1111/j.1471-0366.2006.00125.x.

Cooter, R.D., 1991. 'Kin Groups and the Common Law Process.' In P. Larmour (ed.), *Customary Land Tenure: Registration and Decentralisation in Papua New Guinea*. Port Moresby: Institute of Applied Social and Economic Research (Monograph 29).

Crocombe, R., 1971. *Land Tenure in the Pacific*. Melbourne: Oxford University Press.

Crocombe, R. and R. Hide, 1971. 'New Guinea: Unity in Diversity.' In R. Crocombe (ed.), *Land Tenure in the Pacific*. Melbourne: Oxford University Press.

Curry, G.N., 1997. 'Warfare, Social Organisation and Resource Access amongst the Wosera Abelam of Papua New Guinea.' *Oceania* 67: 194–217. doi.org/10.1002/j.1834-4461.1997.tb02604.x.

Curry, G.N. and G. Koczberski, 2009. 'Finding Common Ground: Relational Concepts of Land Tenure and Economy in the Oil Palm Frontier of Papua New Guinea.' *Geographical Journal* 175: 98–111. doi.org/10.1111/j.1475-4959.2008.00319.x.

Curry, G.N., G. Koczberski and J. Connell, 2012. 'Introduction: Enacting Modernity in the Pacific.' *Australian Geographer* 43: 115–125. doi.org /10.1080/00049182.2012.682291.

Curry, G.N., G. Koczberski, E. Omuru and R.S. Nailina, 2007. *Farming or Foraging? Household Labour and Livelihood Strategies amongst Smallholder Cocoa Growers in Papua New Guinea.* Perth: Black Swan Press.

Epstein, A.L., 1969. *Matupit: Land, Politics and Change among the Tolai of New Britain.* Canberra: Australian National University Press.

Filer, C. and M. Lowe, 2011. 'One Hundred Years of Land Reform on the Gazelle Peninsula: A Baining Point of View.' In V. Strang and M. Busse (eds), *Ownership and Appropriation.* Oxford and New York: Berg (ASA Monograph 47).

Fingleton, J., 2004. 'Is Papua New Guinea Viable without Customary Groups?' *Pacific Economic Bulletin* 19(2): 96–103.

——, 2008. *Pacific Land Tenures: New Ideas for Reform.* Rome: UN Food and Agriculture Organization (FAO Legal Papers Online 73).

Forge, A., 1972. 'The Golden Fleece.' *Man* 7: 527–540. doi. org/10.2307/2799947.

Foster, R.J., 1995. *Social Reproduction and History in Melanesia: Mortuary Ritual, Gift Exchange, and Custom in the Tanga Islands.* Cambridge: Cambridge University Press.

Gilberthorpe, E., 2007. 'Fasu Solidarity: A Case Study of Kin Networks, Land Tenure and Oil Extraction in Kutubu, Papua New Guinea.' *American Anthropologist* 109: 101–112. doi.org/10.1525/ aa.2007.109.1.101.

Goddard, M., 2005. *The Unseen City: Anthropological Perspectives on Port Moresby, Papua New Guinea*. Canberra: Pandanus Books.

GoPNG (Government of Papua New Guinea), 2001. *National Population and Housing Census 2000*. Port Moresby: National Statistical Office.

——, 2007. *The National Land Development Taskforce Report: Land Administration, Land Dispute Settlement, and Customary Land Development*. Port Moresby: National Research Institute (Monograph 39).

Gosarevski, S., H. Hughes and S. Windybank, 2004. 'Is Papua New Guinea Viable?' *Pacific Economic Bulletin* 19(1): 134–148.

Imbun, B., 2013. 'Maintaining Land Use Agreements in Papua New Guinea Mining: Business as Usual?' *Resources Policy* 38: 310–319. doi. org/10.1016/j.resourpol.2013.04.003.

Jackson, R., 1977. 'The Growth, Nature and Future Prospects of Informal Settlements in Papua New Guinea.' *Pacific Viewpoint* 18: 22–42.

Koczberski, G., G.N. Curry and B. Imbun, 2009. 'Property Rights for Social Inclusion: Migrant Strategies for Securing Land and Livelihoods in Papua New Guinea.' *Asia Pacific Viewpoint* 50: 29–42. doi.org/10.1111/j.1467-8373.2009.01379.x.

Larmour, P., 1991. 'Registration of Customary Land: 1952–1987.' In P. Larmour (ed.), *Customary Land Tenure: Registration and Decentralisation in Papua New Guinea*. Port Moresby: Institute of Applied Social and Economic Research (Monograph 29).

Lea, D., 1997. *Melanesian Land Tenure in a Contemporary and Philosophical Context*. Lanham (MD): University Press of America.

——, 2002. 'Are there Advantages to Maintaining Customary Land Tenure in Papua New Guinea?' *Pacific Economic Bulletin* 17(2): 42–55.

Levine, H.B. and M.W. Levine, 1979. *Urbanisation in Papua New Guinea: A Study of Ambivalent Townsmen*. Cambridge: Cambridge University Press.

MacWilliam, S., 1988. 'Smallholdings, Land Law and the Politics of Land Tenure in Papua New Guinea.' *Journal of Peasant Studies* 16: 77–109. doi.org/10.1080/03066158808438383.

Mandeville, E., 1979. 'Agnation, Affinity and Migration among the Komno of the New Guinea Highlands.' *Man* 14: 105–123. doi. org/10.2307/2801644.

Martin, K., 2007. 'Land, Customary and Non-Customary, in East New Britain.' In J.F. Weiner and K. Glaskin (eds), *Customary Land Tenure and Registration in Australia and Papua New Guinea: Anthropological Perspectives.* Canberra: ANU E Press (Asia-Pacific Environment Monograph 3).

——, 2013. *The Death of the Big Men and the Rise of the Big Shots: Custom and Conflict in East New Britain.* New York: Berghahn Books.

Meggitt, M.J., 1965. *The Lineage System of the Mae-Enga of New Guinea.* London: Oliver and Boyd.

——, 1971. 'The Pattern of Leadership among the Mae Enga of New Guinea.' In R.M. Berndt and P. Lawrence (eds), *Politics in New Guinea—Traditional and in the Context of Change: Some Anthropological Perspectives.* Nedlands: University of Western Australia Press.

Numbasa, G. and G. Koczberski, 2012. 'Migration, Informal Urban Settlements and Non-Market Land Transaction: A Case Study of Wewak, East Sepik Province, Papua New Guinea.' *Australian Geographer* 43: 143–161. doi.org/10.1080/00049182.2012.682293.

Peters, P.E., 2007. 'Challenges in Land Tenure and Land Reform in Africa: An Anthropological Perspective.' Cambridge (MA): Harvard University, Centre for International Development (Working Paper 141).

Reay, M., 1971. 'Structural Co-Variants of Land Shortage among Patrilineal Peoples.' In R.M. Berndt and P. Lawrence (eds), *Politics in New Guinea—Traditional and in the Context of Change: Some Anthropological Perspectives.* Nedlands: University of Western Australia Press.

Ribot, J.C. and N.L. Peluso, 2003. 'A Theory of Access.' *Rural Sociology* 68: 153–181. doi.org/10.1111/j.1549-0831.2003.tb00133.x.

Sillitoe, P., 1999. 'Beating the Boundaries: Land Tenure and Identity in the Papua New Guinea Highlands.' *Journal of Anthropological Research* 55: 331–360. doi.org/10.1086/jar.55.3.3631390.

Standish, W., 1984. 'Big Men and Small: Simbu Politics in the 1970s.' In R.J. May (ed.), *Social Stratification in Papua New Guinea*. Canberra: The Australian National University, Research School of Research School of Pacific Studies, Department of Political and Social Change (Working Paper 5).

Ward, R.G., 1997. 'Changing Forms of Communal Tenure.' In P. Larmour (ed.), *The Governance of Common Property in the Pacific Region*. Canberra: The Australia National University, National Centre for Development Studies and Resource Management in Asia-Pacific Program.

Ward, R.G. and E. Kingdon, 1995. 'Land Tenure in the Pacific Islands.' In R.G. Ward, and E. Kingdon (eds), *Land, Custom and Practice in the South Pacific*. Cambridge: Cambridge University Press. doi. org/10.1017/CBO9780511597176.003.

Weiner, J.F., 2007. 'The Foi Incorporated Land Group: Group Definition and Collective Action in the Kutubu Oil Project Area, Papua New Guinea.' In J.F. Weiner and K. Glaskin (eds), *Customary Land Tenure and Registration in Australia and Papua New Guinea: Anthropological Perspectives*. Canberra: ANU E Press (Asia-Pacific Environment Monograph 3).

Yala, C. and K. Lyons, 2012. 'The National Land Research Framework for the Papua New Guinea National Land Development Program.' Port Moresby National Research Institute (Discussion Paper 122).

Zimmer-Tamakoskhi, L., 1997. 'Everyone (or No One) a Winner: Gende Compensation, Ethics and Practices.' In S. Toft (ed.), *Compensation for Resource Development in Papua New Guinea*. Port Moresby: Law Reform Commission (Monograph 6).

6

The Formation of a Land Grab Policy Network in Papua New Guinea

Colin Filer

Introduction

Papua New Guinea (PNG) possesses a very unusual—probably unique—legal institution whose abuse lies at the heart of current public debate about land grabbing. This institution is commonly known as the lease-leaseback scheme. It was invented in 1979 in order to compensate for the absence of any other legal institution that would enable customary landowners to register titles to their own land. This absence was seen as an obstacle to rural development because 97 per cent of PNG's total land area was still customary land, and the ownership of this land was almost entirely illegible to the state and to private capital. The idea behind the lease-leaseback scheme was that groups of customary landowners could lease some of their land to the government, which would then create a formal title over it and lease it back to the landowners. The landowners would then have a piece of paper that they could use as security for a bank loan or as the basis for granting a sublease to a third party for some developmental purpose. The current legal form of the lease-leaseback scheme is represented in two sections of the Land Act. Section 11 says that the minister 'may lease customary land for the purpose of granting a special agricultural and business lease of the land', while Section 102 says that 'a special agricultural and business lease shall be granted: (a) to a person or persons; or (b) to a land group, business group or other incorporated body, to whom the customary landowners have agreed that such a lease should be granted'. Section 11 also says that:

> an instrument of lease in the approved form, executed by or on behalf of the customary landowners, is conclusive evidence that the State has a good title to the lease and that all customary rights in the land, except those which are specifically reserved in the lease, are suspended for the period of the lease to the State.

PNG is also unusual (if not exactly unique) in the propensity of its national government to reveal the dark underbelly of its own dysfunction through the establishment of commissions of inquiry and the eventual dissemination of their findings. The establishment of a commission of inquiry into the operation of the lease-leaseback scheme was announced by PNG's Acting Prime Minister, Sam Abal, in May 2011. In June, the National Executive Council (PNG's cabinet) formally endorsed its establishment and imposed a moratorium on the further grant of special agricultural and business leases (SABLs) and related licences until the Commission reported its findings to Parliament. Three senior lawyers, led by former Chief Magistrate John Numapo, were appointed as commissioners. The commissioners began their hearings in August 2011, and continued to gather evidence until March 2012. An interim report of their findings was presented to Prime Minister Peter O'Neill in March 2013, prompting him to voice his impatience over the length of time that was being taken to produce a final report (Nicholas 2013a). In response, the three commissioners cited a variety of political and bureaucratic obstacles that had hindered the progress of their work, but promised that a final report would be submitted by the end of April (Pok 2013). John Numapo and one of the other commissioners, Nicholas Mirou, submitted separate reports at the end of June (Mirou 2013; Numapo 2013), but the third commissioner, Alois Jerewai, refused to follow suit. When the Prime Minister tabled the two reports in Parliament in September 2013, he threatened 'disciplinary action' against all three commissioners (Nicholas 2013b). Commissioner Jerewai claimed that he had finished his own report in 2012, but he thought there should be one final report, co-authored by all three commissioners, and threatened legal action against all the other parties, including the Prime Minister and the other two commissioners, for failing to insist on this outcome (Kelola 2013). Nothing more was heard from him, and no 'disciplinary action' was taken.

The interim report, the two final reports, and most of the transcripts of the hearings conducted by all three commissioners, were posted on the Prime Minister's departmental website at the end of November.

This chapter describes the formation of a land grab policy network as a two-stage process. The first stage is the one that led to the government's decision to establish the Commission of Inquiry in April 2011. The second stage is the one in which the network changed its shape during the period that elapsed between the start of the Commission's hearings and the public release of its findings. My account of this process is based on the information that I was able to gather in my own capacity as a participant observer. Other participants would no doubt tell a different story, but all such stories must necessarily be partial.

The Network Assembled, 2008–2010

The Commission's terms of reference made specific reference to a manifesto known as the 'Cairns Declaration', which had been produced in March 2011 by 'a large group of environmental and social scientists, natural resources managers and non-governmental organizations [sic] staff from Papua New Guinea and other nations [who] met in James Cook University in the city of Cairns, Australia to discuss the future management and conservation of Papua New Guinea's native forest'. At the same time, the terms of reference noted that '[m]any segment [sic] of the community throughout the country, including civil society organisations, prominent leaders and landowner groups are increasingly objecting to SABL approval and management processes in recent times' (GoPNG 2011: 2).

In a report later published by Greenpeace, Paul Winn also made reference to the Cairns Declaration,[1] but assigned even greater significance to a please-explain letter that the PNG government had received from the UN Special Rapporteur on the Situation of Human Rights and Fundamental Freedoms of Indigenous People following a complaint lodged by PNG's Centre for Environmental Law and Community Rights and the UK-based Forest Peoples' Programme (Winn 2012: 15). By this account, the government was primarily responding to a campaign

---

1   Paul and I were both among the 26 signatories to the Cairns Declaration.

organised by what I have previously called PNG's 'conservation policy community' (Filer 2005)—an interest group in which Greenpeace itself has long played a prominent role.

It seems rather unlikely that PNG's National Executive Council would have responded so rapidly and decisively to this kind of pressure if it had not been reinforced by pressure from other quarters over a longer period of time. Furthermore, such a decision would normally have to be based on a submission made by one or more cabinet ministers, and it is not obvious which ministers or departments would have taken this responsibility, nor is there any obvious reason why they would have been especially responsive to the arguments of conservationists. I suggest that the pressure came from a number of distinct interest groups that came to be joined up in a single policy network. One of the policy brokers who assembled this network is Paul Barker, the Director of PNG's Institute of National Affairs, which might best be described as a civil society think-tank. He was one of the first people to apply the phrase 'land grab' to the systematic abuse of the lease-leaseback scheme, and he did so in the title of a feature article published by one of PNG's national newspapers in May 2009. Paul Barker summarised his evidence as follows:

> Over recent months about two million hectares of land across lowland provinces have been granted as Special Purpose Agricultural/Business Leases under the Land Act, with seven of these areas (in Western, Sepik, Central and Oro Provinces) each exceeding 100,000 hectares.
>
> As with a 38,000 ha Collingwood Bay scam launched in 1995, and finally thrown out of court in 2001, many (if not all) of the 50 known schemes have apparently lacked due process, with landowners never granting their 'informed consent' for the State to lease their land and subsequently reallocate it to various named (largely overseas-controlled) interests (Barker 2009).

Members of the land grab policy network were essentially people who came to share the view that the land contained in SABLs of a certain size had indeed been 'grabbed', since it was not possible to imagine that the customary owners had given their free, prior and informed consent to the lease-leaseback process. However, it took some time for this network to be established, and it was never more than a 'rainbow coalition' of different interest groups.

The List of Dodgy Deals

One thread in our story began with the appointment of Puka Temu as Minister for Lands and Physical Planning in January 2005. The new minister thought he had a mandate to discover more efficient and effective ways of mobilising customary land for urban and rural development. With this aim in mind, a National Land Summit was convened in August that year, and this was followed by the construction of a National Land Development Taskforce (NLDT) whose final report was ceremonially launched in February 2007. The 54 recommendations of the taskforce emerged from the deliberations of three different committees dealing with 'land administration', 'land dispute settlement', and 'customary land development'.

While Minister Temu later showed great enthusiasm for the lease-leaseback scheme as a means to 'mobilise' customary land, the report of the NLDT barely mentioned it—and then only to endorse its limited use by the existing oil palm industry (GoPNG 2007: 117). This is understandable, because the exponential growth in the number of large blocks of customary land alienated in this way had only just begun when the report was drafted in 2006. The taskforce was far more interested in plugging the legislative hole that had originally prompted the invention of the lease-leaseback scheme in 1979, and that was the absence of any legal mechanism by which incorporated groups of customary landowners could register formal titles to their land.

In August 2007, Brian Aldrich sent an email to Thomas Webster, with a copy to Pepi Kimas, expressing his concern about the number of SABLs that were being granted to private companies over large areas of customary land for the maximum allowable period of 99 years. Brian is a private land consultant and long-term PNG resident who had once worked as an expatriate contract officer in the Department of Lands and Physical Planning and was a member of the NLDT committee on land administration. Thomas Webster had been appointed to chair the NLDT in his capacity as Director of the National Research Institute, which is a government-funded think-tank accountable to the Minister for National Planning. Pepi Kimas was the Secretary of the Lands Department and had been a member of the NLDT committee on land dispute settlement.[2]

---

2   He had delegated one of his senior officers to participate in the central committee of the taskforce.

Brian's interest in the issue derived from the fact that he had played a key role in helping the oil palm industry to establish 'mini-estates' on relatively small areas of customary land by arranging for SABLs to be granted to incorporated groups of customary landowners so that they in turn could issue subleases to the oil palm companies and receive a range of economic benefits in return.[3] His view was that the Land Act should never have made provision for SABLs to be granted to anyone other than the families or land groups that had agreed to lease their land to the state in the first instance. His email included a table showing that 10 leases over a combined area of more than 270,000 hectares had been granted to private companies since October 2005. This was in fact an underestimate, since his reading of the *National Gazette* later led him to discover another 10 leases, with a combined area of roughly 130,000 hectares, which had been granted to private companies over the same period. So the area of concern already contained about 400,000 hectares of customary land that could have been alienated without the informed consent of the customary owners.

It is important to note here that the relevant notices in the *National Gazette* are somewhat mysterious, in the sense that they specify the size of the lease (in hectares), but they do not specify its actual boundaries, nor do they state how these relate to the boundaries of PNG's provinces and districts, which are the political entities represented by members of parliament. Instead, they make reference to portion numbers on a national collection of provincial land survey maps that are used to record the creation of formal land titles (see Figure 6.1). These maps are not readily available to members of the public, so even those few people, like Brian, who make it their business to read every issue of the *National Gazette* would not be able to tell where each of the leases was located. What Brian did was to construct a spreadsheet in which he recorded the date of each gazettal notice that struck him as being suspicious, and then recorded most of the other details of the lease in question in the other columns.

By his own account, Brian met with officers of the Lands Department in November 2007, and was assured that no more leases would be granted directly to private companies. However, by the time Secretary Kimas responded to Brian's original email, 12 months after it had been sent,

---

3 The mini-estates deserve their name because none of them covers more than 7,000 hectares of land. The total area covered by SABLs granted to local land groups for this purpose between 1998 and 2007 was less than 20,000 hectares.

his officers had issued another 15 leases to private companies, with a combined area of more than 625,000 hectares, thus taking the total area covered by such transactions to more than 1 million hectares. At this juncture the Secretary stated that he would hold a meeting with his officers 'to address this issue further and to explore ways of informing the public of the potential risk involved'.

Land Act No. 45 of 1996

———

NOTICE OF DIRECT GRANT UNDER SECTION 102

I, Pepi S. Kimas, OL., Delegate of the Minister for Lands and Physical Planning, by virtue of the powers conferred by Section 102 of the *Land Act* No. 45 of 1996 and all other powers enabling me hereby directly grant a Special Agriculture and Business Lease to [A] over the land described in the Schedule hereunder.

1.   The lease shall be used bona fide for the purpose specified in the Schedule.

2.   The lease shall be for a term specified in the Schedule commencing from the date when the land was leased from the customary landowners to the State under Section 11 of the *Land Act* 1996.

3.   The lease shall be rent-free for the duration of the lease.

4.   Provision of any necessary easements for electricity, water, power, drainage and sewerage reticulations.

———

SCHEDULE

———

A Special Agriculture and Business Lease for a period of [number] years over all that piece of land known as "[B]" surveyed and legally described as Portion [number], Milinch of [C], Fourmil of [D] in [E] Province with an area of [number] hectares as registered on Survey Plan Catalogue No. [number].

Dated this [numbered] day of [month], [year].

P.S. KIMAS, OL.,

Delegate of the Minister for Lands & Physical Planning.

Figure 6.1 Format of notices advertising the grant of special agricultural and business leases in the *National Gazette*.
Source: Author's rendition of common features of notices published in the *National Gazette*.

In an email sent to John Numapo shortly afterwards, Brian observed that no one appeared to be taking the issue seriously aside from himself and two other white men, Norm Oliver and Tony Power. John was at that time PNG's Chief Magistrate, and had chaired the NLDT committee on land dispute settlement. Norm was a former Land Titles Commissioner whom Brian had engaged to assist the oil palm industry in the establishment of 'mini-estates' by means of the grant of SABLs to incorporated land groups (Oliver 2001). Tony had long been an advocate for land group incorporation as a means of empowering customary landowners in the process of large-scale resource development (Power 2008), but also had a personal interest in the matter of current concern because land belonging to his wife's clan (in East Sepik Province) had already been included in an SABL granted to a foreign company.[4]

Brian continued to update and circulate his spreadsheet until it finally became the basis of the list of 72 leases, covering a total of 5.2 million hectares, which the Commission of Inquiry was directed to investigate when its terms of reference appeared in the *National Gazette* in July 2011.[5] By that time, the number of people who had seen at least one version of Brian's spreadsheet was much larger than it had been in 2008, but this new audience was not exactly his own creation. Once I started to receive copies of the spreadsheet in 2009, I noticed that he hardly ever sent them to more than three or four people, and although there were some variations in the identities of the recipients, there would not have been more than 10 recipients in the whole of that year. Thomas Webster was still one of them, but Pepi Kimas was not. Paul Barker was also one of the new recipients, and unlike Brian or Thomas, he was now prepared to turn the whole issue into a public scandal. If the land grab policy network therefore began to take a more public shape after the publication of his newspaper article in May 2009, who should be counted among its members by the end of that year?

The Land Development Group

At that juncture, it was possible to identify two distinct interest groups within the network, which I propose to call the 'land development group' and the 'oil palm industry group'. The land development group consisted of people who were actively involved in efforts to implement the recommendations of the NLDT, including some who had been

---

4   Neither Norm nor Tony had been members of the NLDT or any of its three committees, but could still be counted as members of the land grab policy network.

5   Brian's spreadsheet was never a complete list of all the SABLs granted to private companies, but it did include all of the leases that had been granted to private companies since 2003 and covered areas of more than 100 hectares. The Commission of Inquiry eventually dealt with 75 leases granted to private companies (Numapo 2013: 3).

members of the taskforce itself or one of its three committees. In theory, this should have been quite a large group. The recommendations were now known as the National Land Development Program (NLDP), and this program was meant to have a Project Implementation Unit that reported to the Management Committee, which in turn reported to the Economic Ministerial Committee, which was a committee of the National Executive Council. In addition, there was meant to be a National Land Development Advisory Group (NLDAG) providing the Economic Ministerial Committee with independent advice on the implementation of the program (Levantis and Yala 2008).[6] This organisational cluster should have come to life in 2008, but an 'implementation plan' produced by the Management Committee in 2010 revealed that little progress had been made by the end of 2009 except for the drafting of amendments to the Land Registration Act and the Land Groups Incorporation Act, both of which had been passed by the national parliament in March of that year (GoPNG 2008). This document also gave the impression that further progress would substantially depend on foreign aid funding that was yet to be made available.[7]

In these circumstances, it is hard to tell how many people were actively involved in efforts to implement the NLDP, how many of these people were bothered about the land grab unfolding in Brian's spreadsheet, and what, if anything, they were able to do about it. We now know that Thomas Webster and his colleagues at the National Research Institute were bothered about it. The same goes for John Numapo, who was still wrestling with the reform of PNG's land court system. And the same goes for Lawrence Kalinoe, who had chaired the NLDT committee on customary land development and then been appointed Secretary of the Constitutional and Law Reform Commission, in which capacity he had

---

6   The Management Committee was meant to include representatives from 'Magisterial Services, the National Research Institute, the Constitutional and Law Reform Commission, Office of Urbanization, Department of Justice and Attorney General, Department of Provincial and Local Government Affairs, the Department for Community Development, Department of Lands and Physical Planning, Department of Treasury and Department of Planning and Monitoring', while the Advisory Group was meant to include 'Vice Chancellor, UPNG; Head, Social Sciences and Humanities, UPNG; President, PNG Real Estate Association; Head, Land Studies Unit, UniTech; Director, Transparency International; Director, National Agriculture Research Institute; Director, Institute of National Affairs; Director, National Research Institute (Chairman); Chairman of PNG Rural industries Council; President of PNG Bankers' Association; President of PNG Chamber of Commerce and Industries; and the Chairman of PNG Association of NGOs' (GoPNG 2010a: 34–5).
7   The implementation plan was drafted by an Australian consultancy company called Land Equity International (see Chapter 14) and funded by the Australian aid program.

drafted the legislation that would now enable customary landowners to register titles to their own land. However, these people were all public servants, and could not therefore give voice to their concerns in the same way as Paul Barker. Furthermore, it was now evident that Minister Temu, Secretary Kimas and most of the other officials in the Lands Department were *not* part of the land grab policy network but part of the problem that had to be solved, and despite the organisational complexity of the NLDP, officials in other government agencies had no more influence over the Lands Ministry than Paul or Brian had. And even if the NLDP had been implemented with greater speed, they were also hamstrung by the fact that it had nothing to say about measures to stop the abuse of the lease-leaseback scheme.

The Oil Palm Industry Group

Members of the oil palm industry group were bothered about the land grab because they realised that the lease-leaseback scheme was being abused by the proponents of so-called 'agro-forestry' projects. In PNG, the term 'agro-forestry' refers to the practice of clearing large areas of native forest on the pretext of making space for the cultivation of export crops and undertaking to use the revenues obtained from the export of raw logs to defray the cost of developing the plantation infrastructure. This idea originated in the 1990s as a device by which disreputable logging companies could circumvent the onerous regulations associated with the grant of selective logging concessions under PNG's 'sustainable forest management' regime. One of the earliest examples of the lease-leaseback scheme being used for this dubious purpose was the 'Collingwood Bay scam' mentioned in Paul Barker's feature article (Barker 2009), but this project had been blocked by legal action on the part of the customary landowners. The World Bank, in its capacity as one of the main architects of PNG's forest policy reforms, had also made strenuous efforts to block the legal loopholes through which such projects had occasionally gained some form of government approval (Filer 2000: 39–40).

The concept and practice of 'agro-forestry' received a new lease of life in 2005 when Michael Somare's government finally removed the World Bank from the forest policy process and hailed the dawn of a new 'green revolution' (Bonsella 2005). One of the earliest of the big SABLs in Brian's spreadsheet was the one issued to a company called Baina Agro-Forest Ltd in October of that year. This lease covered more than 40,000 hectares of land in Central Province and lasted for 40 years. Even before the SABL was gazetted, the president of the Forest Industries Association, Stanis Bai, was complaining that a logging company, Nasyl No. 98 Ltd, had 'illegally' entered the area on the false pretext of developing an oil palm estate (Anon. 2005a). This complaint was echoed by his brother, Brown Bai, who was chairman of the Rural Industries Council (Anon. 2005b). Their concerns seem to have been justified. The logging company managed to secure a log export licence in 2007, exported a large quantity of logs in 2008, and then disappeared.

Despite the negative publicity that this project attracted in 2005, there was no mention of it in the NLDT report, even though a representative of the oil palm industry, Lillian Holland, was a member of the taskforce committee on land administration. Nevertheless, Mike Manning, who was a member of the central committee, and had preceded Paul Barker as Director of the Institute of National Affairs, voiced another public complaint about 'so-called agro-forestry projects' in September 2007. He did this in his capacity as chair of the PNG National Interpretation Working Group of the Roundtable on Sustainable Palm Oil (RSPO). This group was said to consist of 'all PNG's existing palm oil companies, the Oil Palm Industry Corporation, the PNG Oil Palm Research Association, the Department of Environment and Conservation, the Rural Industries Council and some environmental non-government organisations' (Anon. 2007).

The issue at stake here was that companies wishing to be members of the RSPO were obliged to prove that they were not responsible for the clearance of any new area of primary forest or destruction of ecosystems with high conservation value. Industry representatives were thus opposed to the new generation of agro-forestry projects—especially those that purported to be oil palm schemes—because of the risk they posed to its own reputation as a producer of 'sustainable' palm oil, even if the schemes proved to be illusory. Furthermore, the industry's own use of the lease-leaseback scheme was at risk of being tainted by association with land grabbers who had saved themselves the expense of securing the informed consent of customary landowners to a complex sequence of transactions that Brian Aldrich and Norm Oliver had shown to be required for the creation of new leasehold titles over relatively small areas of land (Filer 2012).

Despite this demonstration of concern, the government proceeded to amend the Forestry Act at the end of 2007 in ways that made it harder for the National Forest Board to refuse the grant of what were now called 'forest clearing authorities' to the proponents of agro-forestry projects (McCrea 2009: 23).[8] Once these amendments had been made, SABLs became the platforms from which landowner companies and their 'development partners' could launch their applications for such permits. That is why Paul Barker, who succeeded Mike Manning as chair of the National Interpretation Working Group, followed his feature article on the 'land grab' with a fresh complaint about the spread of oil palm development proposals that were 'clearly not designed as viable "oil palm" projects' (Anon. 2009). Since Paul had many other hats to wear, the role of representing the oil palm industry in the land grab policy network then fell to Ian Orrell, another member of the working group who was then the head of PNG's Oil Palm Research Association but soon became the head of a new peak body called the PNG Palm Oil Council.

The Silence of the Greens

If the land development group and the oil palm industry group had both established themselves as key constituents of the land grab policy network by the end of 2009, very few members of the 'conservation policy community' appeared to have taken much interest in the issue. This seems rather odd, given that they had played such a prominent role in the defence of customary land rights against the first generation of agro-forestry project proposals, including the 'Collingwood Bay scam' (Seri 2005). Although Paul Barker was forwarding copies of Brian's spreadsheet to other members of the green community throughout the course of 2009, the response was muted.

When I wrote about the conservation policy community in 2005, I discussed the evidence of internal conflict between big international non-governmental organisations (NGOs) and their small local counterparts. Four years later, there was still evidence of a division, but I would now describe it as a split between the 'sustainability group' and the 'anti-dependency group'. Insofar as Paul and I belong to this policy community or network, we would count as members of the sustainability

---

8   The National Forest Board is the decision-making arm of the PNG Forest Authority. Its decisions are implemented by the staff of the National Forest Service.

group because we think it is worthwhile to discuss the achievement of 'sustainable development outcomes' with representatives of the oil palm industry, the mining industry, or even the logging industry. Opponents of the anti-dependency group tend to describe it as an 'anti-development' group, in the hope or expectation that this label will subtract from its popular appeal, but members of this group say that they are only opposed to 'development' in the sense of sharing a belief that large-scale resource development is a bad thing because it induces a form of social and economic dependency at the same time that it causes serious environmental damage. The removal of the World Bank from PNG's forest policy process in 2005 was symptomatic of a change in the constitution of the conservation policy community, because foreign aid agencies and foreign NGOs had less money to spend on forest conservation projects. But if this changed the balance of power within the conservation policy community, it did not enable the anti-dependency group to wield any greater influence over any aspect of national government policy—whether it be forest policy, conservation policy or land policy. If anything, it had the opposite effect.

There was one environmental NGO, the Centre for Environmental Law and Community Rights (CELCOR), which had a representative on one of the NLDT's three special committees, and that was the committee on customary land development chaired by Lawrence Kalinoe. However, there is no evidence to indicate that CELCOR or any of the other organisations in the anti-dependency group endorsed the recommendations of that committee. On the contrary, a meeting of group members in July 2008 expressed strong opposition to the whole idea of registering group titles over customary land (Anon. 2008a). This was consistent with a common belief among members of this group that any legal device for the 'mobilisation' of customary land in Melanesia is the work of a neoliberal conspiracy masterminded by the World Bank and the Australian government (Anderson and Lee 2010), even though the architects of the taskforce had been at pains to exclude all foreign agencies from their deliberations (Levantis and Yala 2008). But it also reflected a total lack of trust in the capacity of the Lands Department to manage a process of registration without somehow turning it into a process of expropriation (Filer 2011a). Some members of the land development group might have felt the same way, but there was hardly any direct communication between the members of these two groups.

Even so, one might have supposed that members of the anti-dependency group would have seized on the evidence contained in Brian's spreadsheet to bolster their case against the registration of customary land. Their initial failure to do so might best be explained by the scarcity of the resources at their disposal and their dedication to campaigns that distracted them from the implications of this evidence. One example of such distraction was the complaint that Damien Ase, CELCOR's executive director, lodged with the World Bank Inspection Panel in November 2009, in which he claimed that a project intended to provide support to smallholders in PNG's existing oil palm industry was in breach of several of the bank's safeguard policies. Given that CELCOR is an organisation whose stated mission is to provide legal assistance to 'landowners affected by large scale environmentally destructive projects including industrial logging, mining and oil palm plantation development' (Ase 2009: 1), it seems rather odd that disgruntled smallholders were still getting more of this assistance than the customary owners of huge tracts of land then being dedicated to the new generation of agro-forestry projects. It certainly seemed odd to members of the oil palm industry group in the land grab policy network.

The REDD Distraction

But in 2009, the biggest distraction of all was the chaos that surrounded the prospect of securing foreign investment in projects designed to reduce carbon emissions from deforestation and forest degradation. These so-called REDD (Reducing Emissions from Deforestation and Forest Degradation) projects had been a matter of interest to national policy makers since 2005, when Prime Minister Michael Somare made PNG one of the founding members of the Coalition for Rainforest Nations—an organisation dedicated to the aim of amending the United Nations Framework Convention on Climate Change in ways that would enable 'rainforest nations' to claim carbon credits from the international community. In 2009, a sort of climate policy group began to take shape as the fifth group in the land grab policy network, but it took such an odd sort of shape that it hardly qualified as a group with any sort of common interest.

The catalyst for the chaos was a notice published in the *National Gazette* at the end of April 2009, advising that a company called Tumu Timber Development Ltd (TTDL) had been granted an SABL over an area of almost 800,000 hectares in Western Province for a period of 99 years.

Several members of the land grab policy network realised that this was the area known to the PNG Forest Authority as the Kamula Doso forest area. The anti-dependency group already had an interest in this area because one of its member organisations, the PNG Eco-Forestry Forum, had issued a legal challenge to a decision made by the National Forest Board to allocate this area to Rimbunan Hijau, PNG's biggest logging company, which already held an adjacent concession. This case was still before the courts. In the meantime, some members of the anti-dependency group and some government officials had separately decided that this would make an ideal site for a REDD project. Among the government officials was Theo Yasause, who had been appointed to head a new Office of Climate Change in the Prime Minister's Department in 2008.[9] Yasause made some sort of arrangement with an Australian entrepreneur, Kirk Roberts, to market carbon credits from the Kamula Doso forest area, and Roberts sought the backing of an Australian carbon-broking company, Carbon Planet, for his own efforts to secure the backing of the TTDL board (Wood 2015).

Some members of the conservation policy community were already making complaints about this sort of arrangement in the middle of 2008 (Melick 2008). Their concerns were reflected in newspaper articles that complained about the state 'grabbing virgin forests' for REDD projects (Anon. 2008b), or warned of an invasion of 'speculators' and 'carpetbaggers' looking to make a fast buck out of the carbon business (Anon. 2008c). When TTDL was awarded its SABL in 2009, they readily assumed that this must be the work of Kirk Roberts and Theo Yasause. Shortly afterwards, the plaintiffs in the long-standing legal dispute over the area therefore asked the National Court to restrain the Lands Department from issuing the SABL on the grounds that Yasause had been wrong to grant carbon trading rights to Roberts. The Court then ordered both parties, along with the Minister for Lands and the Registrar of Land Titles, to be joined with Rimbunan Hijau and the PNG Forest Authority as defendants in the case. Following this order, the Eco-Forestry Forum issued a press release announcing that it had been successful in persuading the Court to grant 'injunctions to stop the Office of Climate Change and the Department of Lands from taking any further steps to issue rights over the forests of Kamula Doso' (PNGEFF 2009a).

---

9   This body was initially known as the Office of Climate Change and Carbon Trade, then as the Office of Climate Change and Environmental Sustainability. In 2010, it became the Office of Climate Change and Development.

The assumption was later shown to be false. The TTDL board contained two different factions, one aligned with Roberts and one aligned with another Australian entrepreneur, Neville Harsley. It was Harsley who arranged the lease, and he had no interest in carbon trading, nor in the kind of agro-forestry project that was agitating the oil palm industry group. But key members of the conservation policy community had now decided to use the Kamula Doso 'carbon credits' as a weapon in their campaign to dislodge Yasause from his post. So they started to circulate evidence of his dealings to journalists whose connections ensured that it would make for an international scandal. In doing so, they made a second assumption that also proved to be false. They thought that Yasause must have been acting on instructions from PNG's 'climate change ambassador', Kevin Conrad, an American friend of the Somare family who was the real architect of the Coalition for Rainforest Nations. The reasoning was that Somare would not have put Yasause in charge of the Office of Climate Change without taking Conrad's advice. And since Conrad's remote control over PNG's climate policy process was a source of great annoyance to many members of the conservation policy community, there seemed to be a chance of killing two birds with one stone. But that did not happen. When the scandal broke, Yasause was removed from his post, official control of climate policy was restored to the Department of Environment and Conservation, and Kevin Conrad retained his own position of influence (Filer and Wood 2012; Filer 2015).

At this juncture, I was asked to advise the department on REDD matters in the lead-up to the United Nations climate change conference (the 15th 'conference of parties') to be held in Copenhagen at the end of the year. This was a source of additional annoyance to members of the Eco-Forestry Forum, who even went to the expense of publishing a full-page advertorial deploring my engagement (PNGEFF 2009b). The reason was that I had previously given advice to Carbon Planet on possible 'benefit sharing arrangements' for REDD projects in PNG, and was therefore thought to be one of the alien 'carbon cowboys' whose wicked schemes had been exposed and denounced in the media scandal that had gotten rid of Theo Yasause. The advertorial had no effect on Wari Iamo, the Secretary for Environment and Conservation, partly because he had already planned to seek my advice before his department lost its official control of climate policy in 2008, but mainly because he had been party to the

National Forest Board's decision to allocate the Kamula Doso forest area to Rimbunan Hijau, and was therefore regarded as a public enemy by members of the anti-dependency group.

It was in fact my interest in REDD matters that led me to take an interest in Brian's spreadsheet at the start of 2009. In the advice that I provided to Carbon Planet in March that year, I observed that there was 'now some evidence that the lease-leaseback scheme has been subject to political manipulation of the sort feared by the opponents of customary land registration in 1995, and on a scale far greater than anything seen in the highland coffee industry or the current lowland oil palm industry', and that '[m]any of these leases are of a size that would rule out any process of informed consent and participation on the part of the customary owners' (Filer 2009a: 24). I made the same point in my subsequent report to the Department of Environment and Conservation (Filer 2009b). Like my opponents in the conservation policy community, I was still under the impression that the SABL granted over the Kamula Doso forest area had somehow been organised by Kirk Roberts, and was therefore suggesting that the lease-leaseback scheme might not be the best way to secure large areas of customary land for REDD projects.

But there was also another issue here. It was already clear that most of the big SABLs were being engineered by the proponents of agro-forestry projects, not forest conservation projects. Since agro-forestry projects entail a substantial increase in the rate of deforestation, and not just in the sort of forest degradation associated with selective logging concessions, it was also reasonable to suggest that the approval of a new generation of agro-forestry projects might cause as much damage to PNG's reputation in the global climate policy domain as it was causing to the reputation of the existing oil palm industry in the global market for sustainable palm oil (Filer 2010). This was a point that I made to Secretary Iamo and his officers (Filer 2009c). The trouble was that he and his department had already been granting environment permits for these projects, and thus facilitating the subsequent grant of forest clearing authorities by the National Forest Board. If other members of the conservation policy community had been paying closer attention, they might have begun to wonder why such permits were being granted, especially when they required the approval of an independent Environment Council that was meant to review the environmental impact statements that were required under the terms of the Environment Act.

The Network Comes to Life

Between the beginning and end of 2009, the area covered by the SABLs recorded in Brian's spreadsheet had grown from just over 1 million hectares to almost 2.5 million hectares. In January 2010, Paul Barker published a second feature article suggesting that the lease-leaseback scheme had been turned into a scam that was 'jeopardising landowners' customary rights over vast areas of the country, without their apparent informed consent' (Barker 2010). According to this article, the discretionary powers granted to the Lands Minister under Section 102 of the Land Act had been systematically abused, and the only way to remedy the situation would be to revoke these powers, cancel the leases that had been granted to private companies, and move ahead with the implementation of the new legislation that would enable customary landowners to register titles to their own land before granting leases to anyone else.

Paul attached a copy of this article, including the latest version of Brian's spreadsheet, to an email that he subsequently sent to 18 other members of the conservation policy community—mostly members of the anti-dependency group—in which he told them to 'get real', stop picking pointless fights with the World Bank and the existing oil palm industry, and start devising a strategy to 'ensure landowners are aware of issues, realities and options before these massive and often bogus new schemes are driven in' to their land. Paul's own strategy was to combine the SABL issue with the REDD issue and make both issues the subject of a multistakeholder workshop at the beginning of March that year.[10] This was the first of several meetings that Paul organised with different groups of stakeholders involved in both of these issues over course of the following 12 months.

Meanwhile, Kevin Conrad seems to have persuaded the National Executive Council to engage McKinsey & Company to develop PNG's climate change policy in the aftermath of the Copenhagen climate change conference. Indeed, they may well have started work on this subject before the end of 2009, since their initial proposal to the PNG government was made in June that year (Lang 2010), but they did not set up shop in the Environment Department until 2010. The McKinsey team had fairly limited contact with other members of the land grab

---

10 The costs of this meeting were largely borne by the Institute for Global Environmental Strategies based in Japan, and a focus on the REDD issue was probably a condition of this funding.

policy network, but they were still quick to appreciate the argument that international funding for REDD projects would be harder to obtain if the PNG government appeared to be promoting an accelerated process of deforestation.[11]

In the second draft of their first policy document, the McKinsey team called for a moratorium to be imposed on the further grant of SABLs pending a review of the social and environmental impact of the country's agricultural development policies (GoPNG 2010b: 29). This document was endorsed by the National Executive Council soon after it was circulated in March 2010 (GoPNG 2010c: 2), and an Agriculture Sector Working Group was established to investigate the workings of the lease-leaseback scheme in the promotion of agro-forestry projects. Three of the four government agencies involved in the process sent representatives to the first of its meetings, but the Lands Department was notable by its absence (Valentine Thurairajah, personal communication, May 2010).[12] The Interim Action Plan drafted by the McKinsey team and published by the newly reconstituted Office of Climate Change in August 2010 included an estimate of the amount of carbon emissions that could be avoided if forest clearing authorities were withdrawn from 60–80 per cent of the area (about 670,000 hectares) for which they had already been granted (GoPNG 2010c: 10).

In July 2010, the National Court finally issued a consent order reflecting the government's admission that the PNG Forest Authority had failed to secure the consent of the local landowners to the grant of a timber permit over the Kamula Doso forest area. This meant that the Eco-Forestry Forum was no longer distracted by the need to pursue that particular case. Meanwhile, some of the customary owners of other areas now covered by big SABLs had begun to seek help from the lawyers in the conservation policy community. These included the customary owners of an area in East New Britain Province where the proponent of an agro-forestry project

---

11   In February 2010, I worked with members of the McKinsey team to locate and digitise all of the environmental inception reports and environmental impact statements for agro-forestry projects that could be found on the shelves of the relevant section of the Environment Department—a total of 19 documents in all. This evidence made it possible to figure out the boundaries of the relevant leases, and also revealed the identities of the foreign companies involved in the projects. This in turn made it possible to hunt down the relevant company records held by the Investment Promotion Authority. At that time, we could not have known that all such information would eventually be tabled at the Commission of Inquiry.

12   This activity did at least result in the circulation of a document that showed that the National Forest Board had approved the grant of 14 forest clearing authorities by April of that year.

proved to be none other than Rimbunan Hijau—public enemy number one for nearly all members of the anti-dependency group (Greenpeace 2004).[13] So Paul Barker's call to arms could finally be answered by plans for a new round of litigation if funds could be raised to pay for it, and that was a hot topic in email conversation among members of the anti-dependency group in November 2010.

This conversation intensified in the wake of a meeting convened by members of the land development group at the National Research Institute, where Damien Ase produced the latest edition of Brian's spreadsheet and demanded to know what former members of the NLDT were going to do about it. In response, Lawrence Kalinoe, now Secretary for Justice, was reported to have said that the Lands Department was 'totally corrupt', because '[o]fficers and certain rouge [sic] landowners are colluding and conniving with each other to sell off customary land for their own benefit and interest while the majority of landowners are left out' (Joku 2010). In the same newspaper article, it was reported that Lawrence called for the department to be subject to a commission of inquiry in order to 'put it back on track'.

To the best of my knowledge, Lawrence was the first person to make this suggestion—at least in public—and it was he who drafted the relevant submission for his minister to present to the National Executive Council in 2011 (Lawrence Kalinoe, personal communication, February 2016). The McKinsey team also took an interest in this cabinet submission when they got wind of it in March that year. They asked me to work out which government ministers were likely to have a vested interest in one or more of the big SABLs that featured on Brian's spreadsheet. By matching the available spatial information to the boundaries of parliamentary electorates, I thought I could identify seven ministers who fell into this category, although Puka Temu was not one of them, because he had joined the ranks of the parliamentary opposition. I was therefore somewhat surprised when the Acting Prime Minister announced the decision to establish a commission of inquiry in May 2011.

---

13   Rimbunan Hijau obtained its forest clearing authority for this area in October 2010, but the company had announced its intention to develop at least one oil palm estate in PNG back in 2006 (Anon. 2006).

As we have seen, the Commission's published terms of reference did point to the Cairns Declaration as a motivating factor, but they also stated that '[i]ssues surrounding SABL management are jeopardising PNG's chances of securing funding for REDD+ and combating climate change', and given PNG's position of leadership in global climate policy debates, the country 'must be seen to live by its words in respect of conserving forests to help reduce the green house gas emission [sic] and its effect on climate' (GoPNG 2011: 2). Kevin Conrad and the McKinsey team had no reason to say any more than this about their own role in the land grab policy network, since this would only have undermined the legitimacy of the Commission.[14] And in any case, the cabinet decision may not have been wholly motivated by the appearance of a cabinet submission, but also by the appearance of a groundswell of public protest facilitated by other members of the network, including the urban representatives of specific rural communities whose land had been expropriated (Filer 2011b).

The Network Reassembled, 2011–2013

The first step in the transformation of the land grab policy network was a radical change in the position of the climate policy group as one of its distinctive elements. Kevin Conrad and the McKinsey team disappeared from the network in August 2011, when the national parliament voted to remove Michael Somare from office and elect Peter O'Neill as his replacement. This did not spell the end of the Office of Climate Change, but the position of that agency was compromised by the decision that it should henceforth be accountable to Belden Namah. Namah had been the Forests Minister who sponsored the 2007 amendments to the Forestry Act, and had subsequently taken advantage of these amendments to secure a forest clearing authority for a very large agro-forestry project in his own electorate. He had been outraged by the decision to establish a commission of inquiry, and might well have taken it as a personal attack, since he had just been elected Leader of the Opposition at the time of its announcement. The price of his support for O'Neill's move against Somare was the position of Deputy Prime Minister, Minister for

---

14   It is equally understandable that the Greenpeace account of what happened also made no reference to their involvement, since Greenpeace has no time for the McKinsey method of calculating the economic costs and benefits of forest carbon sequestration (Greenpeace 2011).

Forests, and Minister for Climate Change. While his occupation of these positions enabled him to get rid of the Conrad-McKinsey group, they did not enable him to interfere with the inquiry.

Following the national elections of July 2012, O'Neill was able to assemble a governing coalition without the support of Namah, who returned to his former role as Leader of the Opposition. The Office of Climate Change was still accountable to the new Forests Minister, Patrick Pruaitch, but its officials no longer had much reason to worry about the findings of the Commission of Inquiry, nor did they have much capacity to influence the government's response. Although they were still charged with the task of producing legislation that would regulate foreign investment in forest carbon projects, it was already evident that the lease-leaseback scheme would not be part of this legal framework. The McKinsey team had left behind a number of policy documents and a very fine suite of PowerPoint slides, but while the legislative task was still unfinished, the Forestry Act remained the most appropriate legal instrument for the control of deforestation and forest degradation. Officials in the National Forest Service therefore included some carbon emission reduction proposals in the latest draft of the National Forest Plan (GoPNG 2012), but discussion of such activities seemed increasingly remote from the debate about what should be done with agro-forestry projects. That is because most members of the land grab policy network now realised that there was no immediate prospect of anyone harvesting a large amount of foreign carbon finance from decisions of the National Forest Board to withhold, revoke or suspend the grant of forest clearing authorities.

While members of the conservation policy community retained some interest in the question of how customary landowners might benefit from a new generation of forest conservation projects, members of the anti-dependency group were now convinced that the new generation of agro-forestry projects was simply the logical extension of a process by which the destruction of native forests was intimately tied to the corruption of the state. As news of the Commission's hearings percolated through the media, evidence of corporate and bureaucratic misbehaviour was used to garner additional international support for a domestic campaign against the foreign capitalists who had supposedly conspired with their local political cronies to undermine the rule of law and deprive innocent customary landowners of their constitutional rights. The amplification of this message entailed a simplification of the problem of consent that the Commission had been asked to investigate. Customary landowners in their right minds could not possibly consent to the theft of their own property, so the state must have been corrupted in a way that enabled the country's political elite to steal the property of their fellow citizens and sacrifice it to the foreign devils of resource development. So the lease-leaseback scheme was just the latest manifestation of the resource curse that had bewitched the nation.

The amplification and simplification of this message did not allow for any further debate about the relative merits of different foreign devils. It made more sense to portray them all in the same bad light, and even to link them together as members of a single community or conspiracy. Greenpeace was the first foreign organisation to support the campaign against the land grab because of the discovery that its old enemy, Rimbunan Hijau (RH), was one of the companies engaged in the practice of agro-forestry. This made it possible for the anti-dependency group to claim that RH must somehow have masterminded the abuse of the lease-leaseback scheme, just as it was previously thought to have exercised some sort of monopoly over PNG's selective logging industry during the forest policy reform process of the 1990s (Filer 1997, 2013). To consolidate this impression, Greenpeace mounted a seaborne expedition to collect evidence of popular discontent at the site of the company's agro-forestry project in East New Britain. This event was carefully timed to coincide with the hearings that Alois Jerewai conducted in that province in October 2011 (see Chapter 7, this volume).

In the blaze of publicity that accompanied this confrontation, the company protested that it was not responsible for any of PNG's other agro-forestry projects, its own project had the full support of the provincial government and most of the local landowners, so it did not deserve this level of critical attention (Gabriel 2015). We do not know what Jerewai would have said about this project in the final report that he did not submit to the Prime Minister, but John Numapo's final report includes an assertion that more than half of the companies holding subleases from the holders of SABLs were 'connected in one way or another' to RH (Numapo 2013: 242). This statement was music to the ears of some members of the anti-dependency group (Act Now 2014a), but it was not warranted by the evidence contained in the transcripts of the hearings conducted by all three commissioners. It is true that RH was found to have some sort of connection to several of the leases that were investigated, but certainly not to half of them, and most of those with which it did have some connection had not become the sites of actual agro-forestry projects. The records of the PNG Forest Authority indicate that RH held only one of the 22 forest clearing authorities that are known to have been granted before the Commission was established, and this was indeed the one that had been granted for the Sigite-Mukus project in East New Britain.

Greenpeace published its own report on the land grab in August 2012 (Winn 2012), shortly after the national elections that enabled Peter O'Neill to consolidate his grip on political power. The report made good use of the evidence presented in some of the Commission's hearings, but it was hard to assess its likely influence on the government's future response to the commissioners' recommendations. My own concern, shared with some other members of the land grab policy network, was that the government might play the national sovereignty card when confronted with a radical populist campaign in which foreign voices made much of the noise. However, the Papua New Guinean members of the anti-dependency group needed money to fund their own domestic campaign, so they stuck to the strategy of broadening their international support network in order to avoid being tainted by association with any part of PNG's private sector, let alone its politicians and public servants.

The next foreign organisations to add their own voices to the campaign were the California-based Oakland Institute and the Fiji-based Pacific Network on Globalisation, whose representatives teamed up with several members of the anti-dependency group to produce another account of the corruption unveiled by the Commission of Inquiry. Their evidence was collected in March 2013, around the time that the commissioners were presenting their first interim report to the Prime Minister, and their own report was published in November 2013, just before the Commission's two final reports were placed in the public domain. Their report did not add much of substance to the information already contained in previous publications, including the Greenpeace report, but was interesting primarily because of its argument that the amount of customary land 'in the hands of foreign corporations' was much greater that the amount covered by SABLs granted to private companies (Mousseau 2013: 4), and the subsequent argument that agro-forestry projects ought to be resisted because of the negative social and environmental impact of the existing oil palm industry (ibid.: 18). The first argument seems to assume that the lease-leaseback scheme did not involve a more complete form of expropriation than the legal arrangements by which customary landowners have agreed to alienate their timber harvesting rights for the purpose of creating selective logging concessions, while the second argument seems to imply that selective logging, forest clearance and the development of oil palm estates are all equally destructive if carried out on a large scale, so the failure of agro-forestry projects to develop oil palm estates with the proceeds of forest clearance might actually be a good thing.

The Pacific Network on Globalisation later added another twist to this line of argument by suggesting that the World Bank was implicated in the PNG land grab because its 'ease-of-doing-business' index had encouraged the government to deregulate the land acquisition process (Act Now 2014b). The idea that the World Bank, RH and New Britain Palm Oil Ltd were the three key players in a global conspiracy to expropriate the poor peasants of PNG might have some appeal to academic anarchists (Anderson 2011, 2015), but it does not reflect the history of forest policy reform in PNG, nor was it likely to influence the direction of the policy process that would follow on from the Commission of Inquiry. Members of the other three groups in the land grab policy network—the oil palm industry group, the land development group and even the sustainability group—were not concerned with the question of how to reverse the alienation of all customary land rights, but rather with the more specific questions addressed by the Commission itself, which was how to rectify the abuse of the lease-leaseback scheme and how to ensure that such abuse could not be repeated in future.

Members of the oil palm industry group continued to gather evidence about the economic credentials of companies that had been granted forest-clearing authorities, and other companies that showed an interest in the future development of agro-forestry projects, even during the period in which the findings of the Commission had not yet been released. They also continued to monitor the progress of existing projects that promised the eventual production of palm oil in order to assess the likelihood that this promise would be kept. The National Forest Board also made some effort to monitor the compliance of existing projects with conditions attached to their forest clearing authorities and, in some cases, this led to a temporary suspension of the permits because the area that had been cleared was too far in excess of the area that had been planted with cash crops. The commissioners also took an interest in such matters, but it was not clear how evidence of this kind might eventually be used to justify the cancellation of the SABLs granted to landowner companies that had then issued subleases to the foreign investors who were clearing the forest.

Some of the senior government officials who were members of the land grab policy network were more concerned by the possibility that the state would be liable to pay these investors substantial amounts in damages if the SABLs were to be cancelled (Lawrence Kalinoe, personal communication, July 2013). Even if the investors had colluded in the process by which the original leases were granted, it might be hard to prove this in court, and if other government officials had already helped the investors to get their hands on the land, they might now help them to get their hands on a financial reward for the opportunity cost of losing control of it.[15] The particular case that prompted this concern was one brought by a company called Albright Ltd, which had entered into a sublease agreement with a landowner company called Mekeo Hinterland Holdings Ltd after the latter had been granted an SABL over a large area of land in Central Province. This SABL was nullified by a decision of the National Court at the end of 2010, before the Commission of Inquiry was established, but in March 2012, Albright claimed damages of more than K153 million from the landowner company and the government, and initially secured a default judgement in its favour when the state failed to file a defence. In July 2013, the state defendants returned to the National Court with a request for this judgement to be set aside on the grounds that they had no 'actionable statutory duty' towards Albright in respect of the sublease agreement. The Court agreed with this argument,[16] but Albright was given leave to appeal to the Supreme Court, and the appeal was finally rejected in May 2014.[17]

Even though the outcome of this case seems to confirm the power of the National Court to cancel SABLs without creating additional financial liabilities for the state, it is not so clear that the National Executive Council or the Lands Minister could exercise the same power in the absence of a case brought by a group of disaffected landowners, and such cases have so far been relatively rare. One such case arose from the decision of the Lands Department to grant a couple of SABLs to landowner companies in Oro Province in July 2012, in apparent defiance of the moratorium imposed when the Commission of Inquiry had been established. It soon transpired that these leases covered the same area that

---

15   The role of government officials in aiding and abetting spurious compensation claims against the state had been the subject of a previous commission of inquiry into the Department of Finance (Sheehan et al. 2009).

16   *Albright Ltd v Mekeo Hinterland Holdings Ltd* [2013] PGNC 262.

17   *Albright Ltd v Mekeo Hinterland Holdings Ltd* [2014] PGSC 30.

had been covered by the SABLs previously granted to another landowner company in the 1990s, which formed the basis for what Paul Barker called the 'Collingwood Bay scam' (Barker 2009). The original leases had been revoked by an order of the National Court in 2002, before the Lands Department began to grant any of the SABLs that the commissioners were investigating. Nevertheless, Thomas Webster took this latest action as proof that the Lands Department was incorrigible, while the landowners who had got the National Court to cancel the original leases were now faced with the prospect of having to engage in a fresh round of legal action to obtain the same result (Pok 2012a, 2012b). They finally won this second battle in May 2014, around the same time that Albright finally lost its compensation claim. Although their victory had no direct bearing on the question of what the government should do with the Commission's recommendations, the case was still significant because the legal action had been backed by the newly elected Governor of Oro Province, Gary Juffa, who declared that there was nothing to prevent members of parliament or provincial governments from taking such action to defend the rights of their constituents (Miae 2014).

The second iteration of the 'Collingwood Bay scam' had a somewhat different significance for members of the land development group and the oil palm industry group. When Thomas Webster deplored the misbehaviour of the Lands Department, he observed that such action was not only a breach of the moratorium imposed by the National Executive Council, but should have been rendered redundant by the fact that customary landowners could now register titles to their own land and issue their own leases to developers of their choice without any need to resort to the chicaneries of the lease-leaseback scheme (Pok 2012a). That is because the amendments to the Land Registration Act and the Land Groups Incorporation Act that had been passed by the national parliament in March 2009 had actually been certified and gazetted in February 2012, shortly before the Commission of Inquiry got to the end of its hearings. However, this legislation posed a new problem because of its requirement that all of the existing land groups in the country, including those that had participated in the lease-leaseback scheme, should undergo a complex process of reincorporation within a period of five years in order to retain their legal status. Only those groups that were incorporated or reincorporated under the amended version of the Land Groups Incorporation Act would be allowed to register titles to their land under the amended version of the Land Registration Act. A new world of properly constituted land groups with registered land titles was one of the ideals of the NLDP, but that program's machinery had almost ground to a halt since the establishment of the Commission of Inquiry, so the implementation of the new legislation was now the responsibility of a Lands Department whose failings had been documented in minute detail.

Conclusion

A commission of inquiry is one phase in the process by which public scandals generate new policies, laws and institutions. The formation of a policy network is one aspect of this process. The number of people and range of interests represented in the network will normally reflect the magnitude of the scandal that starts the process and the amount of time and effort spent on the reforms that bring it to an end. But political cycles of this type do not always run their course in isolation from each other, nor are they always immune from interference by other changes in the political landscape.

The direction of the process started by the land grab scandal has been affected by that of two previous cycles containing their own commissions of inquiry. One was an inquiry into the regulation of the logging industry, whose findings and recommendations started a process of forest policy reform in 1989 (Barnett 1989, 1992); the other was an even earlier inquiry into the regulation of land tenure, whose findings and recommendations started a process of land policy reform in 1974 (GoPNG 1973; Ward 1983). If the recommendations for land policy reform had been implemented in a timely fashion, there would have been a legal avenue for the registration of customary group titles before the end of the 1970s, and the lease-leaseback scheme would never have been invented. The process of forest policy reform did not result in a legal and institutional framework that was quite so obviously incomplete, but it did produce a situation in which the World Bank and its national allies struggled to defend the new framework against the sort of scandalous behaviour that led to that commission of inquiry (Filer 2000; Forest Trends 2006).

The two cycles were briefly entangled in 1995, when the World Bank's investment in forest policy reform was compromised by rumours that it was also in the business of 'stealing the people's land' because it had made a parallel investment in completion of the land policy reform process initiated by the earlier commission of inquiry (Filer 2000: 32–7). This is the point at which the anti-dependency group made its first appearance on the national political stage as a group of people who were equally opposed to the registration of customary land titles and to any industrial exploitation of customary land. But the fuss they made at the time was also the reason why members of the land development group insisted on excluding the World Bank and other members of the 'donor community' from the appearance of any involvement in the next attempt to start finishing the land policy reform process in 2005.

If World Bank staff had any cause for disappointment over this act of exclusion, it would not have matched the frustration caused by their simultaneous exclusion from the cycle of forest policy reform. That wheel soon turned full circle, when amendments to the Forestry Act made it easier for the lease-leaseback scheme to become the site of a new scandal. But this new point of intersection between the cycles of land and forest policy reform had more chaotic effects than the momentary (and largely fabricated) scandal of 1995. Here we had a national conference (the National Land Summit) that was convened to deal with the problems that had arisen from the implementation or non-implementation of the recommendations made by a commission of inquiry more than three decades beforehand. The conference led to the creation of a taskforce (the National Land Development Taskforce) that produced a program of policy reform (the National Land Development Program) whose implementation was rudely interrupted by a new scandal that led to a new commission of inquiry. As a result, the land grab policy network assembled a couple of groups that originated in the process of forest policy reform, a couple of groups that originated in the process of land policy reform, and one group—the climate policy group—that had not been part of either process until the scandal broke. So the process generated by this scandal was almost bound to be a sort of hybrid policy process in which it would not be possible to reconcile the interests of all these different groups in one new package of policies, laws and institutions. The resulting stalemate is explored in Chapter 8.

References

Act Now (for a Better Papua New Guinea), 2014a. 'Rimbunan Hijau, the SABL Puppeteer.' Blogpost by 'rait man', 23 January. Viewed 12 October 2016 at: www.actnowpng.org/content/rimbunan-hijau-sabl-puppeteer.

——, 2014b. 'PANG supports demand for World Bank to end its support for resource grab.' Blogpost by 'Elizabeth1', 6 May. Viewed 12 October 2016 at: www.actnowpng.org/content/pang-supports-demand-world-bank-end-its-support-resource-grab.

Anderson, T., 2011. 'Melanesian Land: The Impact of Markets and Modernisation.' *Journal of Australian Political Economy* 68: 86–107.

——, 2015. *Land and Livelihoods in Papua New Guinea.* Melbourne: Australian Scholarly Publishing.

Anderson, T. and G. Lee (eds), 2010. *In Defence of Melanesian Customary Land.* Sydney: Aid/Watch.

Anon., 2005a. 'Call to Revoke Logger's Licence.' *Post-Courier*, 26 September.

——, 2005b. 'Concern over Loggers' Promises.' *Post-Courier*, 17 October.

——, 2006. 'RH Moves into Oil Palm.' *Post-Courier*, 6 June.

——, 2007. 'Govt Hits Oil Palm Hurdle.' *Post-Courier*, 11 September.

——, 2008a. 'National Land Development Taskforce Report: NGO Response.' Unpublished typescript.

——, 2008b. 'State "Grabs" Forest for REDD.' *Post-Courier*, 31 October.

——, 2008c. 'Carbon Trading or Carpet Baggers.' *Post-Courier*, 22 November.

——, 2009. 'New Palm Oil Firms "a Concern".' *The National*, 25 June.

Ase, D., 2009. 'Request for Inspection: Smallholder Agricultural Development Project—Papua New Guinea.' Port Moresby: Centre for Environmental Law and Community Rights.

Barker, P., 2009. 'Land Grab—A Sinister Cycle.' *Post-Courier*, 11 May.

——, 2010. 'Land Rights Vital.' *Post-Courier*, 7 January.

Barnett, T.E., 1989. *Report of the Commission of Inquiry into Aspects of the Forest Industry: Final Report* (2 volumes). Port Moresby: Unpublished report to the Government of PNG.

——, 1992. 'Legal and Administrative Problems of Forestry in Papua New Guinea.' In S. Henningham and R.J. May (eds), *Resources, Development and Politics in the Pacific Islands*. Bathurst (NSW): Crawford House Press.

Bonsella, B., 2005. 'PM: Green Revolution to Boost Economy by 5pc.' *The National*, 25 July.

Filer, C., 1997. 'A Statistical Profile of Papua New Guinea's Log Export Industry.' In C. Filer (ed.) *The Political Economy of Forest Management in Papua New Guinea*. Port Moresby: National Research Institute (Monograph 32).

——, 2000. *The Thin Green Line: World Bank Leverage and Forest Policy Reform in Papua New Guinea*. Port Moresby and Canberra: National Research Institute and The Australian National University.

——, 2005. 'The Conservation Policy Community in Papua New Guinea.' Canberra: The Australian National University, Research School of Pacific and Asian Studies, Resource Management in Asia-Pacific Program (Working Paper 55).

——, 2009a. 'Institutional Mechanisms for Establishment and Management of Forest Carbon Sequestration Projects in Papua New Guinea.' Unpublished report to Carbon Planet Ltd.

——, 2009b. 'Land Rights and Benefit Sharing Arrangements for REDD Projects in Papua New Guinea.' Port Moresby: Unpublished report to PNG Department of Environment and Conservation.

——, 2009c. 'Drivers of Deforestation and Forest Degradation in Papua New Guinea.' Port Moresby: Unpublished report to PNG Department of Environment and Conservation.

——, 2010. 'Impacts of Rural Industry on the Native Forests of Papua New Guinea.' *Pacific Economic Bulletin* 25(3): 135–153.

——, 2011a. 'New Land Grab in Papua New Guinea.' *Pacific Studies* 34: 269–294.

——, 2011b. 'The New Land Grab in Papua New Guinea: A Case Study from New Ireland Province.' Canberra: The Australian National University, College of Asia and the Pacific, State Society and Governance in Melanesia Program (Discussion Paper 2011/2).

——, 2012. 'Why Green Grabs Don't Work in Papua New Guinea.' *Journal of Peasant Studies* 39: 599–617. doi.org/10.1080/03066150. 2012.665891.

——, 2013. 'Asian Investment in the Rural Industries of Papua New Guinea: What's New and What's Not?' *Pacific Affairs* 86: 305–326. doi.org/10.5509/2013862305.

——, 2015. 'How April Salumei Became the REDD Queen.' In J.A. Bell, P. West and C. Filer (eds), *Tropical Forests of Oceania: Anthropological Perspectives*. Canberra: ANU Press.

Filer, C. and M. Wood, 2012. 'The Creation and Dissolution of Private Property in Forest Carbon: A Case Study from Papua New Guinea.' *Human Ecology* 40: 665–677. doi.org/10.1007/s10745-012-9531-2.

Forest Trends, 2006. *Logging, Legality and Livelihoods in Papua New Guinea: Synthesis of Official Assessments of the Large-Scale Logging Industry*. Jakarta: Forest Trends.

Gabriel, J., 2015. '"Evergreen" and REDD+ in the Forests of Oceania.' In J.A. Bell, P. West and C. Filer (eds), *Tropical Forests of Oceania: Anthropological Perspectives*. Canberra: ANU Press.

GoPNG (Government of Papua New Guinea), 1973. *Report of the Commission of Inquiry into Land Matters*. Port Moresby: GoPNG.

——, 2007. *The National Land Development Taskforce Report: Land Administration, Land Dispute Settlement, and Customary Land Development*. Port Moresby: National Research Institute (Monograph 39).

——, 2008. 'Review of Incorporated Land Groups & Design of a System of Voluntary Customary Land Registration.' Port Moresby: Constitutional and Law Reform Commission.

——, 2010a. 'Papua New Guinea National Land Development Program Phase 1 (2011–2015): Implementation Plan.' Port Moresby: National Land Development Program Management Committee.

——, 2010b. 'Climate-Compatible Development for Papua New Guinea: Second Draft—for Stakeholder Comment.' Port Moresby: Department of Environment and Conservation.

——, 2010c. 'Interim Action Plan for Climate-Compatible Development.' Port Moresby: Office of Climate Change and Development.

——, 2011. 'Commission of Inquiry into the Management Generally of the Special Agriculture and Business Leases and All Matters Relating to the Special Agriculture and Business Leases: Statement of Case.' Port Moresby: *National Gazette* G198.

——, 2012. 'National Forest Plan (Draft).' Port Moresby: PNG Forest Authority.

Greenpeace, 2004. 'The Untouchables: Rimbunan Hijau's World of Forest Crime & Political Patronage.' Amsterdam: Greenpeace International.

——, 2011. 'Bad Influence: How Mckinsey-Inspired Plans Lead to Rainforest Destruction.' Amsterdam: Greenpeace International.

Joku, H., 2010. 'Lands Dept "Corrupt".' *Post-Courier*, 11 November.

Kelola, T., 2013. 'Jerewai Hits Back.' *Post-Courier*, 18 September.

Lang, C., 2010. 'Mckinsey's REDD Plans in Papua New Guinea: Nice Work If You Can Get It.' REDD Monitor blogpost, 7 October. Viewed 5 October 2016 at: www.redd-monitor.org/2010/10/07/mckinseys-redd-plans-in-papua-new-guinea-nice-work-if-you-can-get-it/#more-5966.

Levantis, T. and C. Yala, 2008. 'Breaking Away from the Land Policy Stalemate.' *Pacific Economic Bulletin* 23(1): 99–110.

McCrea, P., 2009. 'Oil Palm Sector Situation and Perception Assessment: Papua New Guinea.' Port Moresby: Unpublished report to World Bank and Oil Palm Industry Corporation.

Melick, D., 2008. 'On-the Ground Role of NGOs with Emerging Carbon Market Issues: Is the REDD Emperor Actually Wearing Any Clothes?' Paper presented to seminar on 'Challenges to the National Implementation of Activities to Reduce Emissions from Deforestation and Forest Degradation (REDD)', The Australian National University, Canberra, 18 June.

Miae, E., 2014. 'Landowners Get Leases Cancelled.' *The National*, 23 May.

Mirou, N., 2013. *Commission of Inquiry into Special Agriculture and Business Lease (C.O.I. SABL): Report*. Port Moresby: Government of Papua New Guinea. Viewed 5 October 2016 at: www.coi.gov.pg/documents/COI%20SABL/Mirou%20SABL%20Final%20Report.pdf.

Mousseau, F., 2013. 'On Our Land: Modern Land Grabs Reversing Independence in Papua New Guinea.' Oakland (CA): The Oakland Institute in collaboration with Pacific Network on Globalisation.

Nicholas, I., 2013a. 'Disappointment over No SABL Report.' *Post-Courier*, 27 March.

——, 2013b. 'Trio Referred.' *Post-Courier*, 13 September.

Numapo, J., 2013. *Commission of Inquiry into the Special Agriculture and Business Lease (SABL): Final Report*. Port Moresby: Government of Papua New Guinea. Viewed 5 October 2016 at: www.coi.gov.pg/documents/COI%20SABL/Numapo%20SABL%20Final%20Report.pdf.

Oliver, N., 2001. 'Lease, Lease-Back: An Instrument for Forestry?' In C. Hunt (ed.), *Production, Privatisation and Preservation in Papua New Guinea Forestry*. London: International Institute for Environment and Development.

PNGEFF (Papua New Guinea Eco-Forestry Forum), 2009a. 'Press Release: Court Stops Carbon Deal.' Port Moresby: PNGEFF.

——, 2009b. 'EFF Calls on Government of PNG, Development Partners and AusAid to Help Protect PNG from Carbon Scams.' *Islands Business* 35(10).

Pok, J., 2012a. 'SABL Abuses Must Be Dealt with Strongly.' *Post-Courier*, 5 September.

——, 2012b. 'Oro SABL's Queried.' *Post-Courier*, 14 September.

——, 2013. 'Shut Up!' *Post-Courier*, 28 March.

Power, T., 2008. 'Incorporated Land Groups in Papua New Guinea.' In AusAID (Australian Agency for International Development) (ed.), *Making Land Work—Volume Two: Case Studies on Customary Land and Development in the Pacific*. Canberra: AusAID.

Seri, L., 2005. 'Land Defrauders: A Close Call.' *Post-Courier*, 19 April.

Sheehan, M., C. Davani and D. Manoa, 2009. *The Commission of Inquiry Generally into the Department of Finance: Final Report*. Port Moresby: Government of Papua New Guinea.

Ward, A., 1983. 'The Commission of Inquiry into Land Matters 1973: Choices, Constraints and Assumptions.' *Melanesian Law Journal* 11: 1–13.

Winn, P., 2012. 'Up for Grabs: Millions of Hectares of Customary Land in PNG Stolen for Logging.' Sydney: Greenpeace Australia Pacific.

Wood, M., 2015. 'Representational Excess in Recent Attempts to Acquire Forest Carbon in the Kamula Doso Area, Western Province, Papua New Guinea.' In J.A. Bell, P. West and C. Filer (eds), *Tropical Forests of Oceania: Anthropological Perspectives*. Canberra: ANU Press.

7

Oil Palm Development and Large-Scale Land Acquisitions in Papua New Guinea

Jennifer Gabriel, Paul N. Nelson, Colin Filer
and Michael Wood

Introduction

Throughout the developing world, large tracts of land are being acquired from customary owners by corporations for the purpose of commercial agriculture (Deininger and Byerlee 2011; Anseeuw et al. 2012). This 'land grabbing' typically occurs in conditions of poor governance and results in benefits to powerful elites at the expense of local populations (Nolte 2014). It has been argued that the loss of access to land by customary owners in developing countries will be offset by investments that will create new jobs and bring new knowledge and infrastructures that will benefit the local population (Toft 2013). However, this process can also entail serious long-term consequences for these same local people (Sayer et al. 2012; Feintrenie 2014; Rulli and D'Odorico 2014). Large-scale acquisitions have been going on for a long time in many regions of the world, but there has been a marked recent acceleration to supply an increasing global demand for food, fibre and biofuels (von Braun and Meinzen-Dick 2009; Cotula et al. 2011; Rulli et al. 2013). Those who advocate for large-scale investments in productive agricultural land point out that measures should be in place to ensure that the benefits are shared equitably with the local populations (Cotula 2013; Toft 2013).

In Papua New Guinea (PNG), the recent large-scale acquisition of more than 5 million hectares of potential agricultural land has been described as the largest land grab in modern history (Global Witness 2014). This has caused great anguish among customary landowners, and was made possible by the abuse of legal loopholes, bureaucratic incompetence, and 'permissive ambiguities' in the leasing process (Numapo 2013: 4). To prevent such abuses in the future, and maximise the benefits of agricultural developments such as oil palm for customary landowners, transparent consultation and agreements between developer companies and representative landowner groups will be needed (Nelson et al. 2014). Our intention in this chapter is to facilitate such change by describing the nature of the actors and their actions to date, with a particular focus on landowner representatives and corporate developers.

We focus on proposed oil palm plantation projects for three reasons. First, oil palm has been the most common crop proposed for large-scale agricultural development schemes in PNG, so oil palm schemes account for 2.2 million of the total of more than 5 million hectares of land that has been alienated through the grant of 'special agricultural and business leases' (SABLs). Second, a focus on this particular industry allows us to assess the nature and activities of players more readily than if we examined all the other proposals for crops with less specific requirements for establishment of a viable economic enterprise. Finally, the palm oil industry has been a major transformer of landscapes and livelihoods throughout the tropics in the recent past, and is likely to remain so in the foreseeable future (Sheil et al. 2009; Cramb and Curry 2012; Sayer et al. 2012).

We reveal examples of complex interactions in specific policy and political contexts between people representing the interests of landowners, companies and government agencies, as well as the failure of government officials to ensure compliance, accountability and transparency in all stages of the leasing process. An understanding of these developments gives insights into how they occurred and how future abuses of people's rights might be prevented. We also identify some opportunities for improved outcomes in programs to rationalise the use of land.

Land Acquisitions for Oil Palm Development

In PNG, the law does not allow for the permanent alienation of customary land. Around 31 per cent of PNG's current palm oil production originates from fruit produced by smallholders, with the remainder originating from the plantations of the two oil palm companies, New Britain Palm Oil Ltd and Hargy Oil Palms Ltd. The smallholders fall into three categories: those who cultivate oil palm on their own customary land; those in occupation of 6-hectare blocks established on state land under so-called land settlement schemes; and those who have gained access to other people's customary land through clan land usage agreements (Koczberski et al. 2013; also Chapter 5, this volume). Most of the plantations operated by the existing two palm oil-producing companies are on land alienated during the time of the Australian administration, although they also operate some 'mini-estates' on land subleased from groups of customary landowners holding SABLs (see Chapter 6, this volume). The two oil palm companies started making use of these lease arrangements in the late 1990s, but the amount of land they acquired through this process is only a tiny fraction of the area of more than 5 million hectares allocated to other companies under SABLs issued since 2003 (Filer 2011, 2012a; Moore 2011; Winn 2012; Nelson et al. 2014). Most of this land has been subleased to foreign investors, which has caused an outpouring of frustration and anger among rural people in many parts of the country about the loss of rights to their land and resources (Mirou 2013; Mousseau 2013; Numapo 2013).

The SABL process was originally designed to enable customary landowners to use their land productively for business development purposes and thereby gain access to the cash economy (Oliver 2002; Filer 2011). The fundamental title remains with the customary owners, but other rights and components of the title can be partially alienated through the SABL mechanism. Land acquisition through this mechanism involves a three-step process (Table 7.1). First, the state acquires a lease over the customary land, sometimes referred to as the 'head lease', which is executed between the customary landowners and the Minister for Lands and Physical Planning on behalf of the state. Then the state issues an SABL to a family or corporate body approved by the customary landowners. This entity may then grant a sublease to a developer or investor on the basis of this SABL. Due to the compensation provisions in many of the development agreements, it is virtually impossible for most villagers to reclaim the land that has been leased or subleased with their supposed approval. In these circumstances, leasing land becomes a form of self-dispossession (Anderson 2010: 13). In some cases, this bureaucratic process of commercialising customary land in effect transfers clan rights to one or more individuals who may not be clan leaders but are supported by a developer who has a close connection with elected politicians or government officials.

While the main justification for the scale of alienation was the establishment of large-scale commercial agricultural ventures, it is now clear that many of the development agreements were being used as a pretext for logging, with many developers having no experience or interest in establishing the agricultural industries promised in the agreements (Nelson et al. 2010, 2014; Filer 2011; Winn 2012).

Table 7.1 Summary of the process intended by government (since approximately 2003) for large-scale agricultural developments in Papua New Guinea, and the variations that have occurred.

Intended process and actors	Variations that have occurred
Customary landowners and developer agree on a development proposal for a particular parcel of land.	Developer and landowner companies frequently changed in structure and ownership.
Customary landowners of land parcel form incorporated land group (ILG) and register it with the state.	Individuals (usually some landowners, not necessarily living on their customary land) formed ILG without full consent of landowners. Multiple dissenting ILGs formed. ILGs initiated negotiations with alternative developers and new projects were formulated, which may or may not involve oil palm.
Land parcel surveyed and Local Land Court approves agreement reached among landowners. ILG registers land parcel for development with the state. Application for lease-leaseback lodged with Provincial Government and forwarded to Department of Lands and Physical Planning (DLPP). Land investigation report prepared by Provincial Lands Office and forwarded to DLPP.	Boundaries were not clearly defined or agreed. Overlapping boundaries for land parcels nominated in competing development proposals. Land investigations and awareness programs funded by entities outside the government and mostly by the developers. Land investigation report not prepared or not properly prepared. Landownership disputes not properly investigated. Landowner representatives and ILG representatives manipulated by developers to fast-track the issuing of the special agricultural and business lease (SABL) titles.
ILG leases land parcel to the Minister of Lands on behalf of the state at no rent ('head lease' or 'customary land dealing'), which formalises the title and allows transfer to non-citizens.	Government departments lost records and acted outside of the law.

Intended process and actors	Variations that have occurred
Minister of Lands grants SABL back to 'a person, group or incorporated body' (e.g. an ILG) approved by customary landowners for a period of up to 99 years for the purpose of agricultural or business development at no rent.	Minister leased land to a company (to whom customary landowners have not agreed such a lease should be granted) rather than ILG. Projects sometimes approved on the basis of agricultural plans submitted to Department of Agriculture and Livestock (DAL) by a developer who is no longer involved in the project.
ILG makes sublease (development agreement) with developer (a registered company). Foreign developers should have Investment Promotion Authority (IPA) certification to conduct oil palm development. Sublease should be registered with DLPP. Full proposal should include evidence of the technical and financial capacity of the developer, land use and capability maps, design and layout of nurseries, plantations and mills, proof of landowner consent and minutes of a public hearing, as well as various endorsed documents from provincial and local-level governments supporting the project proposals.	Brokers negotiated agreements. Agreements lacked transparency in negotiations. SABL grantees often did not return to the DLPP to register their subleases as prescribed. Subleases were transferred between developers without registration. Developers not licensed by the IPA to conduct oil palm development in PNG. Sublease agreements grossly unfair to the landowners in terms of ownership of the infrastructure development and the tree crops. Foreign developers mostly lacked financial backing of an overseas parent company with sufficient experience in oil palm development.
DAL assesses feasibility of the proposal and gives approval.	DAL did not adequately assess proposal or monitor progress. Political pressures placed on government officials by senior ministers and politicians to fast-track SABL applications.
Developer applies to PNG Forest Authority (PNGFA) for forest clearing authority (FCA).	Logging proceeded without FCA. DAL officials supported the view of developers that logging activities within SABL areas were justified in order to fund the proposed agricultural project.
Developer proceeds with forest clearing, establishment and operation of plantation according to sublease agreement, monitored by PNGFA, which ensures that no more than 500 hectares are cleared at one time, and by DAL, which ensures adherence to other applicable regulations and codes of practice.	Developer cleared forest and exported logs from areas much larger than 500 hectares. Developer did not implement agricultural development plan.

Sources: Derived from descriptions by Oliver (2002), Moore (2011), Filer (2012b), Mirou (2013) and Numapo (2013).

Note: There are discrepancies between various versions of the process described here, since the sources focus on different aspects and involve interpretation of several sets of rules that were produced at different times for different reasons.

A commission of inquiry (COI) established by the PNG government in 2011 found much legally questionable activity and serious abuse and subversion of the SABL process (Mirou 2013; Numapo 2013). Commissioner Nicholas Mirou noted 'one unmistakable cry from the vast majority of the rural population of PNG [for] development', along with frustration arising from unmet expectations of benefits from exploitation of their land by developers (Mirou 2013: 167). Two of the three commissioners submitted their reports to the Prime Minister in June 2013, and these were later tabled in Parliament (see Chapter 8, this volume). Along with a number of recommendations to improve transparency, the inquiry recommended that the SABL process be reserved for the development of high-impact projects, with strict conditions to ensure maximum landowner benefit and participation. While in principle these recommendations point to some positive reforms, the government has been slow to remedy situations where evidence of criminality or negligence was uncovered.

Oil Palm Development Proposals

We examined 29 proposed oil palm projects associated with 51 separate SABLs in 10 different provinces (Table 7.2). The areas shown as being earmarked for the planting of oil palm are those specified in the development plans or environmental impact statements submitted to the PNG government. Where these areas are 'unknown', this is normally due to the fact that no such plans have so far been submitted or sighted.

Most of the development proposals we examined are 'agro-forestry' proposals involving oil palm development. The term 'agro-forestry', which is commonly used in the development discourse in PNG, and that we use in this chapter, has a different meaning in PNG to the more widely accepted definition. In the broader literature, 'agro-forestry' refers to a mixed cropping system that includes trees. In PNG, the term refers to clearance of native forest for timber, followed by agricultural development.

Table 7.2 Proposed oil palm projects associated with special agricultural and business leases in Papua New Guinea.

No.	Project name	Province	SABL date(s)	SABL area (ha)	Oil palm area (ha)	FCA date(s)	Log exports 2007–15 (m³)
1	Sigite-Mukus	E.N. Britain	2008	55,400	20,000	2010	864,023
2	Lassul Baining	E.N. Britain	2010	53,480	Unknown	2008	700,243
3	(Lavongai)	New Ireland	2007	93,564	16,000	2010	617,084
4	Wewak-Turubu	E. Sepik	2008	116,840	90,000	2009	558,892
5	Ili-Wawas	E.N. Britain	2008 2011	34,282	24,000	2007	470,509
6	Bewani	W. Sepik	2008	139,909	26,000	2009	347,147
7	Angoram	E. Sepik	2007	25,600	Unknown	2009	336,450
8	Aitape West	W. Sepik	2006	47,630	Unknown	2008	312,259
9	Aitape East	W. Sepik	1995	20,790	20,000	2008	103,086
10	(East Kikori)	Gulf	2008 2009	56,629	Unknown	None	58,087
11	Wammy	W. Sepik	2010	105,200	58,000	2014	56,486
12	(Mekeo)	Central	2007 2008	128,100	40,000	2009 2010	4,234
13	Musa-Pongani	Oro	2009 2010	320,060	100,000	2010	None
14	Nuku	W. Sepik	2009	239,810	25,000	None	None
15	Yumu	Central	2007	115,000	Unknown	2007	None
16	Urasirk	Madang	2011	112,400	75,520	None	None
17	Nungwaia-Bongos	E. Sepik	2011	109,580	89,000	None	None

KASTOM, PROPERTY AND IDEOLOGY

No.	Project name	Province	SABL date(s)	SABL area (ha)	Oil palm area (ha)	FCA date(s)	Log exports 2007–15 (m³)
18	(Wawoi-Guavi)	Western	2009	77,783	Unknown	None	None
19	Mukus-Melkoi	E.N. Britain	2008	68,300	Unknown	2010	None
20	Kerema-Meporo	Gulf	2007	59,640	20,000	None	None
21	Pulie-Anu	W.N. Britain	2008	46,233	32,000	None	None
22	Baina	Central	2005	42,100	29,000	None	None
23	Wanigela	Oro	1995 2012	38,350	Unknown	2010	None
24	Kairak	E.N. Britain	2011	34,536	Unknown	None	None
25	Ainbai-Elis	W. Sepik	2010	22,850	18,000	None	None
26	(Sinivit)	E.N. Britain	2006 2007	21,000	21,000	None	None
27	Vailala	Gulf	2003 2011	11,800	Unknown	None	None
28	Lolokoru	W.N. Britain	2005	1,750	1,750	None	None
29	Akami	W.N. Britain	2008	577	577	None	None

Sources: Papua New Guinea's *National Gazette*; SGS PNG Ltd (annual reports); project development plans.

Note: The titles of agro-forestry projects generally include the name of some geographical area, followed by phrases such as 'agro-forestry', 'oil palm', or 'integrated agriculture'. Such phrases have been omitted from the project names shown in this table. Names that are shown in brackets are those that have been attributed to projects in the absence of any planning documents that contain a title, or those that stand for a combination of different subprojects that are separately named in such documents. For example, Lavongai is the name of an island (otherwise known as New Hanover) that contains three adjoining lease areas—Central New Hanover, Umbukul and Tabut-Mamirum—held by three landowner companies operating in partnership with a single developer.

In Table 7.2, the 12 projects that count as operational agro-forestry projects because of their log exports are listed first in order of the total volume of their log exports over the period from 2007 to 2015. All but one of these projects has been exporting logs under the terms of a forest clearing authority (FCA) issued by the PNG Forest Authority (PNGFA), although some of these licences have been suspended or cancelled at one time or another. Most of the remaining 17 projects have never been granted an FCA, and the revenues from log exports have not been used to finance any kind of agricultural development. These projects are therefore listed in order of the size of the SABLs acquired by their proponents. The last two projects in the list are examples of the 'mini-estates' established in the vicinity of the existing oil palm schemes in West New Britain Province (see Chapter 6, this volume), and they do not count as agro-forestry projects since log export revenues have not been treated as the basis for financing their development.

Table 7.3 shows the identity and origin of each of the 'development partners' who have obtained subleases from the landowner companies holding SABLs. It also shows the dates on which the holders of these subleases were registered with the Investment Promotion Authority (IPA), whether they were registered to undertake oil palm production (ROP), and whether there is documented evidence of their capacity to do so (COP), either on their own account or through their parent companies.[1]

In many cases it was difficult to identify the developers due to frequent changes in agreements and lack of the legally required registration of the participants or their agreements. This is partly due to the developers and landowners trying to keep their involvement in SABLs secret. Logging companies have also been known to set up fake incorporated land groups (ILGs) to further confuse the process (Anderson and Lee 2010: 4).

Data was obtained from the COI reports presented to Parliament by Prime Minister Peter O'Neill in September 2013 (Mirou 2013; Numapo 2013), which cover 49 of the 75 leases investigated by the Commission, as well as the transcripts of COI hearings in individual provinces, especially the hearings conducted by Commissioner Jerewai, who failed to finalise his own report (see Chapter 8).

---

1   In those few cases where the sublease holder is a joint venture between a landowner company and a foreign company, the 'parent company' shown in Table 7.3 is the parent of the foreign company.

Aside from company records filed with the IPA, and the annual reports on log exports by the 'forest industry participants' recognised by the PNGFA, we also consulted company annual reports, industry and media reports, academic articles, stock market announcements, and stock analyst reviews. Company reports provided information on the scale and investment portfolios of public companies in oil palm development and processing, while analyst reviews provided broader information on market trends and industry responses. Information about the existing oil palm plantations and companies was obtained from the PNG Palm Oil Council.

Table 7.3 Developers of proposed oil palm projects associated with special agricultural and business leases in Papua New Guinea.

No.	Sublease holder(s) in 2011	Parent company in 2011	Country of origin	IPA date(s)	ROP	OPC
1	Gilford & Sinar Tiasa (PNG)	Rimbunan Hijau	Malaysia	2007 2010	Y	Y
2	KK Connections	Kerawara	Malaysia	2010	N	N
3	Tutuman Development	Mantorras PNG	Malaysia	1999	N	N
4	Sepik Oil Palm Plantation	Wewak Agricultural Development	Malaysia	2008	Y	n.a.
5	Tzen Niugini & Tzen Plantation	Kenlox Global	Malaysia	2004	N	N
6	Bewani Oil Palm Plantations	PNG Plantations Development	Malaysia	2010	Y	n.a.
7	Brilliant Investment	(None listed)	Malaysia	2005	N	N
8	Vanimo Jaya	(None listed)	Malaysia	1995	N	n.a.
9	Mekar Harvest (PNG)	Brilliant Investment	Malaysia	2007	N	N
10	River Estate Plantations	Reko (PNG)	Malaysia	2007 2011	N	N
11	Global Elite (PNG)	(None listed)	Malaysia	2010	N	N
12	Albright	Willsmart International	Malaysia	2009	N	Y
13	Musa Century	Musa Holdings	Malaysia	2010	N	N
14	Skywalker Global Resources (PNG)	Skywalker Global Resources	Hong Kong	2009	Y	N
15	Aramia Plantations	(None listed)	Unknown	None	N	N
16	Continental Venture	Giant Kingdom International	Malaysia	2010	n.a.	Y
17	SPZ Enterprises (PNG)	Geoff Palm	Australia	2008	N	Y
18	Sovereign Hill	Rimbunan Hijau	Malaysia	1995	N	Y
19	Double Dynasty Lumber	Brilliant Investment	Malaysia	2008	N	N

No.	Sublease holder(s) in 2011	Parent company in 2011	Country of origin	IPA date(s)	ROP	OPC
20	Pacific International Resources (PNG)	Grand Pacific Resources	Malaysia	2006	N	N
21	Monarch Investments	Rimbunan Hijau	Malaysia	1996	N	Y
22	PMS Timbers	(None listed)	Malaysia	None	N	N
23	Ang Agro Forest Management	Collingwood Plantations	Malaysia	2007	N	Y
24	East New Britain Palm Oil (PNG)	Glory Jade Investments	Malaysia	2011	Y	Y
25	Starlink	Brilliant Investment	Malaysia	2010	N	N
26	Feflo Plantation (PNG)	Feflo (PNG)	Malaysia	2009	N	N
27	Sovereign Hill (PNG)	Rimbunan Hijau	Malaysia	1995	N	Y
28	New Britain Palm Oil	Kulim	Malaysia	1999	Y	Y
29	Greenlands Development	(None listed)	Malaysia	2011	n.a.	N

Sources: PNG Investment Promotion Authority and PNG Forest Authority.

State Actors and Their Actions

According to the conventional wisdom, state actors in PNG—whether elected (as politicians) or appointed (as public servants)—should not only represent the interests of the state. They should also favour the interests of customary landowners, who are their own people, against the interests of foreign companies that seek access to customary land. However, the political and bureaucratic process through which SABLs have been granted to private companies, and agro-forestry projects have been granted other permits and licences as a consequence, shows how the capacity of these actors to represent anyone's interest is constrained by their relationship with other actors whose own interests have often been compromised, or whose involvement in the process may have no legal basis.

In order to obtain an FCA under Section 90B of the Forestry Act, the proponents of an agro-forestry project normally had to begin by assembling a set of ILGs whose representatives could alienate a large area of customary land to the state (see Table 7.1). Local politicians and landowner company directors both played important roles in facilitating the process through which a set of land group certificates was presented to the Lands Department in support of an application for 'their' land to be leased back to a company of 'their' choice. By the time this happened, a 'development partner' would normally be party to the process, and may well have helped in its facilitation. In theory, officers of the Lands Department should undertake a 'land investigation' in order to establish the connection between the land group certificates and the customary land under consideration before granting an SABL (Moore 2011). This type of investigation was also meant to establish the free, prior and informed consent of the customary owners to the project for which the land was to be alienated, and that is why the COI went to such great lengths to show that national and provincial lands officers had failed to perform this task in accordance with existing laws and policies.

Once an SABL had been gazetted, if not before, the developer would submit its project proposal to the Department of Agriculture and Livestock (DAL). In order to comply with Section 90B of the Forestry Act, officers of this department were supposed to conduct some form of 'awareness' activity with landowners and other stakeholders to establish the extent of local support for the project. There is some evidence of this activity being undertaken, but the outcomes were not clearly documented. These were likely to be occasions on which the local member of parliament delivered a speech of encouragement to his band of loyal supporters, including landowner company directors, preferably in the company of other political and bureaucratic heavyweights from the national and provincial centres of political power.

Once the DAL staff had placed their stamp of approval on a project proposal, the proponents would attach this to their application for an FCA, which would be sent to the PNGFA.[2] Knowing that the National Forest Board would not normally approve a large-scale conversion concession in the absence of an environment permit issued by the Minister for Environment and Conservation, the proponents would also have initiated a process of environmental impact assessment once the project proposal had been finalised. The National Forest Board also required a recommendation from the relevant Provincial Forest Management Committee before granting an FCA. Landowner interests should have been represented in the deliberations of that committee, but were normally represented by supporters of the project under consideration. Figure 7.1 shows that the

---

2 The PNGFA has three component parts: the National Forest Board, which makes key decisions at the national level; a number of Provincial Forest Management Committees, which make recommendations to the Board about activities to be undertaken in their respective provinces; and the National Forest Service, which implements the decisions made by the Board.

volume of logs exported under FCAs continued to increase, even after the establishment of the COI, and the imposition of a moratorium on the grant of new FCAs, in 2011.

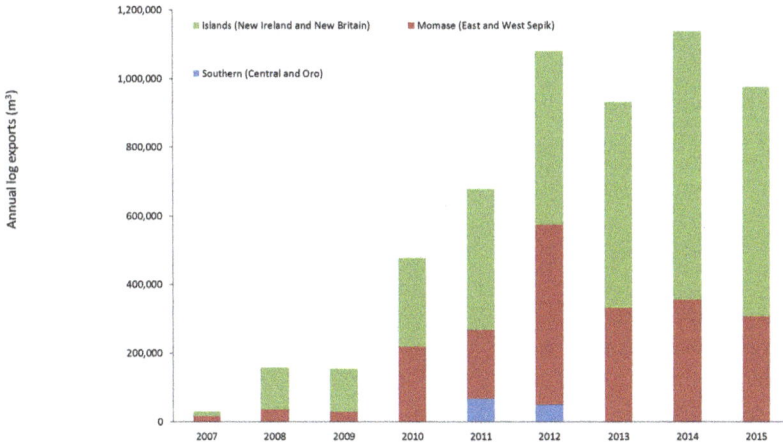

Figure 7.1 Volume of raw log exports from areas covered by FCAs granted to developers of agro-forestry projects, 2007–2015.
Source: SGS PNG Ltd 2008–2015.

In recent years, there has been widespread enthusiasm for agro-forestry projects at all levels of government. This enthusiasm was reflected in the National Agriculture Development Plan (GoPNG 2007), for which DAL is meant to be the implementing agency. Yet DAL staff were also charged with the task of screening and evaluating project proposals to ensure that the proponents had the necessary technical and financial capacities, had conducted the necessary land use assessments, and had produced realistic implementation schedules. However, the COI found 'disturbing evidence' of senior DAL officials simply accepting the idea that logging activities in SABL areas were an acceptable way of financing agro-forestry projects (Mirou 2013: 139; also Chapter 8, this volume).

The perfunctory nature of the project appraisal carried out by DAL staff can also be explained by the institutional disconnection between the national department and its provincial counterparts (Allen 2009). This means that national-level officials had no way to assess the extent of landowner support for a project when it was first presented for appraisal. As Secretary Anton Benjamin explained to the COI:

There are proposals or projects that have come directly to the Department but where the investors have consulted the landowners—and we are not aware of the manner in which this was done—and so they come with landowners to us to assist them. And there are cases where landowners have their differences. There are people in the community or in the village who are not party to that, who have not been consulted and this is where the problem is. After the endorsement is being given by the Department, we get letters from the landowners to us advising us that they have not been consulted, they are not party to this one and they want the project stopped until it is [sic] all been reviewed. So these are some of the issues that arises from the projects that when investors are actually dealing with the landowners themselves without coming to the Department and so those are issues that we are not aware of until after we have given approval, then we start to see this problem arises (Numapo et al. 2011: 24).

Similar sentiments were voiced by other public servants who testified to the COI. They felt they did not have the knowledge or the authority to question the agreements made between landowner representatives and their 'development partners'. And they were even less likely to do so when the 'landowner representatives' included government ministers or other national politicians. For example, the former head of the Lands Department, Pepi Kimas, testified that he was subjected to a lot of 'political pressure ... from the Prime Minister's level down', to grant an SABL for the Bewani oil palm project in West Sepik Province, while the former Provincial Administrator, Joseph Sungi, said that he was 'forced' by officers of the same department to accept a land investigation report that he had not actually sighted (Numapo 2013: 131, 137–8).[3] This does not mean that all elected politicians have been equally enthusiastic in their support of this particular type of development (see Chapter 6, this volume). However, the nature of PNG's current political system does not provide much opportunity or incentive for members of parliament, including government ministers, to obstruct each other's plans for their respective constituencies, especially when these plans are backed by foreign investors. Public servants have therefore been inclined to act on their perception of the weight of political support behind each project, without considering the possibility of political opposition.

---

3   In 2012, Mr Sungi was elected to represent an electorate in which nearly all the land was already covered by SABLs that he had authorised in his former capacity as Provincial Administrator.

Developers and Their Actions

The investors in agro-forestry projects, who have normally been the holders of subleases issued by the holders of SABLs, can be classified by reference to the identity of their owners or shareholders, the assets or experience at their command, the types of licence they have obtained from the PNG government, their relationships to other corporate entities, and various other criteria. In some projects, the leasing arrangements have involved a joint venture between a landowner company and a foreign company, but the majority of projects have involved a sublease by a landowner company to a foreign investor. Some project proponents already have had a track record in the PNG forestry sector, while others have been new to the country, but established companies and new entrants have both been making use of the SABL mechanism to gain access to timber (Filer 2013). In addition to providing access to new sources of timber for export, one of the reasons that SABLs have been attractive to foreign investors is that the value of land and timber assets can be traded on a foreign stock exchange. On the Kuala Lumpur Stock Exchange, for example, land can be traded in similar ways to stocks and bonds.

Our analysis of oil palm SABLs has revealed that around half of the projects involved negotiations with alternative developers before or after the COI hearings, while some have engaged multiple developers. This has been problematic when the project has been approved on the basis of agricultural plans submitted to DAL by a developer that is no longer involved in the project. Part of the problem of regulation, as the COI was told by the Registrar of Titles, is that the SABL grantees rarely returned to the Lands Department to register their subleases, so the Department and the Registrar were often not aware of the transactions that had transpired after the state lease had been granted.

Twenty-six of the 29 oil palm project proposals we investigated involved investors from Malaysia (Table 7.3). The most prominent among these has been the Rimbunan Hijau (RH) group, a large and diverse multinational company, with many business activities in PNG, including logging, in which it is the country's dominant player. RH is involved in logging and oil palm plantations in Malaysia through three public companies—Jaya Tiasa, Subur Tiasa and Rimbunan Sawit. It has approximately 176,000 hectares of land already planted to oil palm in Sarawak.

Nine of the investors had individual shareholders, with no identified corporate entity in the shareholding structure. This form of ownership may be something of an illusion if it constitutes a way of limiting or concealing corporate liability. Where the activities of a corporate group are highly integrated and interconnected, to the extent that each unit can be seen as performing a function conducive to realising the group's common economic goal, regulators can disregard the formal separation between the units and impose liability on the parent, regardless of which members of the group were actually responsible for a particular action (Amnesty International 2014).

Most of the developers could produce no evidence of being licensed to invest in oil palm projects by the IPA, which also functions as a regulator. Only 10 of them could be clearly identified as having the financial backing of an overseas parent company with demonstrable experience in oil palm development, and four of these were RH subsidiaries. One proposal (the Lolokuru estate in West New Britain) was an initiative of New Britain Palm Oil Ltd (NBPOL), the largest palm oil company already operating in PNG, which has recently become a wholly owned subsidiary of the Malaysian multinational Sime Darby. Another of the smaller projects (the Akami estate in West New Britain) would also be dependent on NBPOL as its sole customer. Aside from RH, there were four other foreign investors with some experience of oil palm development, all of them owned by Malaysian shareholders. Some of the investors (including RH) have established markets for non-certified palm oil, and are not members of the Roundtable on Sustainable Palm Oil (RSPO), while others have stated an intention to seek certification. Investors differ in the extent of support they have received from government; RH is known to have the most government support because of the scale and diversity of its past investments in PNG.

The COI highlighted that the legal status of the SABLs is both complex and questionable. Transparent negotiations in the sublease agreements of some of the SABLs were hindered to a significant extent by landowner company directors and foreign investors undertaking negotiations in the nation's capital, Port Moresby. The COI noted with interest, for example, that before an SABL was granted directly to a foreign investor, Brilliant Investment Ltd, this company entered into an agreement with a local landowner company, Marienberg Hills Development Ltd, which invited the former to undertake logging operations within a former logging concession in the Marienberg area. The landowner company representative signed the agreement with the managing director of Brilliant Investment in Port Moresby, yet the transaction was not agreed to by the majority of the landowners, as represented by the shareholders and directors of the company, in contravention of the requirements of the Companies Act (Mirou 2013: 719). Clan signatures collected by government officials, who sometimes never went into the villages to collect the signatures, were often found to be fraudulent and not those of the legitimate clan leaders. This in turn has legitimised the destruction of existing cash crops, such as cocoa and copra, which some villages had spent decades cultivating. These crops have simply been bulldozed to make way for roads and oil palms without the owners being compensated for their losses (Lattas 2014).

Developer actions are driven by global economic factors, corporate and shareholder goals, and the local socio-legal environment. The primary economic factors include strong demand for timber and palm oil, the costs and returns of clearing the forest, establishing and operating plantations and a palm oil mill, and the cost of raising capital. All companies operating in PNG are required by law to register their proposed business activities. In the case of foreign companies entering the country with the express intention to develop large-scale agro-forestry projects, either on their own or in partnership with landowner companies, the IPA's role does not seem to extend beyond the grant of a foreign enterprise certificate (Mirou 2013: 154). It is not given any powers under legislation to specifically require evidence of capital and expertise in the particular type of business activity to be undertaken in a particular area. This has resulted in concessions over many SABLs being given to logging companies with absolutely no agricultural background in their past operations and with a total absence of agricultural specialists among their employees (Mirou 2013: 202–3). In several projects, the terms and conditions in sublease agreements had the effect of putting the SABL title in the control of the developer. In cases such as the Wewak Turubu Integrated Agriculture Project, the sublease holder was a joint venture between a landowner company and a foreign company. Such entities have frequently changed in structure and ownership, and some have acted in the developer's interests rather than that of the landowners.

The COI found that 58 out of 75 SABLs investigated were subleased to developers for 99 years and left no residual rights to the landowners (Numapo 2013: 241). Many of the sublease agreements contain provisions that the COI found to be grossly unfair to the landowners in terms of the ownership of any infrastructure development or tree crops. In the event of objections and disputes arising, legal clauses have been included in a number of sublease agreements that allow the developer to take out restraining orders in the National Court and be compensated for loss of revenue and other costs incurred (Winn 2012: 32; Mirou 2013: 693). In these instances, if the lease is terminated by the landlord (normally a landowner company), then compensation for the tenant's (developer's) loss will be borne by the landlord, including the tenant's projected profit from the harvest of oil palm for the duration of the agreement (Mirou 2013: 781).

Many of the land investigations and awareness programs necessary for securing SABLs were funded by entities outside the government, mostly by the developers (Mirou 2013: 158). The lack of government funding placed government officials in vulnerable positions to the extent that they were easily compromised when developers offered to pay for the cost of carrying out land investigation and awareness programs. The COI found that, in most instances, the reports and recommendations made by the government officials were in favour of the developers, with no proper consent obtained from the landowners, involved erroneous land boundary descriptions, and generally entailed unethical manipulation of both landowners and government officials by the developers (Mirou 2013: 181–2). The COI found instances of landowner company and land group representatives being manipulated by developers to fast-track the issuing of the SABL titles, as in the case of the Musa-Pongani project in Oro Province (Numapo 2013: 239).

Landowners and Developers

In PNG, the 'incorporation' of a customary landowner group means that it is formally recognised as a legal entity, becomes the representative of the customary owners in the formal legal system, and is thus able to enter into agreements and make decisions on behalf of the customary group (Power 2008). However, the complexities of customary land tenure often result in disputes. In new conjunctions of the legal and the social, disputing landowners and marginalised groups have made increasing use of social media, the internet and the mainstream media to pursue their different trajectories of struggle and engagement.

The most frequently expressed motivator for development among PNG landowners is the desire for income, infrastructure and services that may come with agricultural developments. Large-scale oil palm schemes can provide income streams that are sustained over fairly long periods of time, unlike short-term alternatives such as logging (Oliver 2002). Other drivers of landowner actions include existing infrastructure, public services, land use, land availability and competing claims to ownership of land. Processes that lead to loss of control over a resource are complex and multidimensional, but commonly involve power imbalance and complex politics organised around the opposition between development and conservation priorities (Nayak et al. 2014). In the determination of land use options, landowners or their representatives have acted to enter agreements with developers, change developers, form alliances, petition the RSPO, attend RSPO meetings, publicly express disapproval, lodge written complaints to government agencies, and participate in national and international forums.

In SABL areas, where the politics of landownership has generated new forms of inclusion and exclusion, some landowner representatives have been making formal alliances with international and national non-governmental organisations (NGOs) in order to raise awareness of social justice issues involving the development of customary land. These alliances attempt to redress the unequal balance of resources between landowners and developers when it comes to creating, negotiating and contesting leases. Correspondingly, other landowners who prefer the development option draw on support from developers to challenge NGO–landowner alliances. Two case studies, one in Oro Province and the other in East New Britain Province, are presented here to highlight these contrasting strategies.

Ijivitari District, Oro Province

In Chapter 6, Colin Filer has shown how the so-called 'Collingwood Bay scam' featured in the political process that led to the establishment of the COI, and then gained a new lease of life in 2012, after the COI had completed its hearings, when the Lands Department attempted to reissue a pair of SABLs that had been revoked by the National Court 10 years earlier. Since these two SABLs were not thought to be extant when the COI was established, they were not included in the list of 75 leases that were subject to the inquiry. However, the apparent breach of the moratorium imposed on the grant of 'new' leases resulted in a new round of litigation that had the backing of the newly elected Governor of Oro Province, Gary Juffa.

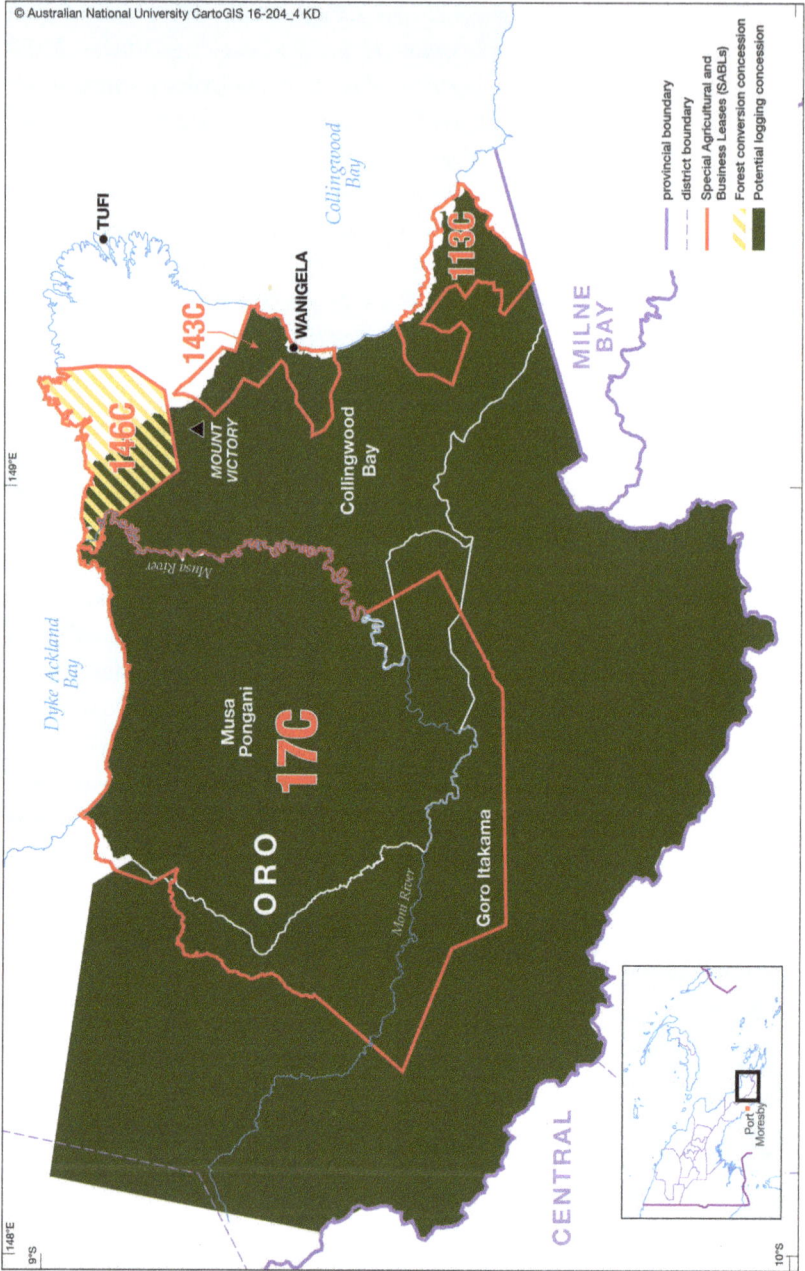

Figure 7.2 Location of SABLs and potential logging concessions in Ijivitari District, Oro Province.

Source: CartoGIS, The Australian National University.

The first of the two leases gazetted in July 2012 covered an area of 21,520 hectares (Portion 113C), and was issued to a landowner company called Sibo Management Ltd for a period of 50 years. The second lease covered an area of 16,830 hectares (Portion 143C), and was issued to another landowner company called Wanigela Agro Industrial Ltd for the same period. Both leases were associated with an oil palm project generally known as the 'Wanigela Integrated Agriculture Project' (which we shall refer to simply as the Wanigela project). These two blocks of land are part of a much larger area of forest in Ijivitari District that has long been regarded by the PNGFA as a cluster of three potential logging concessions known as Collingwood Bay, Musa Pongani and Goro Itakama (Figure 7.2). Two of the SABLs that *were* investigated by the COI (over Portions 17C and 146C) are also located within this larger area of forest. One of these (Portion 17C) was associated with the 'Musa-Pongani Integrated Agro-Forest Project' (which we shall refer to simply as the Musa-Pongani project), while the other one (Portion 146) was associated with the 'Tufi-Wanigela Tree Farming Project'. The second of these projects did not involve any proposal to develop an oil palm estate, so is not included in our list of proposed oil palm projects (Table 7.2).

The Musa-Pongani project has been just as contentious as the Wanigela project, but has not attracted the same amount of national and international publicity. It also covered a much larger area of customary land. In January 2009, an SABL over 211,600 hectares of land was issued to a landowner company called Musida Holdings Ltd (MHL) for a period of 99 years. This followed the production of an environmental impact statement by a Malaysian company called Musa Century Ltd (MCL), which envisaged the cultivation of 100,000 hectares of oil palm and 100,000 hectares of other crops (MCL 2008). However, this document shows that Musa Century Ltd had formed a partnership (in 2007) with another landowner company called Musa Valley Management Company Ltd (MVML). When the SABL was issued to MHL, MCL and MVML took legal action to have the lease revoked on the grounds that the landowners had not consented to it, and they obtained a national court order in their favour in January 2010.[4] Some observers welcomed this decision in the belief that the land would then revert to customary ownership (Pok 2010), as had been the case when the National Court revoked the SABLs over Portions 113C and 143C in 2002. But in

---

4   *Musa Valley Management Company Ltd v Kimas* [2010] PGNC 281.

this case, the Lands Department proceeded to grant a new SABL over a considerably larger area (320,060 hectares) to MVML in September 2010.[5] Meanwhile, in January 2010, a few days after the National Court had made its ruling, the National Forest Board granted an FCA over an even larger area (350,000 hectares) to MVML's 'development partner', MCL, but this licence was later cancelled in August 2011, and no logging has so far taken place.

When the COI came to unravel this case, it was found that the 'successful' landowner company, MVML, had been set up by landowners living in the national capital, Port Moresby, while the other one, MHL, had been set up by landowners living in local villages (Numapo 2013: 208). It was also noted that MVML's apparent success had been diluted by a second court order that granted MHL a right of judicial review, and that seems to explain why the FCA had been cancelled. John Numapo certainly found no evidence to indicate that local landowners had given any more consent to the second lease than they had given to the first one (ibid.: 218–9). From the transcripts of his hearings, it is also evident that MHL had its own 'development partner' (a company called Idamin), that the contest between the two landowner companies had been going on for almost 10 years, and that various politicians and public servants had taken different sides at different points in time. Nevertheless, one witness observed that the directors of the two companies were 'all relatives, very close brothers, uncles, sons, very close', while their former member of parliament compared their relationship to that of 'the Talibans and the headhunters fighting amongst themselves' (Numapo 2012: 88, 95).

A division between the urban and rural branches of a single 'landowning community' may also be part of the history of the Wanigela project, but if so, it has taken a different form because some members of this community have been resolute in their opposition to any form of agro-forestry, and not simply divided in their allegiance to different 'development partners'.

After the Lands Department had granted the SABLs over Portions 113C and 143C in July 2012, a landowner representative claimed that the original leases over these two portions had been granted in January 1998 (Pok 2012). However, the *National Gazette* contains no record of the leases being granted around that time, and other sources suggest that they

---

5   This is the area shown as Portion 17C in Figure 7.2: it includes nearly all of the Musa Pongani forest area and part of the Goro Itakama forest area as well.

may have been granted in 1995, before the Land Act was amended in such a way as to require their gazettal (Barker 2009). The earlier date would certainly seem to be consistent with the fact that the former premier of Oro Province was already supporting a Filipino company's proposal for an agro-forestry project in Collingwood Bay in 1996, and this proposal had already met with opposition from local and international supporters of a forest conservation project in the same area (Filer 1998: 195, 255). Since then, Collingwood Bay has almost attained the status of a 'sacred site' for members of PNG's conservation policy community (Barker 2004), especially members of the 'anti-dependency group' (see Chapter 6, this volume). In Oro Province, this group is primarily represented by the Oro Community Environmental Action Network (OCEAN), and the Collingwood Bay Conservation and Development Authority (CBCDA), but also has strong ties to the Centre for Environmental Law and Community Rights.

Towards the end of 2009, local members of this section of the land grab policy network got wind of the landing of a barge full of logging equipment on the shoreline of Portion 113, and its transportation inland to the adjacent Portion 5.[6] Shortly afterwards, Adelbert Gangai from OCEAN held a 'community consensus meeting' that identified Tony Wong and Vincent Lee as the individuals responsible for this incursion (Gangai 2010). This was a source of some confusion, since these two men were operating out of Tufi, and the companies they represented (Victory Plantation Ltd and Matufi Ltd) were mainly interested in logging the leases associated with the Tufi-Wanigela Tree Farming Project. It was a third company, Ang Agro Forest Management Ltd (AAFML) that was seeking to obtain an FCA over Portions 113C and 143C, and opponents of this Wanigela project thought that Tony Wong and had acquired an interest in it through his relationship with the directors of Keroro Development Corporation Ltd (KDCL), the landowner company to whom the original SABLs had been granted in 1998 or 1995 (Gangai 2010; Nilles 2010). They also believed that Tony Wong was operating as a 'front man' for Rimbunan Hijau (Nilles 2010), as was Eii Sing Hii, who held all the shares in AAFML (OCEAN and CBCDA 2013).[7]

---

6   Portion 5 covers an area of just under 6,000 hectares that was alienated during the colonial period, and was at that time still owned by the government.

7   In 2010, the company records showed that AAFML had been incorporated in 2006, and that Eii Sing Hii held the shares in trust for unspecified financial interests.

In November 2009, the Oro Provincial Forest Management Committee approved the grant of an FCA to AAFML, and this is presumably what triggered the appearance of the logging equipment. The National Forest Board accepted the provincial recommendation in January 2010, but its decision was based on incorrect advice to the effect that KDCL still held the land titles. During the course of that year, the loggers and conservationists took turns at engaging different state actors (including members of the police force) in support of their endeavours (Nilles 2010; Pangkatana 2010). As a result of the attendant publicity, the managing director of the PNGFA announced that no logging operation would be approved until the land tenure issue had been resolved (Anon. 2010). The FCA was formally cancelled by the National Forest Board in August 2011, on the same day that it cancelled the FCA granted to the Musa-Pongani project. In the meantime, in April 2011, AAFML had secured an agricultural lease over Portion 5, but the value of this acquisition was now in doubt.

Gary Juffa was one of the state actors who had supported the conservationists in his capacity as the head of PNG's Internal Revenue Commission. The legal action he supported in his new capacity as Governor of Oro Province was initiated by Lester Seri and six other landowners in November 2012. The defendants in the case were officials of the Lands Department, AAFML and the two landowner companies to whom the SABLs had been granted in July that year. Shortly before the case was launched, one of PNG's national newspapers announced that AAFML's Malaysian parent company, Collingwood Plantations, had been taken over by a much bigger Malaysian company, Kuala Lumpur Kepong Bhd (KLK).[8] A spokesman for KLK was quoted as saying that the takeover 'presents an opportunity for KLK to develop new oil palm plantations in PNG in view of the increasing difficulty and expense to source suitable land in Malaysia and/or Indonesia'. The newspaper story concluded with the statement that AAFML:

> has a 99-year lease on more than 5,992ha in the town [sic] in Northern [Oro], expiring in April 2110; a 49-year sublease on more than [21,520ha] of land in Northern, expiring in August 2061 and a 49-year sublease on more than 16,830ha of land in Northern, expiring in August 2061 (Anon. 2012a).

8   The same article had been published in an English-language Malaysian newspaper on the previous day.

KLK is a public company listed on the Malaysian stock exchange, and had a market capitalisation of approximately RM24 billion in 2013. The company's annual report for 2013 showed that it had paid almost RM11 million for its controlling interest in the Collingwood Bay leases (KLK 2013a: 123). By the time the acquisition was completed in December 2012, the company's managers might have begun to wonder whether they had got value for their money, since they would now have been aware of the court case in which their new subsidiary was one of the defendants. This problem was compounded by the fact that KLK, unlike most of the developers of agro-forestry projects in PNG, is a member of the RSPO, and was therefore obliged to show that it had obtained the free, prior and informed consent of the local landowners to its development proposal.

This created an opportunity for the dissident landowners to lodge a complaint with the RSPO Secretariat in April 2013, in which they stated that 'the Traditional paramount chiefs of the 9 tribes of Collingwood Bay representing 326 clans have irrevocably stated their disapproval … in the strongest possible terms of any plans to introduce the oil palm industry in the Collingwood Bay area', and that KLK personnel had recently sought to overcome this opposition by persuading local villagers to sign a new agreement in exchange for '100 kina, some rice and canned fish' (OCEAN and CBCDA 2013). The dissidents were then able to secure the backing of the Rainforest Action Network (RAN), an NGO with a particular interest in demonstrating the absence of corporate compliance with RSPO standards. With their support, Lester Seri and Adelbert Gangai attended the RSPO's annual meeting in Sumatra in November that year to reiterate their complaint, while Laurel Sutherlin from RAN observed that KLK's project proposal was 'the ugly face of Conflict Palm Oil and … would create an entirely predictable and preventable disaster for the people and wildlife of Papua New Guinea' (Sutherlin 2013).

When the RSPO's Complaints Panel found that there was merit in the complaint, KLK responded with a claim that they had obtained the written consent of all local clan leaders to their project proposal, and this evidence was being presented in the court case over the SABLs. They also denied any link to Tony Wong and Vincent Lee (KLK 2013b). Shortly afterwards, in January 2014, the directors of Sibo Management Ltd, the landowner company that had been granted the new SABL over Portion 113C, published an advertorial claiming that all the genuine landowners were fully in support of the Wanigela project, and those opposing it, such as Lester Seri and Adelbert Gangai, as well as Governor

Gary Juffa, should keep their mouths shut unless they could provide genuine development alternatives (SML 2014). However, this had no material effect on the progress and outcome of the court case.

After the National Court had once again revoked the two SABLs in May 2014, Lester Seri was quoted as saying that:

> The people of Collingwood Bay have spoken clearly through the voices of our chiefs that we are against large scale palm oil development on our lands…. The chiefs of our nine tribes have spoken. Tens of thousands of our international allies have spoken. The Roundtable on Sustainable Palm Oil (RSPO) has spoken. And now the National Court of PNG has agreed: these permits are illegitimate. KLK must leave Collingwood Bay immediately and not return (RAN 2014).

KLK did not leave immediately, since the court decision did not affect its right to occupy the lease over Portion 5, where its base camp was located. However, the cancellation of the other leases effectively meant that the Wanigela project would not be viable unless some other way could be found to access the adjoining areas of customary land in the face of opposition from a well organised group of opponents operating at local, national and global scales.[9] In March 2016, the company announced that it had no personnel in the area, and would remove the equipment still stored on Portion 5 by the end of the year if the 'citizens of the various tribes' with an interest in Portions 113C and 143C did not give free, prior and informed consent to the development of the project (KLK 2016).

Pomio District, East New Britain Province

So long as Gary Juffa remains as Governor of Oro Province, it could be argued that his province and East New Britain Province are at opposite ends of the spectrum of political and public opinion that surrounds the costs and benefits of agro-forestry projects in PNG. With very few exceptions, all of East New Britain's members of parliament, including the governor, have consistently supported the development of new oil palm schemes, especially in the more remote parts of the province. That is partly because they have espoused a conception of 'public–private partnerships' in which the developers of these schemes will fund a major upgrade of

---

9   Industry sources estimate that the capital cost of an entirely new oil palm scheme in PNG would be close to US$100 million, and the investment would only make sense if the investor had guaranteed access to 30,000 hectares of land (Ian Orrell, personal communication, February 2011).

the provincial road network, and partly because oil palm has been seen as suitable substitute for cocoa, formerly the main export crop, which has recently been ravaged by disease (Curry et al. 2011).

The Ili-Wawas Integrated Agriculture Project in the eastern part of Pomio District was the first of this new generation of oil palm schemes in East New Britain, and was heavily promoted by former Member of Parliament Paul Tiensten. It was not investigated by the COI because the SABL that covers the nucleus estate was issued to an ILG rather than a landowner company. Before this lease was issued in November 2008, the developer (Tzen Niugini) had already been logging parts of the project area under 'timber authorities' granted before the Forestry Act was amended in 2007, and continued its logging operations under three FCAs granted in March 2007. These licences covered an area of approximately 50,000 hectares, about half of which was earmarked for the cultivation of oil palm. Tzen Niugini has exported about 500,000 cubic metres of logs from the project area since 2005. The oil palm mill was opened with great ceremony by PNG's Prime Minister and Deputy Prime Minister (the former Provincial Governor) in October 2014.[10]

The Mukus-Melkoi Large Scale Integrated Agriculture Project, on the other hand, is an example of a project that never got off the ground, or to be more precise, has not (so far) gone beyond the paper planning stage. In August 2008, an SABL over 68,300 hectares was issued to a landowner company called Rera Holdings Ltd (RHL) for a period of 99 years. This is the area shown as Portion 2C in Figure 7.3. Company records show that RHL was incorporated in September 2006, and would count as an 'umbrella company', because its shareholders were three other landowner companies.[11] As soon as it had been incorporated, the directors had written a letter of invitation to the general manager of a company called Double Dynasty (or DD) Lumber Ltd (DDLL), and Paul Tiensten had written to East New Britain's Provincial Administrator to express his own support for the project (DDLL 2010; Jerewai 2012). DDLL is a subsidiary of Brilliant Investment Ltd, which was able to secure an SABL (in 2007) and an FCA (in 2009) for the Angoram (Marienberg) Integrated Agriculture Project in East Sepik Province (see Table 7.3), and then proceeded to harvest and export about 340,000 cubic metres of logs from that area between 2010

---

10 Paul Tiensten could not attend the ceremony because he had been convicted of corruption and sent to prison.
11 The three shareholding companies were deregistered in 2009.

and 2013. However, that project did not include any serious plan for the development of an oil palm estate, and DDLL has not even got as far as logging the Mukus-Melkoi project area. It did manage to secure an FCA over the project area in October 2010, on the basis of a proposal to plant 30,000 hectares of oil palm, but the forester who prepared this proposal told the COI that he had no agricultural qualifications and had not even visited the project area (Jerewai 2012: 134, 141). In February 2011, the managing director of the PNGFA advised the company that its forest clearance plans had not been approved (Numapo 2011: 7), and there is no evidence to indicate that new plans have since been submitted.

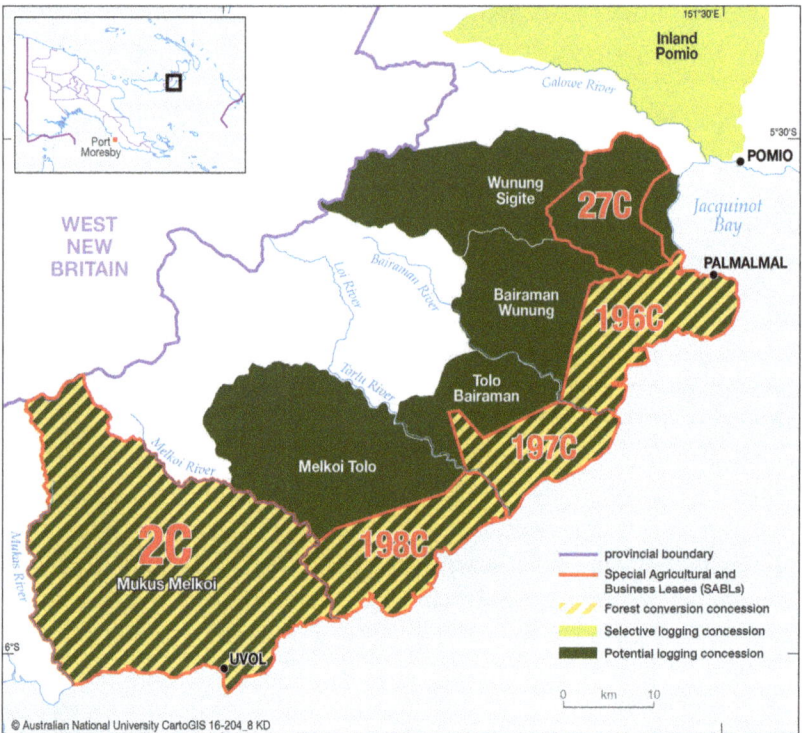

Figure 7.3 Location of SABLs and potential logging concessions in part of Pomio District, East New Britain Province.

Source: CartoGIS, The Australian National University.

The Sigite-Mukus Integrated Rural Development Project is a far more serious venture—more like the Ili-Wawas project. In July 2008, three 99-year SABLs over a combined total of 42,400 hectares of land were simultaneously issued to three landowner companies: Pomata Investment

Ltd (15,000 hectares), Ralopal Investment Ltd (11,300 hectares), and Nakiura Investment Ltd (16,100 hectares). These are the areas shown in Figure 7.3 as Portions 196C, 197C and 198C. In December 2009, a fourth 99-year SABL over 13,000 hectares of land was issued to another landowner company called Unung Sigite Ltd. This is the area shown as Portion 27C. These four landowner companies, along with two other landowner companies called Ura-Mosi Ltd and Mosi-Ngelu Ltd, are shareholders in an umbrella company called Memalo Holdings Ltd (another MHL), which was incorporated in 2004.

Immediately before this company was incorporated, its directors signed a project agreement with Paul Tiensten and a company called Sumas Timber & Development International Ltd (STDIL), in which STDIL agreed to lend K300,000 to MHL and Paul Tiensten so that they could secure the cooperation of the local landowners and later arrange for the loan to be repaid from logging revenues. This agreement was attached to an environmental inception report that MHL and STDIL submitted to the Department of Environment and Conservation in July 2006 (MHL and STDIL 2006). This report indicated that the bulk of the local revenues secured from the logging operation would then be used to fund the construction of a road from the Sigite Gorge to the Melkoi River, as well as a nucleus oil palm estate and an associated corridor of smallholder oil palm blocks between 5 and 10 kilometres inland of the shoreline. The proposed road would have the effect of connecting most of the coastal villages in this coastal corridor with the Pomio district headquarters at Palmalmal, on the shores of Jacquinot Bay, and also with the headquarters of the Melkoi local-level government area at Uvol (Figure 7.3).

By April 2008, MHL had abandoned its former deal with STDIL and had signed a new development agreement with Rimbunan Hijau. At the ceremony held to commemorate this event, a senior official from the Lands Department told the assembled landowner company directors that the lease-leaseback arrangement 'would enable the landowners to have more control over their land, unlike before', while the chairman of MHL, John Parulria, reportedly 'urged the civil society to work hand in hand with the lands, forestry and public services sectors to get the projects going' (Anon. 2008). In October that year, one of RH's subsidiary companies, Gilford Ltd, submitted its own development plan to the relevant government authorities (GL and MHL 2008). This document contains copies of sublease agreements covering Portions 196C, 197C and 198C, over which the SABLs had been granted in July that year.

The East New Britain Provincial Forest Management Committee recommended the grant of an FCA over these three blocks of land in September 2010, and the National Forest Board implemented the recommendation one month later. Shortly afterwards, the vice chairman of MHL, Joe Tali, was reported as saying that 'people were not consulted during the time of the sublease agreement on the selection criteria of the project developer, especially on oil palm', and that 'some non-governmental organisations and stakeholders had caused confusion and in-fighting among landowner companies on the fair distribution of benefits' (Vuvu 2010). This was an allusion to the fact that members of the 'anti-dependency group' were already helping community groups in two of the four SABL areas to mount a legal challenge to the leasing arrangements (Peter Dam, personal communication, February 2011).

Conflict among the landowners became a national issue in April 2011, after Gilford was reported to have moved its logging equipment into the area, and dissident landowners complained of police harassment when they tried to organise a protest (Anon. 2011a). This prompted Paul Tiensten to announce that he would 'not allow any foreign elements to sabotage my projects', while the Provincial Governor, Leo Dion, 'called on all development partners in East New Britain to stand united for the progressive development of the province' (Nicholas 2011). It is not clear whether news of this particular conflict had any direct influence on the national government's decision to establish the COI, but Greenpeace made sure that the story made much bigger headlines when Commissioner Jerewai arrived in the province to conduct his hearings in November that year (see Chapter 6, this volume).

Greenpeace was not the only 'foreign element' that had an interest in opposing the Sigite-Mukus project. In 1995, around the same time that Collingwood Bay became a place of special interest to conservationists, the European Union began to fund the Islands Region Environment and Community Development Programme in West New Britain Province. This was designed to support small-scale community-based 'eco-forestry projects' as alternatives to large-scale selective logging projects (Bird et al. 2007). This program soon extended its reach to East New Britain, and three such projects were established in the three local government wards located along the coastal margin of what is now Portion 197C— Bairaman, Lau and Mauna (Scheyvens 2009). These three projects were still being supported by an NGO called the Forest Management and Product Certification Service (commonly known as ForCert), which is closely related to PNG's Eco-Forestry Forum, which is the body that nominates an NGO representative to the National Forest Board. PNG's eco-forestry projects have been subsidised by a number of foreign organisations (including Greenpeace) over the past two decades.

It is not surprising that the three coastal wards with eco-forestry projects turned out to be home to some of the landowners most strongly opposed to the agro-forestry project, since the clearance of their native forest would destroy their business model (Paniu 2011). Yet these were only three out of a total of 34 wards in the West Pomio/Mamusi local-level government (LLG) area, which is bounded by the Wunung River in the north and the Melkoi River in the south (Figure 7.3). There were other dissidents to be found in the coastal villages located in Portion 196C, but the dissidents were still greatly outnumbered by supporters of the agro-forestry project who lived beyond the zone covered by the FCA. The political geography of the project area was further complicated by a cultural division between speakers of the Mengen language, who occupy these coastal villages and others around the shores of Jacquinot Bay, and speakers of the Mamusi language, who occupy the coastal villages located in Portion 198C and nearly all of the hinterland villages as well.[12] The available evidence suggests that the hinterland people have generally supported the agro-forestry project, not only because it promised to provide them with better road access to the outside world, but also because it would not destroy their existing land-based livelihoods (Pangkatana 2011; Tiden 2011). The same could even be said of John Parulrea, the chairman of their umbrella company, whose own (Mengen-speaking) village is located at the northern tip of Portion 196C. Aside from his role as chairman of MHL, he is also the chairman of Unung Sigite Ltd, the holder of the SABL over Portion 27C, which is located in the Central/Inland Pomio LLG area. Whether or not the forest in this block of land is eventually cleared for oil palm cultivation, it does not include the adjacent coastal zone from which local villagers derive most of their subsistence (Figure 7.3).

The 2008 development plan (GL and MHL 2008) included a map showing the division of a much larger area, extending inland to the border with West New Britain Province, between six 'consolidated land blocks'. These were the six blocks supposedly represented by the six landowner companies covered by John Parulrea's umbrella company. This

---

12 There are two wards in the far north of the LLG area, close to the provincial boundary, where another language (Wasi) is spoken.

map represents a peculiar reconfiguration of this part of Pomio District, which had the effect of eliding the political boundary between two LLG areas at the same time that it distorted the biophysical boundaries between potential logging concessions that had been inscribed in the National Forest Plan.[13] It is not clear who was responsible for this act of 're-territorialisation', but it seems to have ensured that the coastal Mengen-speaking villagers would be a minority of the landowners represented by 'their' three landowner companies.

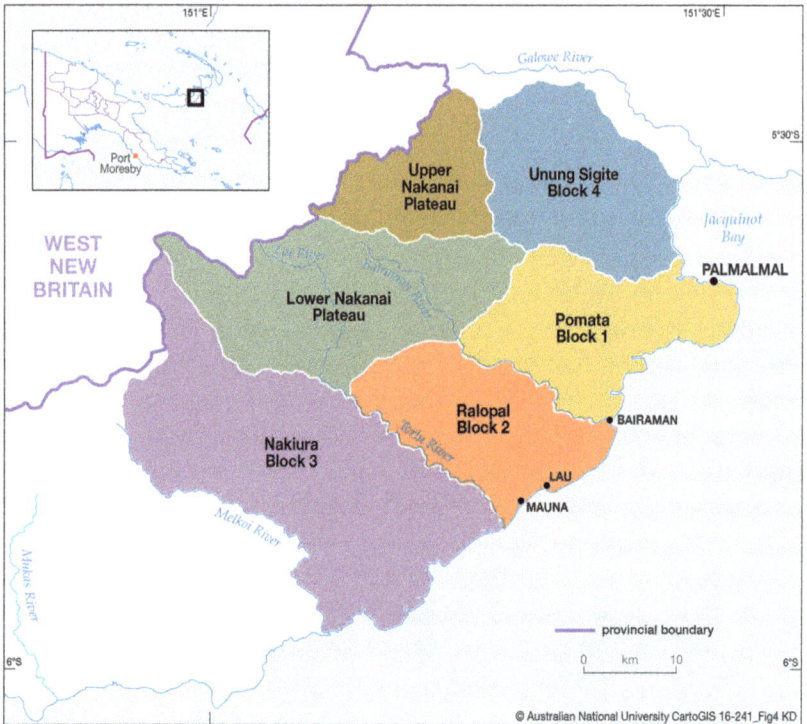

Figure 7.4 Division of the Sigite-Mukus project area into six blocks, with the location of Bairaman, Lau and Mauna council wards in Block 2.
Source: CartoGIS, The Australian National University.

Commissioner Jerewai took no interest in these spatial fault lines. He noted that he could not find any sign of opposition to the project when he visited the area at the end of October 2011, but was interested to discover that the first three witnesses to testify at the first day of hearings

---

13   In 1995, the National Forest Service had recognised the Upper and Lower Nakanai Plateau areas as potential logging concessions, but not with the same boundaries as those shown in Figure 7.4.

in Kokopo were all opposed to it (Jerewai 2011a). He then spent two days trying to persuade the landowner company chairmen that their sublease agreements with Gilford were thoroughly unfair and unreasonable (Jerewai 2011b, 2011c). At one point, he chided the chairman of Nakiura Investment Ltd:

> It is like you have been placed in a boxing ring, pushed into one corner and you cannot get out of it. The only way is to go down—it is a knock-out (Jerewai 2011b: 102).

Jerewai's other main concern was to figure out why men had occupied all the positions of authority from which the leasing arrangements had been negotiated, when the local custom of matrilineal inheritance surely meant that women were the true landowners (Jerewai 2011d, 2011e). One of the male witnesses explained this apparent paradox as follows:

> Yes, it is true that the women are—through women, land is passed on. But in the Pomio custom, man is in charge of partaking in discussions about land matters, dealing with land boundaries, and dealing with disputes within the clan or among clans, and dealing with the houseboy where important issues about the lives of Pomio people are discussed by men … (Jerewai 2011e: 5).

In May 2012, Greenpeace produced a press release declaring that the Supreme Court had upheld an appeal by MHL against previous court decisions that would have allowed for judicial review of the leasing arrangements for the Sigite-Mukus project (Greenpeace 2012). We have not been able to discover the trail of court proceedings, which had apparently begun when Gilford landed its logging equipment in April 2011, and there is some confusion about which court made what orders at what point in time. In any case, the dissident landowners and their allies now switched the main focus of their campaign from the problem of consent, as investigated by the COI, to the problem of violence, as manifested in a sequence of police raids that also began when the logging equipment was first landed in the area (Anon. 2011a; Makis 2011; Tiden 2012a, 2012b). In October 2012, a 'fact-finding mission' arrived in the area to investigate previous allegations of police brutality against the residents of five villages—including Bairaman, Lau and Mauna—in light of an announcement previously made by the police commissioner that he had ordered 'the withdrawal of all police personnel from logging camps following allegation of abuse of power against them' (Anon. 2011b).

This expedition seems to have been organised by the Eco-Forestry Forum, but supposedly included representatives from a number of government agencies, including the police force itself. The resulting report documented several instances of police brutality, some of which had not been reported in the national newspapers, and concluded that the officers responsible had been 'used by Gilford Ltd for their purposes which is to thwart any attempt by the local people to stop the logging operation' (IFFM 2013: 19). However, it also attached a letter in which the police sergeant who accompanied the team acknowledged that the police were accommodated at the logging camp, but 'were there on the request of the landowner company through its chairman to deal with the law and order issues which is [sic] on the rise since the company moved into the area' (ibid.: 24). His argument echoed the line consistently taken in the pages of *The National* newspaper, which happens to be owned by RH, in response to stories published by its opposite number, the *Post-Courier* (Anon. 2011c, 2011d, 2011e, 2012b). As if to anticipate the findings of the 'fact-finding mission', *The National* also published an article reporting that 10 government officials had conducted their own fact-finding mission in September 2012, from which they had concluded that there was no truth to claims being made by opponents of the project that local people had been 'affected by an increase of sexual transmitted diseases, prostitution, pornography, domestic violence in the logging camps and nurseries, gambling, stealing of garden food, academic level of schools declining in the project area, underage employment and chemical contamination' (Apina 2012).

The next round in the contest took place towards the end of 2013, after the publication of the two final reports of the COI, when the dissidents reportedly sent a petition to the Prime Minister demanding the revocation of the SABLs granted over Portions 196C, 197C and 198C (Kolma 2013). When this had no effect, the dissidents took another tack. In August 2014, Bairaman, Lau and Mauna ward councillors, along with the representatives of 15 local land groups, wrote to the chairman of the National Forest Board, requesting that Gilford's FCA should not be renewed when it expired in October 2014. The key point in their argument was that these land groups had been incorporated in 2003, when the eco-forestry projects were initiated, but a different set of land groups had been fraudulently incorporated in 2006 as part of the political process that led to the grant of the SABL over Portion 197C (Samo et al. 2014).

Figure 7.5 Forest cleared for cultivation of oil palm in Portion 196C, February 2015.

Source: Photograph by Simon Foale.

Their request was backed by several local NGOs, and also by the London-based Global Witness, which had come to occupy the space previously occupied by Greenpeace in the land grab policy network (see Chapter 8, this volume). Although the chairman was at that time the board member who had been nominated by the Eco-Forestry Forum, and seems to have sympathised with the request, the National Forest Board accepted the recommendation of East New Britain's Provincial Forest Management Committee and renewed the FCA for a further six years. The dissident landowners then went back to court to obtain another injunction that apparently failed to halt the process of forest clearance (PNGexposed 2014), while Global Witness published a report that showed the extent of the clearance that had already taken place in Portions 196C and 198C (Global Witness 2014). RH responded in the same way that it had previously responded to attacks by members of the anti-dependency group: by hiring the Australian-based consulting firm ITS Global to document the social and economic benefits of the project and refute all claims previously made about its negative social and environmental impact (ITS Global 2014).[14] In 2014, the company managed to export almost 340,000 cubic metres of logs from the project area—100,000 more than it had exported in the previous year.

By the end of 2014, Portion 197C had barely been logged at all, and the court injunction may have served to keep the chainsaws at bay. However, we understand that the injunction was lifted in July 2015, and satellite imagery confirms that forest clearance is now proceeding at a rate equivalent to that seen in the other two portions.

Conclusion

Palm oil companies have been looking to other countries, including PNG, as land availability in the largest producing countries, Malaysia and Indonesia, has been reduced. However, some of the larger palm oil companies have delayed investment in PNG because of problems with the legitimacy (and legal contestability) of the land titles being offered to them (Ian Orrell, personal communication, February 2013). SABLS have failed to offer security of land tenure, largely because relationships between players are dynamic, with changes in bargaining power being fuelled by a discourse that raises rural people's hopes and expectations, driven by actors who benefit from short-term deals.

Some simple changes in negotiation procedures might have a large impact on landowner equity. For example, lease and sublease agreements should be signed in the district where the land is located, or even within the boundaries of the lease area itself, not in Port Moresby or provincial capitals. That might make landowner companies more accountable to the landowners. The land investigation process should also be improved, as Commissioner Numapo pointed out: 'Landowners must be free to attach qualification or conditions to their consent if they wish because merely offering signatures may not reflect their real (contextual or relative) position' (Numapo 2013: 66). The COI recommended a review of the current lease-leaseback provisions under the Land Act, with a 50-year cap on the lease period. The COI also recommended the promulgation of a regulation that clearly sets out the 'processes and procedures' relating to the SABL application, registration, processing, approval and issuance. This would mean that non-compliance with prescribed procedures and

---

14 Their report also purported to show that the local eco-forestry projects produced no benefits at all.

processes (including those related to demonstration of developer capacity) would render the whole SABL null and void (Numapo 2013: 263–4). Transparency in the structure of sublease agreements is also critical to the avoidance of fraud or injustice.

Developers and their relationships with landowners are likely to evolve further in the future. Of the land controlled by companies that have recently acquired an interest in developing plantations, most is under serious legal dispute, which constitutes an obstacle to development, but some of the larger companies could feasibly weather the risks and costs of such problems and eventually develop plantations and mills, perhaps taking over the leases of companies that have failed or have completed logging activities. To manage risks over customary land use for oil palm development, it may be increasingly important for landowners to draw upon the Fairness of Transactions Act, which allows for the re-opening and review of any transaction irrespective of fault and validity, enforceability or effect, of any agreement. This law is intended to ensure the fair distribution and adjustment of rights, benefits, duties, advantages and disadvantages arising out of a transaction, but has hardly ever been applied. It is critically important to address the breakdown and subversion of processes intended for genuine and equitable agro-forestry ventures in PNG, because failed or stalled developments mean that landowners and companies both forego substantial sustained income if agricultural developments do not eventuate. Moreover, if poverty alleviation is a key goal of the mobilisation of customary land for palm oil production, it is important to ensure that the process of establishing and negotiating a lease or sublease for development purposes does not accelerate impoverishment.

Communities across Melanesia have sought to pursue their own 'roads to development' (Curry 2003). Our research has shown how land groups and landowner companies sometimes deal with multiple developers as they attempt to shape the political landscape of large-scale resource development. At the same time, dissenting landowner groups are mobilising the support of international NGOs in the hope of restorative justice. As we have highlighted, one of the key strategies adopted in PNG has been the establishment of linkages between landowners and international NGOs to address the social and political dimensions of palm oil production. To address the power imbalances between developers, state actors and customary landowner groups, the strengthening of long-term relationships built on trust, respect and honesty, as well as transparent communication and information, will be critical. In PNG, increased interaction with accelerated technological developments has resulted in an upsurge in the use of social media and internet forums by PNG landowners, providing a framework for communication and partnership. Although these socio-technical forms of engagement are currently largely restricted to protesting against social injustice in resource projects, the development of resilient network structures may also help marginalised people to pursue other goals. However, unless the PNG government keeps its promise to support positive reform, the legitimacy and equity of foreign investment in new oil palm schemes remains highly questionable.

References

Allen, B., 2009. 'Agricultural Development, Policies and Governance.' In R.M. Bourke and T. Harwood (eds), *Food and Agriculture in Papua New Guinea*. Canberra: ANU E Press.

Amnesty International, 2014. *Injustice Incorporated: Corporate Abuses and the Human Right to Remedy*. London: Amnesty International.

Anderson, T., 2010. 'Land Registration, Land Markets and Livelihoods in Papua New Guinea.' In T. Anderson and G. Lee (eds), *In Defence of Melanesian Customary Land*. Sydney: Aid/Watch.

Anderson, T. and G. Lee, 2010. 'Introduction: Understanding Melanesian Customary Land.' In T. Anderson and G. Lee (eds), *In Defence of Melanesian Customary Land*. Sydney: Aid/Watch.

Anon., 2008. 'Pact Signed to Develop Pomio District.' *Post-Courier*, 15 April.

——, 2010. 'Land Status Halts Oro Agri Projects.' *Post-Courier*, 11 November.

——, 2011a. 'Loggers Enter Land Without Notice.' *Post-Courier*, 8 April.

——, 2011b. 'Top Cop Removes Officers from Logging Camps.' *The National*, 8 December.

——, 2011c. 'Firm Denies Police Went to Arrest Locals.' *The National*, 12 April.

——, 2011d. 'Administrator Denies Brutality.' *The National*, 13 October.

——, 2011e. 'NGOs Told Not to Halt Project.' *The National,* 13 October.

——, 2012a. 'Malaysian Firm Eyes Oil Palm Plantations.' *The National,* 5 October.

——, 2012b. 'Police: Pomio Brutality Claims False and Malicious.' *The National,* 30 April.

Anseeuw, W., M. Boche, T. Breu, M. Giger, J. Lay, P. Messerli and K. Nolte, 2012. 'Transnational Land Deals for Agriculture in the Global South: Analytical Report Based on the Land Matrix Database.' Bern: International Land Coalition.

Apina, A., 2012. 'Pomio Officials Deny Any Social Disorder at Oil Palm Project.' *The National,* 8 October.

Barker, J., 2004. 'Between Heaven and Earth: Missionaries, Environmentalists and the Maisin.' In V. Lockwood (ed.), *Globalization and Culture Change in the Pacific Islands.* Upper Saddle River (NJ): Pearson Prentice Hall.

Barker, P., 2009. 'Land Grab—A Sinister Cycle.' *Post-Courier,* 11 May.

Bird, N., A. Wells, F. van Helden and R. Turia, 2007. 'Issues and Opportunities for the Forest Sector in Papua New Guinea.' London: Overseas Development Institute (Papua New Guinea Forest Studies 3).

Cotula, L., 2013. 'Reshaping Contracts for Quality Natural Resource Investments.' London: International Institute for Environment and Development.

Cotula L., S. Vermeulen, P. Mathieu and C. Toulmin, 2011. 'Agricultural Investment and International Land Deals: Evidence from a Multi-Country Study in Africa.' *Food Security* 3: S99–S113. doi.org/10.1007/s12571-010-0096-x.

Cramb, R. and G.N. Curry, 2012. 'Oil Palm and Rural Livelihoods in the Asia-Pacific Region: An Overview.' *Asia Pacific Viewpoint* 53: 223–239. doi.org/10.1111/j.1467-8373.2012.01495.x.

Curry, G.N., 2003. 'Moving Beyond Postdevelopment: Facilitating Indigenous Alternatives for "Development".' *Economic Geography* 79: 405–442. doi.org/10.1111/j.1944-8287.2003.tb00221.x.

Curry, G., J. Lummami and E. Omuru, 2011. 'Socioeconomic Impact Assessment of Cocoa Pod Borer in East New Britain Province, Papua New Guinea.' Canberra: Australian Centre for International Agricultural Research.

DDLL (Double Dynasty Lumber Ltd), 2010. 'Environmental Permit Application to Discharge Waste: Mukas-Melkoi Large Scale Integrated Agriculture Project.' Unpublished report to PNG Department of Environment and Conservation.

Deininger, K. and D. Byerlee, 2011. *Rising Global Interest in Farmland: Can It Yield Sustainable and Equitable Benefits?* Washington (DC): World Bank. doi.org/10.1596/978-0-8213-8591-3.

Feintrenie, L., 2014. 'Agro-Industrial Plantations in Central Africa: Risks and Opportunities.' *Biodiversity and Conservation* 23: 1577–1589. doi.org/10.1007/s10531-014-0687-5.

Filer, C., 2011. 'New Land Grab in Papua New Guinea.' *Pacific Studies* 34: 269–294.

——, 2012a. 'Why Green Grabs Don't Work in Papua New Guinea.' *Journal of Peasant Studies* 39: 599–617. doi.org/10.1080/03066150.2012.665891.

——, 2012b. 'The Commission of Inquiry into Special Agricultural and Business Leases in Papua New Guinea: Fresh Details for the Portrait of a Process of Expropriation.' Paper presented at second international workshop on 'Global Land Grabbing', Cornell University, 17–19 October.

——, 2013. 'Asian Investment in the Rural Industries of Papua New Guinea: What's New and What's Not?' *Pacific Affairs* 86: 305–326. doi.org/10.5509/2013862305.

Filer, C. with N. Sekhran, 1998. *Loggers, Donors and Resource Owners*. London: International Institute for Environment and Development in association with the National Research Institute (Policy That Works for Forests and People, Papua New Guinea Country Study).

Gangai, A., 2010. 'Collingwood Bay Community Consensus: We Will Be the Masters of Our Own Destiny.' Popondetta: Oro Community Environmental Action Network.

GL (Gilford Ltd) and MHL (Memalo Holdings Ltd), 2008. 'A Development Plan for the Establishment of Oil Palm and Forest Plantations in the Sigite-Mukus Consolidated Land Area.' Unpublished report to PNG Department of Agriculture and Livestock.

Global Witness, 2014. 'The People and Forests of Papua New Guinea under Threat: The Government's Failed Response to the Largest Land Grab in Modern History.' London: Global Witness.

GoPNG (Government of PNG), 2007. *National Agriculture Development Plan 2007–2016* (2 volumes). Port Moresby: Ministry of Agriculture and Livestock.

Greenpeace, 2012. 'Landowners Committed to Fighting Pomio SABLs Despite Court Ruling.' Media release, 2 May.

IFFM (Independent Fact Finding Mission), 2013. 'Investigation of Police Brutality—West Pomio, ENBP.' Viewed 18 October 2016 at: pngexposed.files.wordpress.com/2014/11/investigation-of-police-brutality-west-pomio.pdf.

ITS Global, November 2014. 'Bearing False Witness: A Critique of Global Witness' Anti-Development Activity in East New Britain.' Unpublished report to Rimbunan Hijau (PNG) Ltd.

Jerewai, A., 2011a. Transcript of SABL Commission of Inquiry hearing, Kokopo, 2 November.

——, 2011b. Transcript of SABL Commission of Inquiry hearing, Kokopo, 3 November.

——, 2011c. Transcript of SABL Commission of Inquiry hearing, Kokopo, 4 November.

——, 2011d. Transcript of SABL Commission of Inquiry hearing, Kokopo, 9 November.

——, 2011e. Transcript of SABL Commission of Inquiry hearing, Kokopo, 11 November.

——, 2012. Transcript of SABL Commission of Inquiry hearing, Kimbe, 10 February.

KLK (Kuala Lumpur Kepong Bhd), 2013a. *Annual Report 2013*. Kuala Lumpur: KLK.

——, 2013b. 'Replies to Complaints Made by the Oro Community Environmental Action Network ("OCEAN") and Collingwood Bay Conservation and Development Association ("CCADA") in Respect of KLK's Operations in Papua New Guinea ("PNG").' Letter to RSPO Secretariat, 10 December.

——, 2016. 'KLK Commits to Address Grievances Raised by Rainforest Action Network ("RAN").' Viewed 18 October 2016 at: www.klk. com.my/wp-content/uploads/2016/03/ResponsetoRAN.pdf.

Koczberski, G., G.N. Curry, D. Rogers, E. Germis and M. Koi, 2013. 'Developing Land-Use Agreements in Commodity Cash Crop Production that Meet the Needs of Landowners and Smallholders.' In G. Hickey (ed.), *Socioeconomic Agricultural Research in Papua New Guinea*. Canberra: Australian Council for International Agricultural Research (Proceedings 141).

Kolma, F., 2013. 'West Pomio Landowners Fed Up.' *Post-Courier*, 20 December.

Lattas, A., 2014. 'Logging in Pomio: Violence, Wages, Land and the Environment.' PNGexposed blogpost, 22 September. Viewed 18 October 2016 at: pngexposed.wordpress.com/2014/09/22/logging -in-pomio-violence-wages-land-and-the-environment/.

Makis, M., 2011. 'Pomio DA Refutes Reports of Police Brutality.' *Post-Courier*, 13 October.

MCL (Musa Century Ltd), 2008. 'Environmental Impact Statement for Musa-Pongani Agro-Forestry Project, Safia District, Oro Province.' Unpublished report to PNG Department of Environment and Conservation.

MHL (Memalo Holdings Ltd) and STDIL (Sumas Timber & Development International Ltd), 2006. 'An Environment Inception Report for Sigite-Mukus Rural Integrated Development Project.' Unpublished report to PNG Department of Environment and Conservation.

Mirou, N., 2013. *Commission of Inquiry into Special Agriculture and Business Lease (C.O.I. SABL): Report.* Port Moresby: Government of Papua New Guinea. Viewed 5 October 2016 at: www.coi.gov.pg/documents/COI%20SABL/Mirou%20SABL%20Final%20Report.pdf.

Moore, E., 2011. 'The Administration of Special Purpose Agricultural and Business Leases: Customary Land and the Lease-Lease-Back System.' Port Moresby: National Research Institute (Discussion Paper 118).

Mousseau, F., 2013. 'On Our Land: Modern Land Grabs Reversing Independence in Papua New Guinea.' Oakland (CA): The Oakland Institute in collaboration with Pacific Network on Globalisation.

Nayak, P.K., L.E. Oliveira, and F. Berkes, 2014. 'Resource Degradation, Marginalization, and Poverty in Small-Scale Fisheries: Threats to Social-Ecological Resilience in India and Brazil.' *Ecology and Society* 19(2): 73. doi.org/10.5751/ES-06656-190273.

Nelson, P.N., J. Gabriel, C. Filer, M. Banabas, J.A. Sayer, G.N. Curry, G. Koczberski and O. Venter, 2014. 'Oil Palm and Deforestation in Papua New Guinea.' *Conservation Letters* 7: 188–195. doi.org/10.1111/conl.12058.

Nelson, P.N., M.J. Webb, I. Orrell, H. van Rees, M. Banabas, S. Berthelsen, M. Sheaves, F. Bakani, O. Pukam, M. Hoare, W. Griffiths, G. King, P. Carberry, R. Pipai, A. McNeill, P. Meekers, S. Lord, J. Butler, T. Pattison, J. Armour and C. Dewhurst, 2010. *Environmental Sustainability of Oil Palm Cultivation in Papua New Guinea.* Canberra: Australian Centre for International Agricultural Research (Technical Report 75).

Nicholas, I., 2011. 'Tiensten Warns NGOs with Motives to Stay Out.' *The National*, 19 April.

Nilles, J., 2010. 'Report: Wanigela.' Port Moresby: Centre for Environmental Law and Community Rights.

Nolte, K., 2014. 'Large-Scale Agricultural Investments under Poor Land Governance in Zambia.' *Land Use Policy* 38: 698–706. doi.org/10.1016/j.landusepol.2014.01.014.

Numapo, J., 2011. Transcript of SABL Commission of Inquiry hearing, Waigani, 4 October.

——, 2012. Transcript of SABL Commission of Inquiry hearing, Popondetta, 16 February.

——, 2013. *Commission of Inquiry into the Special Agriculture and Business Lease (SABL): Final Report*. Port Moresby: Government of Papua New Guinea. Viewed 5 October 2016 at: www.coi.gov.pg/documents/ COI%20SABL/Numapo%20SABL%20Final%20Report.pdf.

Numapo, J., A. Jerewai and N. Mirou, 2011. Transcript of SABL Commission of Inquiry hearing, Waigani, 8 September.

OCEAN (Oro Community Environmental Action Network) and CBCDA (Collingwood Bay Conservation and Development Association), 2013. 'Complaint against Kuala Lumpur Kepong.' Submission to RSPO Secretariat, 19 April.

Oliver, N., 2002. 'Lease, Lease-Back: An Instrument for Forestry?' In C. Hunt (ed.), *Production, Privatisation and Preservation in Papua New Guinea Forestry*. London: International Institute for Environment and Development.

Pangkatana, J., 2010. 'Illegal Loggers Nailed!' *Post-Courier*, 18 August.

——, 2011. 'Stop the Land Grab.' *Post-Courier*, 29 October.

Paniu, L., 2011. 'LOs Stage Peaceful Protest.' *Post-Courier*, 10 August.

PNGexposed, 2014. 'Rimbunan Hijau Ignoring Court Order to Stop Logging Operations.' Anonymous blogpost, 24 November. Viewed 18 October 2016 at: pngexposed.wordpress.com/2014/11/24/ rimbunan-hijau-ignoring-court-order-to-stop-logging-operations/.

Pok, J., 2010. 'State to Give Land Back to Landowners.' *The National*, 3 February.

——, 2012. 'Oro SABL's Queries.' *Post-Courier*, 14 September.

Power, T., 2008. 'Incorporated Land Groups in Papua New Guinea.' In AusAID (Australian Agency for International Development) (ed.), *Making Land Work—Volume Two: Case Studies on Customary Land and Development in the Pacific*. Canberra: AusAID.

RAN (Rainforest Action Network), 2014. 'Contested KLK Palm Oil Leases Declared Illegal by Papua New Guinea Court.' Press release, 21 May. Viewed 18 October 2016 at: www.ran.org/contested-klk-palm-oil-leases-declared-illegal-papua-new-guinea-court.

Rulli, M.C., and P. D'Odorico, 2014. 'Food Appropriation through Large Scale Land Acquisitions.' *Environmental Research Letters* 9: 064030. doi.org/10.1088/1748-9326/9/6/064030.

Rulli M.C., A. Saviori and P. D'Odorico, 2013. 'Global Land and Water Grabbing.' *Proceedings of the National Academy of Sciences* 110: 892–897. doi.org/10.1073/pnas.1213163110.

Samo, J., D. Mane, P. Kene, and 15 others, 2014. Letter to Thomas Paka, Chairman of the National Forest Board, 20 August.

Sayer, J., J. Ghazoul, P. Nelson and A.K Boedhihartono, 2012. 'Oil Palm Expansion Transforms Tropical Landscapes and Livelihoods.' *Global Food Security* 1: 114–119. doi.org/10.1016/j.gfs.2012.10.003.

Scheyvens, H., 2009. 'Forest Management and Product Certification Service (PNG): Socio-Economic Impact Survey.' Kanagawa: Institute for Global Environmental Strategies.

SGS PNG Ltd, 2008–2015. 'Log Export Statistics and Export Monitoring Highlights—Table 11: Monthly Actual Shipped Volumes (m3) by Export Company and Project.' Port Moresby: SGS PNG Ltd.

Sheil, D., A. Casson, E. Meijaard, M. van Noordwijk, J. Gaskell, J. Sunderland-Groves, K. Wertz and M. Kanninen, 2009. 'The Impacts and Opportunities of Oil Palm in Southeast Asia: What Do We Know and What Do We Need to Know?' Bogor: Center for International Forestry Research (Occasional Paper 51).

SML (Sibo Management Ltd), 2014. 'Press Release: Collingwood Bay Chiefs of Legigtimate [sic] Clans Speak Out.' *Post-Courier*, 3 January.

Sutherlin, L., 2013. 'Papua New Guinea Tribes under Threat from Conflict Palm Oil.' Act Now blogpost, 13 November. Viewed 18 October 2016 at: www.actnowpng.org/content/papua-new-guinea-tribes-under-threat-conflict-palm-oil.

Tiden, G., 2011. 'Log Ops Stop Bid Opposed.' *Post-Courier*, 19 April.

———, 2012a. 'Police Force Pomio Villagers to Sign Logging Documents.' *Post-Courier*, 7 March.

———, 2012b. '10 Held for Blocking Stream.' *Post-Courier*, 12 April.

Toft K.H., 2013. 'Are Land Deals Unethical? The Ethics of Large-Scale Land Acquisitions in Developing Countries.' *Journal of Agricultural and Environmental Ethics* 26: 1181–1198. doi.org/10.1007/s10806-013-9451-1.

Von Braun J. and R. Meinzen-Dick, 2009. 'Land Grabbing by Foreign Investors in Developing Countries: Risks and Opportunities.' Washington (DC): International Food Policy Research Institute (Policy Brief 13).

Vuvu, E., 2010. 'Oil Palm Growers Warned of Impacts.' *The National*, 23 November.

Winn, P., 2012. 'Up for Grabs: Millions of Hectares of Customary Land in PNG Stolen for Logging.' Sydney: Greenpeace Australia Pacific.

8

The Political Ramifications of Papua New Guinea's Commission of Inquiry

Colin Filer with John Numapo

Introduction

The circumstances surrounding the establishment of the Commission of Inquiry (COI) into special agricultural and business leases (SABLs) in Papua New Guinea (PNG) have already been described in Chapter 6. This chapter deals with the political ramifications of the findings and recommendations that were officially published at the end of 2013, and explores some of the factors responsible for the length of time that it took for the Commission to finish its work, and the length of time that it has since taken for the PNG government to produce a coherent response.

This chapter has two main parts. The first part contains an interview that I (Colin Filer) conducted with Chief Commissioner John Numapo in April 2014, six months after the public release of his final report.[1] The interview was conducted by email correspondence between the two of us. At that juncture, John had been contracted by the Australian aid program to strengthen the magisterial services of Solomon Islands, and

---

1   Another interview with John had been conducted by ABC Radio journalist Jemima Garrett in February 2014 (Act Now 2014a).

was therefore resident in Honiara. His responses to my questions are printed in italics. These responses have only been edited for the sake of stylistic consistency with the rest of the chapter. I have added occasional footnotes to his responses to clarify or query the significance of some of his statements. John has no responsibility for any of the other statements made in this chapter.

The second part of the chapter consists of an account of some of the more significant actions, decisions and arguments that have taken place since this interview was conducted, and that cast some light on the PNG government's response to the recommendations made in John's report and that of his fellow commissioner, Nicholas Mirou. This shows that there is no clear direction to the policy process in which the COI was embedded, and leads to some rather depressing conclusions about the rule of law in PNG.

An Interview with John Numapo, April 2014

COLIN:

Can you tell us what factors delayed the tabling of the Commission's final reports in the national parliament for a period of 18 months after the Commission completed its hearings in March 2012?

JOHN:

Let me start by giving you some background to the whole inquiry itself and how we structured it. The COI adopted a 'four-phased' approach in this SABL inquiry. The first phase was the start of the inquiry in which we focused mainly on receiving <u>preliminary evidence</u> from the principal agencies of government responsible for the management and administration of SABLs. They included the Department of Lands and Physical Planning; the Department of Agriculture and Livestock; the Department of Environment and Conservation; the PNG Forest Authority; and the PNG Investment Promotion Authority. We also received evidence relating to the legislative and policy frameworks that govern the grant of SABLs. The second phase involved <u>provincial hearings</u> whereby the COI was divided into three teams headed by a commissioner and dispatched to the provinces where the SABLs were located to conduct on-site hearings as well as inspecting the actual SABL sites. Phase three was the <u>final hearing</u> conducted by the commissioners separately or *jointly as appropriate to consolidate and adjust evidence gathered during both the preliminary hearings and the provincial hearings. The fourth and final phase involved the final submissions by counsels assisting the inquiry and the write-up of the final reports by the commissioners.*

Phases 2 and 3 activities were disrupted by funding issues, lack of resources and other critical intervening factors that affected the inquiry. The 2012 national elections, the political in-fighting, the change of government, the lock-down of the Government Printing Office that housed the COI and the 'threat' by the new in-coming government to stop the SABL inquiry were some events that directly affected the inquiry. The COI was virtually locked out of the building during the political impasse.[2] This created a lot anxiety and uncertainties amongst the members of the COI. The interruptions went on for weeks. Delays in funding support resulted in personnel engaged by the COI not being paid for months, resulting in people not turning up for work. In fact, the government still owes the commissioners and members of the legal and technical teams 15 months of unpaid allowances and salaries that are still yet to be paid to this day. The delay in the production of the recorded transcripts to assist the commissioners with their final write-ups, and the lack of cooperation and display of arrogance by certain members of the COI, also affected the completion of the final reports by the given deadline. Certain factors that contributed towards the delay were totally beyond our control and were not of our making.

Due to the above factors, I then wrote to the Chief Secretary and the Prime Minister seeking extension of time to submit the final reports. The Prime Minister granted us an extension to the end of June 2013. With respect to the delay in presenting the final reports to Parliament, this is a matter entirely within the jurisdiction of the Prime Minister and Cabinet and I cannot comment on that. What I can say is that we have delivered the final reports by the given deadline. The final reports were submitted to the government on 26 June 2013.

---

2   John appears to be referring to the constitutional crisis that occurred in December 2011, when the Supreme Court ruled that the parliamentary vote by which Peter O'Neill had replaced Michael Somare as Prime Minister had been unconstitutional. This produced a standoff that lasted for several weeks as each man tried to assert his legal authority over the executive arm of the state. O'Neill won this battle because he retained his parliamentary majority, but the authority of the Supreme Court was seriously weakened.

COLIN:

To what extent do you think that the failure of one of the three commissioners to submit his own final report has made it difficult for the government to implement the Commission's recommendations? What is to be done about the 30 or more leases which Commissioner Jerewai investigated, given that his recommendations are not available to the government?

JOHN:

Apart from the delay in submitting the final reports, as alluded to above, Commissioner Alois Jerewai's failure to submit his final report is the biggest set-back to what could have been a very successful inquiry. Commissioner Jerewai blamed lack of funding as a reason for not submitting his report, which I think is an absolute nonsense. If Commissioner Nicholas Mirou and I can complete our final reports, despite financial difficulties, surely Jerewai could have done the same.

Failure by one commissioner to submit his final report should <u>not</u> be an excuse for the government not to implement the findings and recommendations of the two other commissioners. There are two things the government can do under the circumstances. First, appoint a commissioner to conduct a fresh inquiry into the 30 or so SABLs, especially in East and West New Britain provinces and Gulf Province. Secondly, drawing some general conclusions from the findings of the two final reports, the government could assume that the 30 or so leases were also unlawfully issued, like the majority of the other SABLs around the country, and therefore should be revoked. However, this presumption is risky and the government may have to carefully consider that.

COLIN:

At the beginning of your own final report, you recommended 'that the current SABL setup be done away entirely' (Numapo 2013: 4), but towards the end, you recommended that special agricultural and business leases should 'be retained … [as] a national development and customary landowner empowerment mechanism' (ibid.: 255). In his statement to Parliament in September 2013, the Prime Minister himself expressed some surprise that you had recommended retention of the 'SABL setup' after finding that only four of the leases investigated by yourself and Commissioner Mirou had genuine landowner consent. Can you explain this apparent contradiction in your recommendations?

JOHN:

The overall recommendation of the COI is that the current SABL setup is a complete failure and must be abolished. The current setup is riddled with loopholes, shortfalls and inadequacies—so much so that corrupt public officials and unscrupulous individuals are taking advantage of it to enrich themselves. There is simply no transparency and accountability in the whole process, starting from application to processing to the final issuing of SABLs. Although well intended, the SABL concept has lost its meaning over time and is no longer serving the purpose for which it was set. The SABL scheme was conceived as an empowerment option for customary landowners that would facilitate economic opportunities for landowners. It has lost its focus over time as a system and a process to offer financial incentives to the landowners and at the same time protect their interests over their land.

What I am trying to say on page 255 is that SABL as a 'concept' (not necessarily the SABL itself) is good and should be continued in some form (other than the current setup) as it is all about empowering landowners to participate meaningfully in the economic development of the country by freeing up their customary land through the lease-leaseback scheme. Ninety-five per cent of the land in PNG is tied up under customary ownership, and unless that is unlocked, there will be very little in terms of real progress and development. The SABL scheme was introduced because of the long delay in the introduction of customary land registration and the tenure conversion of customary land. Customary land registration was vigorously opposed by the people for fear of losing their land outright. Tenure converted land was subject to very strict limitations which discouraged banks and other lenders from lending money using land as security.[3] The SABL concept seems to provide a good guarantee for the banks (Numapo 2013: 9). It is for this reason that I am suggesting that whilst the concept (lease-leaseback) is good, the abuse and hijack of the current SABL setup has grossly tarnished the integrity of what was once a noble and well-intended concept to allow landowners to partner government in national development through the use of their customary land whilst retaining residual rights to usage and ownership. The time is now ripe for introduction of another viable alternative mechanism that is risk-free, robust, transparent, and landowner friendly.

---

3   This is a reference to the Land (Tenure Conversion) Act that dates from the period of Australian colonial administration and allows for the conversion of customary land to individual freehold titles. Very little use has been made of this legislation, and the National Land Development Taskforce recommended that it be repealed (GoPNG 2007: 96).

COLIN:

At the beginning of your final report (Numapo 2013: 5), you also talk about the need for a 'policy platform [that] will set the foundation for harmonizing the legal framework and pave the way for the State to access customary land in a non-threatening and landowner friendly way'. At the end of your report (ibid.: 261), you call this a 'National Land Policy Harmonization exercise'. What do you think is the single most essential ingredient of such a policy platform?

JOHN:

The policy platform is first and foremost intended to safeguard and protect the interests of the landowners and also to make sure that customary land is not totally alienated under the various acquisition schemes. The current piecemeal and ad hoc approach to acquiring customary land has caused more harm than good because of the different laws and policies that govern it. We hope that the 'harmonisation of laws' and 'standardisation of practice' will bring about some degree of consistency, clarity, parity and regularity in the various land acquisition processes. The policy will provide the basis for streamlining, harmonising and synchronising the various different practices and procedures on 'acquisition of customary land by agreement' for economic development, as in the case of SABLs (under Sections 11 and 102 of the Land Act 1996) and 'compulsory acquisition' of customary land (under Section 12) for national development purposes that are currently managed under different schemes and governed by separate legislations and policies. A number of land acquisition schemes were introduced over the years for 'specific purposes' regulated by different sets of rules and guidelines. Legislative and policy frameworks were done on a piecemeal basis and were, in most cases, ad hoc. Consequently, many land acquisition schemes were created with no proper oversight and control by the relevant agencies of government, resulting in abuses and manipulations by corrupt government officials and unscrupulous foreigners. We believe that, by harmonising the laws and standardising the practices, we will remove ambiguities and generality in the laws and practices. The outcome will then inform the National Land Policy as part of the overall reforms going forward.

COLIN:

At the end of your report (Numapo 2013: 264), you say that special agricultural and business leases should be reserved for so-called 'high-impact' projects that need large areas of land. But, by my calculation, 98 per cent of the land that has been covered by such leases since 1996 has been devoted to projects with a size of more than 10,000 hectares, which their supporters would all probably describe as 'high-impact' projects. So how do you expect the process of acquiring customary land for projects of this kind to be different and better in future?

JOHN:

Let me put some background to it before I attempt to answer the question. There are two types of permission to clear forests. Type 1 is the timber authority issued by Provincial Forest Management Committees to carry out 'small scale agriculture projects' or other land use pursuant to Section 87 of the <u>Forestry Act 1991</u>. Type 2 is the forest clearing authority (FCA) to undertake 'large scale forest clearance' issued by the National Forest Board (NFB) pursuant to Sections 90A, 90B, 90C and 90D of the Forestry Act. For SABL purposes, the FCA applies in most cases. Sections 90A and 90B deal with large-scale conversion of forest for agriculture and other land use, whilst 90C and 90D deal with large-scale conversion of forest for major road construction projects. These are sometimes referred to as 'high-impact' projects.

The Forestry Act requires forest clearance (clear felling) for SABL purposes to be limited to 500 hectares initially on application. This is to ensure that planned agriculture projects are commenced on the initial 500 hectares before the developer moves on to the next 500 hectares. The developer is required to apply to increase the number of hectares, and based on proper assessment and technical advice provided by the Department of Agriculture and Livestock (DAL), the NFB may increase it up to 5,000 hectares. However, in many instances we found that the developers and FCA holders are carrying out 'clear felling' well outside of the 500 hectares covered by their FCA. This is outright illegal and a direct breach of Section 90A of the Forestry Act. DAL has been allowing that clearance to go beyond the required 500 hectares for 'practical purposes' until the maximum land required for the agriculture project is cleared instead of stop-start for every 500 hectares. In addition, the developers are allowed to sell logs of merchantable value to 'raise capital' for the agriculture component. Again, this is unlawful as developers must have sufficient starting capital before getting an SABL in the first place.

To answer the question: yes it is true that the majority of the land that has been acquired is in SABLs that are over 10,000 hectares, and most of these are referred to as 'high-impact' projects because they not only involve large areas of land, but are often associated with large-scale agriculture projects or road line projects that impact on the people and the immediate environment.

The practice to increase the hectares is currently <u>condoned</u> and <u>promoted</u> by DAL and the PNG Forest Authority despite the fact it is unlawful. DAL considers that to be a more 'realistic and practical' approach for agriculture projects as they require land of more than 10,000 hectares. The fact of the matter is that this practice will no doubt continue into the future as it is considered to be a more viable option and an attraction to current and potential investors. What we need to do right now is to properly distinguish between large-scale and small-scale forest clearance permits and introduce different monitoring guidelines for different types of permit to avoid applying the same rules for the two as their impacts are different. This also applies to lease conditions and the types of benefits, royalties and compensation that are paid to the landowners. Those operating large-scale agriculture projects should pay more in consideration of the area of land obtained under the SABL, and should be more accountable under a set of stringent guidelines to ensure that they develop the agriculture projects as required under the terms of the lease and not use it as a pretext for logging operations.

There are currently no FCA monitoring guidelines nor an oversight committee to monitor the FCAs that are issued. It is for this reason that we recommend DAL to implement as a matter of priority the recommendations of the National Agriculture Council to develop proper FCA Project Approval and Monitoring Guidelines and to establish an oversight committee to monitor all FCAs and ensure that they comply with the guidelines and the requirements of the law. Oversight and monitoring of the FCAs is seriously lacking at the present time.

COLIN:

Some senior public servants have been saying that the government is afraid to revoke those leases under which subleases have been granted to foreign investors because of the risk that these investors will sue the government for compensation and the courts will grant their claims. How would you assess the validity of this argument?

JOHN:

I am not surprised at all to hear this. Two separate incidents happened during the course of the inquiry. First, I was approached by a very senior minister of the current government to carefully consider the ramifications of revoking the SABLs that were issued to foreign investors because of the possibility of legal action against the State for compensation due to loss of business. The second incident involved yet another senior minister of the current government telling me in no uncertain terms that the final reports of the inquiry 'will not see the light of day and will be swept under the carpet'. He went on to say that my commissioners and I are wasting our time conducting the inquiry and writing up the reports as it will not be tabled in Parliament and the government has engaged a Queen's Counsel from Australia to go to court to stop the inquiry. I told the two senior ministers that I and my commissioners have a duty to do as required by our terms of reference, and we would continue with the inquiry and deliver the final reports containing our findings and recommendations as we owe it to the people of PNG (especially the customary landowners) to do so. No amount of pressure or threats would deter us from delivering the reports.

Putting one and one together, this is probably the reason why the following things happened:

1. *The Prime Minister went public and threatened to refer me and my other two commissioners to the Fraud Squad to investigate us (for what reasons we do not know to this day).*
2. *There was delay in his tabling of the final reports in Parliament despite the fact that the reports were already submitted to him two months previously (minus Jerewai's report).*
3. *There was criticism of the final reports and misleading of Parliament on the findings and recommendations of the COI.*
4. *There was refusal to pay 15 months' worth of salaries owed to the commissioners and other COI staff.*

The findings of the inquiry are very clear, including the recommendations. Over 95 per cent of the SABLs were unlawfully issued and must be revoked. They cannot lawfully stand in law. Foreign investors, politicians and corrupt public officials have all conspired and colluded to create bad leases and titles over customary land, as was discovered during the inquiry. They are all equally liable and should be investigated and prosecuted as some of them have been named in the reports. The government has no choice but to revoke the SABLs that were illegally issued, as has been recommended. The issue of compensation is a different matter altogether, and should not be used as an excuse not to implement the recommendations of the COI. The threat of compensation claims against the government is yet another excuse not to implement the recommendations.

COLIN:

In March 2011, I wrote a brief for the PNG Department of Environment and Conservation in which I identified eight current government ministers and several other members of parliament who appeared to have vested interests in the grant of SABLs in their own electorates. The current make-up of the national parliament does not seem to be all that different. Given the extent of these vested interests, why do you think the government set up the COI in the first place, and what makes you think that there is enough political will to implement its recommendations?

JOHN:

It's all about 'political correctness' I guess. The setting up of the COI was a reaction to the public outcry over the manner in which SABLs were issued for dubious agriculture and business purposes and instead used as a licence for full-scale logging operations over large virgin forest tracts. It attracted international attention following the James Cook University conference in March of 2011. The government had to act quickly to 'save face' and it decided to set up the COI. For the politicians and those in government there was a lot at stake. It's all about balancing the competing interests of foreign investors on the one hand and landowners on the other. It is common knowledge that some political parties are funded by foreign investors, particularly those involved in logging operations in the country. Many of the SABLs were initiated and driven by politicians as part of 'bringing development' into their electorates. There was evidence of political pressure, influence and interference in the granting of SABLs. This went up as far as the Prime Minister, as in the case of Bewani (Portion 160C in West Sepik Province) and Changhae Tapioka (Portions 519C, 444C, 446C, 517C, 518C, 521C and 520C in Central Province).

Despite the assurances from Prime Minister Peter O'Neill that the recommendations of the COI will be fully implemented, no action has been taken to date to revoke the SABLs that were unlawfully issued, as recommended by the COI. I do not know how long it will take to implement the recommendations as the landowners are already tired of waiting. I think the government is trying to buy time until people forget about it (unfortunately, this is becoming a trend now in PNG).

I have my own doubts about the genuineness of the government's promise to revoke the unlawfully issued SABLs. There is too much at stake, and given the current political make-up and the fact that many of those who were named in the reports are part of the current government, it will be a difficult task for the Prime Minister to live up to his word to revoke the unlawfully issued SABLs. And based on that, I do not know if there is enough political will to implement the recommendations. I doubt it.

COLIN:

At one point in your final report (Numapo 2013: 236), you said that the Commission 'received evidence of undue "political pressures" being put on government officials by senior ministers and politicians to fast-track SABL applications and issue titles'. You gave a couple of examples of such pressures being applied. However, I wonder if you felt constrained by your terms of reference from telling a more detailed story about the extent to which such pressures were driving public servants to neglect their duties.

JOHN:

I am reluctant to go into any more details than what I have already stated in the report, as this might be the subject of another investigation to be carried out in the future, and as we have recommended for such to take place. I do not want to pre-empt or speculate on anything at this point in time. There may also be legal implications. The only thing I can say is that the evidence we received during the inquiry suggests that pressure was applied to government officials to short-cut the processes and procedures to issue SABLs. Threats were issued to sack them if they failed to act, and promises of promotion and a 'good life' were also made. I will stop there.

COLIN:

In September 2013, Prime Minister Peter O'Neill announced that the Minister for Lands would appoint a task force to establish a new legal framework to protect the interests of customary landowners. In February 2014, he said that the ministers of lands, forests and agriculture would oversee the process of cancelling the leases that were acquired illegally. Nothing more has been said in public about the way this process is being organised. How do you think it should be organised?

JOHN:

This is totally absurd and ridiculous. It defies logic and does not make any sense at all. These are the very people who screwed up the SABL scheme in the first place. The whole SABL process was hijacked and mismanaged under their watch. I am at a loss to understand why the ministers for lands, forestry and agriculture have been given the task to implement the recommendations of the COI when it was their respective departments that were responsible for the management and administration of SABLs, and that messed up the whole SABL scheme. Adverse findings were made against these government agencies, including their respective ministers, so how on earth do we expect them to effectively implement the recommendations of the COI? The Prime Minister must re-think the composition of the task force and appoint some independent individuals and entities to implement the recommendations.

I wrote to the Prime Minister when presenting my final report and suggested to him that an independent body such as the National Land Development Program (NLDP) be given the task to study the recommendations of the COI and advise the government on how to implement the recommendations, including the cancellation of the illegally issued SABLs. The NLDP is a multi-government entity made up of representatives from other government agencies, but also including civil society, facilitated by the National Research Institute. It was set up five years ago to initiate some reforms across the board on land management and administration generally, including acquisitions through the various processes. The NLDP has made some headway on some reforms in recent times and is currently ongoing. I made some references to the NLDP towards the end of my final report (Numapo 2013: 262–3).

COLIN:

During the course of the Commission's hearings, you and the other commissioners were sometimes at pains to point out that you were not pursuing an agenda set by local or international environmental non-governmental organisations (NGOs) or 'greenies'. Do you think that the extent of lobbying by these groups could actually be giving the government an excuse to ignore the Commission's recommendations?

JOHN:

I would say 'yes' but I think it would be one of the many reasons why the government would ignore the recommendations or will be slow at implementing them. The SABL scandal has no doubt put PNG on the world map, with NGOs and greenies all over the world criticising the PNG government for the abuse that is going on and not doing anything to stop it. It is a big agenda, especially in the context of global warming and carbon pollution.

During the course of the inquiry we received a lot of requests from NGOs and greenies to make representations at the inquiry and give evidence. Unfortunately, our terms of reference did not allow for that as the inquiry was more focused on landowners and government agencies that were expected to appear and give evidence. We did not have the discretion to invite the public at large, and also time was not on our side. NGOs and others have had a field day in pre-empting the outcome of the inquiry, using social media to discuss specific SABLs and the corrupt activities that went on. One of the dailies (the Post-Courier*) had a field day by publishing the views of NGOs and the greenies nearly seven days a week when the inquiry was still running, prompting Rimbunan Hijau (owners of the other daily,* The National*) to threaten to take the Post-Courier to court for defamation and for pre-empting the outcome of the inquiry whilst it was still going on.*[4] *It was a real circus, and it could have affected us one way or the other, as those of us involved in the COI also read papers and access social media sites. That is why we were at pains to explain that, despite the writings and the newspaper articles, we were not influenced one way or the other, as we have restricted ourselves to making our findings based on the evidence before us, as adduced through the formal hearings of the inquiry. I am glad to say that the final reports reflected the kind of findings one would have expected, based on the evidence presented to the inquiry. Evidence given before the inquiry was on oath and was subjected to the usual examination in accordance with the rules of evidence.*

COLIN:

Some people have argued that amendments recently made to the Land Groups Incorporation Act and the Land Registration Act, which make it possible for incorporated land groups to directly register titles to their customary land and then grant subleases to investors, make the whole of the 'lease-leaseback scheme' redundant, so all reference to special agricultural and business leases should simply be removed from the Land Act. What are your thoughts on this subject?

JOHN:

I disagree. The recent introduction of the Land Groups Incorporation Act and the Land Registration Act is a policy initiative of the government to give the landowners the option to voluntarily register titles to their customary land

---

4   This is a reference to the Greenpeace campaign against the Sigite-Mukus project in East New Britain Province (see Chapters 6 and 7, this volume).

so that the issue of titles is clearly settled before the granting of a sublease, whether it be for an SABL or for other purposes. However, it is not clear if this will replace altogether the 'lease-leaseback' scheme and make it redundant. The option to voluntarily register the title must interface with the concept of the SABL regime so that the lease-leaseback scheme can continue for large-scale, high-impact, intensive land-based development, as I alluded to earlier. Voluntary land registration is best suited as a landowner empowerment option for more general land use (Numapo 2013: 262). Removing the SABL scheme from the Land Act, and replacing it entirely with a new scheme that is untested, is too risky. The SABL as a concept offers opportunities to customary landowners to participate in economic development through a lease-leaseback arrangement, which in itself already guarantees the return of the land after the term of the project has lapsed. The title reverts back to the customary landowners, and that in itself is a form of security. The area that needs to be looked at is the reduction of the lease period from 99 years to something like 50 years as the maximum period for the lease.

COLIN:

In a number of cases investigated by the Commission, it turned out that the landowners opposing the grant of leases to one particular landowner company and its preferred foreign investor were mainly interested in having the leases granted to a different landowner company and another foreign investor. In some cases, you suggested that the competing factions should just sit down, sort out their differences, and come up with a plan on which both sides could agree. As a former chief magistrate, what is your view of the local-level disputes that seem to make land issues so intractable in PNG?

JOHN:

Usually the village court magistrates would try to resolve such a dispute. It is not a land dispute per se, and therefore cannot come before the formal court system because the land is communally owned. It is only a difference of opinion between different members of the landowning clans with respect to which foreign investor they prefer. Unfortunately, it seems that even the village court magistrates are taking sides when dealing with such issues, as it really has got to do with the benefits that flow from the deal, which only adds to the problem. The land issue is always very sensitive and runs deep, with family ties and connections coming into play. We try to encourage the settlement of such disputes through the usual Melanesian ways, where everybody sits down together and talks through things. We believe that, if they resolve the dispute using their own traditional dispute resolution mechanisms, the result will stick. They will also honour it and will abide by it. If it is imposed on them, it might lead to further disputes.

Another Cabinet Decision

When Peter O'Neill presented the two final reports of the COI to the national parliament in September 2013, he declared that '[w]e will no longer watch on as foreign owned companies come in and con our landowners, chop down our forests and then take the proceeds offshore' (Nicholas 2013a). But what was he going to do about it? He initially undertook to establish a ministerial committee that would recommend an appropriate course of action within a period of two months (Nicholas 2013b), but when he tabled the reports in Parliament, he said that the Minister for Lands and Physical Planning would appoint a taskforce to design a new legal framework for the conversion of customary land into leasehold land (Nicholas 2013a). It was not clear whether these were meant to be two distinct initiatives, nor was there any indication of how the new legal framework might relate to the one that had come into effect at the start of the previous year.

Nothing more was heard of the committee or the taskforce until February 2014, when the Prime Minister told a radio audience that the committee would be chaired by the Forests Minister, Patrick Pruaitch, and the other members would be the Lands Minister, Benny Allan, and the Agriculture Minister, Tommy Tomscoll (Nicholas 2014). This news prompted the Eco-Forestry Forum to call for the removal of Pruaitch from the whole process on the grounds that putting him in charge of it would be like 'giving the keys of the blood bank to Dracula' (Act Now 2014b). It is not clear whether this observation was based on the belief that any forests minister would be reluctant to cancel forest clearing authorities or on the fact that two such permits had been allocated to agro-forestry projects in this minister's own electorate. In any case, it does not seem to have been a factor in O'Neill's subsequent decision to give Pruaitch the treasury portfolio and appoint Douglas Tomuriesa as the new Forests Minister. Tomuriesa convened a meeting of the Ministerial Committee in May 2014, and its recommendations formed the basis of a cabinet decision made in June (Act Now 2014c).

KASTOM, PROPERTY AND IDEOLOGY

On the question of how to rectify the previous abuse of the lease-leaseback scheme, there were three key elements to this decision:

- all SABLs that John Numapo and Nicholas Mirou had recommended for revocation were to be revoked;
- the Ministerial Committee was granted leave to make further recommendations on what should be done with SABLs on which Alois Jerewai had failed to report; and
- a Special SABL Taskforce was to be established under the Forests Ministry, reporting to the Ministerial Committee, with a remit to: (a) address matters raised by the findings of the COI; (b) implement recommendations of the COI; (c) investigate SABLs on which the COI made no recommendations; and (d) implement further decisions of the National Executive Council and the Ministerial Committee with regard to SABLs.

In order to ensure that such abuse could not be repeated:

- the Lands Department was directed to keep following the previous instruction not to grant any more SABLs, and the NFB was directed to keep following the previous instruction not to grant any more forest clearing authorities over areas covered by SABLs;
- the Land Act was to be amended to remove the provisions allowing for the grant of SABLs; and
- administration of the land group incorporation process was to be transferred from the Lands Department to the Investment Promotion Authority.

Despite the length of time that had elapsed since the Prime Minister promised to act on the COI's findings, this decision seemed at first sight to satisfy most of the demands that had been made by various members of the land grab policy network, including members of the anti-dependency group.[5] It may have fallen short of their demand for an immediate cancellation of all forest clearing authorities, but it still ignored an earlier ruling of the National Court that said the National Executive Council did not have the power to prevent the NFB from granting such permits

---

5   The decision to remove Sections 11 and 102 from the Land Act actually went beyond the recommendations contained in John Numapo's final report.

in the first place.[6] Tiffany Twivey (formerly Nonggor), who had been a member of the conservation policy community in her capacity as legal adviser to the Eco-Forestry Forum, but was now Peter O'Neill's legal adviser, welcomed the cabinet decision as a great victory for the people of PNG and proof of the Prime Minister's good faith (Act Now 2014d).

But then something strange happened. In July 2014, the Office of the Registrar of Titles in the Lands Department published notices in the national newspapers that summoned the 22 corporate entities holding 29 SABLs to return the original copies of their leases in compliance with the cabinet decision. Fourteen agro-forestry projects were affected by this order, but only three of these had forest clearing authorities that were still valid.[7] Needless to say, the notices made no mention of the 26 leases on which Alois Jerewai had failed to report, but they also left out another 20 leases on which the other two commissioners had provided recommendations. Some of these 20 leases had already been invalidated in one way or another, and some of the smaller ones did not exhibit the sort of abuse that would warrant their cancellation, but eight of them were associated with major agro-forestry projects, and these eight leases should have been revoked if the cabinet decision was going to be implemented (see Table 8.1).

Table 8.1 Agro-forestry projects whose leases were recommended for revocation in June 2013 but were not listed for revocation in July 2014.

Province	Project	SABL area (ha)
Central	Abeda Integrated Agriculture	11,700
Oro	Musa-Pongani Integrated Agro-Forest	320,060
East Sepik	Angoram (Marienberg) Integrated Agriculture	25,600
West Sepik	Aitape West Integrated Agriculture	47,626
West Sepik	Bewani Oil Palm Development	139,909
West Sepik	Nuku Integrated Agroforestry	239,810
New Ireland	Danfu Integrated Agriculture	24,581
New Ireland	Central New Hanover Integrated Agroforestry	56,592

Source: *The National*, 18 July 2014.

---

6   *Musa Century Ltd v O'Neill* [2013] PGNC 152. The case against the state had been mounted by the developers of the largest agro-forestry project in Oro Province. It is not clear whether this project has ever been granted a forest clearing authority.
7   Oddly enough, the list of leases to be surrendered included the one granted to Mekeo Hinterland Holdings Ltd, which had already been revoked by the National Court in 2010.

It was not immediately obvious what these eight projects had in common that might explain their omission from the list. Six of them had been granted forest clearing authorities that were still valid, five were exporting logs in 2012, four were doing so in 2013, and three were still doing so in 2014. One of the two projects that exported logs in all three of those years was the Bewani project in West Sepik Province, but this project was sponsored by Belden Namah, and he was now an enemy of the Prime Minister. The other project that exported logs in all three years was the Central New Hanover project in New Ireland Province, but this project, like the Danfu project in the same province, was sponsored by a former Provincial Premier, Pedi Anis, whose influence over the relevant government ministers was equally tenuous. Perhaps some clue may be found in a statement attributed to the Prime Minister a few days after the cabinet decision, in which he said that 'those SABLs with genuine investors and genuine partnerships with the landowners should work through the Lands Department to acquire new leases to enable them to continue their projects' (Miae 2014), but this does not reflect the decision that was actually made. One might also speculate about the capacity of the various project sponsors or developers to influence the officials in the Lands Department who were responsible for making up the public notices, but one might equally suppose that the latter were guilty of that same negligence for which they had been taken to task by the commissioners. The Forests Minister was later quoted as saying that some SABLs were not revoked because of the amount of money already invested in their development (Tlozek 2015), but this point would hardly seem to apply to the two leases from which no logs had yet been extracted.

The Twists and Turns of Turubu

Another clue to the mystery surrounding the implementation of the cabinet decision may be found in the political and legal history of one big operational agro-forestry project whose SABL *was* included in the public notice issued by the Lands Department. This was the Wewak Turubu Integrated Agriculture Project, generally known as the Turubu project, which operates on a lease of more than 100,000 hectares in the vicinity of Wewak, the capital of East Sepik Province. This is one of several agro-forestry projects, in various stages of development, that have generally been endorsed by local politicians, including the former Prime Minister, Michael Somare, as part of a grand plan to create what is sometimes called an 'economic corridor' running through the middle of the province.[8]

The Turubu project has been established on an SABL that was granted to a company called Sepik Oil Palm Plantation Ltd in 2008. This is actually a joint venture between a local landowner company called Limawo Holdings Ltd and a foreign investor called Wewak Agriculture Development Ltd. The project secured a forest clearing authority in 2009, and more than 400,000 cubic metres of logs were exported from the area over the following five years. Like the Sigite-Mukus project in East New Britain, this project has attracted a good deal of attention from members of the conservation policy community, first because the area is home to an eco-forestry project that has served as a conduit for protests by dissident landowners, and second because it has been claimed that the foreign investor is one of PNG's well-established logging companies.[9] When Nicholas Mirou conducted his hearings in Wewak in February 2012, he was harassed and abused by supporters of the agro-forestry project because they thought he was secretly in league with the dissidents (Mirou 2013: 831–2).

It seems that two different groups of dissident landowners took legal action to get the SABL revoked by the National Court, the first in 2011, the second in 2012 (Sheila Sukwianomb, personal communication, December 2014). The first group obtained a restraining order to halt the logging operation in May 2012 (Matthias 2012), but it does not seem to have had much effect. It was the second group that eventually won its case in July 2014, when Justice Gavara-Nanu nullified the SABL on the grounds that it breached the provisions of the Land Act and the National Constitution.[10] This judgement was delivered during the interval between

---

8   Much of the inspiration for this plan came from Sepik migrants who were involved in the development of the existing oil palm schemes in West New Britain.
9   The logging company in question is WTK Realty Ltd, which has held concessions in West Sepik Province for many years. Its purported link to Wewak Agriculture Development Corporation Ltd was first aired in the Greenpeace report, where the two companies were said to share a common address in Port Moresby (Winn 2012: 33). A more complex set of corporate connections was described in a subsequent report by Oxfam Australia, which aimed to hold Westpac Bank accountable for the Turubu project because of its financial relationship with WTK Realty Ltd (Oxfam 2014: 16). There is no firm evidence to substantiate these claims. The two companies have offices in Port Moresby that are close to each other but are not identical. The connections described in the Oxfam report are supposedly based on evidence provided to the COI, but the transcripts of the relevant hearings show that this evidence has been misinterpreted.
10   *Maniwa v Malijiwi* [2014] PGNC 25.

the cabinet decision and the publication of the notices demanding the surrender of 29 leases, so it might perhaps explain why the Turubu lease was one of them. However, the judgement attracted no publicity at the time, and there is another plausible explanation for its inclusion.

One of the new entrants to the national parliament in 2012 was Richard Maru, who was elected to represent Yangoru-Saussia District in East Sepik Province. He had an interest in the Turubu project because the lease included part of his electorate, and he lost no time in voicing his suspicion that the developers were more interested in taking out the logs than putting in the oil palm (Anon. 2012). This initially led members of the anti-dependency group to hope that Richard Maru would be another champion of their cause, like Governor Gary Juffa, but they were soon disappointed, because it turned out that he was planning to develop another oil palm project in partnership with a different foreign investor. The focal point of this project, which is commonly known as the Sepik Plains project, would be a nucleus estate constructed on a fairly large portion of government land in his own electorate that should not have been included in the Turubu SABL because it had already been alienated by the Australian colonial administration (Anon. 2013).[11] His own promise to cancel the SABL and give the rest of the land back to the customary landowners was thus connected with his plan for them to become smallholders producing raw material for the mill to be built by his own development partners. In his capacity as Minister for Trade and Industry, Maru was also able to secure a major grant from the Treasury to subsidise the development of his own scheme. So he could well have taken some pains to ensure that the Turubu lease would be cancelled by the Lands Department, regardless of what transpired in the National Court.

From a strictly legal point of view, the matter now got quite confusing. Limawo Holdings and its own development partner, Wewak Agriculture Development Ltd, lodged separate appeals to the Supreme Court to overturn the ruling of the National Court, while the landowner company teamed up with the East Sepik Provincial Government to launch a new

---

11   The greater part of the SABL area is located in the neighbouring electorate of Wewak. Jim Simatab, the member of parliament who has represented this electorate in most years since 2007, has been an enthusiastic supporter of the Turubu project. Simatab was the Parliamentary Secretary for Agriculture between 2007 and 2010, and was appointed as Minister for Correctional Services after the national elections of 2012.

case in the National Court to overturn the cabinet decision, and the joint venture company, Sepik Oil Palm Plantation Ltd, did the same thing (Sheila Sukwianomb, personal communication, December 2014).

To the best of my knowledge, only one of these cases had been resolved by the end of 2015, but this was hardly a resolution. In May 2015, Justice Geita began hearing the case brought by the landowner company and the provincial government. Three months later, he ruled that the recommendations of the COI should not have formed the basis for a cabinet decision because the national government had failed to gazette an instrument that would extend the lifetime of the COI beyond March 2012.[12] He also ruled that it was unreasonable of the National Executive Council to include the Turubu lease in the list of 29 that were cancelled in June 2014 without considering the amount of capital already invested in the project. So he reinstated the lease. However, he was careful to say that his own ruling had nothing to do with any future rulings of the Supreme Court in respect of the appeals lodged against the previous ruling of the National Court that cancelled this lease on grounds that were unrelated to the recommendations of the COI. He was also careful to say that his ruling did not necessarily apply to the other 28 leases that the Lands Department had sought to cancel in the wake of the cabinet decision.

Law, Politics and Ideology

Two years after the COI's reports were made available to the public in November 2013, it was still impossible to see an end to the policy process from which it had emerged. It was unclear whether the national government would appeal to the Supreme Court to overturn Justice Geita's ruling, or simply wait to see what the Supreme Court did with the appeals that had already been lodged. The power of the National Executive Council to act on the findings of the COI was as uncertain as the real interest and intent of the ministers responsible for implementing its decisions. By the end of 2015, little more had been heard from the three members of the Ministerial Committee, except for an announcement by the Lands Minister, Benny Allan, that it would not be possible to cancel existing SABLs without enacting some new legislation that his departmental staff would draft 'as soon as possible' (Anon. 2015a).

---

12 *Limawo Holdings Ltd v Numapo* [2015] PGNC 155.

The 'Special SABL Taskforce' seems to have been established at the end of 2014, but then became an 'SABL Implementation Taskforce' reporting directly to the head of the Prime Minister's Department (Anon. 2015b). The recommendations of this body were due to be submitted to the National Executive Council in October 2015, but they had not been made public by the end of that year. To judge by notices published in the *National Gazette*, officials in the Lands Department have not made any further attempt to grant additional SABLs under the current provisions of the Land Act, but there is no evidence that they have drafted amendments to the current legislation that would either get rid of those provisions or change the administration of the land group incorporation process.

For some members of the land grab policy network, the government's failure to take decisive action on this issue is not just a sign of legal complexity or bureaucratic incompetence but proof of systemic corruption at all levels of the political establishment. For members of the anti-dependency group, Gary Juffa, the Governor of Oro Province, is the only member of parliament who has shown that he really cares about the rights and interests of customary landowners, and the only public servants who have shown a comparable concern with the 'rule of law' are members of the judiciary, including John Numapo and Nicholas Mirou. If other politicians and public servants have been unable to avoid the pretence of sharing this concern, then that is only because a new popular front has been mobilised to remind them of their constitutional duties.

Of course, politicians are never immune to public opinion, especially in a country like PNG, where roughly half of the members of parliament have lost their seats at each successive national election. And there is no doubt that members of the anti-dependency group have done a fine job of maintaining a semblance of public outrage through every available medium of communication. In this respect, special credit must go to Effrey Dademo, the founder of an NGO called Act Now (sometimes with an exclamation mark), and Rosa Koian, the campaign manager for another NGO, the Bismarck Ramu Group, which was born out of the ruins of a conservation program funded by the Global Environment Facility in the 1990s (van Helden 2009).[13] Effrey, in particular, has performed a valuable service for all members of the land grab policy network by not

---

13 Effrey and Rosa were two of the 18 members of the conservation policy community who received the email message in which Paul Barker called for a strategy to make landowners aware of the land grab issue back in January 2010 (see Chapter 6, this volume).

only making regular posts to a dedicated section of the Act Now blog, but also harvesting and recycling information from every corner of the internet that serves to keep the scandal alive.

Effrey and Rosa were the primary authors of an 'open letter to the Prime Minister' that was published as an advertorial in one of the national newspapers in December 2013, shortly after the public release of the COI's final reports, but they wrote this on behalf of a group of 20 NGOs that formed the core of the anti-dependency group at that time (Act Now PNG and Bismarck Ramu Group 2013). The letter simply demanded that all the 'unlawful' leases must be revoked, the land covered by the leases must be returned to its customary owners, and all the 'illegal' forest clearing authorities must be cancelled. It also called for the COI's reports to be referred to yet another taskforce known as Task Force Sweep, an agency based in the Justice Department that had been established around the same time that the COI started its hearings, and had a mandate to investigate and prosecute cases of corrupt behaviour on the part of politicians and public servants. By the end of 2014, this body had lost the support of the Prime Minister because it had started to investigate his own behaviour, and it never did get around to investigating the abuse of the lease-leaseback scheme, but the call made by the anti-dependency group still had the effect of aligning the campaign against the land grab with a broader campaign supported by people whose concern with political corruption was not simply a function of their opposition to all forms of large-scale resource development. That is how organisations like Transparency International and Global Witness became part of the reconstructed land grab policy network, almost as if they were occupants of the space vacated by the climate policy group (see Chapter 6, this volume).

Some of the demands made by members of the network since the release of the COI's findings have been somewhat misguided. For example, it is hard to justify the claim that there is anything technically 'illegal' about the grant of forest clearing authorities, and equally hard to see how these could simply be cancelled by the NFB without creating a legal liability to compensate the holders of such permits. As we have seen, the Board has sometimes suspended the permits of companies that failed to comply with their permit conditions, and it does not seem to have granted any new permits until the National Court ruled that the moratorium imposed by the National Executive Council was itself illegal.[14] In October 2014, Act Now teamed up with Transparency International and another local NGO to complain about the Board's decision to renew the forest clearing authority that had been granted to the Sigite-Mukus project four years previously, but were told by forestry officials that nothing could be done so long as the leasehold arrangements were still in effect and the permit-holder had complied with the conditions of its permit (Act Now 2014e). The forest clearing authority that had been granted to Albright Ltd in 2009 does seem to have lapsed when the National Court subsequently nullified the SABL that had been issued to the landowner company, Mekeo Hinterland Holdings Ltd. But if the government had been successful in its defence against Albright's claim for damages as a result of this ruling, that does not mean that it could have defended the breach of a contract in which it did have an 'actionable statutory duty' towards the other party, so if the lease had not been nullified, and the sublease was therefore still valid, then cancellation of the clearance permit would have been a risky move.

A second example of false hope is contained in the demand for Task Force Sweep or other organs of the state to prosecute those individuals whose corrupt and illegal behaviour was documented by the COI. The COI's terms of reference did not really allow for an investigation of the chains of influence or command by which politicians got public servants to evade or ignore the procedures that should have established the consent of customary landowners to the alienation of their land. The commissioners found little evidence of bribery, and they made no specific recommendations for the prosecution of the various lands officers and other public servants whose negligence or incompetence was the focus of their investigation. Furthermore, as they often pointed out in the conduct of their hearings, evidence presented to a commission of inquiry cannot later be used as the basis for a criminal conviction, so prosecutions would have to be based on fresh detective work by the police. And finally, the sort of evidence that might be used to convict someone of 'stealing

---

14   *Musa Century Ltd v Peter O'Neill and Others* [2013]. PNG National Court judgement N5334, 23 August. An 'unidentified source' has been cited as the basis for a claim that the Board granted a new forest clearing authority over 105,000 hectares of land held under an SABL in West Sepik Province in April 2014 (Global Witness 2014: 3). This would appear to be the Wammy project, from which a substantial quantity of logs was exported in 2015 (see Table 7.2, Chapter 7, this volume).

customary land' is actually much harder to assemble than the sort of evidence that Task Force Sweep or the Public Prosecutor has used to convict people of stealing public money.

If it is also unreasonable to expect the government to rapidly concoct some new piece of legislation that would instantly nullify an entire collection of leases and licences without risking a new round of litigation on the part of their current owners, it is certainly not unreasonable to ask the question posed by Gary Juffa, which is why government ministers, provincial governors, or other members of parliament have not been helping specific groups of landowners to take legal action in defence of their own property rights. There are now several cases in which the National Court has nullified an SABL on the grounds that some landowners did not consent to it, and none of these judgements has so far been overruled on appeal to the Supreme Court. If the COI and the media campaign have served to enlarge the population of landowners who have just cause for complaint about the loss of their property, why would their elected political leaders not seek to enhance their chances of re-election by helping to retrieve it?

Many members of the anti-dependency group, or the anti-corruption group, think the answer lies in the subordination of these political leaders to foreign business interests. From this assumption it follows that their complacency about the land grab is an affront to nationalist sentiment, as well as to the 'ideology of landownership' that counts every indigenous citizen as a customary landowner who should be rightly jealous of his or her property. But this argument barely makes sense of a political system in which most members of parliament represent electorates in which most of the voters are customary landowners living on their own land, unless it is also assumed that the foreign companies supply the money with which the politicians buy the votes of the people whose land they have conspired to steal.

An alternative explanation can be found in the testimonies that the COI itself collected from the landowners who had an interest in each of the areas covered by its hearings. The majority of the witnesses who objected to the grant of an SABL said that they were not motivated by opposition to whatever form of large-scale resource development had supposedly justified the creation of this new property right, but rather by their exclusion from the decision-making process by which a landowner company had been formed or a foreign investor had been found. In many cases, different landowner companies, or different factions represented on the board of one landowner company, had formed partnerships with different investors, each one with a view to convincing their partners that they alone were the genuine representatives of all the customary owners of the land to be developed. Members of the anti-dependency group have construed this form competition as evidence that foreign investors 'use local intermediaries who often mislead people and use payments in cash or presents to secure consent', while some of these intermediaries 'made deals with foreign companies on land that was not theirs and was actually used by other communities' (Mousseau 2013: 25). However, those investors who appeared before the COI often appeared to be truly confused by the politics of landowner representation, and there is other evidence to indicate that many potential investors have given up and gone home when they could not see a way to manage this sort of political risk.[15]

Regardless of the power dynamics of this form of partnership and competition, what matters here is that politicians who aspire to be elected or re-elected as members of the national parliament or as presidents of local-level governments may rationally calculate that there are more votes to be gained from promising some form of large-scale resource development than from opposing any form of large-scale resource development on the customary land of their constituents. This certainly seems to be the case in some of the provinces where large areas of customary land have been alienated through the lease-leaseback scheme. When the COI had just started to conduct its hearings, Leo Dion declared that there was no need for any inquiry to be conducted in East New Britain Province, of which he was then the Governor,[16] because agro-forestry projects initiated under the lease-leaseback scheme had broad popular support and exemplified the 'public-private partnerships' that were an integral component of the provincial government's development strategy (Anon. 2011). All of the elected political leaders of that province have consistently toed the same line, so it is not surprising that they have failed to back any legal action taken by groups of dissident landowners who want to get their land back. Indeed, the Prime Minister may have cause to be relieved that East New Britain was one of the three provinces covered in the hearings conducted by Alois Jerewai, so its agro-forestry projects have been saved from any immediate threat to the integrity of their land titles.

---

15   This is a classic example of what economists call the principal-agent problem. The landowners end up with developers who cannot be trusted to produce 'real development' because the landowner representatives cannot be trusted to represent the 'true landowners'.

16   He was appointed Deputy Prime Minister and Minister for Inter-Governmental Relations after the national elections of 2012.

Most members of PNG's national parliament would claim to be customary owners of land in their own electorates. Most of the voters in most electorates reside on what they think is still their customary land, even if the law says that it has been alienated. Only a minority of these electorates contain large areas of customary land that have been legally alienated through the lease-leaseback scheme. But most of the members who represent these electorates believe that their own political fortunes are tied to the promise that these areas will be 'developed', and most of the members who represent other electorates, where this form of alienation has not taken place, appear to share the same belief. But all members would still profess to share Gary Juffa's concern for the rights and interests of customary landowners, since these are the people who constitute the nation.

A grand narrative of bribery and corruption does not really serve to explain this combination of phenomena. If it is unrealistic to portray the land grab policy network as a single community of interest with a common policy objective, it may also be unrealistic to portray the state as an overbearing, monolithic, corrupt and incompetent vehicle for the implementation of a neoliberal policy agenda (Lattas 2011). We need to bear in mind that national government ministers who previously pronounced their public support for the alienation of so many large areas of customary land commonly justified this process by reference to a 'developmental' agenda conceived as a nationalist alternative to the 'neoliberal' policy prescriptions of the World Bank. And in the aftermath of the COI, members of the anti-dependency group have quite correctly asked why a government that is still committed to the same agenda could possibly be expected to halt or reverse the process of expropriation by which it has been implemented. Politicians still talk up the prospects of 'economic corridors', 'special economic zones', 'impact projects' and 'public-private partnerships' in their electorates, but the neoliberal connotations of such terms are given another meaning in the networks of patronage through which they harvest the votes of customary landowners who expect their own leaders to deliver developers to their land. So what seems to be at work here is a contradiction between the ideology of landownership and an ideology of rural or national development that cannot be resolved at any level of political organisation, yet still constitutes a quite distinctive form of political behaviour.

Conclusion

As noted in Chapter 6, the original reason for allowing customary landowners to lease their land to the state and have it leased back to a corporate body of their own choice was the absence of a legal mechanism for the direct registration of customary land titles. That hole in the policy framework has since been plugged with amendments to the Land Registration Act and the Land Groups Incorporation Act. What seems to have bothered John Numapo (and a number of other people) is that these laws may prove to be unworkable, or may only serve to 'mobilise' relatively small areas of customary land. When John said that SABLs should still be the mechanism of choice for what he called 'high-impact' projects needing large amounts of rural land, he had not forgotten the ambitious land mobilisation targets set by the Somare government in a number of policy and planning documents between 2002 and 2011. Richard Maru's solution to this problem, which is to use a large block of public land to form the core of a new rural development project, resembles the policy adopted by the Australian colonial administration when it established the first big oil palm scheme in the 1960s. However, this solution has only limited scope for replication today, not only because of the concentration of such blocks in a narrow coastal belt where they were previously alienated for the development of copra plantations during the colonial period, but also because these blocks are subject to multiple claims of customary ownership that have only grown stronger with the passage of time (Filer 2014).

In the first two years after the new legislation was certified and gazetted, about 15,000 hectares of land had apparently been registered in the names of incorporated land groups, but one of the 11 titles whose registration was advertised in the *National Gazette* accounted for more than two thirds of this land area. More disturbing was a notice published in August 2014, which said that the Lands Department was intending to accept a land investigation report that would establish the ownership of the whole of one local-level government area (more than 470,000 hectares of land) by three incorporated land groups. This example suggests that the problem of consent is not simply solved by insisting that properly constituted land groups be the only legal entities allowed to sublease customary land to private investors, especially if the Lands Department is the arbiter of what constitutes a proper constitution. In this respect, it should be noted that 10 SABLs over areas larger than 10,000 hectares were granted to incorporated land groups before the Commission was established, none of these covered an area larger than 50,000 hectares, all of them look quite suspicious, but only two came to the attention of the Commission.

The size of a block of land is not the only consideration here. One of the SABLs that was investigated by the Commission, and was included in the list of 29 leases that the Lands Department tried to recall in July 2014, covered an area of roughly 25 hectares in the national capital, Port Moresby. Within a month of the publication of the notice of revocation, representatives of one local clan were complaining that officers of the Lands Department had certified the reincorporation of the clan that was implicated in the SABL without providing the legally required opportunity for objections to be made to its original claim to customary ownership of the land in question (Anon. 2014).[17] This is one of several cases in the national capital which suggest that the capacity of some people to appropriate customary land claimed by other people is not so much a function of the land area in question as of the value of the economic benefits to be obtained from its development.

The recommendations of the Commission left open the possibility that land groups already involved in the grant of an SABL could reincorporate themselves under the terms of the amended legislation, register titles to their land, and then grant fresh subleases to investors of their choice. However, the operators of PNG's existing oil palm schemes, who hold a number of subleases under SABLs previously granted to incorporated land groups, have already discovered that this is likely to be a painfully slow process unless the participants, including officers of the Lands Department, are willing and able to bend or break the law. That is why John Numapo, as a member of the land development group in the land grab policy network, doubts the capacity of the new legislation to solve the problem of development, and that is why members of the anti-dependency group consider the new legislation as a mask for the real problem of corruption (Act Now 2014f). The events that have followed the public release of the Commission's findings suggest an additional conclusion: that appeals to the 'rule of law', whether in the form of legislation, litigation or adjudication, will not suffice to settle the contest

---

17   This is one of the SABLs in which Rimbunan Hijau has an economic interest, but it has nothing to do with the practice of agro-forestry.

between the ideologies of landownership and development that is still being played out at every level of political organisation, from the level of the nation-state to the level of the rural or urban council ward.

References

Act Now (for a better Papua New Guinea), 2014a. 'Land-Lease Overhaul Needed: PNG Land Scandal Commissioner.' Blogpost by 'rait man', 14 February 2014. Viewed 12 October 2016 at: www.actnowpng.org/content/land-lease-overhaul-needed-png-land-scandal-commissioner.

——, 2014b. 'Call to Replace SABL Review Team Chairman.' Blogpost by 'rait man', 1 March. Viewed 12 October 2016 at: www.actnowpng.org/content/call-replace-sabl-review-team-chairman.

——, 2014c. 'The Full NEC Decision on the SABL Land Grab.' Blogpost by 'rait man', 27 June. Viewed 12 October 2016 at: www.actnowpng.org/content/full-nec-decision-sabl-land-grab.

——, 2014d. 'PMs Lawyer Joy over SABL Scrapping.' Blogpost by 'Elizabeth1', 20 June. Viewed 12 October 2016 at: www.actnowpng.org/content/pms-lawyer-joy-over-sabl-scrapping.

——, 2014e. 'Forest Authority Not Stopping Illegal Logging in SABL Areas.' Blogpost by 'Effrey', 21 October. Viewed 12 October 2016 at: www.actnowpng.org/blog/forest-authority-not-stopping-illegal-logging-sabl-areas.

——, 2014f. 'New Land Laws Premature—Government Must Deal with Corruption First.' Blogpost by 'Effrey', 29 October. Viewed 12 October 2016 at: www.actnowpng.org/blog/new-land-laws-premature-government-must-deal-corruption-first.

Act Now PNG and Bismarck Ramu Group, 2013. 'SABL Land Grab: An Open Letter to the Prime Minister.' *Post-Courier*, 5 December.

Anon., 2011. 'Dion Wants ENB to Be Excluded from SABL Inquiry.' *Post-Courier*, 1 September.

——, 2012. 'Maru Unhappy with Progress of Projects.' *The National*, 20 September.

——, 2013. 'Landowner Disappointed.' *The National,* 27 December.

——, 2014. 'Clan Land Row Brewing.' *The National,* 8 August.

——, 2015a. 'Govt Plans to Cancel SABLs.' *The National,* 11 August.

——, 2015b. 'SABL Final Report Set to Go before Cabinet.' *Post-Courier,* 5 October.

Filer, C., 2014. 'The Double Movement of Immovable Property Rights in Papua New Guinea.' *Journal of Pacific History* 49: 76–94. doi.org/1 0.1080/00223344.2013.876158.

Global Witness, 2014. 'The People and Forests of Papua New Guinea under Threat: The Government's Failed Response to the Largest Land Grab in Modern History.' London: Global Witness.

GoPNG (Government of Papua New Guinea), 2007. *The National Land Development Taskforce Report: Land Administration, Land Dispute Settlement, and Customary Land Development.* Port Moresby: National Research Institute (Monograph 39).

Lattas, A., 2011. 'Logging, Violence and Pleasure: Neoliberalism, Civil Society and Corporate Governance in West New Britain.' *Oceania* 81: 88–107. doi.org/10.1002/j.1834-4461.2011.tb00095.x.

Mathias, A., 2012. 'Court Restrains Logging on Local Land.' *The National,* 22 May.

Miae, E., 2014. 'State Cancels All SABLs Obtained Illegally.' *The National,* 19 June.

Mirou, N., 2013. *Commission of Inquiry into Special Agriculture and Business Lease (C.O.I. SABL): Report.* Port Moresby: Government of Papua New Guinea. Viewed 5 October 2016 at: www.coi.gov.pg/documents/COI%20SABL/Mirou%20SABL%20Final%20Report.pdf.

Mousseau, F., 2013. 'On Our Land: Modern Land Grabs Reversing Independence in Papua New Guinea.' Oakland (CA): The Oakland Institute in collaboration with Pacific Network on Globalisation.

Nicholas, I., 2013a. 'O'Neill: SABL Success Rates Appalling.' *Post-Courier,* 19 September.

——, 2013b. 'Trio Referred.' *Post-Courier,* 13 September.

——, 2014. 'Govt to Cancel SABLs Obtained Illegally.' *Post-Courier,* 7 February.

Numapo, J., 2013. *Commission of Inquiry into the Special Agriculture and Business Lease (SABL): Final Report.* Port Moresby: Government of Papua New Guinea. Viewed 5 October 2016 at: www.coi.gov. pg/documents/COI%20SABL/Numapo%20SABL%20Final%20 Report.pdf.

Oxfam, 2014. 'Banking on Shaky Ground: Australia's Big Four Banks and Land Grabs.' Carlton (VA): Oxfam Australia.

Tlozek, E., 2015. 'PNG in No Rush to Crack Down on Asian Logging Giants.' *ABC News,* 12 November.

van Helden, F., 2009. '"The Report Was Written for Money to Come": Constructing and Reconstructing the Case for Conservation in Papua New Guinea.' In J.G. Carrier and P. West (eds), *Virtualism, Governance and Practice: Vision and Execution in Environmental Conservation.* New York: Berghahn Books.

Winn, P., 2012. 'Up for Grabs: Millions of Hectares of Customary Land in PNG Stolen for Logging.' Sydney: Greenpeace Australia Pacific.

9

Urban Land Grabbing by Political Elites: Exploring the Political Economy of Land and the Challenges of Regulation

Siobhan McDonnell

Introduction

Internationally there is a large and growing body of scholarly literature that describes problems of 'land grabs' whereby local actors, including indigenous people, lose access to land. This international land grab literature overwhelmingly focuses on large-scale land transformation—on a new scale and with a new intensity—resulting from processes of globalisation, the liberalisation of land markets, and increases in foreign direct investment in land (Deininger 2003; Sikor and Müller 2009; Borras and Franco 2010; Zoomers 2010: 130; Li 2014). In this literature, land is grabbed not only by high-wealth individuals but also by foreign governments demanding a supply of cheap food crops or arable land on which to grow biofuels and non-food agricultural crops (Cotula et al. 2008, 2009; Borras and Franco 2010; Zoomers 2010). Development of nature reserves and conversation areas form another basis for large-scale land transformation (Peluso and Lund 2011; Peluso 2012). The suggested overall trend from land grabbing is a shift in landownership from indigenous people to foreigners (Zoomers 2010: 440). In the work of Derek Hall, Philip Hirsch and Tania Murray Li (2011), this land grabbing is described in terms of the processes of exclusion of people from landscapes.

In contrast with much of this global literature, this chapter seeks to focus on the way in which political elites across Melanesia are instrumentally involved in land transformations, and particularly in the leasing of commercially valuable urban state land. In Vanuatu, state land is defined in Section 9 of the Land Reform Act as public land belonging to the colonial state powers that was vested in the Republic of Vanuatu on the day of national independence.[1] Urban state land is an important site for illustrating the exercise of state power, and in particular for considering in whose interests state actors transact public land. This chapter uses the term 'land grab' in an instrumental way to describe the agency of state actors who lease urban state land without regard to the public interest. Here the act is one of political elites *seizing* land and leasing it in their own self-interest in defiance of the rule of law or administrative requirements. Hall, Hirsch and Li describe these processes as 'licensed exclusion', whereby governments award legal titles to some people rather than others (Hall et al. 2011: 27). This chapter will explore the idea of licensed exclusion and the broader processes of regulation with reference to a case study of ministerial leasing of urban state land in Vanuatu.

Hall, Hirsch and Li view regulation as a set of rule-backed claims over a particular area of land, where rules over land establish boundaries, types of land use, ownership and zoning requirements (Hall et al. 2011: 15–16). While processes of exclusion are informed in significant ways by particular legal contexts, the importance of formal rules can be exaggerated. In this chapter, I argue that the exercise of state power over land is guided by: (1) the operation of the shadow state; (2) the behavioural norms established by political elites in transacting state land; (3) the operation

---

1   According to Section 9 of the Act:

(1) On the Day of Independence all state land shall vest in the Government and be public land and be held by it for the benefit of the Republic of Vanuatu.

(2) The Minister, on the advice of the Council of Ministers, may by Order declare that any land described in the Order ceases to be public land.

(3) In accordance with Article 81 of the Constitution the Minister may, on the advice of the Council of Ministers, by Order vest any public land in indigenous citizens or communities referred to in the Order for such payment by them and on such terms and conditions as may be referred to in the Order.

(4) When an Order is made under subsection (3) it shall provide for payment of compensation to the custom owners by the Government and the amount of such compensation shall be set out in the Order.

of property law; and (4) the organisational 'culture of complicity' in land administration agencies. Rather than enhancing formal rules, these processes can work to establish behavioural norms that often defy the legal frameworks established with respect to land dealings.

Land Transformation in Melanesia

In discussing land transformations in Melanesia, important distinctions need to be made about the scope of customary landholdings and the ambit of states in Southeast Asia—the context that informs the work of Hall, Hirsch and Li—when compared with Melanesia. In Melanesia, the overwhelming majority of land is held under customary tenure arrangements, although both Papua New Guinea (PNG) and Vanuatu have experienced 'land grabs' over customary land in recent years. Written to engage with the broader international debate around land grabbing, Colin Filer's work details the large-scale leasing of customary land in PNG through the grant of 'special agricultural and business leases'. Filer meticulously details the more than five million hectares of customary land (11 per cent of PNG's total land area) 'grabbed' by private companies between 2003 and 2011, while at the same time challenging much of the central 'land grab' narrative in the process (Filer 2011, 2012; also Chapter 6, this volume). In a similar vein, my work documents the processes by which, over the last 15 years, Vanuatu has experienced a dramatic land grab, with more than 10 per cent of all customary land now leased (McDonnell 2016). On Efate Island alone, 56.5 per cent of what was previously held as customary land along the coastline is now leased (Scott et al. 2012: 4; see Figure 9.1). This has the effect of limiting Ni-Vanuatu access to both the most arable land and much of the coastal estate.

In Melanesia, the geographical scope of state authority is more constrained than in Southeast Asia. While formal state law guides the market in land in Melanesia, many local disputes are managed through customary institutions. Land use access and exclusion is often dictated by customary rules enforced by local male leaders in what is described in the introduction to this volume as 'the neo-traditional social order'. Across Melanesia, male leaders, increasingly termed 'chiefs', engage in acts of 'intimate exclusion', validating their own claims of authority over land to the exclusion of the broader landowning group, especially women and young people (Hall et al. 2011: 145; see also Chapter 1, this volume). I call these men 'masters of modernity', rather than 'masters of tradition' (Rodman 1987), because of the way that they have used the power of the state, as well as their claims to customary authority, in attempts to legitimate their dealings with foreign or non-indigenous real estate developers (McDonnell 2013, 2016).

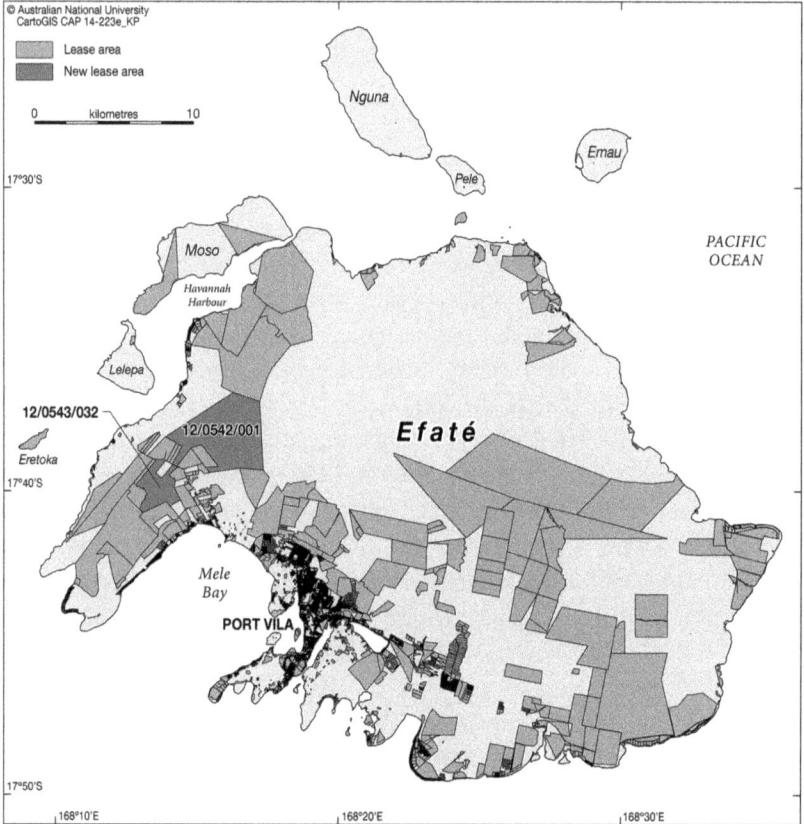

Figure 9.1 Leases on Efate Island as at 2015.

Source: CartoGIS, The Australian National University, based on data provided by the Vanuatu Ministry of Lands.

Note: National lease data indicate that 46 per cent of the Efate land mass is leased, but this statistic was compiled before the leasing of two large areas of customary land in north Efate (titles 12/0543/032 and 12/0542/001).

In spite of some constitutional similarities, the regulatory arrangements over land vary substantially across Melanesia. However, while the rules differ, there are commonalities across the region in how political elites and government officials work to facilitate land transactions, as well as logging deals and mining arrangements, for their own benefit or for the benefit of corporate or individual investor interests.

Hall, Hirsch and Li use the term 'licensed exclusion' to refer to the process by which the state licenses access to land, through a legal title, to some people, while at the same time excluding others (Hall et al. 2011: 27). Licensed exclusion is described through an exploration of land formalisation and land titling projects in Southeast Asia whereby the state makes land 'legible' through surveying, creating categories of ownership, allocating land titles, ultimately allowing for the commodification of land (Scott 1998; Hall et al. 2011: 27–9). The Australian company that has been at the forefront of land registration in several South East Asian countries, Land Equity International (LEI), also operated the Australian government's land program in Vanuatu. Land titling programs based on Torrens Title registration were rolled out through Thailand, Laos, Indonesia and the Philippines (Hall et al. 2011: 35). More recently, LEI has played a lead role in Vanuatu's five-year Land Program, at a cost of AU$23 million, which has been focused on improving the administration of land by government agencies and on the registration of all outstanding leasehold titles. However, these efforts at improving land administration have done little to address what I shall call the 'culture of complicity', which involved the Minister for Lands gifting state land to government officers.[2]

The Impact of the Shadow State on Regulation

Melanesian states are embedded in political economies largely dominated by the exploitation of natural resources associated with mining, forestry, and land itself. These political economies mean that Melanesian states are situated in webs of patronage—global and local—such that political alliances with investors representing transnational institutions inform the exercise of state power. These shifting political networks form the shadow state that operates behind the façade of the formal state, beyond the ambit of written laws and institutional processes (Reno 2000: 434). It is these networks of the shadow state that often guide the operation of state power over customary and state land in Melanesia. Shadow state networks also

---

2   The Australian government and other donors must be cautious of a programmatic approach that creates silos of expertise in which some staff become essential to the land administration process. Where this occurs, it tends to create an opportunity for staff to broker their own individual payments as part of the government land administration process. For example, if only a single staff member can operate a system designed to create maps, then this staff member may demand additional direct compensation for this skill set.

dominate ministerial leasing of urban state land, and across Melanesia, development, planning and environmental regulation is regularly subverted through the alliances of investors with politicians.

Political elites do not always perform land transactions in accordance with the rules written in national constitutions, laws and regulations. Licensed exclusion does not describe the processes by which specific state actors are *included* in this type of performance. The dominance of the shadow state means that, across Melanesia, state actors offer concessional access to land to their investor partners or close business and political associates. Politicians also routinely allocate valuable urban state land to members of their immediate family or wider kinship networks. These acts of *licensed inclusion* affect the access for other rights holders and override public interest or rule of law requirements. In Vanuatu, successive lands ministers have repeatedly acted in contravention of the law by leasing urban state and customary land for their own benefit, or in the interests of investors. Court and Ombudsman decisions detail numerous acts of licensed inclusion: ministers granting land to themselves, close family members, kin, or 'wantoks', as well as political associates and close business associates.[3] For example, the Ombudsman's decision in relation to former Minister for Lands Paul Telukluk found that '15 land titles were improperly allocated by the Former Minister for Lands ... to himself, Members of his Family and wantoks (people of his island community)'.[4] These judgements demonstrate that successive lands ministers have regularly leased urban state land in acts of *intimate inclusion* to immediate family members and kin.

---

3   *Public Report on the Conduct of Messrs Vohor, Dope and Boulekone Regarding an Attempt to Contract with Volani International Ltd* [1998] VUOM 4; *Public Report on the Improper Sale of Government Houses by the Office of the Prime Minister under the former Prime Minister Maxime Carlot Korman* [1998] VUOM 7; *Public Report on the Improper Granting of Land Lease Title 11/0E22/016 by the Former Minister Paul Telukluk and Former Director of Lands Roger Tary.* [1998] VUOM 10; *Public Report on the Granting of Leases by the Former Minister for Lands Mr Paul Barthelemy Telukluk to Himself, Family Members and Wantoks.* [1999] VUOM 6; *Public Report on the Mismanagement of the Tender Sale of the Ten (10) Deportees' Properties by the Former Minister of Lands, Mr Paul Telukluk.* [1999] VUOM 9; *Public Report on the Improper Conduct by Public Officials in Dealing with Mondragon's Proposed Free Trade Zone in Big Bay, Santo* [2001] VUOM 3. See also *Ifira Trustees Ltd v Kalsakau* [2007] VUSC 119.
4   *Public Report on the Mismanagement of the Tender Sale of the Ten (10) Deportees' Properties by the Former Minister of Lands, Mr Paul Telukluk.* [1999] VUOM 9.

Legitimation of State Power over Land

According to Hall, Hirsch and Li, legitimation of state power is the cornerstone of regulation. Legitimation as a process of exclusion 'establishes the moral basis for exclusive claims, and indeed for entrenching regulation … as politically and socially acceptable bases for exclusion' (Hall et al. 2011: 5, 19). Rather than a moral or acceptable basis, legitimation must be understood as central to establishing regulatory authority. Nancy Peluso and Christian Lund describe regulatory processes through the lens of 'legalisation'—the process of defining ownership through claims to property rights. Through legalisation and the associated 'legal titles', certain claims are legitimised, and when enforced, turn previous rights holders into 'poachers and squatters' (Peluso and Lund 2011: 674). Formal rules retain significance because they are the means of 'laundering power' by claiming legitimate authority over land.

Across Melanesia, formal rules are often used erroneously to justify the exercise of state power over land, even where these acts of power are beyond the actual text of the rules. However, establishing legitimate state authority over land can occur almost regardless of the formal rules. In Vanuatu, there are two specific processes that have resulted in the state retaining authority over urban and customary land, even where the land was leased in dubious legal circumstances: (1) the establishment of new behavioural norms, and (2) the tenets of property law.

The behaviour of state actors influences the informal rules that govern land dealings. Governmentality is the 'conduct of conduct'—the attempt to shape the behaviour of citizens by distinctive means so as to create a 'governmental rationality' (Foucault 1991: 93–5). Acts of leasing state land work to establish the governmentality of land by the state, even where this is beyond the formal rules. Where regulatory processes are undertaken by key state actors, they become the embodied practices of governmentality.

In Vanuatu, lands ministers have repeatedly leased state land in breach of the criminal code and the leadership code.[5] The leadership code enshrined in the national constitution specifically requires that members of parliament and government officials do not use their office for 'personal gain or enter

---

5   PNG, Solomon Islands and Vanuatu all have leadership codes in their constitutions that mandate codes of behaviour for politicians and public servants.

into any transaction or engage in any enterprise or activity that might be expected to give rise to doubt in the public mind'.[6] Ministerial leasing of customary and urban state land is legitimated by the failure to prosecute any illegal acts. This failure to prosecute lends an obdurate legitimacy to acts of state power over land.

A minister transacting land with the authority of the state changes the way that the processes of legitimation occur. The behaviour of key actors can comply with, or circumvent, the law (Lund 2009: 139). This is because the legitimation of state power over land involves more than rules:

> what is perceived as legal or illegal may change over time without any change to legislation. Government policies, statements and practices can effectively outlaw certain legal practices and nullify certain established rights (Sikor and Lund 2009: 7; see also Lund 2009).

The Vanuatu example demonstrates that acts of successive lands ministers in leasing state land have operated to nullify established public rights over land without substantial changes to the law as written.

The Register is Everything

The legitimation of state power over land is also established by property law. The effect of property law operates to override the circumstances by which state land transactions occur. The legal foundation of formal property rights in Melanesia is Torrens Title indefeasibility: once a lease is registered it is unable to be broken. The grounds for challenging the registration of a lease are very limited, ensuring the stability of the titling process. By giving effect to registration, the power of the state over land is made legitimate. Property rights in natural resources are 'intimately bound up with the exercise of power and authority' (Sikor and Lund 2009: 1). The acts of lands ministers in Vanuatu provide an illustration

---

6   According to Article 66 of the Constitution:

(1) Any person defined as a leader in Article 67 has a duty to conduct himself in such a way, both in his public and private life, so as not to – (a) place himself in a position in which he has or could have a conflict of interests or in which the fair exercise of his public or official duties might be compromised; (b) demean his office or position; (c) allow his integrity to be called into question; or (d) endanger or diminish respect for and confidence in the integrity of the Government of the Republic of Vanuatu.

(2) In particular, a leader shall not use his office for personal gain or enter into any transaction or engage in any enterprise or activity that might be expected to give rise to doubt in the public mind as to whether he is carrying out or has carried out the duty imposed by subarticle (1).

of the argument that recognition of property works to legitimise the authority of the institution making the determination. Leases allocated by the Minister, even where this is beyond his legal powers, have been legitimated by the operation of the tenets of property law. Once leased by a minister and registered, a lease title over state land becomes indefeasible.

The power of the Minister to create property rights has been repeatedly upheld by the courts in Vanuatu, based on their interpretation of the legislation that governs lease making. Courts in Vanuatu have repeatedly stated that:

> The essential feature of any Torrens System is the indefeasibility of the title of the registered proprietor ... the effect of all these provisions is that *the register is everything*. The title of the registered proprietor ... is protected against any adverse claims or interests not entered in the register except as provided in the Act.[7]

Property interests are detailed in the register, and the register is *everything*. Once the technical requirements of the property transaction and registration are met, the transaction is likely to be held to be indefeasible. Torrens Title registration creates a repository of interests in land so as to 'protect persons dealing in registered interests in land' regardless of 'the circumstances in or the consideration for which such proprietor or any previous proprietor was registered'.[8] The property rights of the titleholder of the registered instrument are backed by the implicit force of the state, thereby excluding prior claims of other groups. The position of the lands minister is legitimated by the power to create property rights, which has been upheld by the courts and backed by the authority of the state. This in turn legitimates the authority of the minister as the state actor who transacts land.

The Organisational Culture of Complicity

Land administration agencies across Melanesia demonstrate a widespread culture of complicity whereby many government officers either support political elites who engage in illicit acts, or themselves facilitate property transactions on the basis of illicit payments. This culture may operate in part because government officers fear for their jobs or face persecution

---

7   *Toro v Kiri* [2013] VUSC 210. Paragraph 8 (emphasis added).
8   See Section 23 of the Land Leases Act.

if they do not comply with directions from their political masters. But it is also clear that some government officers promote illegal acts by key state actors for their own personal gain.

A number of systemic problems with land administration have been identified across the Melanesian region, namely that land administration officials may collude with outside investors to: tamper with or destroy land records; lower valuations of state land so that they do not reflect the market value and to reduce taxes payable; lower land prices or give preferential access to state land to certain investors or politicians; and regularly circumvent planning and environmental processes. However, this does not mean that all officers involved in land administration are inveigled by an organisational culture of complicity.

Minister Kalsakau's Grabbing of Urban State Land

The laundering of state power over land by political elites and the culture of complicity in place in land administration are best understood with reference to a case study from Vanuatu. In 2012, at least 190 leases over state land were approved by the former Minister for Lands Steven Kalsakau to individuals in three general categories: (1) government officers comprising staff from the Department of Lands, the Ministry of Lands, and other related government agencies (including those responsible for agriculture, environment, planning and valuation); (2) Kalsakau's personal business and political associates, comprising his close circle of political advisers and personal staff; and (3) close family members, including his son Periaso Kalsakau, who as a child should not legally have been able to hold a lease interest (GoV 2014: 39).[9] Minister Kalsakau's grants of urban state land leases to his business and political associates, and to close family members, illustrate the processes of regulatory inclusion. For example, the Minister's political associates included his close circle of political advisers and staff members, including his personal driver.

In an illustration of the widespread culture of complicity, leases over valuable urban state land were granted to all 40 staff in the Department of Lands and Ministry of Lands, from senior management to office cleaners. In some instances staff received single leases, but particularly well-connected staff received four or five parcels of state land,

---

9   For this reason, when Ralph Regenvanu became Minister for Lands, he was able to cancel this lease.

or arranged for their wives, sons or close relatives to also be granted leases (GoV 2014: 21). Significantly, 11 staff who were granted leases did not subsequently register their leases over state land (ibid.: 9).

A Public Service Commission investigation into the Kalsakau leases describes the challenges faced by the investigation team as *all* senior staff, and around '80 per cent' of all other Lands Department staff, were implicated in the granting of state land leases (GoV 2014: 41).[10] The entrenched, widespread culture meant that senior government officers felt confident in requesting that the Minister offer them concessional leases over state land. This request was responded to on 3 August 2012 when Minister Kalsakau issued a letter to the Acting Director of Lands:

A lot of staff members have approached me and sincerely requested that they wish to acquire and obtain leaseholds either in Vila or Luganville state lands.

Please find out available plots and allocate each of those staff that has sufficient funds to pay relative fees for the land on the following negotiable arrangement:

1. Pay only 50% of the premium, deposit 10% of the said amount and register the lease and let them organize settlement with the Banks.
2. Must pay full value of all administration fees
3. The lease term to run for fifty (50) years
4. The registered lease would be a non-transferable instrument until the premium balance is fully paid.
5. Type of lease should be classed according to the appropriate zoning and location.

I would expect that you organise this as a priority and forward all certificates and leases to me for approval (Kalsakau 2012).

---

10 A key recommendation of the team's report was that the Public Service Commission: 'formally question the former DG [Director General] of MOLNR [Ministry of Lands and Natural Resources] and the Acting Director at that time, Mr. Peter Pata, as to why they didn't ensure that the officer[s] of the MOLNR and the DOL [Director of Lands] have followed the … [proper] processes … After all, it is the view of the [investigating team] that if the former DG and the Acting Director have properly monitored the processes of lease application and registration done by their officers, they (i.e. the former DG and Acting Director) would have detected the flaws in the process and would have addressed them appropriately' (GoV 2014: 38–9).

Following from this letter, on 4 October 2012, the Land Management Planning Committee (LMPC), staffed by senior Lands Department staff and representatives of other government agencies, approved the registration of the leases.[11] The 10-member committee approved the allocation of leases to themselves and to other staff, thereby breaching the leadership code and requirements under the Public Service Act that government staff do not personally benefit from their positions.[12]

The Kalsakau leases were issued without any regard to existing planning and environmental regulations for the Port Vila and Luganville areas. Leases were issued over many of the remaining public spaces and areas of natural parkland in Port Vila and Luganville. A number of leased areas contain cultural sites such as old *nasara* (dancing) grounds, and trees registered as sites of national heritage by the Vanuatu National Cultural Council.[13]

The Kalsakau leases included numerous leases over commercially valuable real estate with high market value. In Port Vila, leases were issued in Tassariki—the wealthiest residential area—and over part of a luxury resort. Leases were also issued over the site of the former Joint Court House, prime real estate with views across the harbour. Together, the Kalsakau leases involved significant grants of valuable commercial urban state land. The amount of state land leased in Port Vila and Luganville was 128,288 square metres and 67,205 square metres, respectively. The total value of state land leased in Port Vila was approximately VT781,818,000 (approximately AU$8 million) and that of the leases in Luganville was VT181,054,000 (AU$2 million). In numerous instances, the leases also included existing government properties, roads and infrastructure, including existing police housing. In a complete abrogation of government

11 The staff in the LMPC meeting who allocated themselves land were Peta Pata (Acting Director of Lands and chair of the LMPC), Joe Keilson (Lands Department Planning Section and secretary of the LMPC), Phillip Koroka (Lands Department Survey Section), Benuel Tabi (Lands Department Land Lease Section), Gwen Wells (Lands Department Registration Enforcement Officer), Prosper Buletare and Anaclet Philip (Sanma Province representative), Harry Tete (from Luganville Municipality), Philip Banban (from the Department of Agriculture), and Dick Tomker (from the Forestry Department) (GoV 2014: 13).

12 The recipients were mainly located within the Ministry of Lands and Department of Lands but also included representatives from the Environment Office, municipal agencies, and the Department of Geology and Mining (GoV 2012).

13 *Preservation of Sites and Artefacts (Amendment) Act 2008.*

processes, leases were offered to staff without any consideration of their market value or the value of the state properties and assets located on many of them.[14]

Examples of the leases in Port Vila are shown in Figures 9.2, 9.3 and 9.4. The first example, near Independence Park (Figure 9.2), is a lease that was granted to Masoi John Alexine, an associate of Steven Kalsakau. The property was subsequently valued at VT19,500,000. The second example (Figure 9.3) comprises leases issued behind the Malvatumauri chief's nakamal in an area adjacent to Seaside. The third example (Figure 9.4) is a lease that the Minister issued to his own son, covering commercially valuable land located in Tassariki, next to the New Zealand High Commissioner's residence.

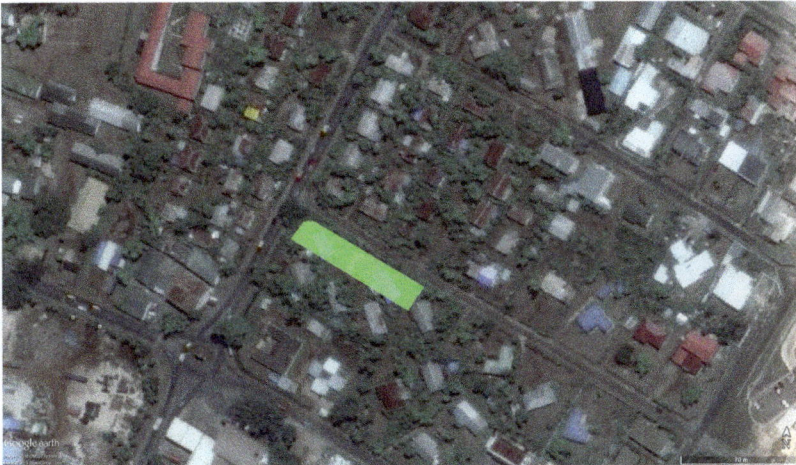

Figure 9.2 Lease titles allocated to staff over state land leased near Independence Park, including two houses.

Source: Author's rendition of Google Earth imagery, overlaid by data obtained from the Vanuatu Ministry of Lands.

---

14 The public interest requirement associated with the leasing of state land and state assets should have at least ensured that the process involved the competitive tendering for land and assets greater than VT5 million, in accordance with the legal requirements of the Financial Services Act.

Figure 9.3 Lease titles allocated to staff over parkland, existing Nasara areas and cultural sites adjacent to Seaside show ground.

Source: Author's rendition of Google Earth imagery, overlaid by data obtained from the Vanuatu Ministry of Lands.

Figure 9.4 Lease title issued by Minister Steven Kalsakau to his son Periaso Kalsakau.

Source: Author's rendition of Google Earth imagery, overlaid by data obtained from the Vanuatu Ministry of Lands.

Like many other ministerial leases over state land, the Kalsakau leases resulted in a loss of substantial revenue to the state. Most government officers paid premiums *of less than 1 per cent of the value of the land*, with at least four staff making no payments at all for their leases.[15] For example, government surveyor Harold Moli registered a lease title over part of the grounds of a luxury hotel without paying any premium for the lease or any administrative fees. While Moli paid nothing, the land was subsequently independently valued at VT8,340,000 (just under AU$100,000) (GoV 2014: 34). These amounts suggest the scale of the illicit financial gains made by government officers who support lands ministers in their gifting of urban land, and who maintain an organisational culture of complicity.

In Defence of the Culture of Complicity

Minister Kalsakau's issuing of leases involved him in an orchestrated bypassing of proper legal and administrative processes that was supported by government officers.[16] In March 2013, Ralph Regenvanu became Minister for Lands and I was appointed as his legal adviser. The new Ministry of Lands team convened a meeting of all government officers involved in Kalsakau's scheme to request that that those who had obtained

---

15   A report prepared by the Valuer-General for the Public Service Commission suggests that all titles were undervalued, premiums were assessed incorrectly based on this undervaluation, some premiums were assessed on a 50-year lease term when the term of the lease was 75 years, and some leases had no valuations done at all (GoV 2014: 35). The grant of leases to staff as gifts is inconsistent with Section 100 of the Land Leases Act, which requires that land be leased for a 'valuable consideration'. It is arguable that this requirement could be used as a basis to cancel the lease instruments where no actual payment was received or—as in the overwhelming majority of leases—where the payment received amounted to less than 1 per cent of the independent valuation of the land. It is likely that similar or greater concessions were offered to the business and political associates of Minister Kalsakau, but statistics related to these land grants are not currently available.

16   Proper administrative process was not followed in the allocation of leases to staff: very few staff actually complied with the ministerial instruction in terms of the amount to be paid; no staff applied for leases over state land following the usual application process; many staff did not pay all of the administrative and registration fees prior to registration—something that in usual circumstances would mean that the lease could not be registered. Administratively, each lease instrument that is submitted for registration should include a 'checklist' to ensure legal and administrative compliance with the requirements of various agencies (State Law Office, Planning Department, Environment Department, and Lands Department). In practice, like the Kalsakau leases, leases are routinely registered in Vanuatu without any reference to this checklist, and with little more than the consenting signature of the minister.

leases 'through flawed processes' surrender them.[17] This request was made in the context of pending court cases and investigations by the Public Service Commission and the Ombudsman.

Standing before a room full of staff in a meeting convened in the Malvatumauri Nakamal (see Figure 9.3), the Minister, lawyers from the State Law Office, members of the Public Service Commission investigation team and I all asked the government officers to surrender their leases. Senior government staff who had orchestrated the arrangement responded with indignation to this request. In the days following the meeting, only one staff member took action to surrender their lease. During the initial meeting and in subsequent discussions, the government officers repeatedly defended the leases on the grounds that the authority of the Minister to consent to the transactions is legitimated by the state, and that this overrides any other legal or process requirements.[18] These arguments were repeated by staff during Public Service Commission interviews where they stated that 'the Minister as Lessor had an agreement with them as Lessee. Thus, according to them [the staff interviewed] when the Lessor gave them the authority to proceed in registering the land, it is a legal instruction' (GoV 2014: 21). Using their expert knowledge of the law, government officers argued that the leases had been consented to by the Minister and subsequently registered, and were now 'indefeasible' property rights that could only be challenged through the courts.[19]

---

17   The meeting was chaired by the Acting Director-General of the Ministry of Lands and was attended by the Chairman of the Public Service Commission, the Public Service Commission investigating team, staff of the Office of the Ombudsman, legal representatives from the Office of the Attorney-General, and the legal adviser to the Minister for Lands. Each staff member was individually handed a letter signed by the Minister that stated, in part: 'I write to you in my capacity as the Minister for Lands requesting that you surrender the lease or leases issued to you over state land by the former Minister for Lands Steven Kalsakau. As you are aware there is currently a court case and two internal investigations being undertaken to identify the current and previous staff of the Department of Lands and Ministry of Lands who have obtained leases in the last 12 months ... The powers of these Public Service Commission and Ombudsman investigations are broad and far reaching. While I await the findings of the inquiries it is highly likely that staff who have been involved in obtaining leases through this process may be subject to disciplinary proceedings and/or prosecution under the Penal Code [CAP 135] and under the provisions of the Leadership Code [CAP 240]. Accordingly I wish to provide staff with an opportunity to surrender the leases that they have obtained over state land through these flawed processes.'

18   The Public Services Act makes clear the duties of all government employees which include: to disclose and take reasonable steps to avoid any conflict of interest (real or apparent) in connection with his or her employment; to use resources and public money in a lawful and proper manner; and not to make improper use of information or use his or her duty, status, power or authority in order to gain or seek to gain a benefit or advantage for himself or herself or for any other person.

19   The usual legal grounds for challenging existing leases are contained in Section 100 of the Land Leases Act.

Government officers also repeatedly referenced previous staff-facilitated leasing of urban state land by other former lands ministers, including Paul Telukluk and Maxime Carlot Korman. In 1994, the Council of Ministers headed by Prime Minister Korman passed a resolution to sell all of the government houses and land that had previously belonged to the former Condominium government. These house and land sales were funded through preferential access to loans from the Vanuatu National Provident Fund.[20]

> In interviews with the Public Service Commission investigation team, [land] officers pointed out that the decision made by the Hon. Kalsakau was not a new decision. Such [a] decision has already been made in the past by the former Minister for Lands namely Hon. Paul Telukluk and the Former Prime Minister, Maxime Carlot Korman (GoV 2014: 32).

Government officers who administratively supported the Korman government in the illegal registration of state land leases personally benefited. Each of the officers involved was granted a lease over an existing parcel of state land including a government house. While the Ombudsman found that the Korman government leases were illegal in terms of the Constitution and other laws, and involved significant breaches of the leadership code, no members of parliament or government officers were ever prosecuted in relation to these matters.[21] When asked about their actions in relation to the Kalsakau leases, government officers repeatedly referenced the actions of former government officers who received Korman state land leases, who remain unprosecuted, and who now occupy senior positions in land administration. These references suggest a long-established organisational culture such that government officers have repeatedly supported successive lands ministers in leasing state land and assets.

---

20 See *Public Report on the Improper Sale of Government Houses by the Office of the Prime Minister under the former Prime Minister Maxime Carlot Korman* [1998] VUOM 7: 10–11. There are a number of similarities between these Korman government leases and the Kalsakau state land leases. First, the Korman government leases were illegal as they failed to follow proper processes and involved a substantial conflict of interest in which key decision makers personally benefitted from the allocation of public assets. This was confirmed at the time by legal advice provided by the Attorney-General to the Council of Ministers which stated that the sale of land and houses to politicians and their political secretaries without competitive tendering was not in accordance with the leadership code or the law. Second, like the Kalsakau leases, the properties and land were seriously undervalued, and third, while the houses were allocated mainly to politicians and political advisers, key government staff located in the Department of Lands who assisted with the scheme were also allocated houses and state land leases.
21 *Public Report on the Improper Sale of Government Houses by the Office of the Prime Minister under the former Prime Minister Maxime Carlot Korman* [1998] VUOM 7: 28–33.

The fragility of governments in Melanesia, and their associated shadow state networks of patronage, also have important implications for the accountability of the bureaucracy. Meeting to respond to Minister Regenvanu's request that they surrender their leases, senior government staff argued in an incendiary fashion that the political cycle was short, that a vote of no confidence would presumably be progressed before any legal action could proceed against them, and that a new government would likely decide not to prosecute staff. These arguments were based on the assumption that a new minister would gain office, supported by investor interests, and would halt any legal action taken against staff. This prediction proved to be correct. On 25 June 2015, newly appointed Minister for Lands Paul Telukluk, well known for previously granting state land to himself, family members and kin, issued an internal memorandum to all Ministry of Lands staff which stated:

> My first priority is to deal with the sale of urban land to staff in the Department of Lands. Last Monday, 15 June I asked the DG [Director-General] and CEO to prepare a COM [Council of Ministers] paper to strike out the court case that the outgoing Minister [Ralph Regenvanu] started against you. My first PA [Principal Advisor] will look over the COM paper to make sure that the government 'cleans the face' of all staff (Telukluk 2015).[22]

This reference to wanting to 'clean the face' of all staff suggests the deep compact that can exist between government officers and their ministers, such that staff and ministers together engage in leasing state and customary land at heavily discounted rates, rather than acting in the interest of the public.[23]

---

22 This is a translation of the Bislama version, which reads: '1) Fes priority, hem I sale blo urban land lo staf blo department blo land. Mi askem finis lo DG mo CEO sins las Mandei 15 June 2015 blo preparem wan COM pepa blo strikem kot kase we outgoing minista I mekem agens yufala. 1PA tu bae I lukluk lo COM pepa ia blo mekem soa se bae gavman I klinim fes.'
23 Minister Telukluk also began a media campaign defending the issuing of leases over state land to government officers by his colleague Minister Kalsakau, and attacking the actions of former Minister Regenvanu in challenging the leases and attempting to prosecute staff (Ligo 2015). See also Makin (2015) for Ralph Regenvanu's response to these statements.

Conclusion: Changing the Rules of the Game

Questions of legality become confused when land dealings are performed by key state actors and upheld by courts as indefeasible lease titles. Understanding the operation of state power over land in Melanesia involves mapping the terrain of politics, the networks of the shadow state: 'who defines the laws, who implements them, who contests them and why?'(Sundar 2009). Political elites and senior government officers act with the imprimatur of the state, such that their actions are the acts of the state. This is the regulatory basis of the political economy of land dealings in Vanuatu, and elsewhere in Melanesia. Lands ministers and senior government officers should be made accountable for illegal acts by the legal institutions of the state, but their actions are the actions of the state. Who then is able to prosecute the illegal acts?

And how does regulation influence the operation of state power over land? Regulation remains an important element in understanding the way in which state power can be laundered to give effect to land transformations. By carefully studying the processes through which state power is laundered, effective regulation can be designed to alter the capacity of state actors to enact state power through property transactions. In this way, effective land reforms can alter the influence of shadow state networks and change the established norms of behaviour of political elites and government officers.

Recent land reforms in Vanuatu will provide an important case study on whether changing the regulatory rules creates substantial, long-term changes to the exercise of state power over urban and customary land. Led by Minister Regenvanu, and drafted by the author of this chapter, radical land reforms have been enacted that remove the powers of the Minister to act unilaterally in leasing urban and customary land.[24] Under the new arrangements, the Minister can only lease urban state land on the advice of a committee made up of representatives from government

---

24   Constitutional amendments and new land laws were debated at length in parliament before being supported by an overwhelming majority of members in December 2013, with the laws coming into effect on 30 February 2014. The land reform package is contained mainly in two pieces of legislation: a new Customary Land Management Act to replace the operation of the existing Customary Land Tribunal Act; and significant amendments to the existing Land Reform Act. As Minister Regenvanu's legal adviser, I was the principal drafter of the land reform package.

agencies under the authority of an independent chair.[25] Predictably, the implementation of the new rules has not received the full support of land administration staff.

Vanuatu's land reforms are designed to ensure that state land transactions are in the interests of the public and follow proper legal and administrative processes. These land reforms substantially change the rules of the game relating to land transformations. For instance, if they had been in place at the time that Minister Kalsakau held office, he would not have been able to unilaterally grant urban state land to either government officers or his close family and business associates.

Regulatory reform can influence the political economy of land by changing the rules of the game. Vanuatu's land reforms represent an attempt to wrestle government from the influence of the shadow state. For this reason they remain vulnerable to the haunting presence of the shadow state and its influence over politics. Already Vanuatu's parliamentary opposition is calling for the removal of these reforms. The question that must be asked is: in whose interests do they act?

References

Borras, S.M. Jr and J.C. Franco, 2010. 'Towards a Broader View of the Politics of Global Land Grab: Rethinking Land Issues, Reframing Resistance.' Rotterdam: Erasmus University, Initiatives in Critical Agrarian Studies (Working Paper 1).

Cotula, L., N. Dyer and S. Vermeulen, 2008. *Fuelling Exclusion? The Biofuels Boom and Poor People's Access to Land.* London: International Institute for Environment and Development.

Cotula, L., S. Vermeulen, R. Leonard and J. Keeley, 2009. *Land Grab or Development Opportunity? Agricultural Investment and International Land Deals in Africa.* London: International Institute for Environment and Development.

Deininger, K., 2003. *Land Policies for Growth and Poverty Reduction.* Washington (DC): World Bank.

---

25   See Part 6B of the amended *Land Reform Act 2015*.

Filer, C., 2011. 'New Land Grab in Papua New Guinea.' *Pacific Studies* 34: 269–294.

——, 2012. 'Why Green Grabs Don't Work in Papua New Guinea.' *Journal of Peasant Studies* 39: 599–617. doi.org/10.1080/03066150. 2012.665891.

Foucault, M., 1991. 'Governmentality.' In M. Foucault, G. Burchell, C. Gordon and P. Miller (eds), *The Foucault Effect: Studies in Governmentality.* Chicago: University of Chicago Press.

GoV (Government of Vanuatu), 2012. Minutes of the Land Management Planning Committee Meeting, Luganville, 4 October.

——, 2014. *Public Service Commission Investigation into Complaints on Corrupt Practices of Lands Officers within the Ministry of Lands.* Port Vila: Public Service Commission.

Hall, D., P. Hirsch and T.M. Li, 2011. *Powers of Exclusion: Land Dilemmas in Southeast Asia.* Singapore: NUS Press.

Kalsakau, S., 2012. 'Allocation of Urban Land to Department of Lands Staff, Both Vila and Luganville.' Letter addressed to the Acting Director of Lands, 3 August.

Li, T.M., 2014. 'What Is Land? Assembling a Resource for Global Investment.' *Transactions of the Institute of British Geographers* 39: 589–602. doi.org/10.1111/tran.12065.

Ligo, G., 2015. 'Telukluk Outlines Five Lands Ministry Priorities.' *Vanuatu Daily Post,* 27 June.

Lund, C., 2009. 'Recategorizing "Public" and "Private" Property in Ghana.' In T. Sikor and C. Lund (eds), *The Politics of Possession: Property, Authority, and Access to Natural Resources.* Chichester: Wiley-Blackwell. doi.org/10.1111/j.1467-7660.2009.01508.x.

Makin, B., 2015 'Response to Article Issued by Telukluk.' *Vanuatu Daily Post,* 28 July.

McDonnell, S., 2013. 'Exploring the Cultural Power of Land Law in Vanuatu: Law as a Performance That Creates Meaning and Identities.' *Intersections* 33.

——, 2016. My Land My Life: Power, Property and Identity in Land Transformations in Vanuatu. Canberra: The Australian National University (PhD thesis).

Peluso, N.L., 2012. 'What's Nature Got to Do with It? A Situated Historical Perspective on Socionatural Commodities.' *Development and Change* 43: 79–104. doi.org/10.1111/j.1467-7660.2012.01755.x.

Peluso, N.L. and C. Lund, 2011. 'New Frontiers of Land Control: Introduction.' *Journal of Peasant Studies* 38: 667–681. doi.org/10.108 0/03066150.2011.607692.

Reno, W., 2000. 'Clandestine Economies, Violence and States in Africa.' *Journal of International Affairs* 53: 433–459.

Rodman, M., 1987. *Masters of Tradition: Consequences of Customary Land Tenure in Longana, Vanuatu.* Vancouver: University of British Columbia Press.

Scott, J.C., 1998. *Seeing Like a State: How Certain Schemes to Improve the Human Condition Have Failed.* New Haven (CT): Yale University Press.

Scott, S., M. Stefanova, A. Naupa and K. Vurobaravu, 2012. 'Vanuatu National Leasing Profile: A Preliminary Analysis.' Washington (DC): World Bank, Justice for the Poor Program (Briefing Note 7.1).

Sikor, T., and C. Lund (eds), 2009. 'Introduction.' In T. Sikor and C. Lund (eds), *The Politics of Possession: Property, Authority, and Access to Natural Resources.* Chichester: Wiley-Blackwell. doi.org/10.1016/j. worlddev.2008.08.010.

Sikor, T and D. Müller, 2009. 'The Limits of State-Led Land Reform: An Introduction.' *World Development* 37: 1307–1316.

Sundar, N., 2009. *Legal Grounds: Natural Resources, Identity, and the Law in Jharkhand.* Oxford: Oxford University Press.

Telukluk, P., 2015. 'Internal Memorandum to Lands Department Staff', dated 25 June.

Zoomers, A., 2010. 'Globalisation and the Foreignisation of Space: Seven Processes Driving the Current Global Land Grab.' *Journal of Peasant Studies* 37: 429–447. doi.org/10.1080/03066151003595325.

10

Making the Invisible Seen: Putting Women's Rights on Vanuatu's Land Reform Agenda

Anna Naupa

> Women in Vanuatu are at a cross road: they live in a society that is both traditional and modern … The gendered roles imposed by society on women has [sic] seen them keep the traditions necessary for the continuation of the culture of their society (Piau-Lynch 2007: 4).

> Kastom has dictated that men are the decision makers and women play a supportive or submissive role. This is often cited as the reason why women are not only involved in decision-making but also do not have a significant voice in the governance of their society. (Tor and Toka 2004: 9).

Introduction

Advocates of Melanesian women's rights have often struggled to find sympathetic audiences among the region's male-dominated societies. Resistance has been rationalised as preservation of cultural values and traditional notions of gendered behaviour, where gender equality advocates have been accused of undermining social cohesion and upsetting the delicate cultural ecosystem (Tor and Toka 2004). Women's traditional gendered roles as mothers and housewives has meant that few women enter positions of seniority in both public and private sectors, resulting in only a handful of champions for women's rights at the national level (Piau-Lynch 2007: 4). While Vanuatu can claim gender equality successes in areas most relevant to women's childcare roles (for example, health and education), there is still a long way to go in other areas (VNGOC 2007).

While land reform was a key political driver of Vanuatu's Independence in 1980, land policy reform only recently returned to the political arena in the mid-2000s. Finding the space to raise awareness about women's land rights in a Vanuatu land reform context is challenged by competing reform priorities, such as redress mechanisms for unscrupulous deals, customary conflict resolution, and anti-corruption measures that had been overlooked for a couple of decades. Predominantly viewed as a male domain, the absence of women is notable in land discussions. Women have been largely invisible in state-managed land decisions, not least due to exclusionary practices by the males who control access to land in the traditional arena. Compounded by the primacy of customary land practice enshrined by Vanuatu's Constitution and state reinforcement of such gender bias, advocating for women's land rights—and women's rights in general—has required culturally and politically strategic approaches to finding a place in the land reform agenda.

This paper analyses the different strategies used to raise awareness and advocate for the recognition of women's rights to land in Vanuatu's policy reform context. Given the cultural context in Vanuatu, it has been necessary to adopt an advocacy model that goes beyond framing the language of rights within accepted socio-cultural constructs, to also address the political-economic dimensions of gendered access to land through identifying male champions, and to combine both upstream (awareness-raising) and downstream (coalition-building) advocacy paths. Future advocacy efforts must include greater engagement by women themselves, not just their advocates, for reform efforts to be sustainable.

Country Context

The Republic of Vanuatu comprises 83 islands in a Y-shaped archipelago, lying south of Solomon Islands and west of Fiji, with a population currently estimated to be about 290,000, of which 48 per cent are women. It is considered to be a lower middle-income country, where the gross national income per capita was US$3,000 in 2012. According to the World Bank's 'country policy and institutional assessment' ranking, Vanuatu scored 3.1 out of 6 for 'social inclusion/equity' in 2012.[1]

The majority of Ni-Vanuatu depend on what are described in Chapter 1 as 'land-based livelihoods', given that roughly three quarters of the population lives in rural areas, and 71 per cent of rural household incomes in 2010 were derived from subsistence production (39 per cent) or the sale of agricultural and other 'home made products' (GoV 2012a: 113–4). For countless generations, the land provided for all members of society, regardless of gender, sustained relationships between groups, and still underpins the identity and self-worth of most Ni-Vanuatu. Most Ni-Vanuatu have access to land through customary systems, and this, combined with the richness of natural resources and social capital, has tended to buffer rural communities from some of the more extreme effects of poverty (AusAID 2009: 5).

The sacred value Ni-Vanuatu place on land, and the central role land plays in cultural identity, are enshrined in Chapter 12 of the Constitution, which articulates the underlying cultural principle of the inalienability of land and universal indigenous access to land for basic livelihoods.[2] Consequently, all of Vanuatu's land legislation recognises the limitations of state governance of customary land. Formalised state protection of traditional land rights, until recently, was only possible in the case of land that was legally titled. Customary landholders governed non-titled land according to the rules of their *kastom*.

A number of development indicators illustrate that women in Vanuatu are disproportionately disadvantaged in society. There is limited access to education, with only 49 per cent of girls completing primary school and just 24 per cent commencing secondary school. In over 30 years of independence, Vanuatu has never had more than one or two female representatives, and currently has none at all, in a national parliament with 52 members. Vanuatu has one of the highest rates of gender-based violence in the world, with over 60 per cent of women experiencing violence (VWC 2011). Women's fertility remains high, with an average

---

1   See: data.worldbank.org/indicator/IQ.CPA.SOCI.XQ/countries.
2   Chapter 12 of the Constitution is devoted to land matters. Article 73 states that '[a]ll land in the Republic of Vanuatu belongs to the indigenous custom owners and their descendants', while Article 74 states that '[t]he rules of custom shall form the basis of ownership and use of land in the Republic of Vanuatu'.

of 4.8 children per mother. While 61 per cent of working-age women participate in the workforce, a significant proportion work in the undocumented informal sector. Women typically access land and property through inheritance and marriage, but very few have recorded a formal claim to land.[3] Nationally, only one in five households is headed by a woman (GoV 2009). The limited cash economy and poor access to credit in rural Vanuatu mean that there are few opportunities for women to earn cash or improve the standards of living of their families. The absence of women from representation in government and in the formal sector, and their limited access to services, point to women being particularly vulnerable in Vanuatu.

As a signatory to the Convention on the Elimination of All Forms of Discrimination against Women (CEDAW) since 1995, the Vanuatu government has been committed to advancing gender equality across several sectors, including that of land governance. However, gender equality has been largely viewed as a foreign import by the representatives of traditional societal structures. Existing land legislation is, at best, gender-neutral, with administrators typically adopting a (cultural) male bias in formal land titling and leasing (Scott et al. 2012). Women face several cultural barriers in exercising their rights to land, as exemplified by Merilyn Tahi's testimony to a Pacific regional meeting on women's access to adequate housing and land:

> I was forced to marry a boy. I had one son and forced to care for three children adopted by my husband, and one son from another woman. I was married to him for 26 years ... he died in 1997 ... all my things were thrown out of my matrimonial house ... I have since found another partner ... [but] according to custom, because of the bride price, I should have remarried my husband's brother, uncle or nephews. So the uncle has vowed revenge if I re-marry someone else ... I still go to the island regularly with my son, but I do not go to my matrimonial home or my husband's family. My husband's sisters no longer speak to me. I have lost everything there (Tahi 2004: 137).

Women's rights to land are not independent of male relatives, and are an extension of their socially constructed gendered roles as daughters, sisters, wives or mothers (AusAID 2008: 82).

---

3   The Department of Lands does not disaggregate land leasing records by gender, but the author's own research has found that rural leases typically do not record Ni-Vanuatu women as lessors (except on Efate Island). In urban areas, the state is the lessor, and Ni-Vanuatu women may be included as joint lessees, but this is rare.

This increases women's economic dependence on men, discouraging them from investing in land as a productive resource beyond subsistence farming, and denies women decision-making rights based on informed consent over land usage, investments and formal agreements on land rights (UNESCAP 2013: 149).

Advocates for women's rights in a male-dominated communitarian context must seek out an accepted cultural space to introduce women's matters into land discourse, overcoming exclusionary practices.

Central to this advocacy is a deep understanding of the nuances between access to land, in terms of rights-based advocacy, and the authority to decide on access to land, which focuses on the political dimensions of exclusion. Various studies have shown that most of Vanuatu's women have access to land in some form (Naupa and Simo 2008; GoV 2012b), but the ability to exert authority over this access is influenced by cultural norms and practice, both in the customary and formal domains. Hall, Hirsch and Li's (2011) framing of exclusion as a political process for determining access—including access to benefits—provides an appropriate lens for unpacking the advocacy approach taken in Vanuatu to elevate women's rights in the land reform agenda.

Land Dualism

As noted earlier, the Constitution of Vanuatu formally recognises the dual system of state and customary governance, particularly in relation to land matters. This dualism has led some (AusAID 2008; Naupa and Simo 2008; Naupa 2009; Stefanova et al. 2012; McDonnell 2013) to question which norms and practices take precedence, particularly where customary practices may conflict with state-condoned international best practice in matters such as women's rights.

Administratively, both the overlaps and differences between the two land governance systems often lead to conflict and confusion. As Rodman (1995) notes, uncertainty about who defines 'custom' lends itself to the emergence of 'masters of tradition' or political elites who direct or manipulate the modern interpretation of custom, and in so doing control it. In such a situation, the foundation of customary land tenure systems becomes challenged and further complicated by the overarching state land administration system that is limited in its ability to verify customary land claims. Siobhan McDonnell introduces the concept of 'masters of modernity'—men who are adept at negotiating the financial, cultural and, to a more limited degree, legal arrangements relating to land matters (see Chapter 9, this volume). This 'mastery' of the processes of the two systems affords certain men additional authority and privileges them as knowledge brokers or gatekeepers.

Where the two systems interact, such as when customary land parcels are formalised through the creation of a land title, a 'hybrid system' emerges that can embed the marginalisation of women in land matters, if rights are defined by the 'masters of modernity'. On many islands in Vanuatu, women do not have a formal role in traditional (or state) land matters, and where they do, this is becoming increasingly marginal (Naupa and Simo 2008). Competing interests in land further compound the ambiguous definition of *kastom* practice in a hybrid system. Whatever minimal protections for women's access to land may exist in traditional customs, which the state has lacked the capacity and the mechanism to enforce, become more threatened in the context of a land grab.

The Global Land Grab Context

Globally, land grabs have accounted for mass marginalisation of local populations, disenfranchised them of their land rights, and have occurred in contexts where the state imposes strict regulations over indigenous or customary land and retains the right to override the social institutions associated with it (Cotula et al. 2009). The displacement of settlements in the name of commerce, whether for large-scale agribusiness or extractive industries such as mining, has been viewed as a necessary price to pay for the greater economic benefit of states and multinational companies, but has also led to greater poverty in many cases, threatening the food security of the poor in particular (Daniel and Mittal 2009).

The global land grab literature and global campaigns to date have primarily addressed the ethics of land grabs or large-scale land investments, with some observers proposing a 'code of conduct' to regulate such land dealings (FAO et al. 2010). For example, Oxfam International's (2012) 'Behind the Brands' campaign has succeeded in getting major multinational brands (such as Coca-Cola) to commit to zero tolerance for land grabs by appealing to their corporate social responsibility.[4]

---

4   www.oxfam.org/en/grow/campaigns/behind-brands.

The focus on transnational commercial land transactions is centred on the production and export of food, biofuel, timber and minerals, where there is a perception of foreign-induced land grabbing (Borras and Franco 2012). The emphasis on the role of external actors in the process has limited the attention paid to the role of domestic facilitators, national elites, and state institutions that enable large-scale access to land, both at a commercial and individual scale (Cotula et al. 2009; Borras and Franco 2010). In Vanuatu, the framing of land issues in terms of foreign-driven investments and deals, enabled by a weak government administration, has tended to overlook the role that traditional institutions and the 'masters of modernity' have played in facilitating these deals.

Verma (2014: 55) has observed that most of the land grab literature has been gender blind (but see Mackenzie 2010). Verma encourages closer scrutiny of the framing of land grab debates, which have tended to

> focus on technocratic and productive values of land, stripping it of the multiple sociocultural, political, historical, and gendered meanings. This affects the processes by which women's and men's differential relationship, access, control, ownership, and security over land are negotiated (Verma 2014: 54).

This chapter explores the role of socially dominant groups and state bureaucrats in consolidating and expanding landholdings and selling or leasing them out to new investors, building on Borras and Franco's (2012) distinction between the *de jure* and *de facto* management of private property in land. It specifically looks at how this experience shaped particular gender advocacy strategies during Vanuatu's land reform process of the mid to late 2000s.

Land Grabs and Vanuatu

Vanuatu's 'land grab' experience is one of weakly enforced land legislation, unlike cases in the African region, and more recently in Papua New Guinea, where the government has strongly exerted its authority in facilitating large-scale land transactions for extractive industries. Vanuatu's 'zone of abandonment' in land governance, exemplified by the limited state oversight of land lease transactions negotiated between customary landowners and interested lessees—both foreign and domestic—is a direct product of Vanuatu's dual land governance system. The enshrining of customary land governance in the Constitution, combined with weak state legislation and regulation, has done little to protect traditional groups from the removal of their access to large tracts of land.

During the late 1990s through to the early 2000s, limited state monitoring enabled exponential growth in land transactions, mostly for speculative purposes. While almost 10 per cent of Vanuatu's land is under leasehold, this is primarily for residential purposes, reflective of the unique real estate emphasis of the 'land rush' during the early 2000s (Scott et al. 2012). The rising tensions between customary land groups and within families, as people—most often women—found themselves suddenly prevented from accessing garden lands, were the subject of much media coverage throughout the 2000s (see Kaloris 2009). Recognising the escalation of land conflict, the Vanuatu Cultural Centre convened a National Self-Reliance Summit in 2005, which led to a National Land Summit in 2006, hosted jointly with the Vanuatu government and the Malvatumauri (National Council of Chiefs). The National Land Summit passed 20 resolutions, committing the country to a long-term land reform process (Regenvanu 2008).

I was drawn into the land reform policy dialogue for both personal and intellectual reasons. As a mixed-race Ni-Vanuatu woman, I was aware that land had always been something that my male relatives talked about, not me. But in 2001, I became involved in researching traditional resource management for the Vanuatu Cultural Centre, which sparked an interest in researching the practical adaptations that occur when various pressures on community land management are prevalent. In the course of conducting research in the peri-urban village of Mele (for a Masters in Geography), it became apparent that I could not ignore the nexus between traditional and state land governance systems. By the time of the 2006 National Land Summit, I was one of only a small handful of women engaged in high-level discourse on this subject. This privilege was in part due to my previous employment at the Vanuatu Cultural Centre, my personal contacts within the Ministry of Lands from conducting my research, and my new job in the Australian government's Pacific Land Initiative.[5]

5   This latter role drew both personal persecution from certain land rights activists who were suspicious of donors' interest in land reform, but also great opportunities to influence the land reform process to address gender issues and women's rights. Cox (2014) has pointed to the role of Melanesia's urban middle class in influencing politics and policy. Though not myself resident in town, I may have fallen into this category.

While the 'land grab' in Vanuatu has largely been facilitated by internal—primarily indigenous—actors (the 'masters of modernity'), certain stakeholders were still focused on the popular framing of land reform to address the threat of foreign-induced land grabs. Framing the land reform process as a battle of 'us versus them', or 'Ni-Vanuatu versus foreigners', failed to recognise the role of indigenous middlemen, and did not allow for the heterogeneity of customary groups, nor the local political dynamics that shape land governance. This demarcation conceals women's rights behind a wholesale image of customary land tenure, and diverts public attention from the more pervasive challenge of local elite capture of custom and formal land governance processes. As a Ni-Vanuatu woman familiar with what Hall, Hirsch and Li (2011) call the 'intimate exclusions' that occur within customary land practice, I regularly advocated for a focus on indigenous facilitation of land grabs, but popular media rhetoric continually presented Ni-Vanuatu as victims of land decisions, belying the active role that Ni-Vanuatu men played in creating situations of land alienation. This framing challenge continues to the present day (Simo 2013).

Gender and Land Context

Eight years ago, my colleague Ketty Napwatt and I stood before an audience of 3,000 men in the national meeting hall of the traditional leaders who had gathered for the 2006 National Land Summit. This was my first public moment advocating for the protection of women's land rights—to speak about the unspoken. Until then, I had been working as a 'behind-the-scenes' policy maker, gathering evidence and applying it to Vanuatu's long-term land reform process. In Vanuatu culture, women do not speak before traditional chiefs; we certainly do not speak publicly in traditional meeting spaces, and we are invisible in land decisions. How then can we get women's perspectives included in the national land reform agenda when the space is typically male-dominated?

Introducing gender rights into the public discourse around land was not only made difficult by cultural attitudes and gendered roles, but also by the modalities of communication. A 2012 survey of citizens' information needs (InterMedia 2013) highlighted that the most preferred method of sharing information about land issues was in person (81 per cent), while radio was the second preferred method (68 per cent). If a trusted source is someone you know, the potential for distortion or influence in information flows is large. Any attempt to help increase women's awareness of their rights to land has to consider how to utilise these communication preferences. Addressing men, as the gatekeepers of knowledge and land decisions, is a prudent way to start to tackle the complex issue of land rights protection for Vanuatu's women.

A Boost for Women's Land Rights: Passage of the Land Reform Act Amendments

The recent amendments to the Land Reform Act signal an important step towards enhanced gender inclusion in the state and customary administration of land. The legislation[6] is the culmination of a seven-year multi-stakeholder effort to formally protect women's land rights, although there is still much work to be done. Careful strategising enabled the attainment of this historic first step towards formalised social inclusion in a country struggling to balance the tension between the traditional and the modern, and between political elites and those without voice.

Advocating for Women's Land Rights

Globally, land rights advocacy typically adopts a cyclical approach of employing a highly visible 'upstream advocacy' that publicises the issue, and the less visible 'downstream advocacy' that involves building consensus, forging alliances, and lobbying. Land rights advocacy efforts have also involved a cyclical approach in which awareness raising and consensus building are followed by: building the capacity of women's organisations; the use of research to educate and mobilise support; various forms of public engagement; and the application of lessons learned to the next stage in the process (ANGOC 2010).[7]

In Vanuatu, advocacy for women's land rights has adopted similar approaches, but adapted to existing power dynamics and the cultural context. While the issue of focus was the protection of women's access to land, the emphasis was on mobilising men rather than women's organisations. This 'downstream' approach was essential to empowering

---

6   *Land Reform (Amendment) Act no. 31 of 2013* and *Land Lease (Amendment) Act no. 32 of 2013.*
7   Some examples of global programs include Terrewode (Uganda), Landesa's Center for Women's Land Rights, and the International Land Coalition's program on Women's Land Rights (see also OHCHR and UN Women 2013).

traditional male leaders to recognise, advocate and protect women's access to land resources. Efforts that began with an overtly public, 'upstream' gender advocacy effort would have hampered subsequent ability to engage male decision makers. Focusing efforts on those in power, rather than mobilising women's organisations, was equally important to ensuring that women's land rights became visible through formal state mechanisms. Commencing with research on traditional rights helped inform stakeholder engagement and mobilisation of men at all levels—from the grassroots to the national parliament. Women's mobilisation had to be the final step in order to ensure initial buy-in from the predominantly male decision makers (see Table 10.1).

The following account of this policy process is largely drawn from a paper presented at meeting on 'Good Practices in Realizing Women's Rights to Land' that was held in Switzerland, not Vanuatu (Naupa 2012).

Table 10.1 Timeline for gender advocacy efforts, 2006–13.

Year	Milestone
2006	National Land Summit Resolutions recognise women's role in land matters ('group ownership').
2007	Research conducted on women's access to land in matrilineal societies (Naupa and Simo 2008).
2008	Vanuatu Cultural Centre's Women Fieldworkers Workshop discusses 'Women's Place on the Land'.
2009	Land Sector Framework 2009–2018 highlights inclusive decision-making processes.
2010	Justice for the Poor Program (World Bank/AusAID) conducts research on group decision making about land on Epi Island (Porter and Nixon 2010).
2011–13	Malvatumauri and Department of Lands build chiefs' awareness, and integrate social inclusion into institutional policy and practice.
2013	Land Reform Act amendments foster inclusive decision making for lease-based land transactions.

Source: Author's summary.

Gathering Evidence for Advocacy Efforts

Cultural resistance to gender equality in land matters can be addressed by sharing evidence of the negative impacts of women's exclusion from land decisions. In 2007 research was conducted on women's traditional roles in land decisions to gather evidence on cultural precedence for women's proactive roles in traditional land matters, led by the Vanuatu Cultural Centre with support from the Pacific Islands Forum Secretariat

KASTOM, PROPERTY AND IDEOLOGY

(Naupa and Simo 2008). This was followed by a 2008 Vanuatu Cultural Centre workshop focusing on women's voice in land matters. By gathering overwhelming evidence that refuted the received notion that decision making about land in Vanuatu was exclusively the realm of men, advocacy efforts could be tailored to make the land reform process more inclusive. Sustaining public attention on the issue required strategic use of the media in accentuating the challenges for women in the 'land for sale' environment on the main island of Efate.

In May 2009, the Cultural Centre's Land Desk gained the support of 100 chiefs to declare opposition to the government's initial land reform efforts through a 'Lamap Declaration' (MILDA 2009).[8] Despite high-level support from the Malvatumauri (the National Council of Chiefs), and its partnership with the Vanuatu government, there was still much suspicion surrounding any land reform efforts. According to the 'traditional guardians' camp, no land reform effort would be genuine without addressing the more fundamental problem of ministerial powers over customary land. However, procedurally, the inclusion of women and youth, as well as chiefs, in the Lamap Declaration was a good example of how to engage the broader community in land matters.

In 2010, the World Bank's Justice for the Poor program (called *Jastis blong Evriwan* in Bislama) collaborated with communities on the island of Epi to research the ways in which customary groups engage in the lease creation process and the subsequent impacts of this process on communities (Porter and Nixon 2010). Community theatre was used to communicate research findings and generate action at the local level. In 2011, the program conducted an assessment of the community dissemination of land leasing research, which found that communities most remembered:

> the importance of land and its protection for future generations in
> the context of a growing population; the need for greater consultation
> and inclusive group decision-making regarding the leasing of land;
> the importance of transparent processes for customary landholder
> identification; the need to understand the social and environmental impact
> of leasing and obtain specialist advice to make informed decisions … and
> the need for benefit-sharing within the group (World Bank n.d.).

---

8   In 2009, opposition to land reform efforts were generalised to encompass any effort by the Vanuatu government to modify the existing (although widely accepted by government as flawed) land administration arrangements. The specific land law reforms mentioned in the bulk of this chapter relate to efforts since 2009.

The value of this localised action research in triggering discussions about inclusive group decision making was considerable and timely, building on the momentum started by the Vanuatu Cultural Centre.

Framing Gender Within Culture: Social Inclusion

Fiercely nationalistic and supportive of the constitutional mandate of the primacy of customary governance systems over land, Vanuatu's traditional leaders have not responded positively in the past to a rights-based approach to gender and land. The framing of women's land rights within the context of family and community, and the broader social and cultural context, helped to gain a foothold in broader high-level discussions about customary land reform, offering a narrative of cultural continuity that sought to accommodate incremental advances for women (Naupa et al. 2006). Framing the issue as one of social inclusion, rather than 'just' a women's issue, tied advocacy efforts closer to culturally respected and valued principles relating to communal livelihoods. It helped to gain credibility for advocacy efforts, and also earned women a seat at the negotiating table for land reform.[9]

The strategic decision to focus on family units, rather than individuals, is one that has met with considerable success in other areas of women's rights. The Vanuatu Women's Centre's 11-year effort to introduce family protection legislation rested on principles of community peace and harmony, highlighting the importance of respect for women and therefore its importance in social cohesion. Working with nominated men and women who deliver community education activities and provide counselling and legal services (through Committees Against Violence Against Women), and a network of male advocates who conduct men-to-men awareness on gender rights, the Centre has successfully integrated a women's rights issue into the social fabric of Ni-Vanuatu lives (Ellsberg et al. 2008: 173, 179–80). For advocacy efforts relating to women's land rights, targeted integration of women into key stages of decision-making processes will be an important next step.

---

9 The author subsequently served as a gender and land policy expert for the Vanuatu government's land reform agenda, was a member of the Vanuatu Land Governance Committee, and served as the Gender Adviser to the 2013 National Land Law Reform Committee. The last two were ministerial appointments.

Tapping into Networks of Power: Male Champions

Advocating for women's land rights in a male-dominated culture necessitated a strategic emphasis on mobilising *men* rather than women to advocate for gender-sensitive land reform. As previously noted, the framing of the issue as a social—rather than gender—issue gave men a role to legitimately support the issue without undermining their own cultural standing. Ni-Vanuatu from both the traditional and state systems could 'buy in' to gender advocacy.

The Vanuatu government appointed a male gender focal point within the Department of Lands, who worked closely with long-time gender equality advocates, such as the author and the Department of Women's Affairs, to achieve a consensus from the traditional chiefly body to formally recognise and protect women's land rights in Vanuatu. The use of male champions enabled a truncated network influence effect that lobbying solely by women's organisations would have taken longer to achieve.[10] This is a practice that women's organisations like the Vanuatu Women's Centre have also employed, using male advocates to champion an end to violence against women. In 2012, a citizens information survey revealed that 70 per cent of those surveyed believed land to be owned by groups, not individuals (InterMedia 2013), thus demonstrating growing public support for formalised social inclusion.

The gender focal point position within the Ministry of Lands ended in late 2013 due to budget constraints, but the importance of using and maintaining networks to ensure the sustainability of these advocacy efforts will remain central to the future effectiveness of the new Customary Land Management Act and the amendments to the Land Reform Act.

In the final quarter of 2013, the Ministry of Lands conducted a nationwide consultation and awareness campaign regarding a proposed Customary Land Management Act (as well as amendments to the Land Reform Act). This would introduce substantial changes to the formalisation process for customary land, not least the process of ownership identification (GoV 2013). Particular attention was paid to ensuring that, at each of the 24 consultation meetings, separate meetings were held with women. Two female staff were appointed to the consultation team to specifically

---

10 Advocacy by women's groups for family protection legislation in Vanuatu took 13 years to have an effect.

facilitate these focused consultations with women on the land reform package.[11] By clearly linking the 2006 National Land Summit resolutions to the proposed land law sections, providing informational material in Bislama, and adopting a multi-media campaign, the consultation process helped to build the momentum that culminated in the passing of the bill during the November 2013 parliamentary sitting. Importantly, these public consultations highlighted the point that, in determining group rights to land, 'women and youth have the right to participate in land decisions' (GoV 2013: 5), and that 'if people did not follow the law, any member of a custom land owning group (e.g., any woman or youth) had the right to make a formal complaint to the newly established Land Ombudsman' (ibid.: 29). The Minister for Lands, Ralph Regenvanu, and the President of the Malvatumauri, Chief Tirsupwe, led the consultations, demonstrating the political and cultural power that supported the inclusion of women's rights in land matters (Anon. 2013a). A month later, the traditional leaders of Vanuatu overwhelmingly supported the proposed legislation, which would also formally protect women's rights and roles in land decisions (Anon. 2013b).

Other Factors: Who Frames the Agenda?

Political commitment enabled the several years of groundwork for women's land rights to be realised. As one aspect of a broader—and contentious—land reform package, there were several moments when the achievement of formal protection of rights was threatened by differing views on traditional rights protection, and by competition from other land policy interests. The genuine fear of codification of customary law, and the potential for diminished flexibility in land rights, as well as a general suspicion of major land reform by the government, led some factions within the Vanuatu Cultural Centre to actively undermine efforts to formally institute protective mechanisms.[12]

---

11   Siobhan McDonnell, personal communication, September 2016.
12   For example, the Land Desk at the Vanuatu Cultural Centre (funded by The Christensen Fund) remained highly critical of government reform efforts throughout.

Closing the Circle

Amendments to the Land Reform Act, gazetted in March 2014, elevate the role of women in consultation processes regarding custom and rights and public awareness of planned land transactions. Section 6(f3) states that:

> Membership of the custom owner group must be determined according to the rules of custom and by customary processes and is to include all indigenous citizens (men, women and children) who hold ownership or use rights over land in accordance with the rules of custom.

And Section 6(j8) states that:

> 'affected groups' must include, but are not limited to all women and young people living in the area concerned, any indigenous citizens who are not custom owners and any community in whose locality the land is situated.

Explicit reference to women in ownership identification and negotiation discussions will be an important guide to land administrators. This is a significant gender equality achievement for Vanuatu's male-dominated culture.

However, while the Customary Land Management Act signals an important first step towards clarifying ambiguity in a hybrid land governance system, it prioritises customary control of land management over social inclusion. Its gender-neutral position with regards to defining land rights does not allow for clear implementation of its intent for an inclusive approach. Women are only mentioned once in the entire Act in relation to group affiliation, where Section 2(1) states that 'members of a *nakamal* include all men, women and children who come under the governance jurisdiction of that *nakamal*'.

There is some irony in advocating social inclusion in land reform while inadvertently excluding women's organisations and networks. The advocacy strategy consciously focused on mobilising men, rather than women, to advocate for women's land rights, in an effort to be culturally sensitive, and therefore more accessible to powerful male decision makers. However, by delaying the focus on the organisational aspects of an advocacy model, Vanuatu now faces the problem of implementing gender-sensitive land law reform without the supporting organisational structures. There remains a role for the Department of Women's Affairs, which was consulted in the land reform process, women's organisations and networks of power, to maintain a focus on the rights issue, specifically through public 'upstream advocacy' efforts and to ensure the sustainability of law reform efforts to date.

The value of this important step in formalising protection of women's rights to land cannot be overemphasised. However, protecting rights to social inclusion in decision making on land-related matters is only part of a bigger package of legal reforms that are necessary to ensure complete protection. Family law, which will address marital property and inheritance concerns, is currently being developed and will demand greater participation by women's organisations and advocates with considerable cultural and formal experience in this area, such as the Vanuatu Women's Centre.

Beyond legal reforms, administrative reforms within both the Department of Lands and related land management entities (at both the state and local levels), as well as reforms within social institutions to incorporate women into traditional decision-making processes, have already begun. Standard policy implementation practices, such as public service training in operationalising legal roles and responsibilities, along with gender training, must be complemented by continued social inclusion campaigns via the media and chiefs' networks. Monitoring mechanisms to track policy implementation, such as six-monthly and annual agency reporting, should include gender-specific indicators to ensure that social inclusion remains visible in both practice and performance. Women's organisations should also play a role in monitoring implementation, using provincial and national networks to provide an independent assessment that can be used to inform improved government practice, through mechanisms like the CEDAW 'shadow reporting' process. Cross-sectoral resourcing of gender equality on land matters is essential for operationalising the current legislation.

Vanuatu's path to emphasise land tenure security for indigenous citizens has its pros and cons. On the one hand, group land rights have the potential to prevent and/or mitigate the negative implications of land grabs if private tenure security is guaranteed—a process that the Vanuatu government has now strengthened. On the other hand, unless the government strengthens its planning regulations and services, the lack of appropriate land advisory services to mitigate bad decisions by private group-based landholders may lead to a repeat of the land speculation of the early 2000s and women's continued exclusion from land decisions. However, the introduction of a set of formal mechanisms that require the involvement of women in the decision-making process goes some way towards mitigating against the lack of transparency in land decisions and the previous scant attention paid to the wider social implications of these land decisions.

References

ANGOC (Asian NGO Coalition for Agrarian Reform and Rural Development), 2010. 'Ideas in Action for Land Rights Advocacy.' Quezon City: ANGOC.

Anon., 2013a. 'Proposed Land Law Changes Consultation Takes Place.' *Vanuatu Daily Post*, 23 September.

——, 2013b. 'Vanuatu's Chiefs Give the Go Ahead to New Land Reform Laws.' *ABC News*, 18 October.

AusAID (Australian Agency for International Development), 2008. *Making Land Work—Volume I: Reconciling Customary Land and Development in the Pacific.* Canberra: AusAID.

——, 2009. *Vanuatu Land Program: Program Design Document.* Canberra: AusAID. Viewed 15 December 2016 at: dfat.gov.au/about-us/publications/Documents/vanuatu-land-program-design-document.pdf.

Borras, S.M. Jr and J.C. Franco, 2010. 'Towards a Broader View of the Politics of Global Land Grab: Rethinking Land Issues, Reframing Resistance.' Rotterdam: Erasmus University, Initiatives in Critical Agrarian Studies (Working Paper 1).

——, 2012. 'Global Land Grabbing and Trajectories of Agrarian Change: A Preliminary Analysis.' *Journal of Agrarian Change* 12: 34–59. doi.org/10.1111/j.1471-0366.2011.00339.x.

Cotula, L., S. Vermeulen, R. Leonard and J. Keeley, 2009. *Land Grab or Development Opportunity? Agricultural Investment and International Land Deals in Africa.* London: International Institute for Environment and Development.

Cox, J., 2014. '"Grassroots", "Elites" and the New "Working Class" of Papua New Guinea.' Canberra: The Australian National University, State Society and Governance in Melanesia Program (Briefing Note 2014/6).

Daniel, S. and A. Mittal, 2009. 'The Great Land Grab: Rush for World's Farmland Threatens Food Security for the Poor.' Berkeley (CA): Oakland Institute.

Ellsberg, M., C. Bradley, A. Egan and A. Haddad, 2008. *Violence Against Women in Melanesia and East Timor: Building on Global and Regional Promising Approaches.* Canberra: AusAID.

FAO, IFAD, UNCTAD and World Bank, 2010. 'Principles for Responsible Agricultural Investment that Respects Rights, Livelihoods and Resources.' Discussion note. Viewed 15 December 2016 at: www.fao.org/fileadmin/templates/est/INTERNATIONAL-TRADE/FDIs/RAI_Principles_Synoptic.pdf.

GoV (Government of Vanuatu), 2009. *National Population and Housing Census—Gender Monograph: Women and Men in Vanuatu.* Port Vila: National Statistics Office.

——, 2012a. *Vanuatu Household Income and Expenditure Survey 2010: Report.* Port Vila: National Statistics Office.

——, 2012b. *Alternative Indicators of Well-Being in Melanesia: Vanuatu Pilot Study Report.* Port Vila: National Statistics Office for Malvatumauri National Council of Chiefs.

——, 2013. 'Plan blong ol Jenis blong ol Loa blong Graon Folem ol Resolusen blong 2006 Nasonal Lan Samit.' Port Vila: Ministry of Lands.

Hall, D., P. Hirsch and T.M. Li, 2011. *Powers of Exclusion: Land Dilemmas in Southeast Asia.* Singapore: NUS Press.

InterMedia, 2013. 'Citizen Access to Information in Vanuatu: Land Issues.' Sydney: Intermedia for ABC International Development and AusAID.

Kaloris, R., 2009. 'Mangaliliu Road Block.' YouTube video, 2 February. Viewed 15 December 2016 at: www.youtube.com/watch?v=zypGJpzLJIE.

Mackenzie, F., 2010. 'Gender, Land Tenure and Globalisation: Exploring the Conceptual Ground.' In D. Tsikata and P. Golah (eds), *Land Tenure, Gender and Globalisation: Research and Analysis from Africa, Asia and Latin America.* Ottawa: International Development Research Center.

McDonnell, S., 2013. 'Exploring the Cultural Power of Land Law in Vanuatu: Law as a Performance That Creates Meaning and Identities.' *Intersections* 33.

MILDA (Melanesian Indigenous Land Defence Alliance), 2009. 'Lamap Declaration 2009.' Posted to MILDA website, 1 May. Viewed 16 December 2016 at: milda.aidwatch.org.au/resources/documents/lamap-declaration-2009.

Naupa, A., 2009. 'iKastom iWomen and Land in Vanuatu.' Paper presented to the World Bank's 'Justice for the Poor Symposium on Legal Pluralism', Jakarta, 4–5 June.

——, 2012. 'Making Change Happen: How and Where to Realize Women's Land Rights in Vanuatu.' Paper presented to the Expert Group Meeting on 'Good Practices in Realizing Women's Rights to Productive Resources, with a Focus on Land', Geneva, 25–27 June.

Naupa, A., K. Napwatt and C. Sparks, 2006. 'Women and Land.' Paper presented at the National Land Summit, Port Vila, 25–29 September.

Naupa, A. and J. Simo, 2008. 'Matrilineal Land Tenure in Vanuatu— "*Hu i Kaekae long Basket?*": Case studies of Raga and Mele.' In E. Huffer (ed.), *Land and Women: The Matrilineal Factor.* Suva: Pacific Islands Forum Secretariat.

OHCHR (Office of the UN High Commissioner for Human Rights) and UN Women, 2013. *Realizing Women's Rights to Land and Other Productive Resources.* New York and Geneva: OHCHR and UN Women.

Piau-Lynch, A., 2007. 'Vanuatu: Country Gender Profile.' Report to the Japan International Cooperation Agency. Viewed 15 December 2016 at: www.jica.go.jp/english/our_work/thematic_issues/gender/background/pdf/e07van.pdf.

Porter, R. and R. Nixon, 2010. 'Wan Lis, Fulap Stori: Leasing on Epi Island, Vanuatu.' Washington (DC): World Bank, Justice for the Poor Program (Research Report).

Regenvanu, R., 2008. 'Issues with Land Reform in Vanuatu.' *Journal of South Pacific Law* 12: 63–67.

Rodman, M.C., 1995. 'Breathing Spaces: Customary Land Tenure in Vanuatu.' In R.G. Ward and E. Kingdon (eds), 1995. *Land, Custom and Practice in the South Pacific.* Cambridge: Cambridge University Press. doi.org/10.1017/cbo9780511597176.004.

Scott, S., M. Stefanova, A. Naupa and K. Vurobaravu, 2012. 'Vanuatu National Leasing Profile: A Preliminary Analysis.' Washington (DC): World Bank, Justice for the Poor Program (Briefing Note 7.1).

Simo, J., 2013. 'Indigenous People, Not Australians, Should Determine Vanuatu's Future.' *Sydney Morning Herald*, 19 November.

Stefanova, M., R. Porter and R. Nixon, 2012. 'Towards More Equitable Land Governance in Vanuatu: Ensuring Fair Dealings for Customary Groups.' Washington (DC): World Bank, Justice for the Poor Program (Discussion Note).

Tahi, M., 2004. 'Testimonies on Violence against Women and the Right to Housing (Vanuatu).' In A.G. Aggarwal, S. Chaudhry and P. Waran (eds), *Our Land, Our Homes, Our Culture, Our Human Rights.* Nadi (Fiji): Proceedings of the Pacific Regional Consultation on 'Women's Rights to Adequate Housing and Land'.

Tor, R. and A. Toka, 2004. 'Gender, Kastom and Domestic Violence in Vanuatu: A Research on the Historical Trend, Extent and Impact of Domestic Violence in Vanuatu.' Report to the Vanuatu Department of Women's Affairs.

UNESCAP (UN Economic and Social Commission for Asia and the Pacific), 2013. *Statistical Yearbook for Asia and the Pacific 2013.* Bangkok: UNESCAP.

Verma, R., 2014. 'Land Grabs, Power and Gender in Eastern and Southern Africa: So, What's New?' *Feminist Economics* 20: 52–75. doi.org/10.10 80/13545701.2014.897739.

VNGOC (Vanuatu NGO Consortium), 2007. *Vanuatu NGO Shadow Report on the Implementation of the Convention on the Elimination of All Forms of Discrimination Against Women*. Port Vila: VNGOC.

VWC (Vanuatu Women's Centre), 2011. *Vanuatu National Survey on Women's Lives and Family Relationships*. Port Vila: VWC.

World Bank, n.d. 'Drama and Legal Awareness Are Effective Tools to Engage Communities Around Land Issues in Vanuatu.' Washington (DC): World Bank, Justice for the Poor Program. Viewed 15 December 2016 at: go.worldbank.org/Z66V7376M0.

11

From Colonial Intrusions to 'Intimate Exclusions': Contesting Legal Title and 'Chiefly Title' to Land in Epi, Vanuatu

Rachel E. Smith

Introduction

Exclusion from land was evidently a pressing social concern in November 2011 in Lamen Bay on Epi Island in central Vanuatu. At a community council meeting I attended a few days after I arrived in my field site, the village chief appealed to the local people to resist registering their land. The chief said that the registration of land under state law (*loa*) would make it vulnerable to leasing by outside 'investors'. He urged people that land should be left for chiefs to manage according to *kastom*. At the time of this council meeting, two major land disputes put the majority of Lamen Bay land under contention. Senior Li-Lamenu[1] men were the principal actors behind these conflicts, both of which involved attempts to register the land. These men had issued eviction letters to their own kin and

---

neighbours, across several different clans (*nasara*).[2] Later in this chapter, I shall discuss these two disputes in order to show how those attempting to exclude kin and neighbours from land in processes of 'intimate exclusion' (Hall et al. 2011: 20), and those trying to prevent these exclusions, deploy different discourses of *kastom* and *loa* to legitimate their actions.

Beyond Efate and Santo islands, where urbanisation and tourism are concentrated, Epi has the next highest degree of land leasing in Vanuatu (Howlett 2012). Lamen Bay is located on the northwest coast of Epi (see Figure 11.1), and is named after the small offshore Lamen Island, whose inhabitants use the bay area for cultivating their gardens. Over the past 50 years or so, Li-Lamenu people have begun to move from Lamen Island to the Epi mainland more permanently and in increasing numbers. Unlike most of the mainland, Lamen Island and Lamen Bay are densely populated, and there are growing worries about future land shortages. The pressure on land could be a reason why Epi islanders see Lamen Bay as a place where land disputes between kin are especially common.

The exclusion of kin and neighbours from land is a process that Derek Hall, Philip Hirsch and Tania Murray Li (2011: 145–66) term 'intimate exclusion'. The authors suggest that such processes are frequently motivated by a desire for wealth and capital. Likewise, in both the land disputes I analyse in this paper, local people saw the attempted exclusions as motivated by a desire for income from rent or leases. Like the Lamen Bay chiefs, many people also perceive exclusionary processes as being facilitated by the creation of formal legal titles to property and state regulation of land titles.

---

2   *Nasara* is the Bislama term most often used by Li-Lamenu people for their primary kinship groups, which I also refer to as clans. Whilst *pamerasava*, the vernacular term, refers to ideals of exogamy, *nasara* is also the Bislama term for a ritual and dancing ground, and thus has more territorial connotations as oral histories relating to such historical sites feature often in land claims. The terms *nasara* and *pamerasava* usually map on to each other, and are often used interchangeably.

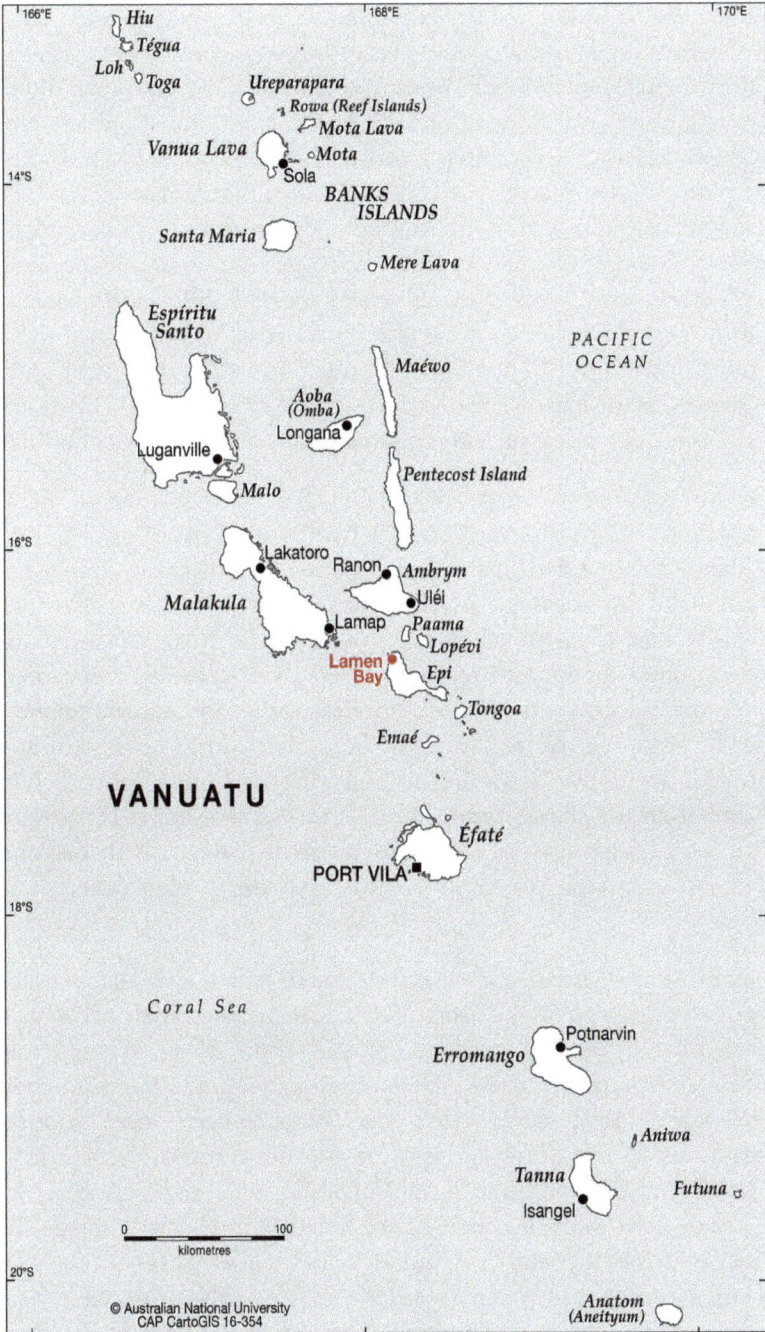

Figure 11.1 Map of Vanuatu, showing the location of Lamen Bay.

Source: CartoGIS, The Australian National University.

Conflicts over land and resources are simultaneously struggles over power, and the meaning and values that give authority to those claims (Hall et al. 2011: 166). As elsewhere in Melanesia (McDougall 2005; Filer 2006), political and moral discourses about land are often articulated in terms of *kastom* and *loa*, or *loa blong waetman* ('white people's law'). *Kastom* denotes knowledge and practices deemed to be indigenous or customary, usually in contradistinction to counterparts characterised as 'foreign'. In Vanuatu, people often say that *loa*—whether relating to land, criminal or civil cases—creates 'winners' and 'losers' (Forsyth 2009: 195), whereas the principle behind *kastom* courts is to restore peaceful and ordered social relations. Nevertheless, I suggest that senior men stand to benefit more than others, as the ideological principle of the restorative power of *kastom* has the effect of reinstating and reinforcing existing hierarchies of power.

As I shall argue in the first part of this chapter, in relation to major land claims on Epi, *kastom* is usually framed in terms of an 'ideology of chieftainship', and claims to 'chiefly title', by which rival claims are judged. Like any ideology, powerful actors can manipulate assertions of 'chiefly title' for personal gain. So, although in Melanesia *kastom* is often conceptually opposed to *loa* in a way that would seem to express an axiomatic distinction between the 'indigenous' (or 'autochthonous') and the 'Western', this duality must be understood as contextual and contested, articulated according to changing and often contradictory political strategies. Furthermore, appeals to *kastom* conceal the way in which local leadership and land tenure systems have been shaped and transformed through interactions with missionary, colonial and state influences.

Although *kastom* and chiefs, *loa* and the state, have a long and complex history of entanglement, they can still act as salient conceptual oppositions, deployed by Ni-Vanuatu people to represent contrasting and conflicting political and moral principles. When local people make the distinction in relation to land tenure today, they often contrast the 'inclusive' principle of *kastom*, ensuring everyone has some access to some land (whilst putting everyone in their rightful place), with the private property regimes of state law, which uphold the 'exclusive' rights of a recognised landholder whilst denying the claims of others altogether (Lea 1997: 12). On Epi, the ideology of chieftainship has also evolved in connection with social processes that (following Hall et al. 2011) I shall term 'intimate inclusions', by which displaced allies from outside were incorporated into kin structures and the 'relational economy' (see Chapter 5, this volume).

In contrast, people on Epi associate *loa* with imported and imposed European legal definitions and procedures, recalling the historical enforcement of processes of exclusion from land by foreign interests. From the late 1890s to Independence in 1980, Epi was one of the centres for European plantations in the archipelago (Bonnemaison 1994: 46–50), but throughout this period local people contested the legitimacy of colonial land titles. In the second part of this chapter, I shall give an account of these political struggles over land, to show how *loa* became a byword for exclusion from land, and *kastom* came to be understood as a compelling political framework for countering these 'foreign' intrusions.

As the phrase *loa blong waetman* suggests, Ni-Vanuatu people continue to associate state law with imported and imposed European legal definitions and the continuation of colonial rule, failing to represent indigenous practices and principles in the post-colonial era. Although land was returned to 'custom owners' following Independence in 1980, the boundaries created by colonial powers, and the legal system that encoded them, continue to be retraced in land disputes and leasing patterns taking place between kin and neighbours. A World Bank survey of leasing on Epi found 23 registered leases, of which 17 were created on land that had been alienated prior to Independence (Porter and Nixon 2010: ii). A subsequent report argued that 'pre-independence land alienation experience shapes land leasing on Epi today' (Stefanova et al. 2010: 2).

In the final part of this chapter, I shall present two case studies that serve to illustrate the micro-level processes by which local actors, usually senior men and self-proclaimed 'chiefs', strategically deploy discourses of *kastom* alongside legal claims for political and economic gain. However, as the second case demonstrates, alternative discourses of *kastom* that emphasise a more 'inclusive' ethic can be deployed as an effective means for countering exclusive legal claims.

Customary Landownership and the Ideology of 'Chiefly Title'

'When you talk about land, you talk about chiefs.' So said the Epi representative on the National Council of Chiefs (Malvatumauri) in a recorded interview.[3]

Kastom and *loa* can be seen as shifting and contested categories that can each incorporate aspects of their conceptual opposite, according to the contexts in which they are applied.[4] As the juxtapositions in the terms 'customary law' and 'custom owner' imply, in post-colonial Melanesian states there is an ambiguity in the relationship between *kastom* and *loa* that allows their configuration to take on an ideological character, concealing changing political and economic relations by presenting a front of time-honoured tradition. For instance, in Papua New Guinea, Filer (2006: 66) argues that the politically salient opposition between custom and law has been eclipsed by an emerging post-colonial ideology of customary landownership, in which indigenous citizenship is increasingly premised on legal status and entitlement within an extractive economy. The new 'ideology of landownership' in this context reflects the desire for resource compensation from mineral extraction and other lucrative development projects, in which claims are structured through the legal framework of membership of incorporated landowning groups.

In Vanuatu, where land leasing and rents rather than resource extraction dominate land transactions, it was the figure of the chief that stepped into the post-colonial space between *kastom* and *loa* to dominate the definition of 'custom ownership'. Following Filer, we might term this an 'ideology of chieftainship', in which the hereditary chief is the personification of *kastom* and rightful guardian of a traditional social order in which he represents the legitimate authority (White 1992: 75; also Chapter 1, this volume). On Epi, major land claims tend to be framed in terms of 'chiefly title', and these often entail contests over land occupied by people other than those of the chief's immediate kin group.

---

3   The chief quoted here is a key claimant in Case Study 2.
4   I am grateful to Keir Martin for helping me to elaborate this argument.

Unlike achieved rank and warrior status, hereditary chieftainship on Epi is traditionally associated with ideals of peace and social order. It is said that, if the chief is of the correct 'bloodline', everything will be 'good' or 'straight' (Lemaya 1996: 78). Although, in recent decades, the village chiefs have instructed each clan to nominate their own 'chief' to help keep order, it is socially recognised hereditary chiefs who tend to be seen as the appropriate candidates to be village chief, and to represent the villagers on the Area and Island Councils of Chiefs.

The role of hereditary chiefs has been transformed, even strengthened, since the early colonial period, relative to other forms of traditional authority. The literature on pre-colonial leadership systems draws a dividing line through Epi between an area of hereditary chiefly titles to the Polynesian-influenced south, and the more relational 'graded society' system to the north (Blackwood 1981; Bonnemaison 1984: 4, 1996: 201; Bedford and Spriggs 2008: 110).[5] However, in practice this line was blurred, and both systems operated flexibly together on Lamen Island (Lemaya 1996: 77–8). On Lamen and in western Epi, grade-taking continued until its demise in the early twentieth century—a period of great depopulation and disruption due to labour migration. And, whilst Presbyterian missionaries at this time looked favourably on the apparently noble institution of hereditary chieftainship, they sought to stamp out the 'morally depraved' grade system (Riddle 1949: 57).

Missionaries appointed Christian men to take on leadership roles as 'elders' and 'chiefs', and in some islands appointed 'paramount chiefs' to oversee the whole island. People today relate how Supabo, an early convert from northeastern Epi, was chosen by the missionaries to oversee a redistribution of land across northern Epi in the early 1900s, including the boundary where Lamen Bay gardens meet those of adjacent villages.

> He was the government of Epi. At the same time, he created some of the boundaries that exist today … They didn't call him chief; they called him government of Epi. He was chief, but at the same time he was government (Village chief of Lamen Island, recorded interview).

From 1911, chiefs were given the role of 'assessors', working alongside government 'district agents' to oversee local disputes. Even after Independence, former 'assessors' continued to use this position to claim

---

5   The 'graded society' was a system in which individual men competed to join successively senior grades or ranks through the distribution of wealth items to other members of their communities.

KASTOM, PROPERTY AND IDEOLOGY

authority and chiefly titles (Lindstrom 1997: 212–3; Rio 2007: 30–1). Thus the redefinition of the 'chief', as the occupant of a Presbyterian or colonial leadership role, has had a direct impact on the role of 'chief' in post-colonial Vanuatu (Bolton 1999: 3–4).

The position of chief as someone who presides over the land access of different clans also evolved in response to a remarkable historical series of 'intimate inclusions', whereby refugees and other incomers were incorporated into local kinship and exchange systems. During the dramatic depopulation of the late nineteenth and early twentieth centuries, depopulated clans, seeking to maintain their population and labour force, took in people from different parts of Epi who had been displaced by land alienation and tribal warfare. Lamen was known to be a hub for returned Queensland labourers (Giles 1968: 63; Docker 1970: 135), and like the Epi mainland, many current residents are descended from colonial-era plantation labourers and refugees from volcanic eruptions. Incomers, especially those from other islands, can be referred to in Bislama as *mankam*—a term which sometimes has derogatory connotations in contradistinction to the autochthonous *manples*. On Lamen today, such terms would occasionally arise in the context of land disputes, especially if the alleged incomers were seen as claiming the right to exclude other people from the land they occupied. However, due to a peaceful and inclusive ethic of respect for kin and neighbours, the word *mankam* is generally suppressed on Lamen.[6]

In fact, it is not those chiefs who claim that they are autochthonous to Lamen Island, but those claiming descent from long-abandoned mainland villages in Epi's interior, who tend to contest control over land in Lamen Bay, based on conflicting claims to 'chiefly titles' on overlapping areas of land, as we shall see in the two case studies that follow. In the past, Li-Lamenu people cultivated land on Lamen Island, and claims to garden land in Lamen Bay derive variously from claims to descent from the mainland, victories in warfare, and the granting of land rights by mainland chiefs.

---

6   See McDougall (2005: 83) for a similar situation in Ranongga, Solomon Islands.

Exclusion and *Loa*: The Historical Experience on Epi

In this section, I outline how processes of state formation and the development of a legal apparatus served to protect rival territorial claims between the two colonial powers. Land law was introduced largely to uphold and formalise land alienation, and so *loa blong waetman* became synonymous with exclusion from land for Ni-Vanuatu people. In the anti-colonial movements that mobilised to contest land alienation, *kastom* was deployed as a salient symbol of opposition, and it retains undertones of resistance to exclusion today. This historical background is crucial to understanding the ongoing politics of land on Epi today, because these legal and political processes of exclusion, and the boundaries they created, continue to be retraced in 'intimate exclusions' between kin and neighbours.

The Nineteenth Century 'Land-Grab'

In the late nineteenth and early twentieth centuries, Epi was at the centre of 'one of the biggest land grabs in the history of the South Pacific' (Van Trease 1987: 26). Unhappy with an 1878 'non-annexation agreement' between the rival powers of Britain and France, New Caledonia-based businessman John Higginson sought to acquire large amounts of land in the archipelago with the ultimate goal of effecting French control. He founded the Noumea-based Compagnie Caledonienne des Nouvelles-Hebrides (CCNH) in 1882, and Epi was a major target for acquisition (Sope 1974: 12; Van Trease 1987: 26).

Barthelemy Gaspard was one of Higginson's two agents in charge of procuring land. Many of these transactions took place on board their vessel, the *Caledonienne*, without any land surveys, and islanders were told to mark a piece of paper in exchange for trade goods and alcohol. Often the purported vendor had no right to the land, or was unaware of the nature of the transaction (Riddle 1949: 69; Weisbrot 1989: 70). Distances and directions were recorded with a deliberate imprecision that allowed them to be stretched far beyond those originally indicated

(Scarr 1967: 183, 199–200; Sope 1974: 14; Van Trease 1987: 27–8).[7] 'Needless to say, these transactions were not worth the paper on which they were written' (Van Trease 1987: 27). People on Epi today continue to relate such stories of fraud and coercion in colonial land transactions, and as Sope (1974: 7–14) argued, it is likely that local landholders would only have knowingly conceded temporary use rights to small areas of land, as was customarily practised, and not freehold title.

The CCNH became the Société Francaise des Nouvelles-Hebrides (SFNH) when the French government took control in 1894, and the French began to settle beyond Port Vila in much greater numbers from the late 1890s (Bonnemaison 1994: 50). The French concentrated their efforts on Epi, where land was split into blocks of 50 hectares to be offered to prospective settlers (Scarr 1967: 212–3; Van Trease 1987: 40). With a Joint Naval Agreement now in place to protect the 'lives and property' of settlers, indigenous people had few options for resistance (Van Trease 1987: 42). Even so, the Presbyterian missionaries on Epi, who were strongly against French annexation, were lending their voices to indigenous protests against the rapid land appropriation (Scarr 1967: 213n; Van Trease 1987: 40).

In 1901, a missionary in western Epi, Robert Fraser, recorded regular incidents between French planters and local villagers, which were published by the Presbyterian Mission Synod to expose France's 'secret plan' for a settlement on the island. The missionaries claimed that the French were appropriating vast areas, including whole inland villages that had never dealt with French agents (Fraser 1900; Paton et al. 1901; Van Trease 1987: 40). However, despite having no official authority over land, the British naval commander gave tacit support to the French planters. 'The forcible occupation of land on the strength of Gaspard's swollen title-deeds was thus facilitated by the unofficial intervention of a body which was formally debarred from deciding land cases' (Scarr 1967: 214).

In the same year, '675 male adults, including 106 chiefs' on Epi signed a petition organised by Fraser,[8] beseeching King Edward VII to annex the island for the British, stating:

---

7   Around the same time, the Australian-owned South Sea Speculation Company was purchasing Epi land in ways that were just as questionable (Van Trease 1987: 28; also Scarr 1967: 202).

8   With support from local missionaries, Epi and Efate chiefs had presented a similar petition intended for Queen Victoria in December 1891 (Anon. 1892).

There are many white men now coming to the New Hebrides, and at the hands of some of these—mostly Frenchmen—we have suffered cruel wrongs. Some have forcibly possessed themselves of our lands, which they have not bought, burnt down houses, shot our pigs, and harassed us in other ways. We wish to live in peace, but at present we feel no protection from such injuries, but we feel that under the shadow of your just Government we would have justice and enjoy peace (Anon. 1901).

With their continued appeals to the British Empire and Commonwealth of Australia to intervene (Paton et al. 1901: 4; Scarr 1967: 218–20), the missionaries played a part in bringing about the Anglo-French Convention of 1906, which led to the formation of the Condominium government (Scarr 1967: 218; Sope 1974: 15; Stober 2004: 14). But with French insistence, the burden of proof regarding disputed land sales was to fall on any challenger. Title deeds relating to the 600,000 hectares purchased before 1896 were very difficult to contest, and the half of these lands that had been acquired by CCNH agents in the mid-1880s were beyond dispute altogether (Scarr 1967: 224–6; Sope 1974: 17).

Resisting the Rule of *Loa*

Throughout the colonial period, people on Epi continually resisted the alienation of their lands, but the balance of 'justice' was very much weighted in favour of the colonial powers. It was a long time before the new government agreed on any legislative measures to deal with disputed land, and in its early decades, land alienation continued to proceed on what was effectively a lawless frontier. A Joint Court was founded in 1910, but was widely seen as inept and ineffective: the Court could only try 'infractions', not major crimes or land disputes (Scarr 1967: 232–3).

In April 1913, two French planters occupied some land in northern Epi that was under cultivation by islanders. When one of the planters attacked local people who refused to leave the land, they fought him and he was killed. The French struck back, and 20 Epi islanders were captured and taken to Vila, including Sam Miley, a leader of indigenous resistance against land alienation. The French pinned Miley with a range of charges, including collecting monies by threat, and attempts to persuade plantation workers to leave their employment (Scarr 1967: 234–40). Miley was tried in secret on board ship, without a hearing, and sentenced to an additional six months' imprisonment. Edward Jacomb, an English lawyer who encouraged indigenous people to resist the appropriation of land by whatever means they could, considered Miley's treatment a 'travesty of justice' (Jacomb 1914: 126), and argued that the French were trying to prevent Miley from finding funds for legal proceedings against the planters.

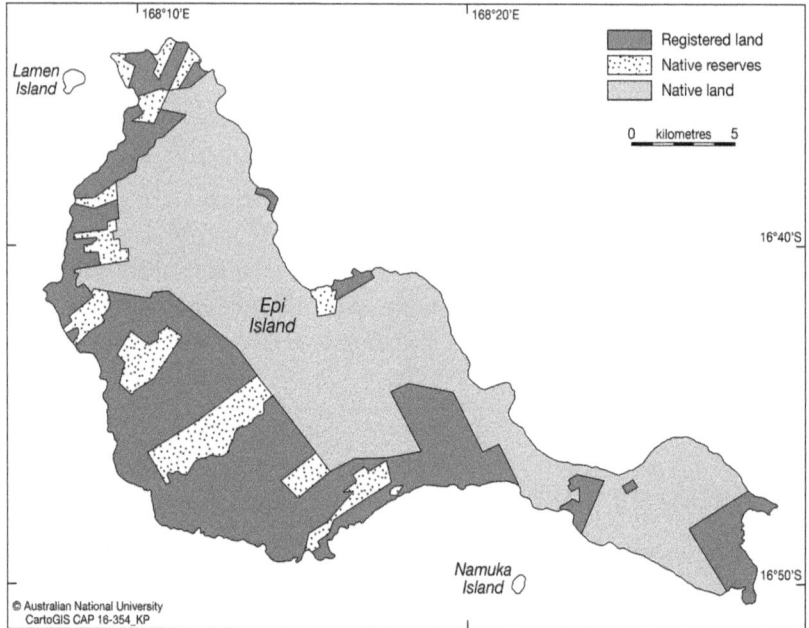

Figure 11.2 Registered land and 'native reserves' on Epi Island.
Source: CartoGIS, The Australian National University, based on a colonial map reproduced in Van Trease (1987: 2).

In 1914 the British and French agreed to a protocol that allowed for the extension of the Joint Court's powers to include land disputes, but even disputed titles would be upheld with a supporting survey and either recognised antiquity or three years' occupation (Scarr 1967: 249–51). It was only in 1935 that the Joint Court finally turned its attention to the 74 applications pertaining to Epi, most held by SFNH, but survey work was halted by hostility from Epi islanders (Sope 1974: 17). Twenty-one of Epi's chiefs had instructed the Court's Native Advocate to counter every one of the SFNH's applications, insisting that the purchases were illegitimate, but without success (Van Trease 1987: 86). The formalisation of the Epi claims was only completed in the 1950s, by which time 15 'native reserves' had been created on the island, including one in the northern part of Lamen Bay (see Figure 11.2). However, this was done with little regard to where people were living, the quality of the land, or how much they required (Van Trease 1987: 80–7). As Sope (1974: 10–11) argued: 'In the judgement of many people the Joint Court was established to legalise land titles which were illegal by European as well as New Hebridean standards.' So it is hardly surprising that people on Epi came to associate *loa* with illegitimate exclusion from land.

Independence and the Rise of *Kastom*

From the 1960s, anti-colonial movements started to gather momentum, which revalorised and propagated *kastom* as a popular symbol to counter land alienation (Weisbrot 1989: 70). Many Li-Lamenu people were drawn to Nagriamel, a movement based on Santo Island that mobilised against further appropriation of land (Kolig 1987).[9] After the New Hebrides National Party (NHNP) was formed in 1971, around half of Li-Lamenu people, mainly from one of its two main villages, withdrew from Nagriamel and joined the new party, encouraged by the Presbyterian Church of Vanuatu. The church made an official declaration of support for the nationalist cause when a resolution was passed at the 1973 Presbyterian Assembly in Tanna, when Li-Lamenu pastor Jack Taritonga was the moderator (Gardner 2013: 138–9; Van Trease 1987: 210).

In 1974, the NHNP produced a number of radical proposals for land reform, stressing the need to return land to customary owners (Van Trease 1987: 213, 217). But when the French intervened politically to prevent the NHNP from achieving the majority required to push through more extensive land reforms, the party resorted to advocating direct action, including the occupation and seizure of alienated land by its Ni-Vanuatu supporters. In 1977 and 1978, supporters of the NHNP, now known as the Vanua'aku ('My Land') Party (VP), set up roadblocks and occupied alienated land. Many VP supporters from Lamen Island and the villages of northeastern Epi occupied the large French-owned Walavea[10] and nearby Ringdove plantations and ousted the plantation owners, seizing their cattle and store goods (Van Trease 1987: 226–30).

---

9   A Nagriamel 'headquarters' was built at Merakup in Lamen Bay, site of the second case study in this paper. This was later to be the site of a showdown between rival Nagriamel and NHNP supporters. When conflict grew between the two movements in the late 1970s, NHNP supporters in northern Epi (according to one of those involved) threatened the Nagriamel group, tore down their flag and burned their copra plantation.

10   The site of Walavea plantation is part of the second case study.

Independence was achieved in 1980, after the VP won a strong majority in the national elections of 1979. The Constitution of the new nation declared that all land belonged to customary owners and their descendants (Van Trease 1987: 238), but did not state how 'custom ownership' was to be resolved.

> The proclamation that all land belongs to the custom owners is, in one sense, an appeal to *kastom* in its oppositional role, and a direct denial of colonial practices of land alienation and of colonial attempts to legislate or police land matters. But the proclamation also created a zone of abandonment by government, in the sense that highly variable customs and the difficulty of identifying custom owners can be glossed over as *kastom* and left alone, beyond state control (Rodman 1995: 66–7).

Meanwhile, the legal system for registration of land was still based on the colonial logic of the 'Torrens system', designed to ease land transactions by facilitating individualised land titling without any checks on existing undocumented claims, and thus difficult to challenge (Rose 1994: 208; McDonnell 2013: 9). This process allowed local people to register land and engage in legal proceedings in Port Vila, often without any prior knowledge or consent from other people using the land, as we shall see in the case studies to follow.

Case Study 1: Appeals to *Loa* and *Kastom*

I shall now discuss the first of the two attempts at 'intimate exclusion' in Lamen Bay that I mentioned in the introduction. This case study shows the legal mechanisms by which colonial boundaries and processes of exclusion continue to be reproduced. Furthermore, it reveals how the indeterminacy of the category 'custom owner' can be manipulated from the angles of both *loa* and *kastom* for personal benefit. As mentioned in court documents, the boundary of the area in question included an airport and—at the time of the original claim—the wharf used by a large commercial cruise ship, and thus was a potentially lucrative source of rental income. In this case, the self-proclaimed chief at the centre of the dispute exploited legal ambiguities to support his highly contested claim to 'chiefly title'.

An Error of Judgement

This dispute stems back to a 2003 Island Court case between a family from nearby Paama Island, and Philip, who acted as a spokesman for four different Li-Lamenu clans. The claimant from Paama had produced a document relating to an 1886 land sale attributed to the infamous French CCNH agent, Barthelemy Gaspard. The claim extended from the northwestern point of Epi to the northern side of Lamen Bay, a region named as 'Velague' and 'Bourgue' in the deeds. These names most likely referred to the areas known today as Vela and Purke, though the disputed boundary extends far from these stretches of shoreline, bearing the dubious hallmarks of Gaspard's hugely exaggerated land claims.

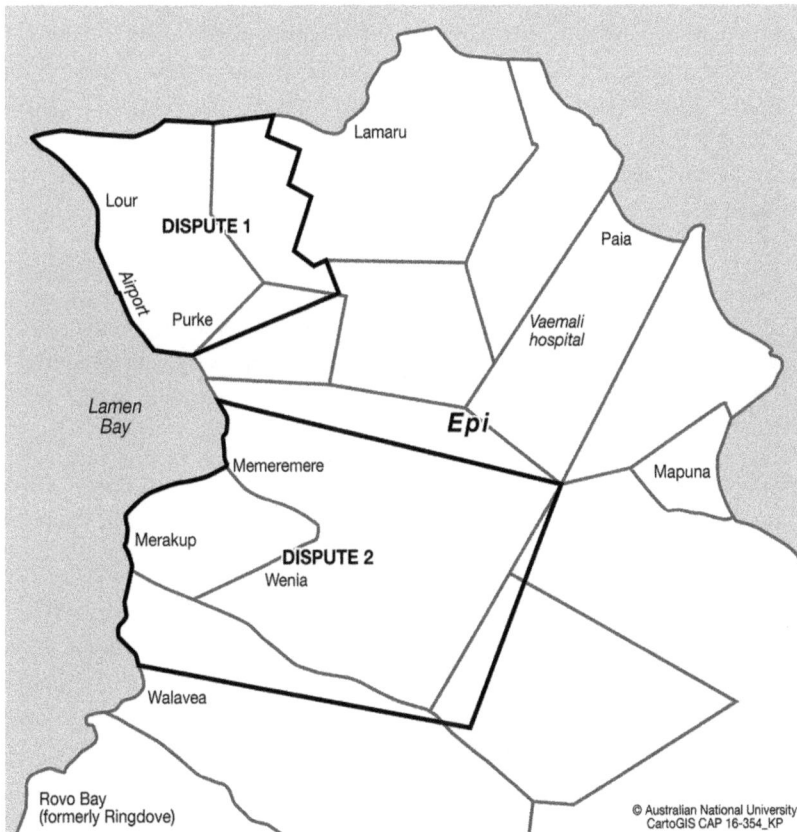

Figure 11.3 Two major land dispute boundaries, Lamen Bay, c. 2012.
Source: CartoGIS, The Australian National University, based on claim documents.

The judgement from the 2003 Island Court case stated that, although the deeds of sale produced by the Paamese claimant appeared to support his claim that his ancestor was resident on 'Velague' land, this was not admissible as evidence for custom ownership, and considered the possibility that it might be based on fraudulent claims:

> We have reminded ourselves to be mindful and conclude that such instrument … is not a decision of a recognized Court that was in existence during the European settler's era in these islands.

Island courts are bound to administer cases according to the 'customary law' of each island or region, so the criteria by which they adjudge cases are open to influence by those who can convince the judges of their superior place-based knowledge. The disputed land included the garden lands or residences of four different *nasara* that had cooperated in the 2003 court case, supporting Philip's claim to be the chief representing one of the original four *nakamal* (communal men's houses) that were historically located on the landscape, with their chiefs' customary ordination stones. In this case the judge was convinced that proof of 'chiefly title' was required:

> It is evident that there is a customary obligation for a Paramount Chief to allocate land to his assistants together with their boundary limits. As a matter of reciprocity a custom lease is normally paid to the Paramount Chief. This Chiefly system and the land tenure system are proved to be intertwined. Thus, any isolation or absence of these founding aspects to land would prove an invalid custom.

Accordingly, the judgement rejected the Paamese claim on the grounds that the claimant could not demonstrate sufficient knowledge of the place and its 'custom', such as knowledge of the chiefly system on Epi.

Furthermore, the Li-Lamenu counter-claims in this case, framed in terms of the 'ideology of chieftainship', also concealed disagreements about claims to 'chiefly title' and the way that these were manipulated to strengthen their case. Although in court the four *nakamal* supported Philip's claim to be descended from a particular high-ranked chief, I later found out that there was an ongoing dispute between two *nasara* as to which could legitimately claim descent from this chief. One man told me that his and the other clans decided to go along with Philip's claims in court, despite the fact that they rejected the truth of these claims, in order to give a united and consistent testimony. That is, by concealing internal rifts and tensions, they could strengthen their claim to superior place-based customary knowledge, which would be difficult for any outsider to challenge. The judge was convinced and the judgement concluded:

> it is this day adjudged that [Chief Philip] representative of the four (4) Nasara of the Lamen Bay community is the rightful owner of the Velague and Bourge [sic] land.

Exploiting Legal Ambiguities

Although the Li-Lamenu strategy of concealing their differences to present a united front was successful in the short term, it had later repercussions. Some years later, when one of Philip's neighbours went to plant some crops near his house, Philip stopped him from doing so and threatened to evict him from the land, claiming that it belonged to him in light of the concluding statement of that poorly worded 2003 judgement. The neighbour told me that he had heard Philip was travelling to Port Vila, and suspected that Philip would try to register the land in his own name, so he phoned a friend at the Lands Department and advised him that the land was under dispute and not to be registered. Nevertheless, Philip had issued a number of eviction notices through a solicitor, ordering local residents off the land. Philip's threat to evict his close kin and neighbours can thus be seen as an attempt at 'intimate exclusion' (Hall et al. 2011: 145)—a process in which kinsfolk and social intimates may be excluded from land, which is often motivated by a desire for rent or resource income.

In 2010, members of the different clans that claimed land within the disputed boundary returned to the Island Court to request a 'judgement clarification' in respect of the 2003 judgement, this time addressing their argument to Philip and making it in Bislama, so it was clear to all. It stated that the land belonged to all four historic *nakamal*, and that each had equal interests. However, given that Philip's opponents have withdrawn their support for his 'chiefly title', and say that he fabricated his genealogy and oral history, this means that even this 'clarified' judgement is still highly contested.

Despite the formal 'clarification', the indeterminacy of customary law means that it could remain open to future attempts at exclusion, or else demands for payments from those occupying the land. The clarification said that residents who were 'non *kastom* owners' have the right to continue to occupy the land provided that they make the 'necessary arrangements such as leasing the land following *kastom* or law', and ordered Philip not to threaten or disturb the people occupying the land unless his notice was 'justifiable and follows law'.

Furthermore, this case illustrates the type of mechanism by which land exclusions today continue to reflect titles created in the colonial period. The boundary claim was originally based on a land purchase document from 1886—a claim that is likely to be fraudulent or exaggerated, given what is known about Gaspard. This document was later deployed to make a post-colonial land claim, despite the fact that colonial titles are supposed to have been erased at Independence. An Island Court decision served to retrace this colonial boundary, but this time through a claim of exclusive ownership by a local man against his own kin.

Case Study 2: Vested Interests

In Vanuatu today, those land disputes that threaten 'intimate exclusions' and evictions tend to be motivated by expected economic gains (Hall et al. 2011: 145) from commercial developments or from leasing the land. These are the disputes that would usually involve attempts to register and secure title to the land. However, many other disputes on Epi did not involve attempts at registration or leasing. Rather, they served as a means to settle political conflicts, aimed more at (re-)establishing social hierarchies between traditional authorities or groups than expectations of economic gain (Epstein 1969: 198; McDougall 2005: 6).

This second case study serves to demonstrate examples of both types of logic and motivation. Whilst the case was triggered by the threat of exclusion from an attempted registration and lease arranged with an expatriate investor, following the logic of exclusive legal title, the same tribunal was used to settle a hierarchical dispute between rival chiefs through a discourse of *kastom*. The chief who arranged the tribunal used a vision of a more 'inclusive' *kastom*—one opposed to exclusive legal principles—to defend his land against the lease. However, this model also served to confirm and reinforce his place in a local political hierarchy, and to help perpetuate the 'ideology of chieftainship' to legitimate chiefly authority over land.

Investors and Leasing

In Vanuatu today, attempts at exclusion are often motivated by the expectation of rent or lease payments, which are enabled by registration of the land, often through collaboration with expatriate 'investors' and with the complicity of powerful political figures (see Chapter 9, this volume).

This is illustrated in a case triggered when John P, originally from Lamen Island but resident in Port Vila, leased an area of land known as Merakup from his own father and brother. John P was a close work associate of an expatriate businessman based in Port Vila who is associated with a number of other land leases in Vanuatu, and it was rumoured that family P wished to subdivide the land for tourism in partnership with this businessman (Porter and Nixon 2010: 60–1; Farran 2011: 261).[11] I was also told that John P had used the colonial title number to register the land, again showing the types of process by which land boundaries created in the colonial era continue to be redrawn.

In 2009, Chief X, and other people in the village of Wenia, close to Lamen Bay, received a letter from a lawyer representing John P, which stated:

> Our client instructs us that you and your immediate family members have been living on the land without knowledge and/or consent of our client who is the registered legal owner of the land.
>
> As such, you are hereby given **Notice** to vacate the land within **twenty eight (28) days** upon the date of the receiving of this letter.

This came as news to the Wenia villagers, who were unaware that the land had been registered at all.

At the time of the dispute, Chief X was representative for Epi in the National Council of Chiefs (Malvatumauri). Thus he was well versed in land matters and well connected in terms of legal and political support. He was also in a strong position to navigate the complexities of *loa* and *kastom* to succeed in regaining control over the land. For Lindstrom (1997: 222–8), Malvatumauri chiefs represent the incorporation and codification of chiefly authority, and operate both inside and outside the

---

11 Family P had adopted the investor in a high profile ceremony in 2010, and this allowed him to run for election as Member of Parliament for Epi in 2011. His victory seemed to reflect a common disappointment with the failure of the post-colonial state to deliver 'development'.

state. In their mediatory role, Lindstrom argues, they serve to sanctify the state as upholding *kastom*, but in their role as authorities of *kastom*, they can also wield their power to oppose the legitimacy of state law. Chief X took the case to the Supreme Court in 2010, on the grounds that the land 'had been registered by fraud or mistake'. He argued that family P had registered the land without the knowledge of other residents, ignoring the ruling of a 2007 area court judgement that indicated Chief X was in charge of the land. On this basis, the judge ordered that the case be transferred to a Customary Land Tribunal.[12]

The 2007 judgement was in fact the result of a long-running dispute over Merakup land between two neighbouring Lamen-based clans from Ngalovasoro village—family P and family Q. The 2007 judgement indicated that both of these Li-Lamenu families had been granted separate areas of land by some chiefly predecessors of Chief X. Family Q supported Chief X in court, confirming that the small area of garden land they cultivated was granted to them by a historical agreement with one of Chief X's ancestors. Those who supported Chief X's claim said that family P originated from another part of Epi, and that Chief X's ancestors had granted them garden land, but a much smaller area than the 115 hectares they had registered (Farran 2011: 261).

Chiefly Rivals

At the same time, Chief X used the opportunity of the Land Tribunal to defend his 'chiefly title' and claim over an adjacent area of land against rival claims by another Li-Lamenu man, James, a member of Y clan from Lamen Island. James was claiming chiefly title as a direct descendant of a past chief of 'Madoga' land, but the boundary of his claim closely matched the boundary of the land claimed by Chief X.

The year prior to the tribunal hearing, James had staged an elaborate ceremony in which visiting chiefs from the villages of Varsu—a separate district in northeastern Epi—conferred a chiefly title on him. Then,

---

12 The Customary Land Tribunal process was introduced in 2001 through a recognition that state courts were not a legitimate location for the resolution of land disputes, which required local knowledge (Rousseau 2004: 76). However, it drew criticisms from chiefs and others who asserted that it contravened customary norms, such as the right of chiefs to take charge of decision making (Farran 2008: 97–8; Regenvanu, 2008: 65). The World Bank research team (Porter and Nixon 2010: 20n) found that Epi chiefs had initially resisted the idea of a Tribunal, but then in 2009 had formally requested one for Epi to address major disputes. Their request was initially refused but eventually granted.

shortly before the hearing, James held another impressive ceremony with the same Varsu area chiefs to open a *nakamal* newly built on the disputed land, and even tried to bring the hearing to this new *nakamal*, rather than the one at Wenia, where Chief X resided. These ceremonies were provocative political statements because Chief X was then involved in land and title disputes with the same Varsu chiefs who were supporting James. Chief X and the Varsu chiefs were of the same language group, and claimed descent and titles from long-abandoned villages in Epi's interior. James and Chief X told me, at the time of the dispute, that rival chiefs in the two districts were planning a series of meetings to try to resolve their disputes according to a 'chiefly structure'.

James and his family had been locked in another dispute with a family Z, belonging to another Lamen clan, who were neighbours of his, and built a church close to James's house. In court, the members of family Z corroborated Chief X's statement that he had given them the right to work on the smaller area of land that they occupied, and said they had made two customary transactions to him in the 1980s. Thus we can see volatile relationships between different Li-Lamenu clans (P and Q, Y and Z), based on historic alliances and claims relating to 'chiefly titles' on the mainland.

Despite these conflicts, neither James nor Chief X ever threatened to evict the other groups occupying or cultivating the land. In fact, during the council meeting I described at the beginning of this chapter, James had stood up to speak in agreement with the Lamen Bay chief, to say that they were all 'Christian' men and should trust each other to resolve the dispute locally. This suggests that James and Chief X were more interested in asserting rival claims to be the 'bigger chief', higher up in the social hierarchy, than to profit from leases or commercial development of the land.

Intimate Inclusions and Relative Exclusions

In an interview, Chief X told me that a big chief's role is to 'manage' the land and everything within it. He argued that Epi *kastom* does not permit exclusive legal claims, and it is the chief's responsibility to ensure that all the clans using the land, and their descendants, have enough land on which to subsist.

Today, many people do not want to do what *kastom* tells them. They say 'The land is mine', but no, *kastom* does not say that ground belongs to you. *Kastom* says that land is for all of us, but that you, the chief, must make sure that you manage the land well so that my children can eat from the land, and when they die their children will still eat from the land. It's simple.

Chief X argued that, when it came to a land dispute, the claimant should not only demonstrate knowledge of genealogical connections, and customary landmarks and boundaries, but also prove where he is properly located in a 'chiefly structure'. To prove that he is a 'big chief', a claimant must prove that he has a set of 'small chiefs' as his 'clients'. Equally, if someone arrives from 'outside', the chief can allocate land to him, but the newcomer must recognise that he is 'under' that chief.

For this tribunal hearing, Chief X presented a list of eight points that he used as 'proof' that he was the 'big chief' of the land in question, and had control over the landholdings of four different Li-Lamenu families (P, Q, Y and Z) involved in the dispute:

I am a chief that has other chiefs below me, with all our 'clients', following the chiefly structure.

Following number 1, they have their own *nasara* and their stones.

I went through an ordination ceremony to take back my title Chief X, and I have a stone.

In 1988, Tarbumamele Council [the Epi Island Council of Chiefs] decided that [Z] family that work in Madoga hill must make a *kastom* [transaction] to me, because we gave them the right to work on that land.

Our ancestors gave the right to the [Y] *nasara* a long time ago, and they have already made a *kastom* [transaction] to us.

In 2007 Varmali Area Council made the decision that Chief X would take the [Q] family and show them their boundary.

We also gave the right for Epi High School to work on the land.

My ancestors gave a piece of land to the family [P]. I don't know if the family [P] knows this or not?[13]

---

13   These statements have been translated from a document written in Bislama.

In the 2012 tribunal hearing, it was adjudged that Chief X was the 'big chief' in charge of the Wenia land whose boundary encompasses Merakup and Madoga (see Figure 11.4). Chief X was implored not to exclude those who were occupying the land:

> Following this agreement, that you are the big Chief that oversees the Wenia boundary, do not endanger those people that stay under your care.

Thus, even though family P were deemed to be immigrants from another part of Epi, the judgement sought to protect their right to remain on the land, alongside the access rights of the other clans allocated adjacent areas.

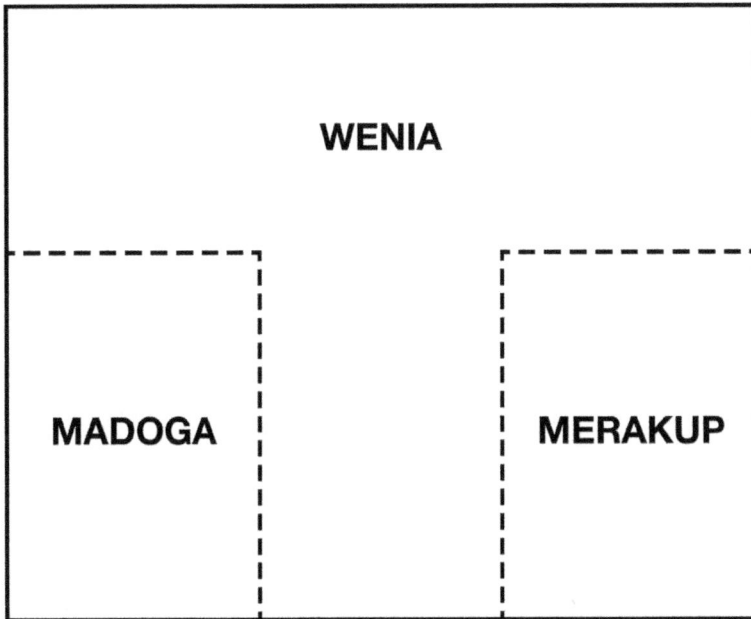

Figure 11.4 Model of land boundaries according to tribunal judgement.
Source: CartoGIS, The Australian National University, adapted from 2012 Land Tribunal judgement.

This version of the ideology of chieftainship takes the form of a layered model of overlapping land rights, where the 'big chief' maintains administrative control, alongside an inclusive ethic that all have rights to use some land. Gluckman (1963: 90–8) argued that, in areas of shifting agriculture, land tenure systems were likely to take the form of layers of different rights administered through a status hierarchy, and those rights depended on the fulfilment of obligations to others. Epstein (1969: 114–6) refined this concept to better fit the kinds of systems found in Melanesia, whereby various overlapping rights and interests in land may apply through membership of a descent group, but also through ties of kinship with other groups, as well through interpersonal transactions. However, changing political and economic circumstances may be leading to a greater emphasis on exclusivity, at the expense of wider obligations and 'interlocking reciprocal claims', as Martin (2013: 35) observed amongst the Tolai people whose customs had previously been described by Epstein (1969).

The promotion of this layered model of land tenure can also be seen as a means for self-proclaimed chiefs to assert their positions in a political hierarchy and, in doing so, perpetuate and even strengthen the 'ideology of chieftainship'. Although this may be more 'inclusive' in terms of allocation of access to land across kin groups, it can be exclusive in terms of restricting decisions about land to senior men, and the voices of women and younger people are often not heard in land debates (see Chapters 10 and 13, this volume).

Conclusions

The concepts of *kastom* and *loa* dominate the terms of debate about land exclusions on Epi today. *Kastom* and *loa* came to be conceived as oppositional terms articulating a history of mutual entanglement, a shifting form of 'double movement' (Filer 2014, following Polanyi 2001: 138), but the way that this is manifested is always contextual and contested. Due to Epi's experience of historical land alienation, and the formalisation of land titles by the incipient state, state law often invokes bitter memories of the appropriation of land to support foreign commercial and political interests. It is little surprise, then, that people on Epi came to associate *loa* with exclusion and domination. Later, in the lead-up to Independence, *kastom* was reshaped and revalued as a potent oppositional symbol of resistance against land alienation.

The post-colonial period represents a further shift in the relations between *kastom* and *loa*, as attention has turned to the identification of 'custom owners'. On Epi, the hereditary chief, as the personification of *kastom* and an arbiter of peace and social order, appeared as the natural figure to take control of the articulation between *kastom* and *loa*. However, this 'ideology of chieftainship' conceals the way in which the position of chief has been transformed, and even strengthened, through missionary and colonial influences. Furthermore, like any ideology, powerful actors can manipulate discourses of *kastom* and claims to 'chiefly title' for personal gain. So *kastom* is not a straightforward articulation of autochthony or indigeneity against alien *loa*. Rather, each concept is able to take on aspects of the other according to the contexts and purposes of its deployment.

Attempts at 'intimate exclusions' of kin from land usually invoke claims of 'chiefly title' as 'custom ownership', but also legal processes of land registration and leasing, often motivated by the promise of economic benefits. Furthermore, boundaries created around land alienated in the colonial era have not been fully erased after more than three decades of independence, and can be retraced in ongoing land claims by senior men who use old title numbers and colonial documents to support their legal claims. Thus *loa* continues to be understood as a continuation of the logic and instruments of colonial rule, facilitating the dispossession of customary owners.

However, alternative and more inclusive discourses of *kastom* can act as effective political frameworks for resistance in denying the legitimacy of exclusive legal property claims. Popular moral narratives of *kastom* tend to give authenticity to those claims that demonstrate a peaceful and inclusive ethic, respecting people's interlocking claims to access land and subsistence security, as opposed to the exclusive land rights associated with state law and capitalist engagements (Carrier 1998; also Lea 1997: 12). The reassertion by councils of chiefs of a layered model of land tenure, which is embedded in social relationships and the 'relational economy', has remained the most compelling form of resistance against 'intimate exclusions' by safeguarding access to land by different clans. However, this model also serves to reinforce and perpetuate existing hierarchies, in which 'land' becomes synonymous with 'chiefs', and so often women and younger people can be excluded from decision-making processes.

Recent (2014) land reforms give good reason to be optimistic that the types of exclusionary processes outlined in the above case studies will not continue to be enabled by political and legal systems as they have been before (McDonnell 2016). Registration and leasing should no longer be able to take place without the knowledge and consent of the community. Perhaps this means that, in future, *kastom* and *loa* can become more conceptually aligned in the minds of Ni-Vanuatu people. And given the oppositional capacity of *kastom* to signify inclusive, consensual, peaceful and relational ethics against exclusionary or individualising processes in shifting political contexts, there may be potential for it to adapt to incorporate increasing community participation and strengthen the values of consensual decision making in future.

References

Anon., 1892. 'Australian Press Comments, Reports, etc., upon Affairs in the New Hebrides.' London: Foreign and Commonwealth Office Collection. Viewed 14 December 2016 at: www.jstor.org/stable/60228992.

———, 1901. 'The New Hebrides. French v. English. Petition for Annexation.' *The [Adelaide] Advertiser*, 11 April. Viewed 14 December 2016 at: trove.nla.gov.au/ndp/del/article/4831227.

Bedford, S. and M. Spriggs, 2008. 'Northern Vanuatu as a Pacific Crossroads: The Archaeology of Discovery, Interaction, and the Emergence of the "Ethnographic Present."' *Asian Perspectives* 47(1): 95–120. doi.org/10.1353/asi.2008.0003.

Blackwood, P., 1981. 'Rank, Exchange and Leadership in Four Vanuatu Societies.' In M. Allen (ed.), *Vanuatu: Politics, Economics and Ritual in Island Melanesia*. Sydney: Academic Press.

Bolton, L., 1999. 'Chief Willie Bongmatur Maldo and the Incorporation of Chiefs into the Vanuatu State.' Canberra: The Australian National University, State Society and Governance in Melanesia Project (Discussion Paper 99/2).

Bonnemaison, J., 1984. 'Social and Cultural Aspects of Land Tenure.' In P. Larmour (ed.), *Land Tenure in Vanuatu*. Port Vila: University of the South Pacific.

———, 1994. *The Tree and the Canoe: History and Ethnogeography of Tanna*. Honolulu: University of Hawaii Press.

———, 1996. 'Graded Societies and Societies Based on Title: Forms and Rites of Traditional Power in Vanuatu.' In J. Bonnemaison, C. Kaufmann, K. Huffman and D. Tryon (eds), *Arts of Vanuatu*. Honolulu: University of Hawaii Press.

Carrier, J.G., 1998. 'Property and Social Relations in Melanesian Anthropology.' In C.M. Hann (ed.), *Property Relations: Renewing the Anthropological Tradition*. Cambridge: Cambridge University Press.

Docker, E.W., 1970. *The Blackbirders: The Recruiting of South Seas Labour for Queensland, 1863–1907*. Sydney: Angus and Robertson.

Epstein, A.L., 1969. *Matupit: Land, Politics and Change among the Tolai of New Britain*. London: C. Hurst & Co.

Farran, S., 2008. 'Fragmenting Land and the Laws that Govern It.' *Journal of Legal Pluralism and Unofficial Law* 40: 93–113. doi.org/10.1080/07329113.2008.10756625.

——, 2011. 'Navigating Changing Land Use in Vanuatu.' *Pacific Studies* 34: 250–268.

Filer, C., 2006. 'Custom, Law and Ideology in Papua New Guinea.' *Asia Pacific Journal of Anthropology* 7: 65–84. doi.org/10.1080/14442210600554499.

——, 2014. 'The Double Movement of Immovable Property Rights in Papua New Guinea.' *Journal of Pacific History* 49: 76–94. doi.org/10.1080/00223344.2013.876158.

Forsyth, M., 2009. *A Bird that Flies with Two Wings:* Kastom *and State Justice Systems in Vanuatu*. Canberra: ANU E Press.

Fraser, R.M., 1900. 'Renewed French Aggression in New Hebrides.' *The [Hobart] Mercury*, 13 October.

Gardner, H., 2013. 'Praying for Independence.' *Journal of Pacific History* 48: 122–143. doi.org/10.1080/00223344.2013.781761.

Giles, W.E., 1968. *A Cruize in a Queensland Labour Vessel to the South Seas* (ed. D. Scarr). Canberra: Australian National University Press.

Gluckman, M., 1963. *The Ideas in Barotse Jurisprudence*. Manchester: Manchester University Press.

Hall, D., P. Hirsch and T.M. Li, 2011. *Powers of Exclusion: Land Dilemmas in Southeast Asia*. Singapore: NUS Press.

Howlett, N., 2012. 'Leases in Vanuatu: Key Data from the World Bank Jastis Blong Evriwan Vanuatu National Leasing Profile.' Washington (DC): Justice for the Poor Program.

Jacomb, E., 1914. *France and England in the New Hebrides: The Anglo-French Condominium*. Melbourne: George Robertson & Company.

Kolig, E., 1987. 'Kastom, Cargo and the Construction of Utopia on Santo, Vanuatu: The Nagriamel Movement.' *Journal de la Société des Océanistes* 85: 181–199. doi.org/10.3406/jso.1987.2578.

Lea, D., 1997. *Melanesian Land Tenure in a Contemporary and Philosophical Context*. Lanham (MD): University Press of America.

Lemaya, J., 1996. 'Nimangki-Vara.' In D. Tryon (ed.), *Nimangki: Wokshop Blong ol Filwoka blong Vanuatu Kaljoral Senta 1994*. Port Vila: Vanuatu Cultural Centre.

Lindstrom, L., 1997. 'Chiefs in Vanuatu Today.' In G.M. White and L. Lindstrom (eds), *Chiefs Today: Traditional Pacific Leadership and the Postcolonial State*. Stanford (CA): Stanford University Press.

Martin, K., 2013. *The Death of the Big Men and the Rise of the Big Shots: Custom and Conflict in East New Britain*. New York: Berghahn Books.

McDonnell, S., 2013. 'Exploring the Cultural Power of Land Law in Vanuatu: Law as a Performance That Creates Meaning and Identities.' *Intersections* 33.

——, 2016. My Land My Life: Power, Property and Identity in Land Transformations in Vanuatu. Canberra: The Australian National University (PhD thesis).

McDougall, D., 2005. 'The Unintended Consequences of Clarification: Development, Disputing, and the Dynamics of Community in Ranongga, Solomon Islands.' *Ethnohistory* 52: 81–109. doi.org/10.1215/00141801-52-1-81.

Paton, F.H.L., T. Smaill and R.M. Fraser, 1901. *Memorial on French Aggression in the New Hebrides from the Presbyterian Mission Synod: With a Narrative of Land Disputes in Epi and Efate*. Melbourne: James Arbuckle & Company.

Polanyi, K., 2001 [1944]. *The Great Transformation: The Political and Economic Origins of Our Time*. Boston (MA): Beacon Press.

Porter, R. and R. Nixon, 2010. 'Wan Lis, Fulap Stori: Leasing on Epi Island, Vanuatu.' The World Bank, Washington (DC): World Bank, Justice for the Poor Program (Research Report).

Regenvanu, R., 2008. 'Issues with Land Reform in Vanuatu.' *Journal of South Pacific Law* 12: 63–67.

Riddle, T.E., 1949. *The Light of Other Days*. Christchurch (NZ): Presbyterian Bookroom.

Rio, K.M., 2007. *The Power of Perspective: Social Ontology and Agency on Ambrym Island, Vanuatu*. New York: Berghahn Books.

Rodman, M.C., 1995. 'Breathing Spaces: Customary Land Tenure in Vanuatu.' In R.G. Ward and E. Kingdon (eds), 1995. *Land, Custom and Practice in the South Pacific*. Cambridge: Cambridge University Press. doi.org/10.1017/cbo9780511597176.004.

Rose, C.M., 1994. *Property and Persuasion: Essays on the History, Theory, and Rhetoric of Ownership*. Boulder (CO): Westview Press.

Rousseau, B., 2004. The Achievement of Simultaneity: Kastom in Contemporary Vanuatu. Cambridge: University of Cambridge (PhD thesis).

Scarr, D., 1967. *Fragments of Empire: A History of the Western Pacific High Commission, 1877–1914*. Canberra: Australian National University Press.

Sope, B., 1974. *Land and Politics in the New Hebrides*. Suva: South Pacific Social Sciences Association.

Stefanova, M., R. Porter and R. Nixon, 2010. 'Leasing in Vanuatu: Findings and Community Dissemination on Epi Island.' Washington (DC): World Bank, Justice for the Poor Program (Briefing Note 5.4).

Stober, W.E., 2004. 'Isles of Disenchantment: the Fletcher/Jacomb correspondence letters exchanged between R.J. Fletcher and Edward Jacomb, 1913–1921.' Canberra: The Australian National University, Pacific Manuscripts Bureau (MS 1243).

Van Trease, H., 1987. *The Politics of Land in Vanuatu: From Colony to Independence*. Suva: University of the South Pacific.

Weisbrot, D., 1989. 'Custom, Pluralism, and Realism in Vanuatu: Legal Development and the Role of Customary Law.' *Pacific Studies* 13: 65–97.

White, G.M., 1992. 'The Discourse of Chiefs: Notes on a Melanesian Society.' *Contemporary Pacific* 4: 73–108.

12

Landownership as Exclusion

Victoria Stead

Introduction

Across the Pacific, as across much of the post-colonial world, various practices of land formalisation—particularly land titling—are posited as remedies to the exclusion of peoples and groups from land, as well as from the promises of 'development' and from participation in the globalising market place and in the political and social space of the nation-state. This is particularly so in the case of indigenous, poor, women, and other marginalised peoples. In Melanesia, land formalisation generally involves mechanisms for codifying or translating elements of customary land systems in order to make them commensurable with the forms and requirements of modern systems of governance and economic production and exchange. Invariably, this involves establishing relations of property ownership—making land into property and people into 'landowners' (including 'customary landowners').

Drawing on an ethnographic analysis of communities living in the vicinity of industrial tuna fishing and processing facilities in Madang Province, Papua New Guinea (PNG), this chapter explores and critiques some of the claims which are made by proponents of land formalisation in PNG. Far from securing people's access to the promises of development, globalisation, and statehood, it argues, mechanisms of land formalisation for these communities have, in many cases, facilitated and exacerbated experiences of exclusion. The chapter considers two key ways in which this has occurred: first, through the introduction and privileging of particular practices of boundary making associated with modernist and regulatory approaches to land organisation; and second, through the use of incorporated land groups and lease-leaseback schemes which claim to reconcile customary and modern land systems. The intention here is not to suggest that all forms of legislative response to issues of land organisation should be avoided. Indeed, as the Madang communities find themselves entangled with the structures of both globalising capital and the nation-state, forms of institutionalised response can become both necessary and desirable. The argument, simply, is that more critical acknowledgement be made of the ways in which mechanisms of land formalisation can, themselves, function to exclude.

Land Reform in Papua New Guinea

Land reform in PNG has long been a contested affair. The enshrining of customary land tenure in the country's Constitution upon Independence in 1975 reflected a broader political commitment to a vision of small-scale development embedded in Melanesian culture—the 'Melanesian Way'. This was, in many ways, a radical and far-reaching vision for the birth of a new nation-state (James et al. 2012). It also, however, reflected a continuation of colonial policy grounded in elements of paternalistic 'social protection' (Filer 2014). Indeed, as Colin Filer observes, the creation of the Papua New Guinean nation-state rested on something of a 'founding fiction' (Filer 2014: 82), which overstated the distinction between colonial and post-colonial land policies, and which instituted a national 'ideology of landownership' as a basis for the new state's self-imagining and social relations. The national ideology of landownership declares all indigenous citizens to be customary landowners, it denies the possibility of waste or vacant land, it identifies clans as the foundational social unit of the nation, and it establishes rent or resource compensation (paid to 'customary landowners' whose land or natural resources are subject to commercial exploitation) as a principal mode of income and the predominant means of accessing 'development'.

If the ideology of landownership remains a potent political force 40 years after Independence, however, a key change in the political landscape over that period has been the emergence of neoliberalism as a dominant political-economic ideology both on the global stage and within key sections of the national stage. This has had significant—if often ambiguous—implications for the imaginings both of 'development' and of land policy. Globally, organisations such as the World Bank began arguing through the 1980s and early 1990s for the introduction of individual freehold land titles (see Deininger and Binswanger 1999). Drawing on the ideas of influential international economists such Hernando de Soto (1989), the argument made was that such reform was a necessary precondition for economic growth, and hence 'development'. In PNG, attempts by the state to introduce mechanisms for the registration of customary land in 1995 were abandoned amid popular opposition, which was sparked by rumours that the World Bank was demanding individualised registration of customary land as part of the conditionality for receiving its loans. In fact the contentious loan condition was rejected by the PNG Department of Finance, but suspicion of land registration, and of both the PNG state and international donor organisations as actors that stood to gain from such registration, remained powerful. And, indeed, the argument for land titling—and for an associated model of large-scale resource extractive 'development'—increasingly took hold among much of the country's political elite, including many individuals who two decades before, had been vocal advocates for the Melanesian Way. Throughout the early 2000s, a number of Australian policy advisers influential in shaping Australian foreign policy in regards to the Pacific also argued strongly for land titling and tenure conversion (Curtin 2003; Gosarevski et al. 2004a, 2004b; Hughes 2004).[1]

In the absence of mechanisms for widespread land registration, two key legal instruments have been used in the post-Independence period to facilitate what is widely described in PNG as the 'mobilisation' of customary land 'for development'. Principal among these are the *Land Groups Incorporation Act 1974* and the lease-leaseback scheme. In the first of these, legislation allows for the incorporation of landowning groups as legally recognised entities, able to contract with other entities, particularly corporations. In the lease-leaseback scheme, land is leased from customary owners by the state, which then leases it on to another entity, usually a corporate developer (see Chapters 6 and 7, this volume). In 2009, land reform legislation—the Land Groups Incorporation (Amendment) Act and the Land Registration (Customary Land) (Amendment) Act—was passed to entrench the use of land groups, particularly, and also to enable these groups to register titles to their land. The passing of this legislation

---

1   For critiques of their position, see Fingleton (2005) and Allen (2008).

reflects, in part, a broader policy shift away from straightforward tenure conversion (from customary tenure to a private property regime), towards hybrid systems that seek to find a 'middle way' between customary land tenure and modern, Western legal frameworks (Deininger and Binswanger 1999; World Bank 2003; AusAID 2008). In part, as well, it reflects what is arguably a growing acceptance of a mainstream developmentalist paradigm in PNG, which takes cash income, formal sector economy, and business-led development as its key criteria of value. It is notable that, notwithstanding opposition from some non-governmental organisations, and the recent anger over the revelation of the 'land grab' facilitated by long-term special agricultural and business leases (Filer 2011; Winn 2012; also Chapters 6 and 7, this volume), the 2009 legislative amendments encountered substantially less popular opposition than did previous attempts at land reform.

In their analysis of land exclusion in Southeast Asia, Derek Hall, Philip Hirsch and Tania Murray Li (2011) identify regulation—including mechanisms for land formalisation and titling—as one of four key forces propelling processes of exclusion from access to land, along with the market, the use or threat of force, and legitimation. This is in spite of the fact, they observe, that proponents of land formalisation efforts most frequently describe them not in terms of exclusion, but *inclusion*. Hall, Hirsch and Li's four 'powers of exclusion' do not operate in isolation, but are mutually affecting and mutually enforcing. Particularly relevant for this discussion is the intertwining of legislation and legitimation, which is the force that 'establishes the moral basis for exclusive claims, and indeed for entrenching regulation, the market and force as politically and socially acceptable bases for exclusion' (Hall et al. 2011: 5). On Madang's north coast, we shall see that the use of both land groups and land leases has been central to the dynamics of the tuna industry, and to the relationships between local communities, the PNG state, and corporate and non-corporate outside actors. In the development of the tuna industry, as well as of the mission-operated plantation industry that preceded it in the late nineteenth and early twentieth centuries, regulation has been a basis for exclusion of (some) people and communities from key sections of land. Across this history, such regulation has been closely bound up with both normative and ideological discourses of legitimation. At the same time, local negotiations and strategic engagements with both legislation and legitimation have given rise to forms of 'intimate exclusion' (Hall et al. 2011: 145) within which some people are excluded from land, not simply by state or corporate actors, but also because of the actions of neighbours and relatives.

Across PNG, arguments for land formalisation invoke normative and ideologically laden ideas of development, citizenship, and progress. Literature produced by the National Land Development Taskforce, for example, features repeated references to 'mobilising', 'freeing up', or 'making available' customary land 'for development' (GoPNG 2007), while elsewhere the aim of the Taskforce is stated as being to 'make land more productive' (Fairhead et al. 2009: 1). With the 'security' of rights, titles and codified ownership claims, proponents of land formalisation insist, people can use their land as collateral for loans, engage in transactions with resource developers and others, and in so doing can access 'development' and its many promises. The Australian aid agency AusAID—influential in guiding land policy in PNG as well as elsewhere in the Asia-Pacific region—likewise talked about land formalisation 'making land work' (AusAID 2008). Such legitimating discourses assume a model of development predicated on the extension of capitalist production and exchange and, within this context, they assume very particular ideas of what it means for land, and people, to 'work' (Stead 2014). In the context of state-building processes, they form part of the project of making citizens, and incorporating people and places within the political space of the nation-state (Scott 1998; Lund 2011). Simultaneously, people and places are incorporated within the economic space of globalising capital. Papua New Guinean civil society organisations, and some landowners and communities, have critiqued these legitimations for land registration and codification, arguing that they ignore the ways in which land already 'works' within communities, and the ways in which 'security of tenure' is provided not by land titles but by customary systems of governance, kinship and oral tradition (Anon. 2008). In turn, they offer their own legitimations, for local small-scale models of 'development', for the efficacy of customary tenures, and so for other visions of statehood and nationhood.

Tuna Fishing in Madang

On most afternoons, the informal fish market near the Madang harbour, easy walking distance from the main Madang market, is brimming with colours, sounds and smells. Small reef fish—brightly coloured and variously shaped—are sold fresh or else cooked up on skewers or wrapped in banana leaves and ready to eat. These fish come in close to the shore and can be caught in shallow waters from boats, or even with lines thrown into the water from on land. It is women, usually, who fish for these small catch, both to feed their own families and to market for cash to supplement a predominantly subsistence livelihood. Among the larger fish on sale are tuna—skipjack, yellow-fin and big-eye—which can be caught out in deeper waters with nets or with lines cast, usually by men, from small outboard motor boats or even wooden canoes. Increasingly, though, the tuna being caught in the waters off the coast of Madang are not being eaten, or sold, by Papua New Guineans, but are caught by large industrial tuna fishing vessels that fly the flags of various countries— Taiwan, Japan, Korea, the United States and the Philippines. Instead of lines and small nets, these use purse seines, huge round nets up to 2,000 metres in diameter, which are dropped from the boats and then drawn together (pursed) so that they enclose whole schools of fish. For the most part, these vessels pay licence fees to the PNG state for the right to fish in PNG waters, and they take their catches—and most of the profits associated with them—to third countries where the fish are processed and exported for sale. Recent efforts to develop the onshore tuna processing industry represent attempts by the PNG state to move from this so-called 'first-generation strategy' to a 'second-generation' one, whereby tuna will be processed onshore and exported—ideally to the lucrative European Union market. This is an attempt, in other words, to move up the global tuna commodity chain, one that will 'bring development' in the forms of increased gross domestic product, employment, and cash income (Havice and Reed 2012; Stead 2014).

Currently, there is one tuna canning facility operating in Madang. This is run by the Philippines company RD Tuna Canners Ltd (RD Tuna) on a piece of land titled Siar Portion 1004, just north of the boundary of Madang town. RD Tuna also operates a wharfing facility, the Vidar Wharf, approximately twenty kilometres further along the north coast highway. The Vidar Wharf, like the cannery, is located on land previously alienated in the period of German administration, when Lutheran and Catholic missionaries alike arrived in the late nineteenth century and began establishing coconut plantations as a lucrative side business to the saving of souls. The area surrounding the Vidar Wharf—216 hectares in total—now stands to be developed as the Pacific Marine Industrial Zone (recently renamed the Madang Industrial Park, but still widely referred to as the PMIZ), a 'special economic zone' that is forecast to house up to 10 new canning facilities, with additional wharfing and berthing facilities as well. Initial funding for the PMIZ was reported to have been secured in 2011 in the form of a 74 million kina concessional loan from China (Anon. 2011), but construction has stalled amid disputes with landowners, legal challenges, political wrangling, and allegations of corruption and mismanagement. Recently, though, more Chinese money has been secured, and construction is once again set to commence.

Among the communities negotiating the presence and extension of the tuna industry are the Kananam, whose customary land includes the site of the present Vidar Wharf, and Rempi, whose people also claim part of the land that is now being developed as the PMIZ. Both are largely subsistence communities, with some supplementary cash income gained through copra production, as well as through the roadside sale of fish in Kananam, and *buai* (betel nut) in Rempi. In both communities, as well, much of what is claimed as customary land is in fact alienated freehold. The 216 hectares of the PMIZ site is part of a larger 880-hectare block previously alienated by the Catholic Church during the colonial period, and used for coconut plantations (the Vidar plantation) and for housing the Alexishafen mission station. In Rempi, leaders of the Bomase clan tell stories about how their ancestors were tricked by missionaries into selling their land in exchange for a pot full of trinkets and quantities of salt, signing their names on papers they could not read and did not understand. In the 1990s the land was returned by the Catholic Church, not to its original owners, but to the state. It was subsequently sold by the corporate arm of the Madang Provincial Government to RD Tuna, which then proceeded to build the Vidar Wharf. RD Tuna subsequently sold back to the national government that section of the former plantation which has now been demarcated as a special economic zone. The making of customary claims on formally alienated land speaks to a 'double movement' of property rights in PNG which has, in the post-Independence period, involved both the 'partial alienation of customary land' and the 'partial customisation of alienated land' (Filer 2014: 82, 89). It is a double movement that blurs the oft-made distinction between customary and freehold land in the country.

Twenty kilometres down the road, at the site of the existing RD Tuna cannery, the Siar and Nobnob communities claim customary ownership of land from which they are, in practice and in legal fact, excluded. Here as well, the access to land enjoyed by global corporate actors today is made possible by prior acts of alienation during periods of colonisation and missionisation. In this case, 540 hectares of land was alienated to form the Siar coconut plantation in the late 1800s, which was administered through the period of German colonialism in close collaboration with Lutheran missionaries (Sinclair 2006: 48). Siar Portion 1004—the 6.5-hectare block on which the cannery stands—forms part of this larger plantation area. As with Rempi and Kananam, the original claiming and titling of this land provided a basis for the land subsequently being claimed by the state, before then being leased to RD Tuna in the mid-1990s as part of a package—along with a ten-year tax holiday, and cheap fishing licences—to incentivise it to establish the cannery.

Both at the PMIZ site and at the RD Tuna cannery, then, large sections of the land, which local communities claim as their customary inheritance, have been subject to the various titling and codification practices advocated by proponents of land formalisation. In differing ways, each community has at times contested the 'mobilisation' of their land for the development of the tuna industry, as they have previously contested its mobilisation by missionaries, plantation bosses, and colonial officials. They have done this both by challenging the ownership claims of outsiders, and by asserting their own claims for recognition as 'customary landowners'. As an oppositional self-referent (Keesing 1989; Kirsch 2006), one that employs a modernist terminology to assert a claim in the face of modernist, and modernising outsiders, 'customary landowner' is one that has been learned through harsh experience. In recent years, the primary way in which this claim has been leveraged has been through the constitution of incorporated land groups as legally recognised bodies capable of entering into contractual relationships, lodging and contesting judicial claims, and claiming compensation and 'spin-off benefits' from developers. In other words, the Rempi, Kananam, Nobnob and Siar communities have each sought, or else been compelled, to *become landowners* in a way that is 'legible' (Scott 1998) to the sites and agents of the state and globalising capital. Doing so involves not simply a translation, but a transformation of the nature of connection to land.

Exclusion 1: Making Landowners/ Boundary Creation

Practices of land formalisation are exercises in boundary making, and this is a key way in which they function to exclude. Incorporated land groups make landowners, in effect, by drawing boundaries around them. They provide a mechanism for determining who is and is not a recognised right-holder, and for grouping them together to form a singular entity with which courts, companies, and state agencies can easily transact. Land groups and other processes of formalisation similarly draw boundaries around land, recording clear and fixed parcels of land that can be identified and known independently of the site of the land itself and of the memories, bodies and social relations of those who claim connection to it. Of course, the making of boundaries is not a uniquely modernist preoccupation, but rather a deeply human practice of marking difference, including the difference between inside and outside. Exclusion, similarly, is not a uniquely modern phenomenon, but a fundamental part of how land is accessed and organised in all times and places (Hall et al. 2011). The types of boundaries that are drawn, however, and the ways in which they are made, maintained, and adjudicated, are not uniform. What is significant about the extension of modern, formalised systems of land titling and codification is not that they introduce boundaries, but rather that they introduce and privilege particular types of boundaries, and in doing so, particular types of exclusion. The social implications of this are far-reaching.

In Rempi, the power of boundary making as an exclusionary force is narrated in the stories through which members of the Bomase clan recount the trauma of their ancestors' dispossession. In the words of the leader of the clan, an old man named Peter Gau Sabum:

> The mission marked out huge areas of land and put borders around it to indicate the boundaries. When they finished, they gave presents to the people … The missions then wrote our ancestors names and told them to sign. Our ancestors did not know how to write so they just hold the pen and did some marks on the agreement paper and the mission said, that mark is enough to say that you agree to the sale of the land. That's how the mission took this land (Peter Gau Sabum, personal communication May 2010).

Bomase ancestors, the old man stressed, did not know they were selling their land. The missionaries did not explain, and they could not read the contracts they were asked to sign in return for what they believed to be 'presents'. More fundamentally, though, how *could* they know that they were selling their land? The type of exclusion that the missionaries orchestrated was, in an important sense, inconceivable within a customary understanding of land and people as mutually constitutive (Stead 2012). The types of boundaries that have customarily separated clan groups or tribes have, indeed, functioned as exclusionary mechanisms—this is what boundaries do—but they have been embedded in the histories and ongoing social relations of the people and land that they both separate and join together. Recorded and narrated through oral history, customary boundaries have qualities of flux. The oral and relational practices through which they are maintained and contested take place on the land to which they relate. They are, as many have pointed out in the context of the Pacific and elsewhere, 'fuzzy' (Rivers 1999; Wainwright and Bryan 2009), pertaining to multiple levels and forms of claims, relating to land itself as well as the resources found within it.

The boundaries marked out by the mission were not fuzzy. The old Bomase leader tells how, after they were marked out and the performance of a sale enacted, the mission poured concrete to mark where the boundaries now stood. 'So the mission lived on one side,' the old man said, 'and we lived on the other side'. The types of boundaries that the mission made were not recorded and maintained in oral tradition or through the ongoing lived practices of exchange—although the mission and clan did indeed become embroiled in one another's lives—but rather on maps and in titles. The mission's ownership of the land became something that existed in the abstract; the land itself became something that could be bought, sold or otherwise transacted. It became something from which people could be both analytically and physically separated, a fact of which the Rempi people and their Kananam neighbours were made painfully aware when the land passed back, not into their hands, but into the hands of the government, and then of the company. As initial, albeit stunted, phases of the PMIZ construction have commenced, fences have been constructed around the perimeter of the special economic zone. Tall, metal, the opposite of fuzzy, the fences are glaringly conspicuous against the grasses, coconut palms and trees which surround them. In 2010, the sons and nephews of Peter Gau Sabum took me walking along the perimeter, pointing through the bars of the fence as they told stories about the land on the other side.

As the Bomase walked the boundaries of the PMIZ, the stories they told were not simply about the loss of gardens and land to build houses, but about the histories and movements of their ancestors, about recognition, and about the humiliation at being made, as one informant described it, into 'beggars on their own land'. It is a stark reminder that questions of access to, or exclusion from, land have significance that go beyond resource access and the possibilities for livelihood. Connection to land speaks to culture and spirituality, to identity, belonging, knowledge, and to structures of governance and authority; in other words, to social life in its fullest sense. Hall, Hirsch and Li (2011) suggest that *access* to land is the opposite of exclusion, but it might also be thought of as *belonging* (Trudeau 2006: 423). Practices of boundary making create and transform relations of belonging, as well as of access and exclusion. Boundaries define what belongs, as well as what does not, with far-reaching social implications.

However, if the varied boundary-making practices evident at the PMIZ speak to very different ways of being in the world—different forms and expressions of belonging—it is not the case that the introduction of modernist systems of land titling and ownership represents a definitive shift from one way of relating to land to another. The boundary between the customary and the modern, as it were, is far from clear-cut. Rather, the differing articulations of exclusion, access, and belonging are 'entangled' in shifting and dynamic configurations (Stead 2013). Entanglement offers its own possibilities for creative expressions of agency and negotiation, but it can also be destabilising in ways that themselves function to exclude local communities both from land and from power. The development of the PMIZ is bringing to a head the complexities of such entanglement for the Bomase and their neighbours. For the Nobnob and Siar communities, this process began more than a decade ago with the establishment of the RD Tuna cannery.

Exclusion 2: Land Groups and Land Claims/ Codifying Custom

The RD Tuna cannery stands in the middle of a complex of claims made by local people identifying themselves as 'landowners'. These claims are made, first, against the company. Second, to the extent that both the national and provincial governments are involved in RD Tuna's operations (having originally invited the company to establish a factory as part of its development strategy, and themselves party to negotiations and agreements with both the company and local communities), these claims are also often made against the state. Third, to the extent that many of them are in competition with one another, they are also claims made by groups within the Nobnob and Siar communities against other groups within those same communities. The primary vehicle for asserting these claims has been the codification of various 'landowning' groups and clans, including a 'landowner company', within legal negotiations, documentation, and contractual agreements entered into with the state and RD Tuna. These are the types of 'middle-way' mechanisms that are so often upheld as means of inclusion with market, state and nation. Yet the codification of custom is never simply a process of translation (Gewertz and Errington 1991; Keesing 1992), and codifications of customary land systems can have far-reaching effects (Weiner and Glaskin 2007; Chesters 2009). Unpacking just some of the experiences of the Nobnob and Siar communities reveals the complex ways these land reform mechanisms have also functioned to exclude.

In field research conducted in 2010—in the villages of Matupi, Baitabag and Nobnob, all within the larger Nobnob area—a total of eight distinct Nobnob clan groups were identified. These were: Ditipa, Gidigdi and Abdah (these three clans together forming the Mamagtub tribe), Inad, Sasagas (with three distinct subclans identified by respondents), Dadolkud, Hibutpa, and Badalon (this latter grouping being sometimes identified as a clan and other times as a subclan, with allegations also made that it is an altogether fictitious or invented clan—a point to which we shall return). It should be noted, however, that the exact nature and relation of different social groupings within Nobnob is contested. There are claims from some community members that some of the groups presenting themselves as clans are in fact not original landowners but descendants of labourers brought to work on the colonial plantations. Indeed, usage and manipulation of terms such as 'clan', 'subclan' and 'tribe' have been widely incorporated into the strategies and narratives of many different claimants across the area, with accounts of the structuring of social groups in relation to one another varying over time as alliances and imperatives shift. Added to this is the erosive impact that the intertwined histories of corporate, church and colonial presence have had on local customary knowledge (Sullivan et al. 2003), which further complicates the task of presenting an authoritative picture of social organisation in the area, if, indeed, such a thing were ever possible.

The arrival of RD Tuna in Madang marked the beginning of the series of protracted legal and extra-legal conflicts within the community, related particularly to who was to enjoy recognition as the landowners of Portion 1004 by the state and the company, and the distribution of benefits (primarily, contracts to run 'spin-off businesses'—cleaning, security, transport, etc.) from the project. In July 1995, prior to the commencement of the cannery's operations, a 'deed of concern' was reportedly signed between RD Tuna and a man named Bantam Dabid, signing as representative of the 'Badalon clan'. Three months later, a statement was signed by representatives of the Sasagas, Hibutpa (identified here as 'Hibutpa No. 2') and Ditipa (identified as 'Didipa Kunta') clans,[2] calling for the withdrawal of the deed of concern on the basis that Badalon were not in fact the landowners of Portion 1004. The following year, the Madang Development Corporation issued RD Tuna with its lease, and construction on the project began. Another year later, a memorandum of agreement was signed between the State of PNG, Madang Provincial Government, RD Tuna, and representatives of the identified landowners. Here, the three clans identified in the letter of protest—Ditipa Kunta, Sasagas, and Hibutpa No. 2—are included, and the representatives signing for them are the same men who signed the letter two years prior. A fourth man, Salib Pasagai, is also a signatory, signing as the representative of 'Badalon *subclan*' (emphasis added).

Dan Jorgensen, writing about land claim processes in the area surrounding the Nena/Frieda mining project in PNG's West Sepik Province, describes those processes in terms of 'clan-making' and 'clan-finding'. Telefolmin claimants in the area around the mine site, he writes, fashioned their claims in the language of clans and subclans, despite this being contrary to the actual nature of their social organisation: the Telefolmin do not have clan-based societies. Explaining the fiction, Jorgensen argues that 'the state's commitment to customary tenure is framed in terms of the state's own ideas of what customary tenure looks like' (2007: 66), which is to say a model of clans and subclans. The state looks for clans, and accordingly the Telefolmin 'create' clans that the state can find. A similar, if less dramatic, manipulation of the language of clans and subclans is evident in the claims surrounding Siar Portion 1004. While the Nobnob and Siar communities, like other communities in the Madang area, do have a clan-based system of social organisation, the language and processes of land group incorporation are creating new opportunities for this system to be manipulated.

Such observations fit—to a degree—with the argument that custom is elicited by the state and modernity. James Weiner and Katie Glaskin, in this vein, have argued that 'the customary is a product of the expansion of

---

2   Throughout the written documentation, as well as in people's recountings of the land claim disputes, a variety of different spellings occur (for example, 'Didipa' and 'Ditipa'), as well as slight variations in naming.

state and capital formations, rather than foreign or external to it' (2007: 2; see also Weiner 2006). To a degree they are incorrect, but it is also possible to distinguish between customary forms of sociality, on the one hand, and custom—or *kastom*—as a modernist *idea* of what that sociality entails, on the other. In doing so, we recognise that land groups do not only elicit custom, they draw together customary and modern ways of being in complex ways. However unwittingly, the argument that custom is elicited by the modern accords a problematic ontological priority to the latter. Customary forms of connection to land are indeed transformed through processes of land group incorporation, but this is not to say that land groups are solely modernist phenomena. Indeed, it is their entangled character, not simply their modern-ness, that makes them so destabilising of the social and political landscape.

The manipulation of clan identities is evident in Nobnob and Siar, particularly in allegations that the 'Badalon clan'—on whose behalf Bantam Dabid signed the 1995 deed of concern with RD Tuna—is not a clan at all, but rather a group made up of the descendants of plantation workers brought to the area during the late nineteenth and early twentieth centuries. After many generations living at Siar, complicated by the realities of extensive intermarriages, there are no customary 'homes' to which the plantation workers' descendants can return. Their connection to the Siar land is not customary, in the sense that it is not land to which they claim an ancestral connection, but they have nonetheless been drawn into customary forms of community social relations (including social relations of conflict) through their residence on that land. In seeking a share of the benefits that they hoped the RD Tuna cannery would bring, the plantation descendants fashioned themselves in the form that would best support their claims. As the 'Badalon clan', they were able to present themselves as a legitimate, and 'legible' (Scott 1998), entity, securing both a modern legal and 'customary' basis from which to assert themselves in negotiations.

In objecting to the deed of concern signed by Bantam Dabid, the representatives of the Sasagas, Hibutpa and Ditipa clans rejected the Badalons' claim to be rightful owners of Siar Portion 1004. Nevertheless, the Badalon group was included as a signatory in the 1996 memorandum of agreement with the company and the state, suggesting some reconciliation between the groups. The reasons again point to the manipulation of clan identities and the legal process of negotiation. Unpacking the different narratives surrounding the signing of the memorandum of agreement, a picture emerges of shifting alliances between clans and social groups, playing out within the new legal-political domain of land groups and benefit-sharing agreements. Within this domain, the two contesting claims for ownership of Portion 1004 came from Badalon and from the Sasagas clan (the latter supported by Hibutpa and Ditipa).

There is, however, another claim made outside of this domain. The Dadolkud clan, another of the eight primary clan groups identified in the Nobnob area, also claims customary connection to the land on which the cannery has now been built. Nongoi, the head of the Dadolkud clan, repeats the assertion made by others, that the Badalon 'clan' are in fact descendants of settlers from the plantation days. All of the eight clans, Nongoi and his supporters insist, '*know*' that Dadolkud is the rightful landowning clan. Nonetheless, Dadolkud has been completely excluded from all of the legal negotiations related to RD Tuna's operations. In this context, the shifting alliances of the Badalon appear in a different light. Their own claim to be customary landowners of the cannery site is widely disputed, with no support from any other clans. In contrast, the leaders of the Sasagas clan—particularly Kumai Musas Mumum and his son John Musas—were able to mobilise support from the Hibutpa and Ditipa clans, and in doing so defeat the Badalons' own claims. Subsequently bringing the Badalons into their alliance, the Sasagas clan was able to further bolster the support for their own claim, and entrench the exclusion of the only other primary claimant, the Dadolkuds. Relegating the Badalon to the status of a 'subclan' rather than a 'clan,' the representatives of Sasagas, Hibutpa and Ditipa were able to further manipulate the language and relations of clans to give legal effect to the Badalons' junior position within their alliance, and within their negotiations with RD Tuna and the PNG state.

The alliance, however, was not long-lasting. Centrally positioned within it, the Sasagas leaders were able to establish the Daghan landowner company, which became the legal entity contracted by RD Tuna to run the 'spin-off businesses' that were to be the main source of income for the Nobnob and Siar communities. If the national ideology of landownership locates the clan as the paramount building block of national society, it similarly locates the landowner company as the core unit of the national economy. In Nobnob and Siar, the business activities of the Daghan landowner company—providing security and cleaning services, running a transportation service and canteen for factory workers—were operational for a short time, but collapsed in 2000 amid conflicts within the Nobnob communities and between the landowner company and RD Tuna. Having positioned themselves as the major powerbrokers within Nobnob, the leaders of the Sasagas clan were subsequently accused by the other clans of monopolising the landowner company and the benefits derived from it. More specifically, John Musas was accused of running the company so as to directly benefit his family and members of the particular subclan *within* Sasagas of which he is a part, the Damon subclan. Allegations of financial mismanagement were made, and another land group, presenting itself as the 'Sasagas No. 2 clan' was formed. In September 2010, a violent attack on the Musas family was made by other residents of the Siar area, including members of the Hibutpa and Ditipa clans. Amid the confusion and conflict, RD Tuna chose to terminate their agreement with the Daghan landowner company, giving as reasons the mismanagement of the money paid to the company, and the fact that it was solely, they alleged, benefiting John Musas and his kin.

Following RD Tuna's termination of the memorandum of agreement, Musas Mumum (as representative of the Sasagas clan) and his son John Musas (as representative of the landowner company) initiated legal action against RD Tuna, the PNG state and the Madang Provincial Government for their breach of the agreement, as well as against the Hibutpa No. 2, Ditipa Kunta and Badalon clans. The case ultimately fell apart because lawyers could not be organised, and because of internal tensions within Sasagas. The result, then, is that John Musas and his father are now relatively marginalised. When RD Tuna began talks in 2009 to build housing for its employees on a piece of land adjacent to the cannery site—Portion 1005—Musas and the Damon subclan were excluded from the negotiations, with RD Tuna talking instead to representatives of the Ditipa, Inad and Hibutpa clans, as well as the new splinter 'Sasagas No. 2' grouping. Back in Nobnob, the now isolated John Musas began reaching out to Nongoi, the leader of the Dadolkud clan whose own exclusion Musas was responsible for engineering more than a decade ago. Meanwhile, as the internal lines of alliance and division continue to shift and re-form, none of the 'spin-off benefits' forecast for the Nobnob communities have eventuated (Sullivan et al. 2003; Stead 2014). RD Tuna's operations continue.

Shifting the Sites and Centres of Power

What does the conflict in Nobnob reveal about the politics of becoming landowners? Where does power sit within this contested landscape, and with whom? To an extent, the manipulation of identities, histories and representations within the land group system—including the alleged 'invention' of the Badalon clan—is itself consistent with the exercise of power within customary sociality. The narration of custom in oral traditions, as the French anthropologist Jean Pouillon describes it, is never fixed or exact, but rather 'a structural ensemble which tolerates, and even favours, a form of creativity' (quoted in Rouland 2001: 15). Annette Weiner, similarly, has pointed to the central role of memory and oral communication in the political domain of customary community, including the manipulation of details of land tenure and the deployment of 'fictively arranged' genealogies (Weiner 1976: 42). The fluidity of land claims in Nobnob, and the accommodation of tension and argumentation within everyday relations, resonates too with the accounts of other scholars describing customary land systems, including in PNG (Sillitoe 1999), Samoa (Olson 1997), and Africa (Berry 2002; van Leeuwen 2010). To this extent, then, and remembering Hall, Hirsch and Li's (2011) proposal that exclusion and access be seen as conjoined conditions, the entanglement of custom and modernity with the land group system can be seen to offer new opportunities for creative agency, and hence for claiming access to land.

A normative valorising of 'negotiability', however, is to be cautioned against. Pauline Peters, writing about customary land tenure in Africa, argues that, in place of such an uncritical privileging, more emphasis needs to be placed by researchers on who benefits and who loses from instances of 'negotiability' in access to land (Peters 2004: 270). Her argument connects strongly with Hall, Hirsch and Li's (2011) critique of the impulse to see exclusion from land as innately negative, and their proposal to inquire, instead, into its effects and consequences. Peters (2004: 270) calls for a shift towards an approach 'that is able to identify those situations and processes (including commodification, structural adjustment, market liberalization and globalization) that limit or end negotiation and flexibility for certain social groups or categories'. It is by doing so that we illuminate the new exclusionary potentials—and implications—inherent within land groups and practices of land formalisation.

The introduction of practices of land formalisation brings into being a whole new system and structure of knowing and governing land. Abstracted from the intimate and particular relations of belonging—defined through new practices of boundary making—land is stripped of its own agentive capacity and potential, and customary communities' autonomy over their own land similarly diminishes. As the adjudication of land claims shifts to the administrative and judicial processes of the state, the governance of land shifts from the site of land itself, which is the grounding of customary power and authority, to the sites of land titles commissions, courtrooms, and government offices. So too is knowledge disembedded from the land to which it pertains, recorded in titles and registration documents rather than in the embodied, situated memories and stories of people who are connected to land. Through these abstracted structures of law, regulation and administration—structures of boundary maintenance—particular human agents are invested with power in relation to land: lawyers, bureaucrats, policy makers, judges, cartographers. Collectively, these agents, institutions and structures form the foundations of a modernist cartography of power in relation to land, and it is these that are privileged over customary agents, institutions, and structures as the authoritative basis for adjudicating, recognising, or rejecting claims of access. In this way, landownership can function to exclude those whose customary claims to access and use land, or whose practices of access and use, fall outside the structures of governance and organisation to which 'ownership' gives rise.

Customary forms of relating to land, though, are not expunged. In Nobnob, the dynamic and relational process of claims and counter-claims continues. Yet as much as this negotiability persists, the danger here is that it is against the modernist, definitive statements of 'fact' that these claims are measured and assessed. Indeed, the final termination of the benefit-sharing agreement in Nobnob speaks profoundly to this possibility. As much as the Nobnob and Siar communities were able to engage with the legal system in such a way that allowed some continuation of customary practices of disputation and communication, ultimately it was the company, against which all of those communities were positioned, which acted unilaterally and, to date, definitively in simply terminating the agreement.

On the site of the old Siar plantation, our attention is also drawn to the implications of landownership for power relations *within* communities, as well as between communities and external actors. That is to say, we see practices of 'intimate exclusion' (Hall et al. 2011: 145) directed by local Papua New Guineans at neighbours and kin, as well as processes of exclusion attributable to the regulatory or legitimating forces of state or corporate actors. What we see, in these local and intimate relations of landownership, is that power often goes to those able to translate across ontological difference. That is, power goes to those who are best able to position themselves within, and across, both modernist and customary systems of land use and governance. Peters (2004: 279) comments on the theme of negotiability, that 'not everyone is able to be an interlocutor, and many lose in such negotiations and "conversations"'. Her comments are made particularly in the context of negotiability within customary land systems, but the point is perhaps all the more salient in the context of negotiations, or translations, across different systems of boundary making and boundary maintenance. Similarly, Benjaminsen and Lund (2002) point to the ways in which those who most often benefit from land formalisation titles are those, often elites, who are most able to work across the spaces of both tradition and the formal institutions of the state.

In the disputes between the Nobnob claimants, the representative of the Damon subclan within the Sasagas clan, John Musas, emerges as someone who was able to gain and assert power within the intertwined communities through his negotiation of both customary and modern forms of land systems. Through customary practices of negotiation between different clans, he secured support for the Sasagas claim over the land on which the RD Tuna cannery was built. Through his familiarity with the mechanisms of courts and administrative processes, he was able to assert this claim within a modernist framework as well, establishing a landowner company to enter into a contract with RD Tuna and the state, while also demoting the rival Badalon claim through the letter of challenge and through the subsequent designation of Badalon as a 'subclan'. In contrast, Nongoi, the leader of the Dadolkud clan, has been unable to translate his customary claims within a modernist legal context, and the effect of this has been the clan's exclusion. Of course, whatever power John Musas was able to garner through his negotiation of the customary and the modern needs to be set within the context of his ultimate failure to hold on to it. The cancelling of the Daghan landowner company's contract highlights the fact that possibilities for agency by local communities are made within the context of structures of power that can be weighted against them.

Conclusion: Dilemmas of Ownership

In each of the Madang communities negotiating the development of the PMIZ—Nobnob, Siar, Rempi and Kananam—contemporary experiences of exclusion cannot be understood outside of the context of prior acts of colonial alienation some 100 years ago. In the claiming of land for plantations at the turn of the twentieth century, land itself became a commodity—something that could be parcelled, sold, leased, 'developed'—and it is as a commodity that it is now being 'mobilised' for use in the burgeoning tuna industry. The alienation enacted by the missionaries and colonial administrators instigated particular practices of boundary making that drew lines around parcels of land and so separated them, analytically and categorically, from the emplaced, contingent relationships of those who claim belonging to them. Land and people became ontologically separable, and this process of abstraction was the first act of regulatory exclusion. At the same time, however, colonial attempts at alienation were never complete. The introduction of modern relations of property and landownership does not expunge customary ones, and even in places where land formally exists as freehold property, dynamic forms of customary practice continue. Processes of land formalisation, meanwhile, have themselves given rise to ideas and identities of 'customary landownership', which are wielded in ongoing relations through which exclusion is practised, contested, legitimated or decried. Dramatically different forms of connection to land exist, but these are entangled in dynamic configurations.

Exclusion from land is not, as Hall, Hirsch and Li (2011) point out, an innately negative phenomenon. Relations of exclusion and inclusion are inherent to all systems of land use and organisation. As these relations take different forms, however, we need to also take account of the consequences of the entanglement of these differing forms. These are far-reaching, not only for issues of access to resources and livelihood opportunities, but also for issues of identity, culture, and belonging. Attention needs to be paid, too, to the legitimating discourses through which some forms of exclusion/access are privileged, and others devalued.

In PNG, the 'mobilisation' of land is heralded as a mechanism for securing access to the promises of 'development', by which is meant a contingently modernist vision of formal sector employment, cash income, and participation in capitalist systems of production and exchange. Drawn into modernist cartographies of power through which land use is governed and adjudicated, these communities who live on and around the Siar and Vidar plantations have indeed been drawn into the social and political space of the nation-state, and through their negotiations with state and corporate actors they find themselves embroiled in the relations of capital and the global market. These 'inclusions', however, have only been made in the most marginal and unequal of ways. The entanglement of custom and modernity has offered some space for creative negotiation and for the deployment of 'customary landowner' identities as a basis for making claims against both state and company, but ultimately the promises of land mobilisation remain elusive.

References

Allen, M., 2008. 'Land Reform in Melanesia.' Canberra: The Australian National University, State Society and Governance in Melanesia Program (Briefing Note 6).

Anon., 2008. 'National Land Development Taskforce: NGO response,' Unpublished typescript.

———, 2011. 'PNG Govt secures K74m from China for the development of Pacific Marine Industrial Zone.' *Pacific Islands News Association*, 15 June.

AusAID, 2008. *Making Land Work—Volume One: Reconciling Customary Land and Development in the Pacific*. Canberra: Australian Agency for International Development.

Benjaminsen, T.A. and C. Lund, 2002. 'Formalisation and Informalisation of Land and Water Rights in Africa: An Introduction.' *European Journal of Development Research* 14(2): 1–10. doi.org/10.1080/714000420.

Berry, S., 2002. 'Debating the Land Question in Africa.' *Comparative Studies in Society and History* 44: 638–668. doi.org/10.1017/S0010417502000312.

Chesters, T., 2009. 'Introduction.' In T. Chesters (ed.), *Land Rights: The Oxford Amnesty Lectures 2005*. Oxford: Oxford University Press.

Curtin, T., 2003. 'Scarcity amidst Plenty: The Economics of Land Tenure in Papua New Guinea.' In T. Curtin, H. Holzknecht and P. Larmour, 'Land Registration in Papua New Guinea: Competing Perspectives.' Canberra: The Australian National University, State, Society and Governance in Melanesia Program (Discussion Paper 2003/1).

de Soto, H., 1989. *The Other Path: The Invisible Revolution in the Third World.* New York: Harper and Row.

Deininger, K. and H. Binswanger, 1999. 'The Evolution of the World Bank's Land Policy: Principles, Experience, and Future Challenges.' *World Bank Research Observer* 14: 247–276. doi.org/10.1093/wbro/14.2.247.

Fairhead, L., G. Kauzi and C. Yala, 2009. 'Land Reform in Papua New Guinea: Quantifying the Economic Impacts.' Port Moresby: National Research Institute.

Filer, C., 2011. 'The New Land Grab in Papua New Guinea.' Paper presented at the International Conference on Global Land Grabbing, Institute of Development Studies, University of Sussex, 6–8 April.

——, 2014. 'The Double Movement of Immovable Property Rights in Papua New Guinea.' *Journal of Pacific History* 49: 76–94. doi.org/1 0.1080/00223344.2013.876158.

Fingleton, J. (ed.), 2005. *Privatising Land in the Pacific: A Defence of Customary Tenures.* Canberra: Australia Institute (Discussion Paper 80).

Gewertz, D.B. and F.K. Errington, 1991. *Twisted Histories, Altered Contexts: Representing the Chambri in a World System.* Cambridge: Cambridge University Press. doi.org/10.1017/CBO9781139166430.

GoPNG, 2007. *The National Land Development Taskforce Report: Land Administration, Land Dispute Settlement, and Customary Land Development.* Port Moresby: National Research Institute (Monograph 39).

Gosarevski, S., H. Hughes and S. Windybank, 2004a. 'Is Papua New Guinea Viable?' *Pacific Economic Bulletin* 19(1): 134–148.

——, 2004b. 'Is Papua New Guinea Viable *with* Customary Land Ownership?' *Pacific Economic Bulletin* 19(3): 133–136.

Hall, D., P. Hirsch and T.M. Li, 2011. *Powers of Exclusion: Land Dilemmas in Southeast Asia.* Singapore: NUS Press.

Havice, E. and K. Reed, 2012. 'Fishing for Development? Tuna Resource Access and Industrial Change in Papua New Guinea.' *Journal of Agrarian Change* 12: 413–435. doi.org/10.1111/j.1471-0366.2011.00351.x.

Hughes, H., 2004. 'The Pacific is Viable!' Sydney: Centre for Independent Studies (Issue Analysis 53).

James, P., Y. Nadarajah, K. Haive and V. Stead, 2012. *Sustainable Communities, Sustainable Development: Other Paths for Papua New Guinea.* Honolulu: University of Hawai'i Press. doi.org/10.21313/hawaii/9780824835880.001.0001.

Jorgensen, D., 2007. 'Clan-Finding, Clan-Making and the Politics of Identity in a Papua New Guinea Mining Project.' In J.F. Weiner and K. Glaskin (eds), *Customary Land Tenure and Registration in Australia and Papua New Guinea: Anthropological Perspectives.* Canberra: ANU E Press (Asia-Pacific Environment Monograph 3).

Keesing, R.M., 1989. 'Creating the Past: Custom and Identity in the Contemporary Pacific.' *Contemporary Pacific* 1: 19–42.

——, 1992. *Custom and Confrontation: The Kwaio Struggle for Cultural Autonomy.* Chicago: University of Chicago Press.

Kirsch, S., 2006. 'Property Limits: Debates on the Body, Nature and Culture.' In E. Hirsch and M. Strathern (eds), *Transactions and Creations: Property Debates and the Stimulus of Melanesia.* New York: Berghahn Books.

Lund, C., 2011. 'Fragmented Sovereignty: Land Reform and Dispossession in Laos.' *Journal of Peasant Studies* 38: 885–905. doi.org/10.1080/03066150.2011.607709.

Olson, M.D., 1997. 'Regulating Custom: Land, Law and Central Judiciary in Samoa.' *Journal of Pacific History* 32: 153–179. doi.org/10.1080/00223349708572836.

Peters, P.E., 2004. 'Inequality and Social Conflict over Land in Africa.' *Journal of Agrarian Change* 4: 269–314. doi.org/10.1111/j.1471-0366.2004.00080.x.

Rivers, J., 1999. 'Formulating Basic Policy for Community Relations Programs.' Canberra: The Australian National University, State, Society and Governance in Melanesia Project (Discussion Paper 99/1).

Rouland, N., 2001. 'Custom and the Law.' In P. de Deckker and J.-Y. Faberon (eds), *Custom and the Law.* Canberra: Asia Pacific Press.

Scott, J.C., 1998. *Seeing Like a State: How Certain Schemes to Improve the Human Condition Have Failed.* New Haven (CT): Yale University Press.

Sillitoe, P., 1999. 'Beating the Boundaries: Land Tenure and Identity in the Papua New Guinea Highlands.' *Journal of Anthropological Research* 55: 331–360. doi.org/10.1086/jar.55.3.3631390.

Sinclair, J. 2006. *Madang.* Madang: Divine Word University Press.

Stead, V., 2012. 'Embedded in the Land: Customary Social Relations and Practices of Resilience in an East Timorese Community.' *Australian Journal of Anthropology* 23: 229–247. doi.org/10.1111/j.1757-6547.2012.00183.x.

——, 2013. 'Greeting the State: Entanglements of Custom and Modernity on Papua New Guinea's Rai Coast.' *Anthropological Forum* 23: 16–35. doi.org/10.1080/00664677.2012.724008.

——, 2014. 'The Price of Fish: Problematising Discourses of Prosperity at the Pacific Marine Industrial Zone.' In J. Ritchie, M. Verso and E.P. Wolfers (eds), *Securing a Prosperous Future: Papers from the Second Annual Alfred Deakin Research Institute Papua New Guinea Symposium 2012.* Goolwa (SA): Crawford House Publishing.

Sullivan, N., T. Warr, J. Rainbubu, J. Kunoko, F. Akauna, M. Angasa and Y. Wenda, 2003. *Tinpis Maror: A Social Impact Study of Proposed RD Tuna Cannery at Vidar Wharf, Madang.* Madang: Nancy Sullivan Ltd.

Trudeau, D., 2006. 'Politics of Belonging in the Construction of Landscapes: Place-Making, Boundary-Drawing and Exclusion.' *Cultural Geographies* 13: 421–443. doi.org/10.1191/1474474006eu366oa.

van Leeuwen, M., 2010. 'Crisis or Continuity? Framing Land Disputes and Local Conflict Resolution in Burundi.' *Land Use Policy* 27: 753–762. doi.org/10.1016/j.landusepol.2009.10.006.

Wainwright, J. and J. Bryan, 2009. 'Cartography, Territory, Property: Postcolonial Reflections on Counter-Mapping in Nicaragua and Belize.' *Cultural Geographies* 16: 153–178. doi. org/10.1177/1474474008101515.

Weiner, A.B., 1976. *Women of Value, Men of Renown: New Perspectives in Trobriand Exchange.* Austin: University of Texas Press.

Weiner, J., 2006. 'Eliciting Customary Law.' *Asia Pacific Journal of Anthropology* 7: 15–25. doi.org/10.1080/14442210600551842.

Weiner, J.F. and K. Glaskin, 2007. 'Customary Land Tenure and Registration in Australia and Papua New Guinea: Anthropological Perspectives.' In J.F. Weiner and K. Glaskin (eds), *Customary Land Tenure and Registration in Australia and Papua New Guinea: Anthropological Perspectives.* Canberra: ANU E Press (Asia-Pacific Environment Monograph 3).

Winn, P., 2012. 'Up for Grabs: Millions of Hectares of Customary Land in PNG Stolen for Logging.' Sydney: Greenpeace Australia Pacific.

World Bank, 2003. *Land Policies for Growth and Poverty Reduction.* Washington (DC): World Bank.

13

The Politics of Property: Gender, Land and Political Authority in Solomon Islands

Rebecca Monson

Introduction

In his 2012 New Year's address to the nation, Solomon Islands' Governor-General Sir Frank Kabui warned that land tenure had become the issue most likely to spark conflict within the scattered archipelagic nation. He went on to outline a number of issues he perceived to be a problem, including: the 'communal' ownership of land by kin groups and the need to register land in order to make it 'marketable'; the inequitable distribution of natural resource rents; and the 'illegal occupation' of land in the vicinity of the national capital, Honiara, by migrants from other islands. He exhorted Solomon Islanders to 'adjust our mindset' or remain 'caught between our cultural way of life and the cash economy' (Damosuaia 2012).

The core themes of Sir Frank Kabui's address—transformations in customary tenure, social differentiation, and capitalist development—occupy a prominent position in politics, not only in Solomon Islands, but across Melanesia. Indeed, recent conditions and events in Solomon Islands have sometimes been seen as exemplifying regional concerns about land, development and conflict in the wider region. From 1998 to 2003,

Solomon Islanders experienced a period of civil conflict, popularly known as 'the Tension', during which hundreds of people died, tens of thousands were displaced, and the country's economy collapsed. Although land scarcity is not a major issue in Solomon Islands, Solomon Islanders continue to perceive disputes over customary land to be a major source of social inequality and conflict.

As is the case elsewhere in Melanesia, the state in Solomon Islands is often described as 'weak' when it comes to land governance and administration, and in any event, most land is formally governed by customary tenure. In broad terms, this means that land tenure revolves around the occupation and use of a named place, by a named group, whose members trace their descent through men, women or both, to an apical ancestor or ancestors. Landholding and social ordering vary immensely across the country, but people generally lay claim to both land and membership of a kin group by invoking histories of their ancestors' origins and migrations. These stories are etched out across the land and sea, punctuated by important sites such as abandoned villages, old gardens, and significant trees. Contemporary land tenure therefore hinges on received ancestral models of land, territory and kinship. However, these models have also been recalibrated as people have engaged with Christian ideas and institutions, state laws and institutions, and an economy that is highly dependent on extractive industries. One of the most striking features of land tenure in Solomon Islands—in some parts of the country more than others—is the extent to which Solomon Islanders establish, assert, and defend their claims, not only by drawing on customary and state-based norms and institutions, but also norms and institutions rooted in Christianity. Contemporary land tenure is therefore characterised by multiple, overlapping arenas, norms and institutions emanating from *kastom*, Christianity and the state as they vary from one community to the next (Monson 2012; see also Scott 2007).

This means that land tenure in Solomon Islands is far from static, but dynamic and negotiable, with people asserting claims to land by drawing on a range of vocabularies, narratives and institutions. These qualities of indeterminacy and negotiability have been emphasised in much of the recent scholarship on land and natural resource tenure in Melanesia. This literature often draws on ethnographic research in Papua New Guinea, and focuses on innovations in landholding and sociality elicited by mining and forestry (Brown and Ploeg 1997; Wagner and Evans 2007; Weiner and Glaskin 2007). While attention has been paid to the ways in which the negotiation of 'ownership' is linked to increased social and economic differentiation (Rodman 1987; Zimmer-Tamakoshi 1997; Koczberski and Curry 2004; Bainton 2008), the links between 'local' contests over land and wider processes of state formation remain relatively under-explored. This is a theme that has received far greater attention in the literature on sub-Saharan Africa, which emphasises that the negotiation of land tenure is bound up with the contestation and assertion of political authority and leadership, whether by 'local' actors such as chiefs, or by representatives of the post-colonial nation-state.[1]

This chapter links questions about social differentiation in land relations in Solomon Islands to debates about gender inequality in the exercise of formal political authority. I demonstrate that, although land tenure is dynamic and contested, different people are differently positioned to influence the outcomes of negotiations over land. In particular, once contests over land enter the arenas established by the state, it is primarily male leaders—often referred to as 'chiefs'—who perform, endorse and reject claims to land as property. While the dominance of senior men in these arenas is often perceived by foreign observers as rooted in 'customary' ideas about 'who may talk' about land matters, I suggest that it is also linked to long-term processes of colonial intrusion, missionisation, and capitalist models of development.

In this chapter, I argue that an individual's ability to solicit the state's recognition of claims to land is not merely linked to their political authority, but that property and authority are in fact mutually constitutive. As is the case in neighbouring Papua New Guinea and Vanuatu, the Solomon Islands' economy has always been heavily dependent on agricultural development and exploitation of natural resources. This means that soliciting the state's recognition of claims to land, trees and other resources has become a vital avenue to economic and political power and prestige in contemporary Solomon Islands.

The relationship between property and authority also means that land disputes have implications that stretch far beyond the local contexts in which they initially arise. The recursive constitution of property and authority through the state tends to consolidate control over land in

---

1   As Sara Berry puts it, 'contests over land involve contests over authority as well as resources: they draw on and reshape relations of power as well as property' (Berry 2002: 656; see also Lund 2008; Sikor and Lund 2009).

the hands of a small number of men, while reproducing state norms and institutions as a masculine domain. Thus contests over land not only reflect social differentiation but constitute it; and processes of inclusion and exclusion at the national level are intimately entwined with the construction and re-inscription of categories of difference through contests over the 'ownership' of land at the local level.

Property and Emergent Inequality

Land tenure systems in Solomon Islands are dynamic, with multiple pathways for making, contesting and sanctioning claims through *kastom*, Christianity and the state. However, not all people are equally well positioned to influence the outcomes of negotiations, particularly as they occur across different arenas. Indeed, once contests over land enter the arenas established by the state, such as land acquisition procedures, it is primarily male leaders who perform, endorse and reject claims to land as property. Women are rarely listed as land trustees or timber rights holders, and they are largely absent from records of public hearings, suggesting that their role within the formal legal system is constrained. This is not to suggest that women—or indeed many men within communities—are unable to exert *any* influence over land deals and disputes. As I have argued elsewhere, women have had highly visible roles in all of the customary feasts I have observed, and their strategies for influencing land deals range from informal conversations within the household to staging large-scale protests (Monson 2011, 2012, 2014). However, across Solomon Islands, men and women alike express concern that logging, mining and the sale or leasing of land are occurring to the benefit of a small number of men, while many men and most women are excluded both from negotiations regarding these arrangements and the financial benefits that flow from them. Notably, all of these arrangements involve particular claims to land (or, in the case of logging, trees) being recognised, legitimated and consolidated by state legal and administrative systems. Thus, while Solomon Islanders gain and maintain *access* to resources in a variety of ways, it is primarily senior male leaders who are involved in making and adjudicating claims to land as *property*; and it is often senior male leaders who stand to gain the most from the legitimation of property by politico-legal institutions such as chiefs and courts (see Sikor and Lund 2009; Hall et al. 2011).

These inequalities are thrown into sharp relief in struggles over land in Kakabona, a series of densely populated settlements built along the coastline to the immediate west of the Honiara town boundary.[2] These villages are occupied by a number of matrilineages, widely referred to in Pijin as *traeb* ('tribes') and *subtraeb* ('subtribes'). Each of these matrilineages is associated with one of two moieties, and there is a prohibition on intra-moiety marriage—historically, villages were made up of two intermarrying groups.

Land in Kakabona is held under various tenure arrangements. Most of the land in the immediate vicinity of the Honiara town boundary has been registered and leased under the Land and Titles Act. In formal legal terms, this means that it is no longer considered 'customary land'. These parcels are registered in the names of a small number of male leaders who, under the terms of the Land and Titles Act, are representatives of the landholding group. The extent of registration declines as one moves east along the highway and away from Honiara, and customary land tenure becomes predominant. Significant tracts of land in this area are claimed by the members of one particular matrilineage, who base their claim on their descent from those who originally settled and cleared the land. However, in the last 30 years there have been a series of transactions through which some of this land has been divided up and distributed among a number of landholding groups. While these transactions often involve cash and are increasingly commercialised, they are also rooted in customary practice. Most involve feasting or *tsupu*, the ceremonial exchange of gifts, particularly food and shell money. The maintenance of claims to land depends on these feasts and ceremonies being remembered through oral histories and emplaced genealogies, known as *tutungu* (Scott 2007; Monson 2012).

Oral histories and government records indicate that social conflict and legal disputes regarding land in Kakabona intensified as the urbanisation of Honiara gathered pace during the 1970s. Indigenous villages on the outskirts of Honiara grew as indigenous Guale people relocated from more remote areas. While migrants from other islands initially settled on government land inside the town boundary, these settlements quickly began to spill out onto customary land. By the 1980s, disputes concerning land in Kakabona were regularly coming before the chiefs and courts,

---

2 Despite their proximity to the national capital, villages in Kakabona have received only very limited scholarly attention.

often triggered by attempts to register and then lease or sell blocks of land under the Land and Titles Act. With just one notable exception, all of the disputes I examined involved men coming before the courts to make claims on behalf of the landholding group, and in all of the cases, the members of dispute resolution forums (whether chiefs or courts) were men.

Transcripts of hearings before chiefs and courts reveal that the claims made by senior men revolve around: highly complex and non-linear oral histories of origin and migration; descriptions of boundaries and sacred sites; repeated prestations across several generations; and intermarriage between groups and the birth of descendants. These *tutungu* reveal that land tenure on Guadalcanal was historically characterised by a complex web of nested and overlapping interests, with particular matrilineages living in close proximity to one another and regularly intermarrying. Disentangling the history of territorial claims is further complicated by the fact that oral histories suggest that the population of this part of Guadalcanal was quite mobile well into the twenty-first century. Indeed, it appears that it was not until the 1950s that sizeable, permanent settlements began to develop in Kakabona (Scott 2007; Monson 2012). However, the process of registration under the *Land and Titles Act 1996* requires that land acquisition officers, chiefs and courts legitimate the claims of some kin groups and not others to 'ownership' of the land. While exclusive claims are rarely (if ever) made, courts often construct a hierarchy of claims, describing other groups as 'living under' the identified 'owners'. Under Section 195(1) of the Act, the process of registration also requires the identification of individuals who may be registered as the 'duly authorised representatives' of the landholding group, and joint owners on a statutory trust. These individuals are, with few exceptions, the individuals who appear before land acquisition officers, chiefs and courts, on behalf of the successful tribe; and in the vast majority of cases they are senior male leaders.

Most of the current trustees were initially nominated by members of the landholding group when land registration began to gather pace during the 1980s. All are senior men within their landholding groups, and most are referred to as 'chiefs'. The appointment of these men can in some respects be traced to long-standing models of masculine leadership: historically, a senior male was usually the spokesperson for the family and kin group on all land-related issues. These spokespersons are often described, in Pijin, as having the 'ability to talk' about land matters.

The idea of being 'able to talk' about land is important across Guadalcanal, and indeed many other parts of Solomon Islands. It depends partly on an individual's level of education and skill in managing land relations within the landholding group, as well as with outsiders. Since women often have less access to education than do men, they are often less likely to possess the skills necessary to negotiate the state legal system and manage land transactions. Further, according to some Guadalcanal people, custom dictates that women *no save tok* ('cannot or should not talk') about land. People in Kakabona often explain that women should 'stand behind' the men when it comes to speaking about land and dealing with land in public arenas. This norm is often explained by reference to the role of men as warriors and protectors of women.

It is a principle of both *kastom* and the state legal system that these trustees consult with other members of the landholding group before dealing with the land.[3] However, there is evidence that trustees have often failed to fulfil this obligation. Land in Kakabona has often been sold to migrants from other areas, as well as to local landholders who wish to move into new areas and establish new hamlets or gardens. Many of these sales have been made by trustees, although other members of landholding groups have also sold land. These deals are often struck by individuals in exchange for cash rather than through the traditional *tsupu* (feast), without adequate consultation of other members of the landholding group, and without distributing the proceeds of sale. As a result, land transactions are often highly controversial and a significant source of conflict.

This suggests that received ancestral models of leadership are now being translated into the state legal system in a manner that turns the customary 'ability to speak' about land into increasingly individuated control over land. People often explain that these trustees were nominated at the time of registration because they were 'big men' and skilled spokespersons who were trusted to represent the interests of the group. However, registration fixes their control over land and the wealth that flows from it, enhancing their authority over land vis-à-vis other members of the landholding group even further. Thus, while the dominance of senior men in state legal arenas may be partially traced to 'customary' ideas about 'who may talk' about land matters, it also needs to be understood in terms of the structural characteristics of the state legal system, which have worked to

---

3   See, for example, the then Chief Justice Muria's comments in *Kasa v Biku* [2004] SBHC 62.

facilitate the simplification of the land tenure system and enable certain male leaders to consolidate their authority over land, people and *kastom*. Furthermore, I suggest that the dominance of senior men in state legal arenas also needs to be understood in terms of long-term processes of colonial intrusion, missionisation, and capitalist models of development.

The Recursive Constitution of Property and Authority

An individual's ability to solicit the state's recognition of claims to land is closely entwined with the political authority they enjoy. Indeed, following Christian Lund (2008), I suggest that property and authority are in fact mutually constitutive. Since the earliest period of colonisation, the pursuit of control over natural resources in Solomon Islands has been tightly bound up with the assertion, consolidation and dispersal of political authority. This has occurred at multiple scales, ranging from localised struggles over the territory between adherents to different missions, to constitutional debates about federalism and freedom of movement.

With the notable exception of Alice Pollard's work (2007), the scholarly literature on Solomon Islands focuses on male institutions of leadership and pays very little attention to the political roles and power of women prior to colonisation. Two key characteristics emerge from this literature. First, in many societies, male leadership appears to have been characterised by a triumvirate of idealised leadership functions involving a leader in warfare; an entrepreneurial feast giver; and a religious leader.[4] For example, on Guadalcanal, these idealised masculine roles were concentrated in the *taovia* (often referred to in Pijin as *jif* or big man), *malaghai* (warrior), and *vele* (sorcerer). It is important to note that oral histories in Guadalcanal, as in many parts of Solomon Islands, clearly indicate that the idealised roles of the chief and warrior often overlapped and found expression in a single person (Aswani 2008).

Second, in many parts of Solomon Islands, male leaders gained prestige primarily by winning followers and mobilising people and resources in warfare, feast giving and ceremonial occasions. The *taovia* of Guadalcanal

---

4   For Malaita, see Hogbin (1939) and Keesing (1978); for Marovo, see Hviding (1996); for Guadalcanal, see Kabutaulaka (2002).

were never assured of their status as leaders, but required to constantly compete with others by: making prestations of pigs and shell valuables; mobilising dancers and bamboo pan pipers; establishing large gardens; and leading warfare (Hogbin 1934, 1937, 1964; Bathgate 1993). Hereditary preference played a larger role in some parts of the country, but still depended largely on the ability to gain prestige. In the New Georgia group, the role of the *bangara* was generally achieved through a combination of male primogeniture, alliance through marriage, and leadership ability (Hviding 1996). A man who demonstrated exceptional skill as a warrior and leader, and who built up and distributed wealth, might become a *bangara*; and equally, a young man who lacked these qualities might be overlooked in favour of a more capable uncle, brother or cousin. Political leadership was therefore achieved more than it was ascribed, and characterised by a high degree of contestation.

Missionisation, the development of the cash economy, and the 'pacification' policies of the colonial authorities all worked to transform these pre-colonial systems of male leadership. The idealised masculine role of the warrior receded with the cessation of warfare; and though the fear of the power of pre-Christian religious authorities never disappeared altogether, it probably abated in the face of the new source of spiritual power promoted by Christian missionaries. European missionaries often regarded feasts as a waste of resources and actively discouraged them, contributing to a decline in an important path to prestige and increasingly individuated control over wealth. While wealth had previously been distributed throughout the community in order to gain prestige, it was increasingly used by the individual who earned it (Hogbin 1934: 252). However, many of the old avenues to prestige were in decline just as new opportunities to assert and consolidate authority were opening up. The 'big men' within communities were among the first to engage in commercial trade, and the language and commercial skills they acquired through trade with Europeans soon enabled them to sell land to Europeans and retain the financial benefits of such transactions. Those men who could speak English or Pijin were able to further consolidate their authority following the implementation of a system of indirect rule that involved the identification and appointment of 'village headmen' and 'constables'.[5] Indirect rule, like the new commercial opportunities opened

---

5   British colonial regimes in Melanesia, like those elsewhere in the world, sought to establish and exercise administrative control through a version of indirect rule (see Berry 1992).

up by colonisation, provided new avenues for the enactment of political authority and territoriality—opportunities that were overwhelmingly concentrated in the hands of those men who were able to convince British colonial officers and foreign planters to recognise them as leaders, 'chiefs', and the 'owners' of the land.

Processes of rearrangement of customary tenure and leadership therefore worked to legitimate and consolidate the authority of some segments of customary polities while de-legitimating and undermining others. In particular, leadership roles historically associated with women were usually overlooked and ignored. While existing scholarly literature pays very little attention to the political authority of women prior to colonisation, oral histories often attest to its importance. For example, the Bareke people of central Marovo Lagoon frequently refer to the fact that they historically had three important institutions of leadership: the *bangara*, *siama*, and *vuluvulu*. The *bangara* is often translated in Pijin as *jif* (chief), while the role of the *siama* was tied to pre-Christian religious beliefs and pre-colonial warfare. The term *vuluvulu* has multiple meanings, one of which refers to the people who constitute the blood core of a matrilineage. The term is also used to refer to particular women of high standing and, in this sense, is often translated as meaning the 'first born girl', the 'oldest female', a 'princess' or a 'queen'. However, European missionaries and colonial administrators alike consistently recognised some segments of the local polity, notably the idealised masculine role of the *bangara*, while seemingly unaware of the *vuluvulu* and actively undermining the *siama*. For example, European missionaries incorporated the term *bangara* into Christian liturgies and hymns, and Protectorate officials perceived *kastom* as collapsing political authority and control over land into the single figure of the *bangara* (Monson 2011). This enabled the *bangara* to convert their historical roles as group leaders to those of 'chiefs' and 'landowners', strengthening their political power in a context where customary forms of land tenure and leadership were already being renegotiated, and customary leaders were struggling to secure their continued relevance.

Perhaps the pre-eminent example of such a leader is Ngatu, a man from Marovo Lagoon who successfully negotiated the multitude of changes occurring during the early twentieth century. Despite being unable to assert his authority as a warrior due to the 'pacification' policies of the colonial authorities, Ngatu was able to negotiate new paths to prestige by attaching himself to the new orders of the church and state. He introduced Methodism to Marovo and became a critical leader within the Methodist mission. He was able to use his reputation as a 'chief' or 'big man' to sell land to the government, and to generate cash through the establishment of a large-scale cooperative scheme of copra production, transport and marketing (Bennett 1987: 116, 224). The introduction of indirect rule consolidated Ngatu's authority even further—he was appointed District Headman for Marovo, and held the post until it was abolished in the 1940s, at which point he became a member of the Native Court instead. Court records, oral histories and written histories all indicate that Ngatu was very heavily involved in determining land disputes (Carter 1981: 60). His position as *bangara* and his appointment by Protectorate officials must have had a recursive effect, for in the process of legitimating some claims to land, and not others, Ngatu's authority was simultaneously reinforced. Put another way, as local claimants sought to secure their rights to land by having their claims recognised by Ngatu, that process worked to consolidate Ngatu's authority in the eyes of both local people and Protectorate officials. Indeed, Ngatu was so successful in consolidating his authority within each of the arenas of *kastom*, church and state that he ultimately became regarded as the 'chief' of a huge area, from Nggatokae to Ramata.

Processes of adaptation, contestation and legitimation of claims to both natural resources and politico-legal authority have therefore worked to benefit some segments of the customary polity more than others, with implications for property and authority today. Marovo is well known not only as a major tourist destination in Solomon Islands, but as the site of some of the most socially and environmentally destructive logging in the country. This occurs under the *Forest Resources and Timber Utilisation Act 1978*, which provides (in Section 7) that any person who is interested in logging customary land must apply to the Commissioner of Forest Resources for consent to negotiate with the relevant government authorities and the 'owners' of land and timber rights. In theory, under Sections 8 and 9, the relevant provincial government then holds a 'timber rights hearing' at which it determines a range of issues, including who holds timber rights; who the customary landowners are; and how profits are to be shared.[6] This information is then recorded in a 'certificate of customary ownership', commonly known as a 'form two'. The individuals

---

6   Note also that the courts have interpreted the Act to distinguish between ownership of customary land and ownership of trees: *Allardyce Lumber Company Limited* [1989] SBHC 1; *Gandley Simbe v East Choiseul Area Council* [1997] SBHC 67; *Mateni v Hite* [2003] SBHC 144. This distinction has added to the complex maze of claims, negotiations and contracts associated with logging.

listed in the 'form two' are deemed to be entitled to negotiate with the logging company. Under Part III of the Act, there is a right of appeal to the Customary Land Appeal Court, the decision of which is final and conclusive, subject only to the original jurisdiction of the High Court.

The regulation of forestry in Solomon Islands is notoriously complex, and the problems surrounding logging have stimulated a wealth of research on collusion between foreign logging companies and local politicians, irregularities in the timber rights hearing process, poor monitoring and enforcement, and the uneven distribution of royalties (Frazer 1997; Dauvergne 1998; Bennett 2000; Kabutaulaka 2000, 2001; Wairiu 2007; Wairiu and Nanau 2010; Allen 2011a; McDougall 2011). The Forest Resources and Timber Utilisation Act presupposes that it is possible to identify and mark boundaries between social groups, as well as delineate the 'land' and 'timber' to which they hold 'rights'. As a result, debates about the 'ownership' of land and trees in timber rights hearings and before courts often revolve around competing unilineal interpretations of customary tenure (Hviding 1993, 2002; Foale and Macintyre 2000). The process of making and legitimating claims to land and trees *as property* results in relationships between people bound by generations of shared descent and shared use of the land being fractured or 'cut' (Strathern 1996; Blomley 2011). In at least one instance, the process of disentangling people and marking off social identities and land claims has precipitated protracted litigation between a father and son.[7]

Women and men are differently positioned to influence the outcomes of negotiations with logging companies and contests before provincial authorities and courts. In practice, negotiations between logging companies and landowners have often been underway for a significant period before the issue of a 'form two'. While forested land is widely regarded as being the collective territory of the kin group in Marovo, representatives of logging companies often focus their efforts on negotiating with particular individuals who are identified as being influential with the landowning group and are in favour of logging (Wairiu 2007; Kabutaulaka 2008: 252). In many instances, proponents of logging form 'companies', a process that involves the appointment of particular individuals as company directors (see Scales 2003: 105; also Kabutaulaka 2008: 252, 2011: 7,

---

7   I have not cited the case here in order to preserve the privacy of the parties. However, the ongoing dispute resulted in at least nine determinations in the High Court and the Court of Appeal between 2003 and 2010.

104–5, 185ff). The individuals who are appointed as company directors, involved in negotiations, and signatories to agreements are nearly (if not always) men—some are recognised as chiefs, and some are younger, entrepreneurial individuals who are likely to be recognised as chiefs in the future (Hviding and Bayliss-Smith 2000).[8] Many of the younger men have become powerful due to their relatively high level of formal education and literacy, their understanding of regulatory frameworks governing forestry, and their ability to persuade elderly—sometimes illiterate—senior men to endorse and promote logging.[9] As was the case with traders, missionaries and colonial administrators before them, loggers and provincial authorities today wish to identify and engage with individuals rather than entire matrilineages—a process that is facilitated by the requirements of the state legal system. This has enabled a small number of individuals to carve out a 'big man' status and strengthen their power base within their matrilineage by obtaining and distributing logging revenue (Bennett 1987, 2000; Wairiu 2007). These processes have implications that stretch far beyond the local contexts in which they initially arise.

Property, Authority and Post-Colonial State Formation

Despite the manifest weaknesses of the state in Solomon Islands, it has nevertheless constructed and recognised a structure of entitlements for some people while diluting the claims of others (Lund 2008: 8–9). This has resulted in processes of gendered social differentiation, in which the semantic and institutional structures of the state have been reproduced as masculine domains. It is generally senior men who mobilise the language of state law on behalf of the group before chiefs and courts, men who are constructed as the defenders of the land against incursion, senior men who are constituted as 'trustees', and therefore senior men who control the access to revenue so crucial for participation in provincial and national politics. These processes have not only ensured that land disputes remain a critical arena for the performance of particular models of masculinity, but have produced and reinscribed state institutions as a masculine domain.

---

8   There are also similarities with the practices regarding mining (see Hviding 1993).
9   See also Kabutaulaka (2000, 2001), who emphasised generational differences between men in relation to logging on Guadalcanal.

Since the earliest period of colonisation, economic development in Solomon Islands has been based primarily on the extraction of natural resources by a relatively small number of large-scale, foreign-owned companies. Many of these operations are based on customary land, and the state bureaucracy acts as both regulator and intermediary between local communities and foreign companies. In this context, soliciting the state's recognition of claims to land and other natural resources has become a vital avenue to building economic and political power in contemporary Solomon Islands (Hameiri 2007a, 2009). A number of scholars have noted that parliamentarians in Solomon Islands invariably have substantial logging interests (Bennett 2000; Hviding and Bayliss-Smith 2000; Allen 2011a), and similarly, many of the men who have been successful in establishing themselves as 'trustees' of registered land also hold significant roles in national and provincial politics.

Securing state recognition of territorial authority has therefore become an important means by which to assert authority, not only at the local level, but also in provincial and national politics. Provincial and national political organisation in Solomon Islands, as in neighbouring Papua New Guinea, is extremely unstable and fragmented. For various reasons, governing coalitions in Solomon Islands have been characterised by highly fluid alliances, in which political cohesion is maintained through highly personalised patronage networks, largely involving men (Dinnen 2008a, 2008b; Allen 2011b). Again like Papua New Guinea, Solomon Islands' heavy dependence on primary resources and foreign capital has meant that the bulk of cash required to support these patronage networks comes from the state, from revenues derived from natural resource extraction by foreign-owned corporations, and from foreign donors (Hameiri 2007a, 2007b; Dinnen 2009; Allen 2011a). As Sinclair Dinnen points out, this has worked to maintain social fragmentation and to disperse rather than centralise power (Dinnen 2009). The relative fragility of the state has contributed to a situation that Edvard Hviding has described as 'compressed globalisation', in which a relatively small number of actors engage with a variety of local and global actors, including multinational logging, fishing and mining companies, as well as conservationists and tourists (Hviding 2003).[10] The fragility of government, combined with the relatively small and dispersed population, has allowed foreign commercial

---

10   Knauft (1999: 242) similarly suggests that Melanesia is notable for the ways in which 'the local intersects the global in axiomatically condensed forms'.

actors and non-government organisations alike to largely bypass the central government and negotiate directly with communities. In some senses, this could be praised as contributing to decentralisation and strengthening indigenous control over natural resources. Yet in practice, control over negotiations is concentrated in the hands of a relatively small number of people, primarily male leaders. Thus local contests over land and leadership are entwined with broader processes of social differentiation and state formation that are often extremely condensed in both space and time (Hviding 2003).

The implications of these processes of social differentiation must be understood in symbolic as much as material terms. Land disputes have now become a key arena for the performance of masculine authority and prestige, and the ideal spokesperson of the group embodies not only the oratorical prowess, but also the aggression and independence, that was previously symbolised by the chief and warrior (Scott 2000). Put another way, the forms of authority, prestige and solidarity that were previously associated with chiefs and warriors now find their coalesced expression in the ideal representative of the social group in discussions and disputes regarding land. This serves to construct men, rather than women, as the ideal spokespersons of the group. Furthermore, the performance of authority in state arenas works to entrench the authority of particular male leaders over land, so that the roles of 'spokesperson' and 'trustee' are mutually constitutive.

The implications of these processes stretch from local-level struggles over land through to participation in the exercise of formal political authority at the provincial and national level. Solomon Islands has one of the worst records in the world in terms of women's participation in the national parliament.[11] I suggest that the dominance of male leaders, and the absence of most women and many men from the courts and the parliament, are closely entwined. Soliciting the state's recognition of claims to land has become a vital, if not the pre-eminent, route to building masculine authority and prestige in contemporary Solomon Islands. The recursive constitution of property and political authority through the state therefore works to consolidate control over land in the hands of a small number of men, while simultaneously producing and reinscribing state norms and institutions as a masculine—even *hypermasculine*—domain.

---

11   Only two women have so far been elected to it: Hilda Kari held a seat for two terms in the 1980s, and in 2012, Vika Lusibaea was elected in a by-election for the seat formerly held by her husband.

Conclusion

Customary land tenure in Solomon Islands is highly dynamic and negotiable, comprised of an ever-shifting mosaic of norms and institutions emanating from *kastom,* church and state. Such flexibility undoubtedly opens up multiple pathways for negotiating access to land, but not all of these pathways are equally accessible to all people. While members of landholding communities have a variety of means by which to claim access to land, once contests over land enter the arenas established by the state, it is primarily male leaders who perform and adjudicate claims to land as property. Indeed, these arenas have become crucial sites for the performance of masculine authority and prestige, meaning that property and authority are not only recursively constituted, but inscribed as masculine. Securing state recognition of control over land is therefore intimately intertwined not only with the performance of masculine authority and prestige at the local level, but also in provincial and national politics. The mutually constitutive relationship between property and authority works to consolidate control over land in the hands of a small number of male elites while reproducing state norms and institutions as a masculine domain. This means that contests over land cannot be dismissed as parochial struggles over economic resources, nor do they merely 'reflect' social differentiation. Rather, contests over property emerge from and are productive of social differentiation in ways that are not merely confined to 'the local,' but inextricably entwined with contests over belonging, citizenship, political authority, and state formation.

References

Allen, M., 2011a. 'The Political Economy of Logging in Solomon Islands.' In R. Duncan (ed.), *The Political Economy of Economic Reform in the Pacific.* Metro Manila: Asian Development Bank.

——, 2011b. 'Long-Term Engagement: The Future of the Regional Assistance Mission to Solomon Islands.' Canberra: Australian Strategic Policy Institute (Strategic Insights 51).

Aswani, S., 2008. 'Forms of Leadership and Violence in Malaita and in the New Georgia Group, Solomon Islands.' In P.J. Stewart and A. Strathern (eds), *Exchange and Sacrifice*. Durham (NC): Carolina Academic Press.

Bainton, N.A., 2008. 'Men of *Kastom* and the Customs of Men: Status, Legitimacy and Persistent Values in Lihir.' *Australian Journal of Anthropology* 19: 194–212. doi.org/10.1111/j.1835-9310.2008. tb00122.x.

Bathgate, M., 1993. *Fight for the Dollar: Economic and Social Change in Western Guadalcanal, Solomon Islands*. Wellington: Alexander Enterprise.

Bennett, J.A., 1987. *Wealth of the Solomons: A History of a Pacific Archipelago 1800–1978*. Honolulu: University of Hawai'i Press (Pacific Islands Monograph 3).

———, 2000. *Pacific Forest: A History of Resource Control and Contest in Solomon Islands, c. 1800–1997*. Cambridge: White Horse Press.

Berry, S., 1992. 'Hegemony on a Shoestring: Indirect Rule and Access to Agricultural Land.' *Africa* 62: 327–355. doi.org/10.2307/1159747.

———, 2002. 'Debating the Land Question in Africa.' *Comparative Studies in Society and History* 44: 638–668.

Blomley, N., 2011. 'Cuts, Flows and the Geographies of Property.' *Law, Culture and the Humanities* 7: 203–216. doi. org/10.1177/1743872109355583.

Brown, P. and A. Ploeg (eds), 1997. *Change and Conflict in Papua New Guinea Land and Resource Rights*. Special issue 7(4) of *Anthropological Forum*.

Carter, G.G., 1981. *Ti é Varané: Stories about People of Courage from Solomon Islands*. Rabaul: Unichurch Publishing.

Damosuaia, D., 2012. 'Land Likely Cause of Conflict, G.G. Warns.' *Solomon Star*, 4 January.

Dauvergne, P., 1998. 'Corporate Power in the Forests of the Solomon Islands.' *Pacific Affairs* 71: 524–546. doi.org/10.2307/2761083.

Dinnen, S., 2008a. 'State-Building in a Post-Colonial society: The Case of Solomon Islands.' *Chicago Journal of International Law* 9: 51–78.

——, 2008b. 'The Solomon Islands Intervention and the Instabilities of the Post-Colonial State.' *Global Change, Peace and Security* 20: 339–355. doi.org/10.1080/14781150802394063.

——, 2009. 'The Crisis of State in Solomon Islands.' *Peace Review* 21: 70–78. doi.org/10.1080/10402650802690094.

Foale, S. and M. Macintyre, 2000. 'Dynamic and Flexible Aspects of Land and Marine Tenure at West Nggela: Implications for Marine Resource Management.' *Oceania* 71: 30–45. doi.org/10.1002/j.1834-4461.2000.tb02722.x.

Frazer, I., 1997. 'The Struggle for Control of Solomon Islands Forests.' *Contemporary Pacific* 9: 39–72.

Hall, D., P. Hirsch and T.M. Li, 2011. *Powers of Exclusion: Land Dilemmas in Southeast Asia.* Singapore: NUS Press.

Hameiri, S., 2007a. 'The Trouble with RAMSI: Re-Examining the Roots of Conflict in Solomon Islands.' *Contemporary Pacific* 19: 409–441. doi.org/10.1353/cp.2007.0052.

——, 2007b. 'Failed States or a Failed Paradigm? State Capacity and the Limits of Institutionalism.' *Journal of International Relations and Development* 10: 122–149. doi.org/10.1057/palgrave.jird.1800120.

——, 2009. 'State-Building or Crisis Management? The Regional Assistance Mission to the Solomon Islands and the Limits of State Transformation.' *Third World Quarterly* 30: 35–52. doi.org/10.1080/01436590802622276.

Hogbin, H.I., 1934. 'Culture Change in the Solomon Islands: Report of Fieldwork in Guadalcanal and Malaita.' *Oceania* 4: 233–267. doi.org/10.1002/j.1834-4461.1934.tb00110.x.

——, 1937. 'The Hill People of North-East Guadalcanal.' *Oceania* 8: 62–89. doi.org/10.1002/j.1834-4461.1937.tb00406.x.

——, 1939. *Experiments in Civilization: the Effects of a European Culture on a Native Community of the Solomon Islands.* London: Routledge.

——, 1964. *A Guadalcanal Society: The Kaoka Speakers.* New York: Holt, Rinehart & Winston.

Hviding, E., 1993. 'Indigenous Essentialism? "Simplifying" Customary Land Ownership in New Georgia, Solomon Islands.' *Bijdragen tot de Taal-, Land- en Volkenkunde* 149: 802–824. doi. org/10.1163/22134379-90003114.

——, 1996. *Guardians of Marovo Lagoon: Practice, Place and Politics in Maritime Melanesia.* Honolulu: University of Hawai'i Press (Pacific Islands Monograph 14).

——, 2002. 'Disentangling the *Butubutu* of New Georgia: Cognatic Kinship in Thought and Action.' In I. Hoëm and S. Roalkvam (eds), *Oceanic Socialities and Cultural Forms: Ethnographies of Experience.* New York: Berghahn Books.

——, 2003. 'Contested Rainforests, NGOs, and Projects of Desire in Solomon Islands.' *International Social Science Journal* 178: 539–554.

Hviding, E. and T. Bayliss-Smith, 2000. *Islands of Rainforest: Agroforestry, Logging and Eco-Tourism in Solomon Islands.* Aldershot: Ashgate.

Kabutaulaka, T.T., 2000. 'Rumble in the Jungle: Land, Culture and (Un) sustainable Logging in the Solomon Islands.' In A. Hooper (ed.), *Culture and Sustainable Development in the Pacific.* Canberra: Asia Pacific Press.

——, 2001. Paths in the Jungle: Landowners and the Struggle for Control of Solomon Islands' Logging Industry. Canberra: The Australian National University (PhD thesis).

——, 2002. *Footprints in the Tasimauri Sea: A Biography of Domeniko Alebua.* Suva: Institute of Pacific Studies.

——, 2008. 'Global Capital and Local Ownership in Solomon Islands' Forestry Industry.' In S. Firth (ed.), *Globalisation and Governance in the Pacific Islands.* Canberra: ANU E Press.

Keesing, R.M., 1978. *Elota's Story: the Life and Times of a Solomon Islands Big Man.* St Lucia: University of Queensland Press.

Knauft, B.M., 1999. *From Primitive to Postcolonial in Melanesia and Anthropology.* Ann Arbor: University of Michigan Press. doi. org/10.3998/mpub.10934.

Koczberski, G. and G.N. Curry, 2004. 'Divided Communities and Contested Landscapes: Mobility, Development and Shifting Identities in Migrant Destination Sites in Papua New Guinea' *Asia Pacific Viewpoint* 45: 357–371. doi.org/10.1111/j.1467-8373.2004.00252.x.

Lund, C., 2008. *Local Politics and the Dynamics of Property in Africa.* Cambridge: Cambridge University Press.

McDougall, D., 2011. 'Church, Company, Committee, Chief: Emergent Collectivities in Rural Solomon Islands.' In M. Patterson and M. Macintyre (eds), *Managing Modernity in the Western Pacific.* St Lucia: University of Queensland Press.

Monson, R., 2011. 'Negotiating Land Tenure: Women, Men and the Transformation of Land Tenure in Solomon Islands.' In J. Ubink (ed.), *Customary Justice: Perspectives on Legal Empowerment.* Rome: International Development Law Organization.

——, 2012. *Hu Nao Save Tok?* Women, Men and Land: Negotiating Property and Authority in Solomon Islands. Canberra: The Australian National University (PhD thesis).

——, 2014. 'Unsettled Explorations of Law's Archives: The Allure and Anxiety of Solomon Islands' Court Records.' *Australian Feminist Law Journal* 40: 35–50. doi.org/10.1080/13200968.2014.931882.

Pollard, A., 2007. *Painaha*: Gender and Leadership in 'Are'Are Society, the South Seas Evangelical Church and Parliamentary Leadership. Wellington: Victoria University (PhD thesis).

Rodman, M., 1987. *Masters of Tradition: Consequences of Customary Land Tenure in Longana, Vanuatu.* Vancouver: University of British Columbia Press.

Scales, I., 2003. The Social Forest: Landowners, Development, Conflict and the State in Solomon Islands. Canberra: The Australian National University (PhD thesis).

Scott, M., 2000. 'Ignorance is Cosmos, Knowledge is Chaos: Articulating a Cosmological Polarity in Solomon Islands.' *Social Analysis* 44(2): 56–83.

——, 2007. *The Severed Snake: Matrilineages, Making Place, and a Melanesian Christianity in Southeast Solomon Islands.* Durham (NC): Carolina Academic Press.

Sikor, T. and C. Lund, 2009. 'Access and Property: A Question of Power and Authority.' *Development and Change* 40: 1–22. doi.org/10.1111/j.1467-7660.2009.01503.x.

Strathern, M., 1996. 'Cutting the Network.' *Journal of the Royal Anthropological Institute* (NS) 2: 517–535. doi.org/10.2307/3034901.

Wagner, J. and M. Evans (eds), 2007. *Customs, Commons, Property, and Ecology.* Special issue 66(1) of *Human Organization.*

Wairiu, M., 2007. 'History of the Forestry Industry in Solomon Islands.' *Journal of Pacific History* 42: 233–246. doi.org/10.1080/00223340701461684.

Wairiu, M. and G. Nanau, 2010. 'Logging and Conflict in Birao Ward of Guadalcanal, Solomon Islands.' Honiara: Islands Knowledge Institute (Working Paper 1).

Weiner, J.F. and K. Glaskin (eds), 2007. *Customary Land Tenure and Registration in Australia and Papua New Guinea: Anthropological Perspectives.* Canberra: ANU E Press (Asia-Pacific Environment Monograph 3).

Zimmer-Tamakoshi, L., 1997. 'When Land Has a Price: Ancestral Gerrymandering and the Resolution of Land Conflicts at Kurumbukare.' *Anthropological Forum* 7: 649–665. doi.org/10.1080/00664677.1997.9967478.

14

Afterword: Land Transformations and Exclusion across Regions

Philip Hirsch

Introduction

The preceding chapters of this book give a central place to the *Powers of Exclusion* framework for understanding transformations in land relations, as developed in our 2011 book on Southeast Asia (Hall et al. 2011). A couple of the main aspects of the two books make for an interesting comparison. The first is that each employs a regional frame of reference to explore themes in changing land relations. The second is their respective development and application of a common conceptual framework. These commonalities beg the twin questions I seek to address in this chapter:

- Are there particular regional characteristics and dynamics that mark land relations with reference to exclusionary processes?
- Is the conceptual approach developed in one region applicable or adaptable to another?

These questions are explored first by considering what a regional approach to land relations might mean. The main part of this Afterword then makes a number of comparative observations between Melanesia and Southeast Asia, drawing out implications for the ways in which powers of exclusion help frame our understanding of commonalities and differences between regional patterns of changing land relations. The essay concludes with a recap of tensions between common forces reshaping land relations across both regions, on the one hand, and regional specificity on the other.

A Regional Approach to Land Relations

During our several writing retreats as we co-authored *Powers of Exclusion*, Derek Hall, Tania Murray Li and I wondered out loud on a number of occasions whether there would be uptake of our approach at a wider geographical and interdisciplinary level, with reference to country cases beyond our regional area of interest in Southeast Asia, or—and most ambitiously—with specific reference to other world regions. Reviews, informal discussion, and feedback from colleagues working in the field of agrarian studies and land-oriented activism in Africa, Latin America and South Asia have been positive in this regard, and they have encouraged us with the sense that the *Powers of Exclusion* framework does indeed have wider geographical resonance. However, not until the present volume has there been a sustained monograph-length effort to test the framework with reference to another world region.

What does a regional approach to understanding changing land relations entail? Unlike 'fugitive' resources that move across jurisdictions, such as water in transboundary river basins, or riverine and ocean migratory fisheries, and unlike environmental pollution such as smoke haze or greenhouse gas emissions, land is fixed in space and hence is not often treated as a transboundary resource. Land is also jealously protected as a national asset that is subject to national policy prerogative and ownership, or to more locally specific arrangements associated with ethnic identity. Yet despite this fixity of land in particular locales and national spaces, land is also subject to regional analysis in at least three main respects.

First, regions are often defined by particular characteristics that have relevance to land relations. Cultural norms such as patron-clientage, reciprocity, structures of political authority, and religious affiliation have regional associations, albeit in ways usually much more complex than simple stereotyping allows for. Also, regional location has both historically and in a more contemporary sense subjected land relations to external economic influences in particular ways. Different world regions have been subjected to quite specific colonial and post-colonial influences, and to Cold War and post-Cold War changes. Agro-ecological patterns of farming characterise regions, with implications for land use, land tenure, and rural social relations. Similarly, population dynamics within and between regions are location-specific, with implications for pressures on land.

Second, regional political-economic dynamics are integral to the defining of regions beyond more archaic and static cultural bases for regional demarcation. The discursive construction of regions is closely linked to these dynamics, so that, for example, Southeast Asia and subregions within it have been associated with institutionalised regional arrangements such as the Association of Southeast Asian Nations and the Greater Mekong Subregion. Regions are also naturalised around river basins, shared maritime zones, island groups, and so on. The governance of natural resources within, and with reference to, these regional constructions is in part shaped by institutionalised arrangements, aid programs, and other interventions that adopt a regional approach. In Southeast Asia, for example, the Greater Mekong Subregion's neoliberal agenda of facilitating private sector-led infrastructure development and transboundary flows of goods and investment capital brings with it a suite of policy and legal reforms geared to strengthening private property rights in land, enhancing wealth creation through markets (not only in mobile goods and services but also through mortgageable land), and through other measures. In the Pacific, regional arrangements and external interventions through aid flows appear to be much more circumspect in the ways in which they intervene in customary property arrangements.

Third, intra-regional flows and regional interaction with the global economy bind regions, internally and externally, in ways that have significant implications for land relations. In particular, concern during the past decade over land grabbing plays into regional dynamics. But these dynamics are often quite specific to one region or another. In Southeast Asia, transboundary land deals dominate the investment in boom crops such as rubber and sugar. In mainland Southeast Asia, or the Greater Mekong Subregion, investments by Chinese, Thai and Vietnamese companies in Cambodia, Laos and Myanmar respectively forge a particular regional dynamic, which is matched to a lesser degree by Malaysian and Singaporean investments in oil palm in Indonesia. In Melanesia, in contrast, this intra-regional dynamic is lacking, and indeed, much of the investment through land deals is from the region's northern neighbours.

Some Comparative Reflections Between Melanesia and Southeast Asia

Regional patterns of changing land relations in Melanesia and Southeast Asia reflect each region's historical experience of colonisation and state formation, as well as innate cultural and agro-ecological specificities. We can explore commonalities and contrasts with reference to the four key powers of exclusion that we set out (in Hall et al. 2011): markets, regulation, force and legitimation. First, however, it is useful to consider the respective regional contexts in which the powers operate.

The Politico-Historical Regional Backcloth

Agrarian structures are the basis on which property relations in land develop. Southeast Asian and Melanesian societies have quite different backgrounds in their pre-colonial and colonial-era structuring of land and labour vis-à-vis capital and central authority.

Historically, paddy rice has been the staple crop in lowland parts of both mainland, and insular and peninsular, Southeast Asia; and even in upland areas dominated by swiddening, rice has provided a main staple. Rice is commonly associated with smallholder peasant farming (Bray 1986), and historically irrigation systems have associated such cultivation with wider patterns of kingship, quasi-feudal land relations, and patronage. Of course, smallholder farming varies across the region, and histories of colonialism, revolution, land reforms, and other processes are quite diverse and country-specific. Nevertheless, land issues were prominent in most of Southeast Asia's anti-colonial grievances, in post-Independence conflicts, in the left-right struggles of the Cold War, and in the post-revolutionary regimes and subsequent reforms of Indochina.

In Melanesia, on the other hand, swidden cultivation systems and the absence of pre-colonial or colonial state involvement in small-scale agriculture, which has been mainly swidden-based, provides a very different backcloth for land relations. This is related to the absence of large-scale kingship, and the tribal, clan and lineage basis for authority, including assignation of individual and communal rights over land. Similarly, the decolonisation process in Melanesia reinforced the quite different agrarian structure and the role of the post-Independence states, which were shaped much less by Cold War dynamics than in Southeast Asia.

Additional to the different colonial and post-colonial histories of the two regions, the scale at which society is organised around land influences the nature of exclusion in the two regions in question. The intimate exclusions discussed in *Powers of Exclusion* are considered in terms of familial and neighbourly relations at the village level. In the smaller scale societies of the Pacific, personal ties also operate within the government system to a greater degree and in a seemingly more obvious sense, and with greater impunity, than in larger bureaucracies. The quasi-feudal arrangements around land and labour in Southeast Asia that have shaped revolutionary and reform programs alike are more or less absent in Melanesia, and the tribal rather than peasant-based nature of society has, as a result, tended to show greater persistence than in Southeast Asia.

Land is political everywhere, but in some cases it is more overtly related to big-picture political agendas than in others. The politics of exclusionary processes around land have had quite different meanings in the two regions in question. Rural support for anti-colonial movements in Southeast Asia was closely linked to resentment over impositions on land and labour (Scott 1976, 1985). Land-to-the-tiller campaigns became embroiled in Cold War tensions, both through revolutionary movements and in counter-revolutionary pre-emptive reforms. Some socialist experiments went beyond land redistribution, with programs of cooperativisation and collectivisation, including the extreme example of Khmer Rouge elimination of all individual claims to, and family working of, land.

In Melanesia, the politics of decolonisation were nowhere near as closely tied up in agrarian grievances as they were in Southeast Asia. Land reform has never assumed the redistributive agenda that it has in Southeast Asia (Chapter 1, this volume), whether through the vehicle of successful communist revolutions or as a pre-emptive measure against revolutionary movements. Ironically, because of this absence of socialist land reform, Melanesia has also not been subject to exclusions associated with the post-socialist market-based reforms, which has been one of the strongest forces for renewed concentration of land in Cambodia, Laos, Vietnam and— in a different geopolitical and structural context—Myanmar (Hirsch and Scurrah 2015).

Markets: Boom Crops and Land Grabbing

The phenomenon of land grabbing has drawn global attention to injustices associated with unequal political-economic power and has revived interest in land questions around the world more generally. Driven in particular by the 2008 food price spike and concerns over underinvestment in agriculture that encouraged or legitimised a spate of 'land deals', land grabbing has increasingly come under scrutiny at a number of levels, one of which is definitional. Land grabbing is not only open to discursive interpretation, but it also manifests itself in regionally specific ways.

In mainland Southeast Asia, the so-called land grab takes a number of forms. Most often discussed is the rush of transboundary investment in agricultural and other land-hungry resource projects by commercial interests from the more industrialised and land-scarce countries of China, Thailand and Vietnam in the perceived land and natural resource-abundant countries of Cambodia, Laos and Myanmar. In reality, domestically driven land grabbing by the military in Myanmar, and by crony tycoons in Cambodia, is equally significant. Large-scale land accumulation has also accelerated in Thailand, historically a country of smallholders (Laovakul 2015). In insular and peninsular Southeast Asia, Malaysian investment in oil palm in particular is associated with dispossession of ethnic minorities and with forest clearing. Despite the global legitimation of land grabs by concern over food shortages, the boom crops behind much of Southeast Asia's land grabbing are mainly industrial, including rubber and crops grown for biofuels. The latter are often what have been termed 'flex crops' (Borras et al. 2014), such as oil palm and cassava, but the driving force for their expansion has mainly come from the biofuel sector. While market demand has driven expansion, the large-scale concessions granted to transnational regional capital have been facilitated by the neoliberal notion of underutilised lands whose suboptimal use can be corrected by market-based measures. This follows longer standing colonial practices that often characterised swidden fallows as 'wastelands' (Ferguson 2014).

In Melanesia, the land onto which oil palm and other boom crops have expanded has nominally remained in customary hands. However, arrangements for alienation of such lands are evident in various forms, including the special agricultural and business leases (SABLs) in Papua New Guinea (PNG), which provide an institutional means for concentration of land in the hands of corporate interests while maintaining nominal customary tenure (Chapter 6, this volume).

Regulation: Land Formalisation Through Titling

In Southeast Asia, marketisation of land often goes hand in hand with formalisation through land titling. Whether marketisation creates the demand for titling or vice versa remains an open discussion. In Melanesia, given that only a very small proportion of land is under freehold or state land leases, land exclusions are driven by market pressures through informal transactions, for the most part on customary land (Chapter 5, this volume). This implies that *kastom* provides a sound basis for relational market transactions that tend to fly in the face of conventional thinking about formalisation and individualisation of property rights as a basis for market transactions in much of Southeast Asia. Yet at the same time, formalisation works within the framework of customary arrangements around land to privilege certain groups with respect to boundary making and to catalyse innovative exclusionary institutional arrangements that exclude even in the absence of fully individualised land title (Chapter 12, this volume).

The authors of the introductory chapter to this volume follow Rose (1994) in suggesting that social relations embedded in property in the Spearhead states of Melanesia are concealed by formalisation through registration under Torrens Title. Most of the land titling in Southeast Asia has similarly been carried out under programs employing the Torrens system of title by registration, that is, without reference to historical lineage of possession. Land titling programs have received significant technical and financial support from the Australian government and the World Bank. Most have been run by the Australian company Land Equity International, an offshoot of the surveying arm of the Australian mining giant BHP Billiton. Thailand's land titling program, established in the mid-1980s, served as a model that was adopted in Laos, the Philippines, and to varying degrees in other Southeast Asian countries. While these programs were the target of critique, and have faced significant challenges in their importing of particular assumptions about property rights systems developed in capitalist economies under mainly liberal democratic governance, there has been relatively little resistance to their adoption. In part, this may be attributable to the post-socialist economic contexts in which market-based institutions are being developed quite aggressively by the respective governments of countries such as Laos, Cambodia, Myanmar and Vietnam.

In Melanesia, in contrast, the usurping of customary land tenure by individualised property rights has been subject to heated debate (Hughes 2004; Fingleton 2005). The same company that implemented the main Torrens Title-based land titling programs in several Southeast Asian countries, Land Equity International, has more recently led Vanuatu's Land Program, but without succeeding in overcoming the nepotistic or otherwise corrupt practices of ministers gifting land to government officers. Because of the patronage relations in a small-scale society, this leasing of state land is referred to as another level of 'intimate exclusion' (Chapter 9, this volume).

An interesting point of comparison emerges in the formalisation of customary land tenure. On the one hand, the restriction of title to collectively managed land subject to rights of use by association with a particular community, clan, or other group serves as a protection against alienation of individual land title, whether through voluntary decision or as a result of distress sale. In parts of Southeast Asia, customary rights associated with locale or ethnic distinction continue to play a role in negotiating tenure arrangements that push back on the neoliberal model of fully alienable property rights in land. In eastern Indonesia, for example, farmers appear to give priority to security against alienation rather than individually mortgageable and alienable property rights following the neoliberal model (Kristiansen and Sulistiawati 2016). In northeastern Cambodia, the 2001 Land Law has provided the basis for community title in indigenous communities, albeit following a convoluted and expensive bureaucratic process. But, at the same time, formalisation of customary lands also raises the spectre of 'powerful men', comparable with those mentioned in Chapters 1 and 9 in this volume, excluding fellow members of the customary group and even leasing out the land in question in a process echoing *Powers of Exclusion*'s 'intimate exclusions' (Chapter 6, this volume). Milne (2013) presents an interesting such case in northeastern Cambodia, where some farmers have opted for individual over community title out of concern that the latter can be exploited by unscrupulous leaders. These intimate exclusions also take on an important gender dimension in Ni-Vanuatu social relations in the process of formalisation (Chapter 10, this volume).

Force: Scales of Authoritarianism

In *Powers of Exclusion*, our consideration of force as a power of exclusion looks largely at the ways in which violence or threats of violence serve to exclude, beyond the enforceable regulatory power of the state and often by extra-legal means. In Southeast Asia, state authoritarianism has waned and waxed, and it has taken various forms ranging from outright military dictatorship to illiberal communist regimes, including regimes best characterised as 'neoliberal authoritarian' (Springer 2009). Control over land and restrictions on land-based activism or right of redress for land grabbing and related injustices are a significant part of the extra-constitutional exercise of authority, such as that exerted in the enforced disappearance of community development leader Sombath Somphone in Laos in December 2012.[1] Elsewhere, notably in Cambodia and the Philippines, violence with impunity is carried out or threatened by those with direct vested interests in land, often supported by connections in high places. As land prices have skyrocketed across the region, so the threat of violence has pervaded land disputes.

The association between state power and local violence is not so apparent in this volume. Rather, local and highly gendered structures of authority appear to wield this power of exclusion more autonomously. This is not to suggest that such power is unrelated to wider developments. On the contrary, in Vanuatu we see local powerful men acting as 'masters of modernity' (Chapter 9, this volume), and an interweaving of property and authority in Solomon Islands such that 'land disputes have now become a key arena for the performance of masculine authority and prestige' (Chapter 13, this volume). Furthermore, also in Solomon Islands and perhaps related to the relatively small-scale society within which violent or potentially violent land disputes are played out, conflict is constitutive not only of local social relations but also of wider political authority in a manner that helps shape state formation (Chapter 13, this volume).

Both Melanesia and Southeast Asia exhibit violence in exclusions based on ethno-territorial claims (Hall et al. 2011: 11; Chapter 2, this volume). But in Melanesia, such violence extends into peri-urban and even urban zones, whereas it tends to be concentrated in peripheral frontier lands in Southeast Asia. The centrality of clan, tribe and lineage in social and political organisation in Melanesia means that state and *kastom* co-exist

---

1   See the website www.sombath.org/en/.

within a more singular polity, particularly with reference to land, than in the more centralised and much larger states of Southeast Asia. The fact that the ruling regimes in the latter are all associated with a numerically dominant ethnic majority claiming national patrimony also gives ethno-territorial land claims a different place and role with respect to the distinction between extra-legal force and state-sanctioned violence.

Legitimation: Custom, Conservation and Developmentalism

In Melanesia, the status of customary landholder carries a great deal more weight in legitimising smallholders, not only to farm and live on the land in question, but also to derive resource rents or compensation payments when outsiders extract value from the land (Chapter 1, this volume). However, the role of *kastom* is complex. At one level, it is often understood as an inclusive basis for counter-movements to keep exclusionary market forces at bay. At another level, however, *kastom* can be a legitimating power of 'intimate' exclusion in its own right, particularly as it interacts with rights of chiefly authority (Chapter 11, this volume).

In both Melanesia and Southeast Asia, conservation has been a legitimating pretext for exclusion. In particular, forest carbon schemes (Hall et al. 2011: 84; Chapter 8, this volume) have facilitated the identification of areas to be excised from agricultural use in the name of forest protection. It is noteworthy that market principles underlie such schemes, illustrating the overlaps in powers of exclusion in both cases.

In both regions also, large-scale land acquisition has been legitimated by the investment that large plantation schemes attract for relatively high value 'boom crops', which we described as cases of 'volatile exclusion'. In PNG, oil palm dominates this kind of investment (Chapter 7, this volume), and SABLs are the key vehicle for investors to gain access to customary land. They do so through a process facilitated but not brokered by state authorities. This valorisation of land potential in pursuit of productivity and profits is a response to market forces, but more immediately it is legitimised by the promises of modernity contained in the land use itself and the associated infrastructure that it attracts. These developments are typically carried out as 'agro-forestry' projects, although it should be noted that this term denotes a peculiar set of practices in Melanesia—logging followed by plantation or agricultural development—whereas in Southeast Asia, it refers to integrated land uses mixing annual and perennial crops, or sometimes—as in the colonial-era *taungya* system in Burma—a progressive succession of swidden systems into silvicultural systems as shifting cultivation is phased out in favour of long-term teak rotations.

There are commonalities between upland Southeast Asia and Melanesia in the legitimation of possession in shifting cultivation systems through the act of cultivating the land. In both regions, such possession is traditionally a temporary right of exclusion (Chapter 1, this volume), albeit one whose form and relative impermanence varies greatly from one agro-ecological and ethnic context to another. Similarly, in both regions, there are many cases where exclusive tree ownership may not coincide with the recognition of landownership of the plot on which the trees are growing (Peluso 1995).

A key contrast in the legitimation of exclusion through colonial or post-colonial state-assigned property rights occurs in the realm of customary tenure. Whereas land alienated by titling in most Southeast Asian countries is more or less off-limits for customary claims, Torrens Title continues to be contested in all of the Spearhead states discussed in the current volume, and Vanuatu even went to the extent of abolishing freehold land after Independence (Chapter 1, this volume). *Powers of Exclusion* tends to focus on state lands, notably the untitled 'political forest', as sites of contestation in Southeast Asia that are subject to legitimacy-based claims, with more emphasis on market-based exclusions in the case of titled lands. The situation in Melanesia appears to be considerably more open, fluid and contestable, presumably because of the continuing debate on the suitability, necessity, or otherwise of alienable property rights in the development context of Melanesian societies (Fingleton 2005).

These tensions over property rights find their way into public discourse and debates in different ways in each region. In both Melanesia and Southeast Asia, the neoliberal argument that legitimates exclusion through individualised, alienable land title has considerable traction (Chapter 1, this volume), but more so in the latter than in the former. The argument tends to be rolled out in Melanesia by certain neoliberal economists as an explanation for continuing underdevelopment (Hughes 2004), a notion hotly contested by others (Fingleton 2005), whereas in Southeast Asia the post-facto neoliberal economic discussion on land titling has long sought to measure its effect on productivity (Feder 1987)—a discourse that is less challenged, but that raises conundrums on the extent to which public cultivated land in particular should be fully titled (Hirsch 2011). In Melanesia, the experience of land tenure reform that violates the moral basis of customary land principles through excessive individualisation has been one of failure. This does not necessarily exclude outsiders from access rights to land, but it requires that such rights are contingent on establishing place-based social relationships and enduring goodwill between in-migrants and existing customary landowners (Chapter 5, this volume). Nonetheless, neoliberal ideology holds increasing sway, even in the absence of a Torrens Title system, legitimating exclusionary arrangements such as SABLs (Chapter 7, this volume) and 'special economic zones' (Chapter 12, this volume).

In one respect, the requirement to formalise at the level of customary land, rather than by individualisation of titles, has provided a partial protection against land alienation in Melanesia. However, it has by no means pre-empted land grabbing. The lease-leaseback system in PNG allows wholesale alienation and abuse of authority by those in positions of power at the community level, who are thereby empowered to do documented land deals with external investors (Chapter 6, this volume). While the form of such exclusions may be different from state-brokered deals in Laos and Cambodia, for example, the effect is not altogether different. Nevertheless, land tenure reform in favour of customary group title registration in Melanesia might afford greater protection against such land grabbing.

The Melanesian ideology of landownership described in this volume (Chapter 1, this volume), based in membership of tribes or clans or lineages, is quite different from much of what we encounter and describe for Southeast Asia in *Powers of Exclusion*. The formalisation of these links as a key process of state formation is similarly difficult to recognise in the historical experience of Southeast Asia. The role of land titles in identification with the state as a form of urban and even national citizenship appears particularly strong in the urban context of Port Moresby (Chapter 4, this volume)—a phenomenon that remains under-explored in Southeast Asia, although a recent study in Bangkok suggests important links between land security and a sense of urban belonging in 'informal'—albeit long-established—settlements (Herzfeld 2016).

Conclusion

What do the foregoing comparative comments reveal about regional processes and conceptual applicability of the *Powers of Exclusion* framework across regions? We see a number of common external forces pertinent to land relations in both regions: both have been shaped by colonial and post-colonial histories that incorporate land as a site of contestation at the state-society nexus. Both regions have gone through processes of marketisation and formalisation of bounded property arrangements. Both are subject to transnational investment and policy reform inspired by neoliberal development agendas. Both have seen the emergence and problematising of land grabbing. Corruption and violence enters the field of land relations in both regions, and in both there have been challenges to full commodification of land.

Yet we have also seen regionally specific dynamics. History and culture are of paramount importance, but there is also a need for caution in explaining regional dynamics in overly simplified historico-cultural terms, particularly in a region such as Southeast Asia, which is often considered to be an imagined or constructed entity rather than having an innate geographical logic (Acharya 2013). The political economy of land grabs differs fundamentally between the two regions. In part this may be an issue of scale. In the introduction to this volume, the authors raise the question of whether the quantum difference in population size of the countries in Melanesia and Southeast Asia makes a difference to the conceptual framework's application across regions. For example, we have seen that the more 'intimate' nature of the political systems in Melanesia raises questions of exclusions based on personalised aspects of the political process. But beyond scale, the nature of state authority, the very different experiences of the Cold War and subsequent reforms, and the difference in the drivers and shape of land reform initiatives, also set the regions apart.

A final key difference between land struggles in Southeast Asia and Melanesia is the significance of urban land conflicts in the latter (Chapters 2–4, this volume). This is not to suggest that urban land issues are insignificant in Southeast Asia, but there are three reasons for the relative absence of urban considerations in *Powers of Exclusion*. The first is simply that we wrote the book as part of a project concerned with the agrarian transition in Southeast Asia, and scoped it mainly as a rural-based analysis. The second is that much of the literature and public discussion on land issues in Southeast Asia is based on rural land conflicts, which have a history of political salience in the region. And the third is that most—although far from all—urban land in Southeast Asia is registered with private land title, and exclusions are therefore largely market-based, so that conflict tends to be less overt in urban than in rural areas. This is in direct contrast to the situation in Melanesia. With this in mind, there is still much to learn from this volume in re-addressing urban land questions in Southeast Asia through the lens of exclusion.

References

Acharya, A., 2013. *The Making of Southeast Asia: International Relations of a Region*. Ithaca (NY): Cornell University Press.

Borras, S.M. Jr, J.C. Franco, R. Isakson, L. Levidow and P. Vervest, 2014. 'Towards Understanding the Politics of Flex Crops and Commodities: Implications for Research and Policy Advocacy.' The Hague: Transnational Institute Agrarian Justice Program.

Bray, F., 1986. *The Rice Economies: Technology and Development in Asian Societies*. Oxford: Blackwell.

Feder, G., 1987. 'Land Ownership Security and Farm Productivity: Evidence from Thailand.' *Journal of Development Studies* 24: 16–30. doi.org/10.1080/00220388708422052.

Ferguson, J.M., 2014. 'The Scramble for the Waste Lands: Tracking Colonial Legacies, Counterinsurgency and International Investment through the Lens of Land Laws in Burma/Myanmar.' *Singapore Journal of Tropical Geography* 35: 295–311. doi.org/10.1111/sjtg.12078.

Fingleton, J. (ed.), 2005. *Privatising Land in the Pacific: A Defence of Customary Tenures*. Canberra: The Australia Institute (Discussion Paper Number 80).

Hall, D., P. Hirsch and T.M. Li, 2011. *Powers of Exclusion: Land Dilemmas in Southeast Asia*. Singapore: NUS Press.

Herzfeld, M., 2016. *Siege of the Spirits: Community and Polity in Bangkok*. Chicago: University of Chicago Press. doi.org/10.7208/chicago/9780226331751.001.0001.

Hirsch, P., 2011. 'Titling against Grabbing? Critiques and Conundrums around Land Formalisation in Southeast Asia.' Paper presented at the International Conference on Global Land Grabbing, Institute of Development Studies, University of Sussex, 6–8 April.

Hirsch, P. and N. Scurrah, 2015. 'The Political Economy of Land Governance in the Mekong Region.' Vientiane: Mekong Region Land Governance.

Hughes, H., 2004. 'Can Papua New Guinea Come Back from the Brink?' Sydney: The Centre for Independent Studies (Issue Analysis 49).

Kristiansen, S. and L. Sulistiawati, 2016. 'Traditions, Land Rights, and Local Welfare Creation: Studies from Eastern Indonesia.' *Bulletin of Indonesian Economic Studies* 52(2): 1–29. doi.org/10.1080/000749 18.2015.1129049.

Laovakul, D., 2015. 'Concentration of Land and Other Wealth in Thailand.' In P. Phongpaichit and C. Baker (eds), *Unequal Thailand: Aspects of Income, Wealth and Power*. Singapore: NUS Press.

Milne, S., 2013. 'Under the Leopard's Skin: Land Commodification and the Dilemmas of Indigenous Communal Title in Upland Cambodia.' *Asia Pacific Viewpoint* 54(3): 323–339. doi.org/10.1111/apv.12027.

Peluso, N.L., 1995. 'Fruit Trees and Family Trees in an Anthropogenic Forest: Ethics of Access, Property Zones, and Environmental Change in Indonesia.' *Comparative Studies in Society and History* 38(3): 510–548. doi.org/10.1017/S0010417500020041.

Rose, C.M., 1994. *Property and Persuasion: Essays on the History, Theory, and Rhetoric of Ownership*. Boulder (CO): Westview Press.

Scott, J.C., 1976. *The Moral Economy of the Peasant: Rebellion and Subsistence in Southeast Asia*. New Haven (CT): Yale University Press.

——, 1985. *Weapons of the Weak: Everyday Forms of Peasant Resistance*. New Haven (CT): Yale University Press.

Springer, S., 2009. 'Renewed Authoritarianism in Southeast Asia: Undermining Democracy through Neoliberal Reform.' *Asia Pacific Viewpoint* 50(3): 271–276. doi.org/10.1111/j.1467-8373.2009.01400.x.

www.ingramcontent.com/pod-product-compliance
Lightning Source LLC
Chambersburg PA
CBHW040146270326
41929CB00025B/3385